SO, ABOUT MODERN

SO, ABOUT MODERN EUROPE . . .

A CONVERSATIONAL HISTORY FROM THE ENLIGHTENMENT TO THE PRESENT DAY

David Imhoof

BLOOMSBURY ACADEMIC
LONDON • NEW YORK • OXFORD • NEW DELHI • SYDNEY

BLOOMSBURY ACADEMIC
Bloomsbury Publishing Plc
50 Bedford Square, London, WC1B 3DP, UK
1385 Broadway, New York, NY 10018, USA
29 Earlsfort Terrace, Dublin 2, Ireland

BLOOMSBURY, BLOOMSBURY ACADEMIC and the Diana logo are trademarks
of Bloomsbury Publishing Plc

First published in Great Britain 2021
Reprinted 2021

Cover Design: Ben Anslow
Cover image: © Miguel Navarro / Getty Images

A catalogue record for this book is available from the British Library.

Library of Congress Cataloging-in-Publication Data
Names: Imhoof, David Michael, 1970– author.
Title: So, about modern Europe. . . : a conversational history from the Enlightenment to the
present day / David Imhoof.
Description: London ; New York : Bloomsbury Academic, 2021. | Includes bibliographical
references and index.
Identifiers: LCCN 2020035927 (print) | LCCN 2020035928 (ebook) |
ISBN 9781350148697 (hardback) | ISBN 9781350148680 (paperback) |
ISBN 9781350148703 (ebook) | ISBN 9781350148710 (epub)
Subjects: LCSH: Europe–History–1492–
Classification: LCC D208 .I47 2021 (print) | LCC D208 (ebook) | DDC 940.2—dc23
LC record available at https://lccn.loc.gov/2020035927
LC ebook record available at https://lccn.loc.gov/2020035928.

ISBN: HB: 978-1-3501-4869-7
       PB: 978-1-3501-4868-0
       ePDF: 978-1-3501-4870-3
       eBook: 978-1-3501-4871-0

Typeset by RefineCatch Limited, Bungay, Suffolk

To find out more about our authors and books visit www.bloomsbury.com
and sign up for our newsletters.

CONTENTS

LIST OF FIGURES AND MAPS

Figures

Maps

ACKNOWLEDGEMENTS

You better get comfortable, because I've got about 1,500 people I need to thank here. Seriously. But don't worry, I'm not going to name them all. I'm talking about all the students I've taught modern European history for twenty years, mostly at Susquehanna University. They served as guinea pigs and helped me figure out the main points in this book, and which attempts at humor totally bombed.

A number of student readers helped fine-tune this book: Adam Unger, Trevor Diggan, Derek Dengler, Brandon Sorge, Robert Masters, Meredith Lemons, Lauren Imhoof, Jay Gegner, Nicole Flemming, and Sasha Fields, as well as the fabulous AP European History teacher Bill Switala. Some of them offered concrete suggestions; some told me when I was trying too hard.

Big props to the super smart readers Bloomsbury lined up. They really whipped me into shape. I appreciate their attention to the book's topics and tone and their advice on how to make it more inclusive, not to mention their faith that this kind of thing might actually work.

I may be revealing dirty secrets here, but you have to know stuff better when you're writing it than when you're just rambling about it in class. Susquehanna librarians Ryan Ake, Meg Garnett, Rob Sieczkiewicz, and Nici Baer helped get me up to speed on the, uh, one or two things I needed to learn. Above all Veronica Polyniak helped tremendously with research and source collecting

I've mentioned Susquehanna[1] already a couple of times. This university I call home has given me the ability to try out crazy ideas and the time necessary to write this book. I appreciate the role students, staff, and faculty have played in assisting me with this work.

When I told my editor Rhodri Mogford about this idea, I kind of thought he'd laugh uncomfortably and change the subject quickly. Instead, he said he'd like to work on a foul-mouthed, Enlightenment-obsessed textbook trying to connect with undergraduate students who may not love history as much as we do. He and Laura Reeves have made working with Bloomsbury a pleasure and a process that has taught me a great deal. They have been exceedingly helpful.

Finally, my wife Leslie Imhoof deserves credit for pretty much any good idea I'm connected to, and this one is no exception. After ploughing through my first book, she

---

[1]Yeah, it's a long Algonquin (Native American) name that refers to the river nearby. If you want to sound smart to locals, you pronounce it "sus-kwu-hae-na."

wondered if, well, maybe I could do something with, you know, not so many footnotes. She suggested I try to write something that was closer to what I do in the classroom. She and our three kids (Lauren, Natalie, and Austin) have put up with my discussing a lot of random stuff at dinners and have been massively supportive. I love them and thank them for it and dedicate this book to all four of them.

I KNOW YOU SKIP INTRODUCTIONS, BUT HERE'S WHY YOU SHOULD READ THIS

No one reads introductions. I get it. They're boring and just repeat what the book is actually going to say. But you need an introduction to a history book because it gives you the main point, the big picture, or the argument. Yes, this textbook on modern Europe has an argument. Think of the argument as a knife that cuts away what doesn't matter and leaves you with the important stuff. That's not so bad, right? A history book telling you what you can leave out!

Every time you tell a story, you are making an argument in the present about the past. If I asked you what you did over the summer or last weekend, you would be deciding *right now* what matters to share about those past experiences. Don't be fooled. All histories have arguments, just like your story about last weekend does. The past is behind us, but history is formed in the present. There's a lot of past, right? An argument allows the author to say, okay, we can't cover it all, but here's what I think matters. A lot of people don't like history because they're taught a ton of details and then expected to make sense of them. But that's backwards. Let me first give you the big picture, and then the chapters that follow, or details, will hopefully make more sense.

The main point of this book is that big ideas that came mostly from the eighteenth-century[1] Enlightenment have shaped the lives of everyday people and continue to do so. We'll define the Enlightenment soon enough. Before that I'll hit you with the Renaissance and Scientific Revolution because those big developments set up the Enlightenment. This book will look at the impact of concepts like freedom, capitalism, socialism, democracy, feminism, nationalism, and fascism. Starting in the 1800s many people believed in them strongly enough to fight, die, and kill for them, and they still do today. This book looks chiefly at Europe because that's where these ideas came from, but Europeans took them all around the world. Americans and other people have used them too.

What even is a "conversational history"?

This book is called "A Conversational History from the Enlightenment to the Present Day". That means it's written like we're just talking. Sort of. I take seriously the importance

---

[1] It's okay if you're a little unclear about whether the eighteenth century was the 1700s or 1800s. It works like this. In the modern world we generally use dates based on the birth of Jesus, which of course shows the lingering influence of Christianity. The first century AD—*Anno Domini* or after Christ—was years 0–99. The second century was years 100–199. And so on. That's why the fourteenth century was the 1300s, the eighteenth century was the 1700s, and we live in the twenty-first century, or the 2000s.

of this history, and I need to share some info with you to make the big point. But I don't take myself too seriously in how I relate it to you. If you saw me teach in the classroom, you'd watch me jump up and down, be sarcastic, use bad accents, and make history dad jokes. I'm hoping some of that approach comes across in these pages. I also want you to consider the main point but not stress so much about the details. Unfortunately, a lot of history books seem to make the details the main point. My students constantly tell me that they don't like history because it's, like, a huge litany of facts, names, places, events, etc. By writing more casually, I try to make the details less overwhelming and hope you can fit them better into the big picture. I will include a "building the argument" section in each chapter to connect the parts of this book.

This book may seem a little irreverent, certainly not like a traditional work of history. I've written those and consider them important. But much of what historians write is aimed at each other and assumes the reader knows a lot already. That's how academics work in every field. If you're reading these pages, though, you have at least some motivation to understand modern European history. Maybe you feel that you *have* to, that someone's *making* you, but that's enough of a start. If I can show you that my perspective on this era is valuable, interesting, and perhaps even a little entertaining, then you are more likely to remember it.

So, what is the main story here, and why should I care?

Let's take those questions in reverse order. First, you should care about this story because it informs almost everything you do today, whether you realize it or not. That's right, almost everything. Why do we talk about the left and the right in politics? French Revolution, baby. When did people start killing in the name of democracy? World War I, if not before. Why are you, no matter how much money you have, relatively rich in this world? Imperialism. Why do we expect technology to save us or destroy us or maybe both? Industrialization. Why do we define ourselves by what we consume? Capitalism. Many other issues that we still worry about—racial tensions, globalization, education, gender inequality, environmental concerns, and so on—can be traced back to the big ideas we'll study here. Like I said, history is today, and this book aims to explain important concerns we face in the twenty-first century.

I'm not going to threaten you with that "those who ignore history are doomed to repeat it" crap. History does not repeat. Every situation is different. However, it's a lot easier to take lessons from the past, with hindsight, than from the present. We can use lessons from the past to ask about what we're doing today and what we should do in the future. So, you should care about the story here because it will help you understand our society with all its problems and promises. And if you figure out the twenty-first century, maybe you can help fix what's wrong or avoid problems in the future. Please.

My story here goes something like this. The Renaissance gave some thinkers and leaders new ways of looking at people and how they organize themselves. Science then built upon those perspectives to define truth as something concrete and measurable.

Enlightenment philosophers used those concepts to come up with rational, secular ideas for all of society that would both liberate and control people. Very important: the Enlightenment = good and bad. Europeans didn't make all these ideas. Some of them were around in other places, at other times. But Europeans took credit and put them to work (something we'll see happens a lot). The French Revolution and its aftermath showed how awesome and terrifying those ideas could be, when armed with modern weapons. The nineteenth century was kind of about figuring out how all that worked. Industrialization during this same time period raised the stakes by offering folks more opportunities, giving leaders new ways to control people, and by making bigger and badder weapons. Over the course of the nineteenth century, most Europeans came to believe that these big ideas—nationalism, democracy, capitalism, socialism, feminism, science, etc.—were improving people's lives. And then Europeans took that action on the road, forcing the rest of the world to consider these ideas, usually at the barrel of a gun. So, yeah, by the end of the nineteenth century, Europeans were feeling pretty good about themselves.

Now, a few intellectuals around that time raised their hands and said, "well, maybe we're not *all* good." Writers like Friedrich Nietzsche and Sigmund Freud were not convinced that Europeans were all cool and rational and making the world better. But most people ignored these weirdos until the destruction of World War I. Then folks were, like: oh, I see. But instead of trying to replace or improve (Enlightenment) ideas that had nearly killed a whole generation, the leaders and citizens of most Western countries doubled down on those promising, dangerous concepts. And of course, they kept making bigger guns. The period after World War I produced some cool culture and interesting thoughts, but also more death and destruction: World War II, the Holocaust, and nuclear weapons. After World War II, good old Enlightenment ideas kept liberating people (end to imperialism, gay rights, second-wave feminism), but the darker side pushed the world to the brink of nuclear war (thanks, Cold War!) and tightened Western control on the rest of the planet. When the Cold War ended around 1990, major ideological conflict also slowed down. But I'm sorry to say that fighting about big ideas has definitely continued. Identity politics have helped expand human rights but also given us more to argue about. And technology has certainly advanced. It's curious, though, how much technological development has created products to sell rather than sending folks to Mars or finding a cure for cancer. Anyway, that's my story.

Almost done

Just three final points. First, I will not be covering everything in this book. Most likely that will be a cause for rejoicing since historians are not known for their brevity. I won't talk about every country in Europe. And while we'll consider the interactions of Europeans with non-Europeans, this book mainly focuses on Europeans' experiences. Because of what I leave out, some people may accuse me of bias. But that's how you build an argument or tell a story. If I ask you about your weekend, there's a lot you will leave out, depending on what point you want to make. History is always written from a point of view, and I'll try to be up front about mine.

Next, I will talk about music. I like music, I play music, I always have music in my head. I use music to introduce all my classes. It wakes students up and helps them hear what the past sounded like. Music can convey important points about the past, like how the Renaissance worked or how Africans used imperialist tools against imperialism. Besides, culture especially matters in the modern world because it gives people the opportunity to express both who they've been and who they aspire to be.

Finally, this book looks at how ideas developed and what they meant for average people. I believe we should take seriously the experiences of regular people in the past, not just the wealthy and the powerful. At the same time, this book also looks at thinkers who usually had more money and time than most people did, so they could sit around and think up those big ideas. And we will also deal with leaders who convinced or forced average people to support their ideas. This book will therefore show the impact leaders and thinkers and average people all had on each other. It's up to you to decide if it works.

CHAPTER 1
(RE)BIRTHING NEW IDEAS IN THE RENAISSANCE

Why do the French get to name the cool stuff, like "The Renaissance"? After all, the most important *Germanic* king and first Holy Roman Emperor everyone calls "Charlemagne" (pronounced "shar-le-main"), even though he was really *Karl der Grosse*. We call a big, awesome home a *mansion* (Old French for "house"), not a *Haus* (German for "house"). Then there's the Renaissance, which means "rebirth" in French but was mainly an Italian thing. This explosion of rediscovered classical learning and new ideas began in Italy around 1350. Maybe the Italian *Rinascimento* would be too hard to pronounce! Whatever the case, we use the French word *Renaissance* to describe the process of how Italians first and then other Europeans started thinking, wow, there are some cool old ideas from ancient Greece and Rome and the Muslim world that we could use right about now. The Renaissance wrapped up around 1600, at which point leading thinkers started getting more scientific. We'll look at that in the next chapter.

This book is about the impact of ideas, especially the ones that came out of the Enlightenment—big ideas like democracy, capitalism, communism, nationalism, and feminism; ideas that gave Europeans the ability to rework society and take over the world. The Renaissance created the basic framework of thinking that would help generate those world-changing concepts. Renaissance thinkers, to put it simply, decided that humans matter and that the human experience should decide the value of art, science, religion, politics, whatever. They weren't necessarily inventing new ideas—hence the term "rebirth"—like the champs after them did. But Renaissance thinkers' focus on humans and their push for education created the space for the big thinking that followed. These Renaissance types also ramped up the tension between religious and secular or non-religious world views. They didn't mean to, since they were all solid, God-fearing Christians. But people after them would wonder, hmm, if we should focus on improving human lives, where does God fit into that? We'll get to that later.

Building the argument

So, my Introduction laid out the basic argument of this book. Historians write arguments, not just a bunch of names and dates and stuff. The basic story in this book looks like this: Renaissance Humanism → Scientific Revolution → Enlightenment Ideas → French Revolution → All Hell Breaking Loose → Modern World.

This book will trace the history of big ideas in the modern world—freedom, democracy, human rights, how Sweden produced ABBA, totalitarianism—that sort of thing. I'm trying to get you to realize that these big ideas have dramatically impacted the daily lives of average people in Europe and in the world. Your life too. We'll talk a lot about intellectuals because they're the ones coming up with this stuff, but also pay close attention to what those ideas do for regular people. Big ideas are sort of like politics or The Beatles. You can ignore them or pretend you don't care about them, but sooner or later, you're going to have to deal with their influence on your life. It is therefore worth understanding these concepts and where they came from. One of the main places they came from was from Italy, from the Renaissance.

Renaissance thinkers took humans seriously. And that shift from only focusing on God toward *humanism* is going to have a huge impact on how people look at the world. That's the main point of this chapter. The next chapter will deal with the way that focus on humans helped produce the Scientific Revolution. Then after that we'll see how humanism and science produced the Enlightenment.

I will use these "Building the argument" sections to show you the development of this book's argument. I hope that doing so will help you understand this book better and will teach you how to write your own arguments. I mean, you do that all the time anyway. If you can figure out how to do it with the old stuff covered in this book, you will (a) understand better where you come from and (b) know how to rock arguments in all areas of your life. Basically, you'll be unstoppable. People will love and fear you. But first let's talk about music.

The Renaissance in a song

One of the best ways to understand the issues and conflicts in the Renaissance is to listen to choir music. Now, unless you're majorly into singing with a choir, you probably don't listen to a lot of choral music. But check it out for a few minutes. Go find Robert Ramsey's (1590s–1644) song "How the mighty are fallen." It's pretty awesome, haunting stuff. It was church music, used in worship. This music reveals important points about the Renaissance.

First, the words from the Bible (2 Samuel 1:25–27) are in English. During the Renaissance, some writers moved away from writing in Latin and toward what they called "vulgar" languages. No, they didn't swear and tell dirty jokes (well, some). "Vulgar" means common, or of the people. Ramsey and others were using words that average people could understand. Latin had been the language of the Church since about the fourth century. It was handy to have one language that people working for the Church all over Europe could understand.[1] Since the Catholic Church pretty much had a monopoly on learning in Europe, Latin was also the language of writers and intellectuals. But our man Bobby Ramsey had other ideas. Of course, he wasn't the first to start writing in vulgar languages. Dante did it in Italy; Shakespeare, in England; Rabelais, in France. Like other writers in the Renaissance, Ramsey wanted people actually to understand what he was saying.

---

[1] A bit like English today, right?

Next, this kind of music uses multiple overlapping parts—in this case three female and three male—to create tension. Every so often all these separate lines come together to form a really satisfying chord, usually a major triad, something that Western music has programmed us to believe is positive and strong and just feels good. In the first minute-and-a-half of this piece, all these competing melodies are echoing everywhere (remember we're in a big church). But then, boom, that chord forms, and all is right with the world. You really hear it in the last thirty second of the song. Even non-choir nerds may get some chills when Ramsey pulls it all together at the end and says, "and the weapons of war are destroyed"! (There are worse ways to end a song.) The tension and release that Ramsey uses here reflect the debates among thinkers at this time about the world, people, and God. But they all came together in sweet, sweet harmony around a common belief in God. That tune will change as we get further into this book, both literally and figuratively. But for now, common faith brought even competing ideas together in the Renaissance.

There were no atheists in the Renaissance

Right. So, pretty much everyone in Europe during the Renaissance believed in Christianity. Now, this book is going to detail conflicts between religion and science, or at least between religious thought and secular thought. And (spoiler alert) religion is going to lose. We live in a scientific world. And no matter how you feel about faith, your everyday life is all about the science. The basic conflict about whether we understand the world through human or divine experience began in the Renaissance. But it was kind of an accident.

The Catholic Church was the most important institution in Europe at the time of the Renaissance. By 1350, the Church dictated pretty much all learning, morals, and much of human behavior. Rome had been the center of the Church, and the Pope (Archbishop of Rome) was the head of the Church and also a powerful secular ruler by this time.[2] There were still some lingering "pagan" ideas and "superstitions" in Europe (like knocking on wood). But by the 1300s, the Church had either rooted out most of these older beliefs or incorporated them into its larger belief system. The best example of the Church folding pagan ideas into its program was Christmas, which fit with older celebrations of the winter solstice, even though Jesus was probably born in March. Until well into the 1500s, there were no major challenges in Europe to the Catholic Church's claim to universal spiritual authority. Jews were a tiny, scattered minority, and Muslims represented a military, not a spiritual threat. The Greek and Russian Orthodox Churches were distinct institutions that mainly believed the same thing as the Catholics.

The Church thus shaped everyone's belief system by defining the basic outlines of how the world worked:

---

[2]Meaning he controlled land and ruled just like any other ruler who didn't wear a robe and tall pope hat. "Secular" means non-religious.

- God created the world and sent his son Jesus to save it spiritually.
- The Catholic Church was the manifestation of Christian beliefs.
- The Bible was God's word on how the world worked and how people should live.
- Average people connected with God through representatives of the Church.

The Church shaped daily life by controlling the most important rituals and events everyone experienced: birth and baptism (into the Church), marriage, and death. And in a world without clocks, church bells rang throughout the day to mark when to get up, when to work, when to go to church, holidays, danger, etc. The Church thus counselled, cared for, and regulated the everyday lives of Europeans at all levels of society, from the wealthiest and most powerful to the poorest and most marginalized.

Not that all was well with the Catholic Church by 1350. From 1309 to 1377, the French kings basically kidnapped the Pope and moved the seat of the Church to Avignon, in southeastern France. Score one for secular rulers over the Church. And then from 1378 to 1417 there were *two* popes, one in Avignon and one in Rome. Score another for worldly rulers. These divisions in the One Church (that's what "catholic" means) weakened its authority. Perhaps not surprisingly, popes at this time focused more on their role as rulers and their conflicts with states than they did on their job as number one spiritual guy. That attention to the secular away from the religious had some real benefits for Renaissance artists and architects wanting to build awesome things for the Church. However, those secular moves encouraged lots of folks in the Church to call for reform to improve the spiritual lives of all believers. And that brings us back to the choral music of our man Ramsey: tension resolved by common belief in God.

Even the most radical humanist thinker of the Renaissance did not propose that the Church or the Bible was wrong. No one questioned whether God existed. Renaissance thinkers explored ideas that would lead to the development of science, and that world view will present great challenges to religious authority later in this book. Likewise, the attention these guys paid to human beings will eventually make other thinkers focus more on secular answers to major questions about the world and social organization. Certainly questions about how humans relate to the divine will create major division in Christianity in the form of the Reformation in the sixteenth century. But for now, during most of the Renaissance era, common belief in God and the Christian Church brought people together like those major chords in Ramsey's music.

Why Italy?

Why did the ideas of the Renaissance first get going in Italy, especially since, like, there was no "Italy"? Yes, people recognized the "boot" to be an area called "Italy," but it was not a country until 1871, something we'll look it later in Chapter 5. So why did these super-important ideas originate in this area? The basic formula looks like this: legacy of Rome + strong cities + conflicts between pope and major secular leaders + the Black Death = Renaissance. Let's take that apart.

During the Middle Ages—from about 400 until the start of the Renaissance around 1350—Italy was kinda backwards. Then, like now, the former home of the Roman Empire was a favorite destination of tourist barbarians. Back then the barbarians from Northern Europe did more than just take selfies. They ripped apart the Roman Empire and left Italy weak and disorganized. In fact, from about the 400s until the 1400s, what was left of the Roman Empire was based in what is today Tukey and Greece. Together the Italians and the barbarians didn't exactly maintain the greatness of Rome. At this time, Islamic states coming out of Arabia and North Africa boasted a more advanced culture, as their bloody take-down of the once-mighty Roman Empire in 453 indicated. During the Middle Ages, plenty of important ideas in science, medicine, and math had thrived in the Muslim world more than in Christian Europe. Europeans had discovered some of that in the Crusades, when they kept trying to capture parts of the Middle East from Muslims (and killed lots of Jews and Muslims along the way), starting in 1095. They never managed to hold on to those places, but they did bring back some smart ideas. So, yeah, why *did* the Renaissance start in Italy in the 1350s?

Well, the Roman Empire may have been gone, but it was not forgotten. Evidence of Roman greatness was still most present in Italy. Many of the buildings, aqueducts, and other visible accomplishments were still standing and, in many cases, still used. The books and great ideas had not gone away either. Religious leaders and other intellectuals read Latin, and some of them read Greek too. There were copies of important Greek and Roman writings all around Europe, and leading thinkers of the Middle Ages knew them. So classical ideas were there.

Next, northern Italy turned out to be a perfect incubator for rediscovering past learning. Cities like Florence, Venice, Genoa, Bologna, and Padua developed new and powerful economies starting in the 1200s, chiefly based around trade. These more urban places didn't have tons of land, so well-connected and smart people there figured out that they could make money trading with other places. That was pretty unique in Europe, where people usually amassed wealth by owning land. Cities based on trade, on the other hand, developed very different social set-ups and cultures. This commercial revolution promoted a different kind of rich man from the traditional landed nobility in medieval Europe. Urban Italian elites needed to be polite, well-connected, and literate, wear cool shoes, understand the different cultures with whom they traded, and be good at negotiations. Those were very different skills than those of a powerful landed nobleman. Italian merchants also needed employees who were educated in Latin, math, and the art of international trade. Like successful entrepreneurs in the twenty-first century, these merchant elites had to walk a fine line between showing how great and rich they were vs. cooperating with colleagues and promoting helpful organizations. This set-up, first of all, made big money in Italy. It also promoted a new kind of education and created incentives for building big, beautiful things. Likewise, these elites experimented with the best government for their interests. And they were constantly fighting with and against each other, expanding and contracting their territories on the Italian peninsula.

Italian city states found political and economic space between the Church and major secular rulers (Kings up north), who were in constant conflict. Popes, archbishops,

Map 1.1 Renaissance Italy.

monastic leaders, and others in the Church were of course also secular rulers. That whole "render unto Caesar that which is Caesar's; and unto God that which is God's" line from Matthew 22:21 got a little confusing when folks were repping for both God *and* Caesar. But the big players like the Holy Roman Emperor (who was German … don't ask), the Pope, and kings of France and Spain found it lucrative to let Italian city states serve as independent trading points with Turks, North Africans, Middle Easterners, and even the Chinese. Remember that Marco Polo, who hung out with Chinese emperors and Kublai Kahn, was a merchant from Venice at this time. The Church remained supremely important in northern Italy but also made money off Italian merchants and needed Italian bankers.

Finally, the Black Death. Whatever you know about the bubonic plague, you've got to be asking yourself: how did *that* help promote the Renaissance? The Plague (*Yersinia pestis*, which just sounds nasty) came to Europe in 1347, carried by rats on merchant ships from Asia. It spread so rapidly and killed so many people, that many Europeans thought it was the end of the world. The disease wiped out about 60 percent of Europe's population within seven years. Think about that. About 740 million people live in Europe today. Imagine if, say, 444 million of them died from the Covid-19 virus within five years or so. Or consider Australia's current population going from 25 million to around 10 million. Needless to say, the Plague marked a dramatic end to about three centuries of population growth in Europe.

Basic economics would tell you that this event initially caused a depression because goods could not find markets. Once mercantile Italian city states recovered somewhat, however, they had to expand trade networks and methods to unload those products. In the countryside the resulting massive labor shortage helped spur new ways to farm that ultimately made European agriculture more efficient, which then freed up more people to participate in other forms of employment. While medieval medicine did not understand the disease, the Plague did prompt cities and medical professionals to implement public health policies that improved cramped city life. It's no surprise that folks ran screaming from the Black Death. But only the wealthy could really afford to move out of Plague-ridden cities for a while, something portrayed in Giovanni Boccaccio's *The Decameron* (1353), one the greatest and most inspiring works of Renaissance literature (not to mention a fine collection of dirty jokes). So, another unfortunate upside of the Plague's destruction was to remind rich people they needed to have the means to escape when things got ugly. That realization encouraged more economic activity. The writing of Boccaccio and others made clear that innovative culture might grow from that privileged economic space. Here we see an important theme in European history: wealthy people find ways to thrive even in dark times, while poor folks usually suffer.

Together, these strange circumstances—Rome's legacy, a new merchant elite, conflicts between church and state, and the Plague—created conditions in northern Italy especially that gave rise to Renaissance thought and art. As the name "rebirth" implies, many of the ideas came from the past.

Unfrozen voices from the ancient world

Another great (and satirical and dirty) Renaissance book, François Rabelais's *Gargantua and Pantagruel* (1564), talks about "unfrozen voices." That's what one historian has called ancient writers that got Renaissance thinkers excited.[3] Now, Renaissance intellectuals

---

[3]John Hale, *The Civilization of Europe in the Renaissance* (New York: Atheneum, 1994), 189–90.

didn't discover some hidden trove of texts from ancient Greece and Rome like in a *National Treasure* movie. Most of the great Greek and Roman writers that Renaissance thinkers admired had been studied in the Middle Ages too. But starting with writers like Boccaccio in the late fourteenth century, some Italian intellectuals rediscovered the value of these pre-Christian writers such as Aristotle, Plato, Cicero, and Virgil. What did Renaissance thinkers learn—or *relearn*—from ancient Greek and Roman authors? It boils down to three main points.

1. *Ideas and texts matter*

Specifically, those by *people*, not just from God (i.e., the Bible). Renaissance intellectuals took inspiration from ideas of the ancient world about how to live a good life, how best to organize society, and how the world worked. What people write, in other words, can help us improve and is worth studying. This realization reinforced the value of academic subjects that study ideas and texts: philology (the history of language); rhetoric, grammar, and logic (which explain how to use language convincingly); moral philosophy, history, and poetry. These subjects became important in the Renaissance because they enabled readers to pull as much as possible out of texts. They also became the basis of modern university education by the way.

2. *People can use reason*

Medieval writers used reason and logic, too. But unlike ancient authors, they always had a big trick up their sleeve. When Christian writers wanted to bring down the hammer, they would pull out the Bible as The Ultimate Support. Mic dropped, game over. Ancient Greek and Roman authors, on the other hand, lacked one definitive religious text as the litmus test for truth, so they had to *convince* their readers. They appealed to logic, common experiences, and concrete evidence. Ancient writers also employed emotion and sometimes humor, but they ultimately had to build convincing arguments with reason and evidence. Renaissance writers realized that such approaches could explain many things and reveal ways to improve one's life.

3. *The way you write also matters*

By the same token, if you don't have the Bible as ultimate validation, you've got to write well to convince people. You need to make your argument clear and support it well. You should present your thoughts in a well-organized fashion. Being a little entertaining or funny helps. And stringing together beautiful words may make your readers more apt to buy what you're saying. Renaissance thinkers appreciated ancient authors' oratory skill and their style. And it wasn't just for show: ancient writers demonstrated that eloquence and moral virtue actually reinforced each other.

These big ideas from dead guys inspired Renaissance intellectuals to think differently about the world, re-examine their relationship with the past, and consider new ways to educate people (mostly men). From the Greeks they reconsidered how the natural and social world worked. Aristotle taught them the value of models and natural laws. From Euclid and Ptolemy they learned mathematical, quantitative concepts, setting the stage for modern science. Renaissance intellectuals also learned a lot about the natural world from medieval Arab mathematicians and doctors, who had developed the concepts from ancient Greeks far more than Christian writers in Europe had. As well, Plato's ideas about governance, especially the concept of the Philosopher King, suggested that wisdom and reason should govern over tradition and emotion.

The Greeks may have been the Big Daddies of ideas, but Renaissance writers really liked the Realistic Romans. Authors like Virgil and Cicero used beautiful writing to explain the complexities of politics in first century BCE[4] Rome. Virgil's *Aeneid*, modeled on Homer's *Iliad* and *Odyssey*, combined mythology and history to offer moral lessons about politics and how to treat other people. The great Renaissance poet Dante Alighieri (1265–1321) fashioned his *Divine Comedy* trilogy partly on the *Aeneid*. Renaissance writers really admired Cicero's writing skill and the fact that he lived the things he wrote about. Cicero had served in important capacities in the Roman Republic and shared his firsthand knowledge about conflicts between ideals and the reality of governance. The fact that Cicero chilled with Julius Caesar and lost his head to Marc Anthony only gave him more street cred with Renaissance writers.

These noobs also wanted to figure out how the thoughtful, educated man might aid his city or country—though ideally without being decapitated. Cicero taught Renaissance thinkers that poetry and good writing had civic value, that a broad education was important for leaders, and that educated men should be skeptical. All of these ancient types, Greek or Roman, reminded intellectuals in the Renaissance that humans were capable of great things. Renaissance intellectuals did not believe that those pagan writers challenged their Christian faith. They thought these ancient "unfrozen voices" demonstrated that God gave humans the ability to observe and think for a purpose.

Rediscovered ancient voices encouraged Renaissance thinkers to reject some medieval learning that focused on the Bible as sole source of truth. You may have heard medieval Europe described as the "Dark Ages," a bleak time when leaders and average people alike lived in squalor and were driven by mysticism, blind faith, and violence, like in *Monty Python and the Holy Grail*. The term "Dark Ages" was an exaggeration created by Renaissance intellectuals, who drew a direct line between classical thinkers and themselves. Yet during these supposedly dark times, folks in the less smelly, more scientifically advanced Arab world developed ideas from Greeks and Romans. This myth of the "Dark Ages" also allowed modern Europeans to write off events or developments elsewhere in the world as similarly unimportant.[5] Despite these blind spots in their learning, Renaissance thinkers began to use history and empirical (concrete, evidence-based) study to explain the world and how best to live in it. They came to realize that

---

[4]That's "Before Common Era," which is another way of saying "BC" or "Before Christ."
[5]And, guess what! This view made it easier for Europeans to justify taking over other places and stealing stuff. You'll be seeing that a lot in this book.

human experience should be the standard by which ideas about the physical world, social organization, and even God should be judged. Bring on the humanism.

Humanism

Humanism was the defining concept of Renaissance thought and the most important legacy of this era. Humans should be the standards and goals for all things. This concept did not turn away from religion. Instead, Renaissance humanism brought a human focus to Christianity. God remained at the center of people's lives and most intellectual ideas, but Renaissance thinkers paid more attention to human beings in *this* world and their improvement rather than just their salvation. Renaissance thinkers employed human experience rooted in history, observation, art, and the body as evidence alongside the Bible. Let me mention three guys who did this especially well.

Francesco Petrarch (1304–74) was one of the first Renaissance humanists. He was born in Tuscany, not far from Florence, but had an odd childhood. His family moved to Avignon in southeastern France to follow the pope there, when the king of France basically kidnapped him. This time outside Italy introduced Petrarch to other ways of thinking and ancient texts found in the courts of France. He had that familiar, biopic story of the brilliant artist: uprooted and moved around, distant father, found solace in books, etc. Petrarch also caught the travel bug and roamed around his whole life. He even climbed a mountain for fun in 1336. People didn't hike up mountains for the view back then; that's a very modern thing to do. Petrarch loved himself some classical Roman literature but had little time for the medieval culture around him. As a result, he was kind of a pissed-off Renaissance dude.

He wrote poetry in Latin and Italian and is especially known for his letters to dead guys, in particular Virgil and Cicero. In those letters, Petrarch considered the value of ancient ideas and helped create a new relationship with the past. Similarly, he wrote love poems to some married woman named Laura he barely knew. Creepy though they may sound, his letters and poetry seem strikingly modern, almost like the work of Romantic writers 500 years later. His admiration for ancient authors compelled him to work hard to line up those "pagan" writers with his Christian world view. Petrarch also came up with a very unique vision of history, one that also seems more like our modern view. He was the one who labelled the centuries between himself and his Roman heroes the "Dark Ages."

Next, Niccolò Machiavelli (1469–1527) was such a Renaissance bad-ass that his name became a commonly used adverb! "Machiavellian" means behaving in a way in which the ends justify the means, where someone focuses more on expediency than morality. That's probably a little harsh, but it captures important aspects of Machiavelli's contribution to the Renaissance. He grew up in Florence, studying Latin, history, philosophy, and ancient works. Like his father, Machiavelli held important posts in the Florentine government. It was a wild time in Italy though. The pope was using his son to kill off his enemies. Yes, the pope's *son*. The influential Medici family was in and out of power in Florence. The

French king and Holy Roman Emperor were angling for a piece of the Italian action. Machiavelli spent time in prison and was tortured for being on the wrong side of a conflict in Florence. He had to flee to the family farm.

What's a bored, exiled, well-educated political insider supposed to do? How about start the study of political science! Machiavelli wrote a lot but is best known for his book *The Prince* (written in 1513 though published after his death). The book is basically a super-long resume and cover letter to the head of the Medici family. That aim colors what he writes a little. But the main points of this book have become basic tenets in the study of politics: know your enemy, better to be loved than feared, but better to be feared than dead, use history to understand your current situation, take lessons from previous leaders' mistakes, and political virtue should be informed by necessity, not just morality. Like Petrarch and other Renaissance thinkers, Machiavelli assumed that human experience was as important as religious teachings. Machiavelli also demonstrated that Renaissance humanism was definitely expertise for sale.

Finally, Leonardo da Vinci (1452–1519) best embodies the concept of the "Renaissance Man," or someone with skills in several different fields. Above all, da Vinci brought art and science together, as you can see in Figure 1.1. Known as the *Vitruvian Man*, this drawing shows the idealized proportions of man first imagined by the Roman architect Vitruvius (from the first century BCE). Da Vinci also painted probably the most famous portrait of all time (the *Mona Lisa*) and the most reproduced religious painting of all time (the *Last Supper*). He designed versions of the helicopter, submarine, parachute, bicycle, and tank. He helped diagram human anatomy in great detail and imagined civil engineering projects that we still haven't managed to put in place. Naturally he also wrote poetry and invented musical instruments and hydraulic pumps. He grew up in and around Florence. Unlike Petrarch and Machiavelli, he received little formal education and taught himself much of what he learned, starting as a painter's apprentice. Da Vinci lived during the same nutty times as Machiavelli. Da Vinci in fact worked with some of the same folks, finding many ways to sell his expertise as a military strategist, engineer, and artist. His mad skills in so many areas epitomized the broad interests of Renaissance humanism and influenced subsequent thinkers, engineers, and artists. Many of his ideas were so advanced that they weren't even remotely feasible until we had modern industry.

All three of these guys make clear that the Renaissance connected learning and doing. Renaissance thinkers were interested in an intellectual *method*, a process for working through problems or creating something new. These perspectives helped to spawn modern science and the Enlightenment, the subjects of the next two chapters. What mattered to them was not the final answer but the process of getting there. That was different from most thinking before the Renaissance and is one of the most important hallmarks of modern thought. Things change, stuff happens, we don't always know what's going on, but maybe we can set up a method to consider those changing factors. That's very different from the certain and static way of looking at the world in medieval times.

Renaissance intellectuals valued education based on curiosity, problem solving, convincing, debating, working in a world of uncertainty, and figuring out how to advance one's interests in this context. They slowly revolutionized education, focusing on practical

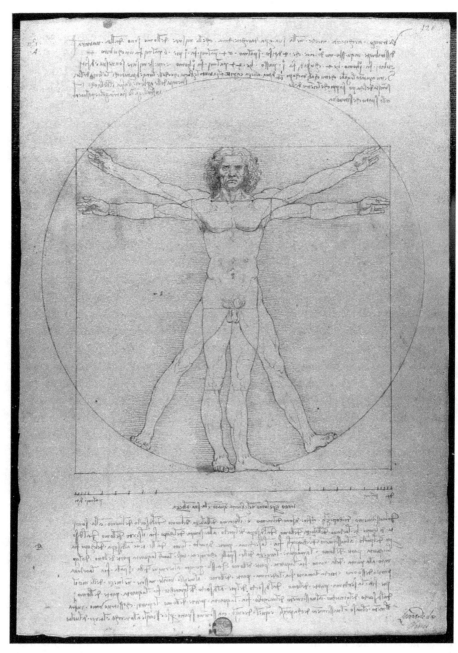

Figure 1.1 *Vitruvian Man* by Leonardo da Vinci

application. Especially in the complex political and economic conditions of Italian city states, a broad, humanist education became necessary for the elite. They needed to use history and philosophy to understand their political situation; art, poetry, and music to comprehend the human spirit; and math and early science to grasp the physical world in which they lived. That wasn't a philosophy exactly but a set of assumptions about human nature that had profound importance in the centuries to follow. Indeed, the form of education that Renaissance thinkers proposed remained dominant until the twentieth century.

The Renaissance in a picture (well, two pictures)

Like with Ramsey's music, we can see many of the qualities of Renaissance humanism reflected in the art of the time. We might as well go big and look at the work of one of the era's greatest masters, Michelangelo di Lodovico Buonarroti Simoni (1475–1564), who was thankfully famous enough just to go by his first name. Michelangelo grew up in Florence, where all that emphasis on humanist, liberal arts education was very strong. He even attended a school based on Plato's ideas. Michelangelo learned the value of art, poetry, history, philosophy, and science, as well as the ability to express himself and convince others. Of course, the dude had skills, but he used his education and eloquence to work well in a complicated political situation. He also got in fights, wore the same smelly clothes all the time, and wrote sexual poetry about various men and women. He was a very *human* humanist. Anyway, like da Vinci, Michelangelo grew from working-class craftsman to wealthy genius, reflecting the practical application of Renaissance learning, not to mention the mega money in Italy to support big artistic projects.

Michelangelo created the marble sculpture *Pietà* (Figure 1.2) in 1499 when he was twenty-four years old. This scene of Mary holding the crucified Jesus is not in the Bible but reflects one of the most poignant and human moments in the Christian story: a mother grieving over the death of a child. Michelangelo rendered it in such exquisite flowing detail that it's hard to believe the sculpture is marble. The idealized image compels viewers to consider the emotions at the heart of the Christian story. (We'll leave alone the fact that Mary looks like a sixteen-year-old girl holding her thirty-three year-old son.) Michelangelo chose to portray a powerful human experience, something all too familiar to people of this era, as a way to reinforce faith and help people of that time feel more connected to the story of Christ's crucifixion.

The *Creation of Adam* portion of the Sistine Chapel (Figure 1.3) portrays perhaps the most human moment in the Bible, when God gave life to Adam. It's right in the middle of the massive set of frescoes that Michelangelo painted between 1508 and 1512 on the ceiling of the pope's main chapel in the Vatican or basically the epicenter of the Catholic Church. Here, too, Michelangelo represented biblical characters in idealized form in order to make the story human: God as kind, all-knowing father and Adam as flawless nude model. Certainly, the over 300 figures on the ceiling represent a master class in painting human form, reflecting Michelangelo's keen observation of human anatomy.

Figure 1.2 *Pieta* by Michelangelo.

Figure 1.3 *Creation of Adam* by Michelangelo.

But his ultimate goal was to illustrate important parts of the Bible. Many other Renaissance artists, sculptors, and architects tried to reveal the divine through this combination of attention to human forms and emotions.

To say that Renaissance art was great is stating the obvious. It's important to stress the economic and social reasons behind it. Wealthy elites in Italian cities set the example of supporting art that reflected Christian, humanist, and classical ideals. Leaders elsewhere in Europe did the same thing. In particular, political struggles on the Italian peninsula and broader religious conflicts in the 1500s prompted the Catholic Church to pour lots of money into big, beautiful churches like St. Peter's Basilica in Rome, which Michelangelo helped design.

This flow of financial support toward the arts helped start a creative revolution. So did intense competition among elites for who could support cooler work. Artists' attention to ancient art and architecture inspired them to create new works that rendered the human form both beautifully and accurately. Their interest in observation, science, and math helped make that possible. In northern Europe, intensely detailed artists like Albrecht Dürer (1471–1528) and Pieter Bruegel (1525–69) did much the same thing with smaller, darker oil paintings, paving the way for subsequent masters of realism like Johannes Vermeer (1632–75) and Rembrandt van Rijn (1606–69). The work of Renaissance artists redirected European art toward human expression, a trend that lasted until the twentieth century.

The Renaissance and all the humans who weren't wealthy, white, Christian men (that is, the majority of the world)

Here's a refrain you're going to see a lot in this book: those in charge found ways to make new, crazy ideas reinforce their control of society. Sometimes their ideas ended up helping average people *despite* the elite's desire to keep power. If you think about it, the big ideas we're discussing here have the potential to help everyone. The defining concept is *humanism*, not wealthy-white-guy-ism. And in some important ways Renaissance ideas did give power to those who lacked money and authority. Leonardo Bruni (1370–1444), another famous writer and historian from Florence, even said that women—at least the really rich ones—should be educated the same way as men. That must have been great for those ladies to be so learned, while they sat at home all day because they couldn't go to university or participate in civic life or get a job. Thanks, Leo.

While the lives of average people didn't change much during the Renaissance, the ideas of this era offered men some greater agency in the world. Writers like Machiavelli encouraged leaders to consider popular opinion in how they ruled, so rulers might have thought a little more about average people when they made decisions. One of the common themes in this book and in modern Europe generally is that liberating ideas that were created for a small group of men ended up improving the lives of other people. The big ideas of the Renaissance, science, the Enlightenment, workers' rights, and human rights all started out being just for straight wealthy white guys but expanded to include women, people of color, the poor, queer people, etc. One question we'll explore in this book is: fine, but who deserves credit for these growing rights—the elites who created them or the regular people who grabbed them and made them universal?

Renaissance thinkers did not plan for their ideas to be the basis of universal human rights or even assumptions that all people are equal in the eyes of God or the state. However, the sum of these ideas indicated that humans mattered and could use reason to improve their lives. If you're a woman, a slave, a worker, an androgynous person, or a peasant, and you catch wind of this idea, you might think: hmm, does that include me too? At the time the answer was "hell, no." So things continued to suck for most of the population, but these concepts did eventually promise more rights and opportunities for average people. Of course, patience is hard to maintain when you live during the Plague. Renaissance thinkers agreed that education was essential to improving things. Getting in on that action was one of the ways that more men and a very few women could make use of Renaissance ideas to improve their lives.

The vast majority of women during this time were too busy having kids, worrying about having kids, raising kids, working, and serving their families to have the ability to pursue any kind of education. And for the tiny number who did have access to education, those magnanimous Renaissance thinkers mainly thought learned women could serve guys better. Reformers like Desiderius Erasmus (1466–1536) and Boccaccio (who wrote the first biography of famous women) wanted to educate women in order to improve their traditional female qualities of beauty, humility, and virtue. Nobody taught women Latin, which was the key to broad, international ideas. Still, gripping how-to books like *Needlepoint Like a Saint* or racy romances like *Thine Heaving Humanist Chest Doth Swell*[6] in vulgar languages provided female readers opportunities to imagine and perhaps create some space for thinking or behaving differently.

A very few women achieved more. For example, Christine de Pizan (1364–1430), a brilliant noble woman born in Venice who became the king of France's astrologer, was the first woman actually to make a living writing. She wrote poetry and prose and defended women, especially in her best-known works, *The Book of the City of Ladies* and *The Treasure of the City of the Ladies* (1405). Her books praised female virtue and encouraged women to find their own meanings and do things that mattered in their lives. Sounds like twentieth-century Second Wave Feminism! Few wealthy women, much less the majority of women, had the wherewithal and good fortune to accomplish so much. But de Pizan demonstrated that Renaissance ideas *could* help expand women's horizons.

Even women's limited roles gave them more opportunity than people of color. Some Europeans at this time came into contact with non-white people through trade, slavery, and war. Not exactly the best conditions for respectful relationships. Most educated people learned about the lives of people in Africa and the New World through the writings of imperialist conquerors or accompanying clerics, who had obvious reasons to approach alien cultures as weird and threatening. Even before *conquistadores* took to the seas in the 1500s, leaders and thinkers in Spain and Portugal had redefined their nation

---

[6]Or something like that.

based on religion and blood, violently pushing out Jews and Muslims. If Spaniards were willing to drive out, forcibly convert, and execute people with similar backgrounds and religious ideas, imagine what they would do to folks around the world who looked and behaved radically differently!

Imperialist expansion thus helped define the Other in the Renaissance according to color and religion. The growth of Atlantic trade relied directly on African slaves. Societies had enslaved other people for millennia. But this was the first time that slave = black (or at least non-white) and master = white. In their efforts to know about and organize information about the world, Renaissance thinkers reinforced this growing racial hierarchy. Dark-skinned people weren't just waiting to get some Renaissance humanism. They were helping to define "The Other" in white European thinking, something that would take a long, long time to undo.

Legacy of humanism

Let's wrap up and get ready for the next chapter by considering the lasting impact of Renaissance humanism. Above all, Renaissance thinkers made clear that ideas and texts by people matter. God may still have been at the center of thought and action, but Renaissance intellectuals showed that we can better understand God, ourselves, and others through *human* observation and experience. Humans thus became the way to determine truth. That radical idea created modern science, gave secular rulers new ways to control people, and would eventually pit religion against science and reason. The rest of this book will chart the way such ideas served both to free and dominate people. Renaissance humanists also demonstrated the value of education, especially one steeped in the liberal arts. Chances are that you are reading this because your university agrees that history (and philosophy, literature, language, and science) will provide you with moral and practical guidance. You've heard this before: a university degree will make you a better person, help you think effectively, and get you a great job! You're welcome.

The Renaissance provided Europeans with new technology and economic development, too. The massive technological leap of the printing press, which Johannes Gutenberg (1400–68) developed in the 1450s, perfected texts and spread them to more people. It's not popular to claim in the twenty-first century, but the printing press represented a greater leap forward in media than did the invention of the internet. Yeah, I said it. Like other Renaissance thinkers, Gutenberg took/stole cues from ancient sources: his press imitated those that the Chinese had been using for 800 years. The printing press helped introduce the ideas of ancient and Renaissance thinkers to more people. The Renaissance also provided the tools and impetus for European imperial expansion. The intoxicating combination of curiosity, technological innovation, and commercial revolution drove European explorers and conquerors to the seas and to new lands. As we'll see, those guys produced rather mixed results at home and abroad.

Two results of the Renaissance that went hand in hand with all this intellectualizing and developing were theft and racism. Renaissance thinkers absolutely took some of their ideas from other places, especially the Arab world. They tended not to give credit to those people for religious and political reasons. Renaissance types did not see Greek and Roman paganism as a threat to their faith, but monotheistic Muslims challenged their world view.[7] Plus, by the 1400s Muslims had taken over what was left of the Roman Empire (based in today's Turkey) and were moving into southeastern Europe. With their Christian beliefs and love of ancient Greece and Rome, Renaissance intellectuals in fact viewed Arabs and other non-white people as different—interesting perhaps and worth studying, but certainly the Other. This dehumanizing side of humanism would help define modern racism and empower Europeans to steal people, resources, and ideas from others. That legacy will run throughout this book.

The impact of Renaissance humanism varied across Europe. Especially north of Italy, these ideas helped produce the massive religious upheaval of the Protestant and Catholic Reformation. Beginning with Martin Luther (1483–1546) in 1517, Protestants decided that their humanist ideal of developing deeper relationships with God could not work within the Catholic Church. Some Catholic leaders responded by reforming aspects of the Church and tightening its control over people's lives. Unfortunately, Renaissance humanism did not prevent both slides from slaughtering each other. Oh, that's another refrain in this book: great ideas usually don't stop people from killing each other and often cause more death. But in addition to division and death, the Renaissance also gave us art, literature, and music about people and for people.

Finally, Renaissance thinkers developed a new love-hate relationship with the past. Those guys took inspiration from ancient thought yet totally rolled their eyes at medieval ideas (not to mention developments from other parts of the world). So, even if they acted a little like teenagers who tire very quickly of what was *so* last year, Renaissance intellectuals were really the first people to understand their place in history. You don't have to be an historian to realize that's kind of a big deal.

---

[7] Another prophet *after* Jesus? Uh, nothing in the Bible about that. Jews presented a similar conundrum to Renaissance Christians: how could anyone who knew about Jesus reject him as the son of God? As a result most Christian rulers legally restricted Muslims and Jews and sometimes, just to be safe, killed them.

CHAPTER 2
SCIENCE IS A HUMAN INVENTION

In 1722 Johann Sebastian Bach (1685–1750) wrote twenty-four short pieces for keyboard called the "Well-Tempered Clavier." The clavier is a keyboard instrument similar to the harpsichord, a precursor to the piano. Why twenty-four pieces? Because there are twelve notes in an octave in the Western music scale. On a piano that would be all the notes—black and white keys—between, say, once C and another. Bach wrote a piece for each of those notes or each possible key, one in major and one in minor, until he had a fine collection in all twenty-four possible keys. Bach went to all this trouble to explore each key on what he called a "well-tempered" or evenly-tuned keyboard. This chapter explains the origins of modern science, and Bach's "Well-Tempered Clavier" shows us how applying science and math to a keyboard could expand the possibilities of writing music.

You might rightly think that the distance between every note on a keyboard has always been the same, that the half-step between a C and C# for Bach was the same as a half-step between an A and A#. Not back in Bach's day. Back then, keyboards were tuned *relatively* or based on one key or another. That tuning meant that you had to retune keyboards a lot. You couldn't modulate or shift from one key to another, and "accidentals" or notes not in the key to which the keyboard was tuned sounded really bad. Bach figured out how to tune his clever clavier so that all the notes were the same distance apart. That made it well-tempered or well-tuned. Then players could easily move between keys and add accidentals, both of which majorly (no pun intended) opened up musical composition. Bach's compositions show how math and science improved music. The system Bach and his buddies created opened up new spaces for composers that radically altered composition, demonstrating one way that science—and math and reason—helped change people's understanding of the world. That's what this chapter is about.

Building the argument

In many ways, science was an outgrowth of Renaissance humanist ideas: humans can use reason to figure things out, human experience should define truth, empirical evidence matters, new ideas should improve people's lives, and we learn a lot from ancient thinkers. Science is, above all, a *way* to learn. Hello, Scientific Method! Like the Renaissance ideas we just studied, early modern scientific thought rejected some medieval perspectives, continued others, and sometimes took ideas from Muslim intellectuals. Also like the Renaissance, there's no clear-cut date on a calendar announcing that, hey everyone, the Renaissance is over, the Scientific Revolution has begun.

The term Scientific *Revolution* is apt here. From about 1500 to 1700, thinkers across Europe came up with a (mostly) new way of studying and understanding the natural world. We also call this period "early modern Europe" since it contained the seeds of modern thought and thus modern Europe. Some crazy, exciting, scary things will follow: the Enlightenment, industrialization, Europeans taking over the planet, the start of global warming, weapons of mass destruction, leaving Earth. Scientific thought has, in the last fifty or hundred years, shaped what most people around the world do. It's the basis of modern, mechanized society. It's the basis of how you think.

People created this new way of looking at the world in the midst of massive battles about religion, so the conflict between religion and science was built into the origins of science. Early modern European scientists pretty much all thought that their work celebrated and explained God. Still, they dropped some pretty radical ideas. They investigated the natural world and believed truth was something observable and measurable. Those secular concepts made some people at the time wonder about God's role in the world and would gradually replace a purely religious world view. The violence in the name of religion going on around them made science seem a little more attractive.

Modern states, which were developing at this same time, harnessed science to become more powerful. Enlightenment thinkers in the next chapter will run with scientific concepts to create new ideas about how humans work with each other and organize themselves. In Chapter 6 we'll talk about industrialization as a very concrete way that science has altered our approach to nature, work, and economic relations. You shouldn't be surprised when we see that science has done a mess of good for people and has helped us really mess up the world. Science is a human invention. It doesn't just *exist* in the natural world, any more than math does. Both science and math are human ways of explaining the world. They have worked pretty well. This chapter explains where the ideas come from and how that history shaped what science has done ever since.

What was (and is) science anyway?

Right. Let's start with a basic definition. Science focuses on the natural world—not the spiritual, philosophical, cultural stuff. Truth is something observable, measurable, and verifiable by mathematical models. Above all, science is a method of searching for answers that should make you skeptical and question existing knowledge. You go, scientific rebels! You probably learned about the Scientific Method at some point. It goes something like this:

- Ask a question (about the natural world).
- Do some background research.
- Form a hypothesis.
- Do cool experiments, ideally ones that other people can do too, to test your hypothesis.

- Analyze the results and draw conclusions.
- If the results agree with your hypothesis, celebrate. If not, feel sad briefly and then try again or get yourself another hypothesis.
- Either way, share your findings, which become part of scientific knowledge. Thanks!

This new way of studying the world grew out of various ancient, medieval, Islamic, and Renaissance ideas—but especially from the Greeks. Yes, the Greeks are back. The term "science" comes from Latin *scientia* or "knowledge." But ancient Greek philosophers gave us a *secular* definition of science based on the concept of the *cosmos*, an ordered universe that people could understand without the help of some supernatural being. Turns out that view was totally unique. Pretty much everywhere else in the world, thinking about the physical world was closely tied to religion. Even pathbreaking scientists in the Arab world, who expanded upon many Greek ideas before Europeans stole them, often connected science and religion.

Very special, those Greek guys. But here's the thing about them. They used their groovy ideas about the cosmos to explain what they assumed were "natural" differences in the world. Male was, for example, *naturally* superior to female; master was *naturally* superior to slave. In other words, their *assumptions* about the *social world* helped define their *observations* of the *natural world*. Basically, they built bias and inequality into early ideas about science. Womp womp. And don't forget that all those fabulous Greek ideas were possible in part because slaves gave toga-clad elites the time and resources to sit around and ponder things. In other words, fundamental ideas from the Greeks offered modern thinkers a way to challenge traditional assumptions but also helped reinforce hierarchy as a "natural" part of the universe.

Normally we'd jump right to those Renaissance thinkers who "rebirthed" ancient ideas. But there's an important and often ignored step between, something that came up in the previous chapter when I talked about the "Dark Ages." See, many early European scientists stole scientific ideas from medieval Muslim thinkers. It was a little like twenty-first century plagiarism: You have to write a paper on some random dead guy, so you do a little searching on the internet. You learn a little, get a few good ideas. You write the paper, and those ideas somehow find their way in there. You didn't *mean* to; you weren't really *trying* to use those exact words as your own. But, buddy, you plagiarized.

Early European scientists likewise believed they were creating all these amazing new ideas, maybe riffing on ancient Greeks, building on the Renaissance. That's true in many ways. But during the Middle Ages, Arab scientists had really developed ancient Greek ideas. European scientists then came along, took those ideas, pushed them forward, but kinda forgot to cite their Arab sources. Arab scientists came up with some of the most basic concepts of the Scientific Revolution: common laws of nature, algebra, medical science, even the notion that the earth might revolve around the sun. They gave us numbers too. Islamic thinkers used the modified Hindu-Arabic number system: 1, 2, 38, 7051, etc. And, boy, it's like an M times easier to do long division with those numerals (including zeroes) or measure planetary orbits than with Roman numbers! This early modern plagiarism doesn't alter the basic story in this chapter about how science changed

Europeans' views on the world. But it does help explain why many Europeans started feeling okay about using their awesome science to take over the world, including those places where these concepts had developed.

Medieval thinkers, next, merged ideas from the ancient and Islamic world with Christian theology. We saw in the last chapter that Christian intellectuals found ways to ignore the "pagan" in "pagan thinkers" from the ancient world. Greek super brain Aristotle gave Christian thinkers a nifty way of ordering everything that supported their assumption that God made them the center of the universe. Renaissance types made clear that human reason and observation could help make things better (at least for some people). That perspective paved the way for the Scientific Revolution, as did the Renaissance interest in understanding and controlling the natural world.

Science was a new way of looking at and using the natural world that came from these various origins. Science marks a pretty dramatic shift in approaching the natural world from most previous thought. Early scientists rejected medieval models of the world that were certain and static. Instead they viewed the natural world with skepticism and the desire to change things. Like science today, a lot of the new ideas came from studying the very big (stars, planets, universe) and the very small (cells, chemical composition, atoms). Early modern scientists particularly rejected the restrictive medieval vision of a solar system based around the earth. Instead, they placed the sun at the center and recognized an infinite universe beyond. That major re-centering, perhaps more than anything else, turned science into a new big way to understand the world that challenged religious explanations. But let me say it again: People invented science; it's a human perception. That human perception came out of a pretty wacky and violent time, so it's no wonder that science has, well, some issues.

Young science comes of age while people fight over religion

How many memoirs have you read or biopics have you seen about people who grew up in hard times and that tough upbringing ultimately molded them into a great individual? Maybe you've had that experience. Science developed like that too. It grew up on the mean streets of Europe without a loving home life. Science got bullied a lot when it was young by both Protestants and Catholics, and it had to find its own way in a big, tough world full of warfare and uncertainty. Cue swelling music. But finally science made it to the top, the very top. Yet no matter how big and famous and powerful it got, no matter how socially acceptable it became, no matter how much love it eventually received, science never forgot that upbringing. In fact that difficult start helped make science who it is. Catholics and Protestants fought about Truth, and Science got stuck between them.

More accurately, religious leaders killed each other about Truth.[1] Plenty of folks had wondered how to reform the Church before Martin Luther, but he made a pretty dramatic

---

[1] That's with a capital "T," friends, because it was more of a mythical concept than real thing.

statement in 1517 about the need to fix some things. Of course neither he nor other Protestants challenged the basic ideas of Christianity (God created the world; His son died to save it and came back to life). Protestants—people who *protested* against how the Catholic Church worked—wanted people to connect directly with God without a priest as a link. They believed everyone should be able to hear or read the Bible. And they thought that salvation came only from the grace of God, not by doing good works. These ideas took off because lots of people wanted spiritual renewal. Plus, many rulers and average people resented the Church's authority. Protestants pretty quickly came up with some ideas and organizations that fundamentally challenged the Catholic Church, so the Church kicked them out. But remember, this isn't the playground. Getting kicked out of the Church didn't just mean that you were sad that they didn't like you. It meant that the Catholic Church viewed you as a heretic, spawn of Satan, and an enemy to be killed. The Protestants thought much the same of the Catholics, going so far as to call the Pope the Antichrist. Both sides were excommunicating, forcing conversion, damning to hell, burning at the stake, and other nasty stuff.

What made it worse was that nobles—folks with money and armies—started taking sides. And, let me tell you, the last thing those people needed was *another* reason to slaughter each other. But now, hallelujah, they could fight for both political *and* religious reasons! For better or worse, new ideas of science could and did serve both sides. Early modern science developed as a part of the religious conflicts that raged in Europe from the early sixteenth to mid-seventeenth centuries. Please see cool chart (Figure 2.1) for a visual representation.

Here comes the Sun

Actually, here comes the Earth around the Sun, but we'll get to that in a moment. First, when was the last time you spent time outside in the night sky identifying constellations or observing changes? Today we may know more about astronomy, but in early modern Europe people spent a lot more time outside in the dark. The sun, moon, stars, comets, etc. were therefore on the minds of average people and intellectuals. That's one of the reasons astronomy was one of the most important areas of study for early in the Scientific Revolution.

RENAISSANCE   (THRU RELIGIOUS CONFLICT) ⟶ SCIENCE

RENAISSANCE	(THRU RELIGIOUS CONFLICT)	SCIENCE
—Classical learning	(Instrumentalizes these things into *ideology*)	— Empirical truth
—Humanism		— Process
—Empiricism		— Assumptions
—Exploration		— Efficiency as good
— Wealth		— Used by states

Figure 2.1 Renaissance morphs into science.

Schema huius praemissae diuisionis Sphaerarum

Figure 2.2 *The Ptolemaic Universe* (from Peter Apian's 1539 diagram).

Medieval thinkers viewed the universe as a nice synthesis of Christian and classical ideas. Christian theology got a boost from two Greek ideas: (1) the universe was an eternal and ordered cosmos, and (2) all things within the cosmos were hierarchically organized into a great "Chain of Being." Centuries of observation demonstrated that everything spun around us, so the Earth was the center of the universe. Above all, the Greek-Egyptian astronomer Ptolemy (who lived around 100–170 CE[2]) crafted a geocentric (Earth-centric) model of the universe based on the ideas of Aristotle and other Greeks. See Figure 2.2.

---

[2]That's "Common Era," another way of saying "AD" or "Anno Domini," in the time of Christ.

Ptolemy was pretty much the Man in astronomy in both the Islamic and Christian worlds thereafter. It helped that he had an amazing beard. Yes, he was burning in hell, but medieval Christian thinkers dug Ptolemy, because his vision of the universe fit with their own observations and their belief that the Earth was the center of the universe in the Bible. After all, the book of Genesis talks about God creating the heavens and the earth (and light, land, winged birds, etc.). And the Bible says God sent a savior to *this* world, not anywhere else. Ptolemy reinforced these beliefs. Medieval astronomers in Europe and the Islamic world generally saw Ptolemy's geocentric system as right and good, although some Arab scientists began revising it in the Middle Ages. But then Copernicus had to mess the whole thing up.

Nicolaus Copernicus (1473–1543) was a Polish monk. Like a good Renaissance thinker, he studied in Italy. As early as 1514 he proposed that the sun was the center of our planetary system. He was motivated by both humanist and religious reasons to overturn Ptolemy's system but was a little worried the Church might not like his heliocentric (sun-centric) ideas. When his big bombshell came out in 1543, though, the response was: meh, cute idea, but it doesn't really work. Other astronomers, especially the Dane Tycho Brahe (1546–1601) and German Johannes Kepler (1571–1630), worked out more sophisticated and accurate orbital patterns for a heliocentric universe that were more convincing. Plus, Brahe had what must have been one the most boss mustaches of his day, and Kepler's goatee could not have hurt his reputation. Still, most religious leaders weren't too worried, especially since these scientists said that their work revealed God and reinforced Catholic faith. All of these sun-chasers helped formalize a method of observation: gather long-term info, analyze it, and create mathematical models to reflect observations. That process was starting to look like what we'd call science. Then Galileo, his fancy telescope, and his gutsy claims kicked the discussion up a notch.

Galileo, science, and the Church

Galileo Galilei (1564–1642) was the most famous scientist of his time. This star-gazing superstar was one of highest paid people at the Tuscan court, who certainly loved the nightlife! He could have gone pro as a lutenist but felt drawn to science, math, engineering, and especially the stars. Speaking of attractions, he started working on some early ideas of gravity by dropping things off the leaning tower of Pisa. Galileo heard about telescopes or "lookers" in Holland created by lens makers. Since he couldn't exactly order one online, he built his own. Smarty pants. He used the thing to observe the Moon, planets, and Jupiter's moons. Galileo enjoyed the support of powerful people in Italy, including the Pope. And like other astronomers, he believed that his work strengthened the Church's position in the world. But by 1616 the Church had decided that a heliocentric universe contradicted the Bible (Psalms 93, 96, and 104; 1 Chronicles 16; and Ecclesiastes 1). And Galileo got into a fight with some Jesuit[3] mathematicians, making some powerful

---

[3]The Society of Jesus or "Jesuits" began in 1540 as part of the Catholic Reformation to advocate for Church reform and combat Protestantism. The current Pope, Francis, happens to be the first Jesuit to be elected Pope.

enemies. Still, his elite support allowed him to publish in 1632 *Dialogue Concerning the Two Chief World Systems*, in which he provided evidence and models for a heliocentric universe. But pride goeth before the fall.

The Church, including the Pope, was cool with the majority of Galileo's book. But Galileo kinda made fun of the Pope in his work. The Pope unleashed the Inquisition[4] on Galileo, forced him to recant, and placed him under house arrest for the rest of his life. (Note to self: if the Pope is letting you skirt the edge of propriety, don't make fun of him.) It didn't help that the Thirty Years War against the Protestants was going poorly for Catholics, and there had been threats on the Pope's life.

Galileo's 1633 trial reveals several important points about the status of science in the early seventeenth century. Unlike previous heliocentric advocates, Galileo used a telescope to gather evidence. Ever since, the advance of science has been directly connected to technological development. Next, after a century of some tolerance and support for science, the Catholic Church drew a sharp distinction between new discoveries and new interpretations of the Bible. The Inquisition threatened to torture poor Galileo, demonstrating that the Church would use its full power to limit any scientific inquiry that interpreted the Bible differently or challenged its authority.

Galileo had been wrestling with that tension for some time. For example, in a 1615 letter to one of his patrons, Galileo appeared to bow to the Church's authority:

> I declare (and my sincerity will make manifest) not only that I mean to submit myself freely and renounce my errors into which I may fall in this discourse through ignorance of matters to pertaining to religion, but that I do note desire in these matters to engage in disputes with anyone, even on points that are disputable.

Good start, G, but what about interpreting the Bible? He writes that "it is very pious to say and prudent to affirm that the holy Bible can never speak untruth—whenever its true meaning is understood." Uh-oh. That last bit seems to imply that *you* can figure out the Bible's meaning better than the Church can, mate. How you going to do that? Galileo appeals to his God-given reason and powers of observation:

> I do not feel obliged to believe that the same God who has endowed us with senses, reason, and intellect has intended to forgo their use and by some other means to give us knowledge which we can attain by them. He would not require us to deny sense and reason in physical matters which are set before our eyes and minds by direct experience or necessary demonstration.

---

[4]This infamous institution within the Catholic Church started in the twelfth century to combat heresy and really got busy in the 1500 and 1600s during the Reformation and religious wars. Inquisitors used threats, torture, slavery, burning at the stake, the usual stuff.

The Bible does a great many things, Galileo argues, but it's pretty vague about astronomy and science. He quotes a Church official: "the intention of the Holy Ghost is to teach one how to go to heaven, not how heaven goes." And besides, Galileo says,

> No one should be scorned in physical disputes for not holding to the opinions which happen to please other people best, especially concerning problems which have been debated among the greatest philosophers for thousands of years.[5]

Unless of course the "other people" happen to be Church Inquisitors or the Pope!

This letter reveals that early modern scientists wanted human observation and reason to be the basis of understanding the natural world. Such ideas echo Renaissance humanism, claiming secular instead of scriptural authority over science. Galileo may not push the issue to its logical conclusion, but we can see here the deeper challenge that science will present to religion in the modern world. Plus, Galileo viewed the scientist's work as part of a long tradition of inquiry, another connection to humanist, Arabic, and ancient thought.

Galileo's trial demonstrates, furthermore, the importance of context. Galileo probably could have gotten away with his heliocentric book if he had complemented powerful people, instead of ridiculing them. I mean, he'd long been using his support from important elites to push his luck. Before this time, his ideas prompted Church officials to roll their eyes. But in the midst of intense religious warfare, they become major threats. While Galileo's case was an extreme example of withdrawn support, it reminds us that wealthy and powerful people have always shaped scientific discoveries. They still do today. In 1992, the Catholic Church formally apologized for its treatment of Galileo.

Most of us today, regardless our religious persuasion, shake our heads at the vicious, ignorant clerics who punished Galileo, especially since we know that he was right. It's often satisfying to look back into the past and pity dead people or decide they were idiots. We know so much more than they did, and isn't it sad that they did cruel things to progressive thinkers like Galileo? Sure, but I want to encourage you not to pat yourself on the back for being so much smarter than those Inquisitors and consider why Church leaders feared the ideas of Galileo and other scientists. Yes, they wanted to hold onto their authority. Yes, they employed cruel and violent methods to keep people from interpreting the Bible themselves. But assume for a moment good intentions on their parts: they were genuinely concerned about people's lives and souls.

Religious wars were killing millions of Europeans at this time. The Thirty Years War (1618–48), which raged during Galileo's trial, wiped out at least 20 percent of the population in the German-speaking part of Europe. Neither Catholic nor Protestant leaders showed a bit of mercy to each other. In our tolerant world, we tend to see people with different ideas about religion as a little off or ignorant or straight-up wrong, but we

---

[5]Galileo, "Letter to the Grand Duchess Christina," In *The Discoveries and Opinions of Galileo* (New York: Anchor, 1957), 50–9.

don't usually view them as Satan's minions. Protestants and Catholics saw each other as eternally flawed and evidence of the devil's work in this world. For Catholic leaders, this whole mess had grown out of some people's desire to interpret the Bible on their own. It's fine to judge clerics' desire to control thinking and their treatment of Galileo, but it's also important to recognize the impulses behind their behavior. That's part of our responsibility as historians.

Some folks had it worse. Even before Galileo's bruhaha, Inquisitors had burned the scientist and Dominican friar Giordano Bruno (1548–1600) at the stake. Now, that guy had claimed that the universe was infinite with no center at all, which meant there was probably no heaven and hell. Oh, and God didn't necessarily create the universe. Bruno then shared all that with Catholics *and* Protestants. He thus articulated the greatest fear of the Catholic Church regarding science: it could not only alter how people understood the universe but in fact replace religion as people's main vehicle for understanding everything. Light him up!

Witches and women of science

Speaking of lighting up, there was another interesting story going on at the same time of the Scientific Revolution in Europe, a great big witch hunt! Between 1450 and 1750 about 90,000 people in Europe and North America were accused of witchcraft, and around 45,000 of them were executed, mostly burned at the stake. Most societies around the world have traditions of witchcraft. But Europeans used systematic violence to try to destroy them. Nowhere else and at no other time were so many people criminally accused of *diabolical* witchcraft—running with the devil. Van Halen would have been proud.

Accused witches were mostly the opposite of the dudes we've been studying thus far. While they came from all ages and social standings, accused witches were overwhelmingly female, poor, uneducated, over the age of fifty, and socially unattached (widowed, unmarried). Larger social and economic pressures help explain this witch hunt, but so does long-standing misogyny at the heart of a strongly patriarchal society. Especially poor older women were often healers, midwives, children's caretakers, and economically vulnerable. In a period of major religious conflict, such women were seen as more likely to turn to dark magic and the devil for some measure of power. Neighbors thought so and often denounced these people as witches.

Perhaps the anxiety-induced killing of vulnerable women for social and religious reasons seems a little out of step with the secular, highfalutin ideas of the Renaissance and Scientific Revolution we've considered. True enough, and the elite's gradual embrace of scientific thought finally ended witch hunting. At the same time, most early modern scientists saw their work as justifying one religious perspective or another, so they sometimes added fuel to the fire (no pun intended).

Similar anxieties drove both witch hunting and clerical concerns about science. Economic changes, population pressures (big growth after the Plague), and dramatic challenges to established religious practices all made many people nervous. Plus, attacking witches, especially women, points to a recurring theme in this book. The very tools that seem most likely to liberate and help people can sometimes be used to reinforce existing social hierarchies. New religious ideas about a personal relationship with God could empower women and other socially weak people. And secular science could challenge the bases of social inequality. However, the early modern witch hunt demonstrates that many men worried about big changes of this era, and elites unleashed those broad fears against some of society's most vulnerable people. Now, imagine me giving you the evil eye and saying, heed ye this warning: when states do give common folk the means to accuse and wage violence on their fellow citizens, bad things will follow. Alongside this here witch hunt, consider ye the French Revolution, Russian Revolution, Nazi Germany, and many other examples. Thou hast been warned.

Women's contributions to early modern science also shows the dual impact of the Scientific Revolution and changes during this era. If the new concept of "science" was about empirical, experimental, practical knowledge, women were actually at the forefront of that work. In some ways they always had been. Across Europe women had been healers, chemists in kitchens, and midwives. Wealthy women, like wealthy men, were able to engage in scientific work and study, often serving as important supporters, sounding boards, and experimental partners with new male scientists. Printing and expanded female education gave women greater access to scientific knowledge and the ability to participate in scientific study. Women also played leading roles in alchemy, a more speculative area of science that blurred lines between science and belief, something that was very common among all early modern scientists. Alchemy was to chemistry a bit like astrology was to astronomy.

The colorful and brilliant Italian countess Caterina Sforza (1463–1509) worked on various alchemical procedures, creating some 400 recipes and publishing many of them in various books. She drew from the home remedies common among wealthy and poor women, as well as from leading scholarly texts and her interactions with other scientists. The fact that history books have viewed her contributions as less important than those of big male scientists says a lot about how science advanced *and* how historians have told its history. Sforza was a leading thinker of her day and a forerunner of modern chemistry. But "science" became defined as something men did with the material world in a public setting. That assumption has literally written Sforza out of the history of science.

Similarly, important pro-science organizations like the Royal Society of London for Improving Natural Knowledge (1660) and the Parisian *Académie Royale des Sciences* (1666) helped institutionalize science as something collaborative, public, and valuable to the early modern state and society. Yet by excluding women from membership, such organizations also institutionalized assumptions that a "scientist" was a man who labored and discovered alone. Assistants, lab technicians, and others who were invaluable to the development of scientific knowledge were all subsumed under the identity of the Great Scientist who got to claim public ownership of knowledge. So not only did men grab the science spotlight, they helped push a "masculine" definition of

So, About Modern Europe …

science (empirical, public, useful for states and business) over a "feminine" concept (both material and spiritual, private, useful for home and family). Given some of the bad things done subsequently in the name of science (weapons, environmental destruction, colonialism), you have to wonder if the scientific vision of women like Sforza would have served the world better.

The modern state and science

Who pays the bills for science? Who benefits from it? In early modern Europe increasingly powerful states shaped and profited from scientific inquiry. During the Scientific Revolution, the modern nation state was developing—states that could influence people's daily lives and even help them define themselves. We often call these states *absolutist*, because they sought absolute authority by trying to influence many aspects of subjects' lives. Some scientists benefitted when these new kinds of state utilized their scientific knowledge to become more efficient and powerful. At the same time, science helped

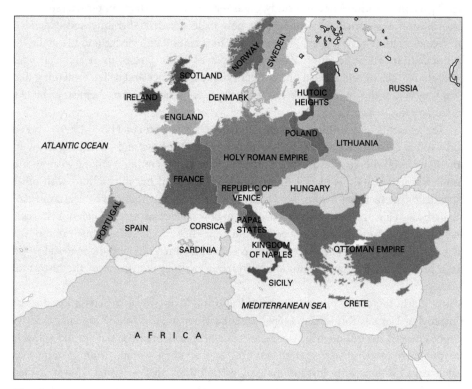

Map 2.1 Europe, *c.*[6] 1500.

---

[6]"C." is short for "circa," which means "around" or "approximately" in Latin.

formulate new ways of thinking to challenge state authority. Let's have a look at three of the most important and powerful states of this era to see how states developed. Then we'll consider how science fit into them.

Spain: the lure of easy money and violent self-righteousness

"Spain" was actually a pretty small and ill-defined place in the Middle Ages. We often assume that countries and cultures we know today have always existed. Definitely not the case for any of the places we're discussing here. We might be able to talk about something like "Spain" starting around 1469 when Ferdinand of Aragon and Isabella of Castile married. Oddly enough, neither of them spoke Spanish. These two monarchs finished in 1491 a task that many rulers of the Iberian peninsula (today Spain and Portugal) had been trying to do since the 700s. They reconquered the area from Muslims who had moved in from North Africa. Then in 1492 they kicked out the Jews (or forced them to convert) for good measure. This process defined being "Spanish" by blood and religion, which foreshadowed modern notions of race and ideology.

You may know that Spain began colonizing the New World in 1492, which was awesome for them, because it literally brought in boat loads of silver and gold stolen from those lands. Having that kind of coin had some dramatic consequences. For one, Spanish kings could wage war pretty much any time they wanted. Also, Spanish elites needed trade from the New World, including the slavery that became part of that system. That set-up made Spanish elites less interested in economic innovation. The success of early colonialism also reinforced in Spain the importance of religion and blood. This system totally worked for the Spanish for a while but didn't help so much going into the modern world. And Spain was not the most hospitable place for science, because the Catholic Church was more powerful and less tolerant there than in Italy. Plus, Spanish leaders generally weren't too interested in science as a tool for technological and economic progress, 'cause they had boatloads of gold and silver rolling in.

France: absolutism as the origins of beautiful palaces, gourmet cuisine, and the French Revolution

When historians talk about absolutism, they usually mean the system that developed in France in the seventeenth and eighteenth centuries, one in which the king wielded great authority through a powerful, centralized state.[7] It was very pretty and generally effective—at least for the top 5 percent of the population. France, too, was disorganized and weak in the Middle Ages with no common language. The decentralized nature of all these places stemmed in part from the organization of European feudalism. In this economic system lords owned all the land and peasants farmed it and gave most what they harvested/earned to the lord.

---

[7]If we're honest, though, "absolute" is a bit of a stretch. The king still had to work with nobles and even some middle-class people. Chapter 4 will be all about how that dramatically fell apart.

King

Prince-Prince-Prince

Duke – Duke – Duke – Duke – Duke

Marquess- Marquess- Marquess- Marquess- Marquess- Marquess

Earl-Earl-Earl-Earl-Earl-Earl-Earl-Earl-Earl-Earl-Earl-Earl-Earl-Earl- Earl-Earl

Viscount-Viscount-Viscount-Viscount-Viscount-Viscount-Viscount-Viscount-Viscount

And so on…

Figure 2.3 Feudalism in a crude chart.

As a political system, feudalism meant that power and money flowed upward. In the much-simplified chart (Figure 2.3), each level of nobility owed allegiance to the noble above them. That relationship required nobles to pass on a little of what they made to their superiors and to provide military support in times of war. Kings at the top therefore received plenty of allegiance *but* were only as powerful as the money and arms flowing up to them. It may be hard to believe, but medieval kings were actually kinda weak, because their support came from those below and could be taken away. You can imagine that plenty of monarchs did not like this arrangement.

The young French king Louis XIII (1601–43) tried to do something about it. He and his main minister, Cardinal Richelieu (1585–1642), wanted to bypass this silly feudalist system by placing the king in control of taxes and the army, both of which were firmly in the hands of nobles. Louis didn't get it all settled, but he managed to make France firmly Catholic and stop nobles from keeping armies. His son Louis XIV (1638–1715) worked out the system during his long rule (seventy-two years!), firmly taking the power to tax and raise armies. He invited nobles to skip all that nasty business of taxing, ruling, judging, and smelling peasants. Louis made his own state representatives (*intendants*) in charge of such duties, freeing the nobles to come and live the good life at Versailles. It was a party, but the king could also keep an eye on them. This highly centralized system revolved around the king himself, which is why he claimed "*l'état, c'est moi*" or "I am the state."

This arrangement made France the most powerful monarchy in Europe, expanded its authority around the world, and made other monarchs super jealous. The French absolutist state also exercised direct control over the economy, a system called *mercantilism*. This political and economic organization ensured that money, power, and innovation flowed from the top down, and it was guaranteed by laws giving great privileges to nobles and the clergy. Such a system weakened innovation and made social and economic inequality into permeant political issues, something that would blow up in the French Revolution in 1789. For scientific development, absolutism was a mixed bag. On the one hand, the French state promoted innovation to advance its mercantilist economy. On the other hand, Catholic dogma, a powerful king with spy networks, limited legal freedom, and centralized control of patronage did not create the most welcoming atmosphere for scientists.

England: absolutist wannabes who stumble into constitutional monarchy

England was in fact the earliest and most unified state in this group. Guillaume or William the Conqueror, who was from Normandy, France, took over England in 1066, unified the island (save Scotland and Wales),[8] built a bunch of fine stone churches, and introduced castles. English tourism has been thankful ever sense. After he gained control of England by the 1070s, William chose to live back in France until he died in 1087. Something about the food and the weather. At any rate, William's need to rule indirectly empowered local nobles to keep things running smoothly. That recognition, especially in the *Magna Carta* or "Great Charter" of 1215, strengthened the feudal organization that kings hated.

Sometimes British history is told as one splendid, intentional step after another toward a modern equitable, democratic society.[9] But make no mistake: early modern English monarchs did not gladly limit their power. They wanted themselves some absolutism and maybe a Versailles too. Beyond those pesky *Magna Carta* rights of landholding nobles, religious conflicts further eroded the English monarch's authority. In the 1530s, Henry VIII (1491–1547) yanked England away from the Catholic Church, creating the Protestant Church of England (with himself as the Head, thank you very much). He did so for both theological and political reasons (like trying to find a wife who could give him a male heir), not to mention his sexual appetites.[10]

Henry and subsequent monarchs demanded religious loyalty. However, there was a lot of fighting in seventeenth-century England about whether England was Protestant or Catholic. And since the monarch was the head of the Church, religious struggles weakened that position. Finally, in 1688 Parliament invited William and Mary of Orange, from the Netherlands, to become king and queen. This move by the nobles, called the Glorious Revolution, settled previous religious and political conflicts. England was Protestant (with some tolerance for other religions), and Parliament held supreme power, not the monarch. English rulers also tried to manage the economy, but they left more room for private or university innovation in science than the French or Spanish did.

---

[8]Yep, you read that right: a Frenchman united England.

[9]God knows US history is often told that way too. Come to think of it, lots of historians indulge in such fantasies.

[10]Henry did have a son with his third wife, but it's one of the great ironies of English history that his daughter Elizabeth from his second marriage became one of England's greatest monarchs. And yes, horny kings screwed a lot of things up in the past. No pun intended.

These modern states became more and more involved in people's lives, including the work of scientists. In France, the state played a very direct role in how science developed. Wars of religion ripped France apart in the second half of the sixteenth century and were one of the main reasons Louis XIII and XIV built that strong monarchy. Perhaps the most innovative French thinker of this time, René Descartes (1596–1650), exemplified the work of scientists in early modern France. He came up with a whole new way to know what we know. That's epistemology, baby! Descartes advanced mathematics, first speculated about inertia, and thought that the universe might be filled with matter, all of which have had profound impact on science ever since. And like other scientists of this time, Descartes assumed his work directly reflected religious morality. In fact, he may be most famous for coming up with a logical "proof" of God's existence. Descartes was mainly a theoretical thinker, and his theories did not challenge the authority of Christian theology or the absolutist state very much. As a result, he generally flourished in the French system, although his hair did suffer a little. Descartes had really nice hair. But the state messed that up later in his life, because balding king Louis XIII began the fashion of men wearing wigs in the 1620s. You win some, you lose some, René.

Hairstyles mattered in England too. After all, one side of the bloody Civil War in the 1640s was labelled the Roundheads, because they had short hair and didn't wear fancy noble wigs. Likewise, religious conflict shaped the development of science in England, especially in the seventeenth century. A number of leading scientists there were Puritans and believed that science should be practical, that is, based on evidence and human observation and aim to improve humans' lives. Some thinkers like Francis Bacon (1561– 1626) and Thomas Hobbes (1588–1679) concluded that a strong state could best guarantee the bounty of science. In 1660, scientists founded the Royal Society of London for Improving Natural Knowledge. This organization became one of the most important locations and models for collaborative scientific work in Europe.

From this context came the most important English scientist, Sir Isaac Newton (1643–1727). He served in important roles for the government and the Royal Society of London for Improving Natural Knowledge. Newton finished the work that a lot of previous scientists had started by figuring out how the planets moved. He discovered gravity, posited basic laws of motion, improved telescopes, and developed theories about color and the speed of sound. Newton also perfected calculus, for which people have both thanked and cursed him ever since. Newton's work was typical of this era. He saw his efforts as strengthening faith in God, yet his ideas convinced some folks that the universe functioned with little or no influence from God.

So, the English and French states both supported science. Good for them. In both places scientists worked to advance the technology and economy of their country. The growth of early capitalism matters here. In fact we might describe the major difference between English vs. French support for science as based on low vs. high trust in market forces.[11] The French state's lower trust in markets ensured royal funding, whereas greater

---

[11]Henry C. Clark, *Compass of Society* (Landham, MD: Rowan & Littlefield/Lexington Books, 2007).

trust in markets in England created more space between government and private activity. In these cases and across Europe, science became a tool to improve people's lives, increase economic opportunity, and expand the power of the state over its citizens. Oh, and eventually take of the world.

Conclusion: the many legacies of science

If you glance at the topics that follow in this book, you'll see that science is literally everywhere. Enlightenment, industry, colonialism, wars, race and identity, material abundance, and so on. All science, all the time—well, pretty much. In the modern world, science has become the primary way to explain and make most things, and therefore it has also helped shape our visions of how humans work together. The concepts we've been looking at here help explain many subsequent developments and ideas.

To wrap up, let's consider the main impacts of the Scientific Revolution:

- **A new definition of truth,** based on empirical evidence and a process we now call the Scientific Method.

- **Conflict between material and religious/spiritual views of the world**. Virtually all early modern scientists saw their work as extensions of their Christian beliefs. Nevertheless, their *material* explanations of things raised potentially tough questions about God's place in the world. They offered a new means to understand the world and maybe even human behavior without relying upon religion.

- **Ways to control Nature**. Theology and science actually reinforced each other in this case. The Christian story of God giving Nature to the care of humans encouraged early modern thinkers to assume it was their job and duty to rule over nature. Science gave them the tools to know the natural world better, control it, and maybe mess it up.

- **Increased power of the state and elites over common people**. From 1500 to 1700 European states grew in power partly by harnessing science and math to improve their economies, militaries, and politics. By the start of the eighteenth century, most elites in Europe more or less understood the world scientifically, whereas average people continued to use a mixture of religion and traditional peasant ideas. This intellectual separation would last until around the start of the twentieth century.

- **The long march of technology**. Scientific knowledge expanded greatly, as more people investigated the natural world. But in early modern Europe, science aimed to deliver new technology to people, states, and businesses. The need to get funding often drove scientists—then as now—to highlight the practical benefits of their work. That desire to make scientific discovery useful, and thus for sale, was there from the start.

- **Tools for controlling the world**. Science reinforced Europeans' assumptions that they could and should remake the world and history in their image. Uh, God complex much?

- **Assumed progress**. Science, finally, convinced those in the know that progress was possible and maybe inevitable. Science became a process for new ideas to compete with old ideas. New discoveries and methods of observation would push and alter what scientists assumed to be true. In other words, things were bound to change. Change, conflicting ideas, and new knowledge were at the heart of the scientific method that developed by around 1700. As scientific thinking became more common, more people believed in the spirit of progress animating science. And that's our cue to move on to the Enlightenment.

CHAPTER 3
THE ENLIGHTENMENT WILL FREE YOU AND MESS YOU UP

Well, this is the main attraction, the big reveal for the book. After all, the Enlightenment is even in the title. The ideas in this chapter are the foundation of modern Europe, the Western world, the contemporary universe! Yes, they are pretty important, and we'll get to them in a moment, but first let me throw one little surprise at you. It's because of the Enlightenment that women, not men, wear high-heeled shoes.

Seriously. Knights in the Middle Ages wore heeled shoes to stay in the saddle. In the seventeenth century women started copying lots of male aristocratic fashion, including higher heels. By the eighteenth century, aristocratic men and women loved to display just how impractical they were by wearing heels—just like being pale showed that they didn't have to work hard outside like everyone else. The Enlightenment, as we'll see, challenged the impractical nature of the aristocracy and helped redefine men's purposes. Aristocratic men began dressing more practically to demonstrate they could do something productive, like own an estate or a factory or command soldiers or rule everyone. Suddenly men's heels were *so* eighteenth century. We'll see below that the Enlightenment was a real mixed bag for women. These fine ideas *might* liberate women someday, but they also helped define women as the "dark" opposite of "enlightened" men. Women's roles didn't change that much. So, wealthy women kept wearing heels because they looked good, and women weren't supposed to be practical, contributing citizens. The Enlightenment thus helped make women into objects, not active subjects, from their shoes up. Depending upon how you feel about heels on women, this lesser-known result of the Enlightenment was either a blessing or a curse.[1]

Building the argument

The last two chapters dealt with some biggies. First, Renaissance thinkers showed us that humans might not be so bad and that it's okay for society to focus on their happiness. The Renaissance encouraged early scientists to use reason and critical inquiry to find answers about the natural world and about people. Then those crazy early modern scientists went further to define truth as something that's measurable by humans. They didn't try to pick a fight with religious leaders. Really. But early scientists were not the most humble bunch, and their ideas that the Bible didn't hold the ultimate truth for everything pissed off the Catholic Church particularly. It didn't help that scientists were

---

[1] Elizabeth Semmelhack, *Heights of Fashion* (Toronto: Bata Shoe Museum, 2008).

making these bold claims while tons of Christians were forming Protestant churches or trying to reform the Catholic Church. As we saw in the last chapter, both the Protestant and Catholic Reformations grew out of new Renaissance humanist ways of thinking about humans' relationship with God. Crazy days.

Now, in this chapter we'll see Enlightenment *philosophes* (a wonderfully pretentious word for "thinker" or "philosopher") build upon the Renaissance and Scientific Revolution. They used rational, scientific, human-oriented thought to propose new ways that people could organize themselves and relate to each other. That's the Enlightenment for you: a little humanism, some science, and the belief that folks could fix their societies. Sounds pretty good, right?

These new ideas are going to be the basis of many great liberation plans right up to today: human rights, democracy, freedom, socialism, EDM, capitalism, etc. But we'll also see in this chapter that Enlightenment thinking included certain assumptions about who gets liberated and who gets controlled. Europeans (and the societies they spawned in North America and Oceania) did not make up all the powerful ideas in this chapter. Some of them we can find in other places at other times. But as we saw in the last two chapters, even when Europeans stole or borrowed others' ideas, they used them to expand their power. The Scientific Revolution may have given Europeans the tools to take over the world, but the Enlightenment created a new "civilization" they thought was worth exporting. The Enlightenment's dual nature will lead us to some pretty dark places, not to mention high heels. Remember the main point of this book? Ideas from the Enlightenment have profoundly shaped our society for good *and* ill. Let's have desert first and begin with the good news.

Humans are good

Think about that for a moment: humans are good. That's our starting point to understand the Enlightenment. These philosophes thought that people were good and could do good things. They could think for themselves and fix things. Now, that's a big change from religious perspectives up until this point. The religious traditions of the West—Judaism, Christianity, and Islam—all said that people were bad to the bone and had to rely on some serious divine intervention to overcome that badness. Those faiths assumed that original sin (Adam and Eve disobeying God) defined humans as evil and living in guilt.

Enlightenment thinkers were like, guys, we are *good*; we've got to get beyond that original sin business! (And, yes, they did mean "guys" only; we'll get to gender in a bit.) Humans are good, but the systems they live under mess them up: political systems, economic and social organizations, even families. Enlightenment philosophes thought that *systems* caused people to do bad things like war, murder, theft, oppression, smooth jazz, injustice, and so on. If we can fix the system to maximize human goodness, then society will be awesome. This shift from seeing people as bad to seeing them as good was the basis of Enlightenment thought. It meant that anything is possible. Machiavelli had shown over 200 years before that political leaders could rethink how they ruled, that they weren't bound to do everything like those before them. Enlightenment philosophes gave leaders *and* average people the hope that they could radically change their society: make it more just, fair, more powerful, or efficient. Of course, all these smart people didn't necessarily agree on what needed to be fixed. But if humans were good and rational, then, by God (or not), they can fix society.

An age of Enlightenment

Immanuel Kant (1724–1804) was kind of a funny guy, at least for an eighteenth-century German philosopher. So maybe he was just being a smart ass, when he said in 1784, "If we are asked, 'Do we now live in an enlightened age?' the answer is 'no.' But we do live in an age of enlightenment." The difference matters. Enlightenment was a process, according to the wry Herr Kant, not necessarily a status one achieves. An "age of enlightenment" meant that lots of philosophers and scientists and others in the eighteenth century were considering changes and hopefully working toward something better. But they didn't believe that their societies were yet "enlightened."

We call the ideas they came up with collectively "The Enlightenment," but there was no unified movement or set of principles to which everyone involved agreed. It wasn't a *thing* that did stuff or accomplished feats. We're talking about a broad group of intellectuals, some European leaders, and a few of the educated elite. Although writers from around Europe contributed, the French probably deserve the right to claim the Enlightenment because of the tension there between political and intellectual development. See, the absolutist state, which French kings really rocked, created an atmosphere in which the government tried to assert control yet had to consider the needs of society. And more than in most places, French intellectuals fought each other about whether ancient or new learning could improve society more. They were really into both. From those conditions, thinkers came up with ideas that criticized the status quo, starting in the early 1700s and ending with the French Revolution in 1789. Enlightenment ideas played a major role in that big event (and in the 1776 American Revolution). More on that next chapter.

Anyway, big-headed philosophes came up with many different ideas about how to understand the world and make society better. They shared them with each other, published books, discussed them, and sometimes got in trouble for what they wrote. But only in 1784, with some early hindsight, did Immanuel Kant identify something called the Enlightenment. We can look back on this era like archeologists or maybe miners, unearthing what seems helpful to explain what followed. After all, that's what historians do. So, let's sit back in our historical armchairs and identify five major themes in Enlightenment thought.

1. Reason and science can explain how humans behave and organize themselves

Scholars have also called this era "The Age of Reason." But what exactly is reason? It's the ability to use logic to draw conclusions from evidence, especially to consider how one thing leads to another. It comes from the Latin verb *reri* or "to think, to consider," and it implies that reason also encourages us to think about new things. Reason usually stands in contrast to emotion, instinct, and religious belief. Science, as we saw in the last chapter, reveals more about the world and the universe by analyzing evidence that can be observed. And when people used reason and science to uncover truth, they sometimes demonstrated that the Bible and religious leaders didn't have all the answers. Enlightenment thinkers lived in this world of science and reason. In fact, many of them were scientists too—doing chemistry in the back yard, reading books on human anatomy, etc. And why not? In the eighteenth century none of this work they did—social theorist, political philosopher, botanist, advocate of freedom, chemist, philosophe—was a profession.[2]

Enlightenment thinkers applied science and reason to human organization. If we can use such concepts to understand the universe better, then, hey, let's use those same cool tools to clarify how people work and improve their lives. Isaac Newton had shown that the natural world could be rationally explained, and that view helped set the stage for Enlightenment thinkers to do the same for human interactions. The Dutch mathematician Baruch Spinoza (1632–77) had the audacity to claim that humans were rational individuals who could understand the universe. What, he thought, if we used science and reason to study the Bible? I bet you can guess how well that was received. Bad boy Galileo had gotten himself excommunicated by noting places where the Bible lacked answers. Spinoza went further. He actually used reason and evidence-based analysis *on* the Bible and thus questioned some basic Judeo-Christian ideas. No wonder Jewish and Catholic leaders banned his books! Fortunately, Spinoza did not make a living as a writer. He worked modestly as a lens grinder, turning his scientific knowledge into practical technology that rested on people's faces. And even his detractors agreed that he was a really nice guy.

Enlightenment thinkers followed these scientists' lead and asked about the rationality of political systems, religious organizations, and social relations. They wanted evidence for why things worked. And when evidence suggested that existing ways of doing things were not working, well, these guys were ready to come up with new ways of running a government or creating laws or whatever. Enlightenment thinkers sought new ways to make society work better. Reason and science gave them the critical tools to ask difficult questions and common standards to judge the answers. Two examples.

First, Charles-Louis Baron de Montesquieu (1689–1755) was one of the most influential political theorists of the Enlightenment. He helped identify different types of government, and he argued that states should separate branches of government and put checks and balances on each other. Needless to say, the absolute monarchs of his day were not impressed. But sly Montesquieu avoided angering the powers that be because of the very scientific and rational way that he built his argument. His *Spirit of the Laws* (1748) reads a bit like a list. He describes the positive and negative points of what he saw as the three main types of government: republic, monarchy, and despotism. Now,

---

[2]Too bad, because "Advocate of Freedom" sounds like a pretty cool thing to put on a business card.

Montesquieu was a baron, but even he couldn't get away with advocating a republic in France. However, he could neutrally *observe* the good and bad in these government systems and let readers draw their own conclusions. In the end, his ideas strongly influenced the constitutions of both the United States and revolutionary France. But his rational, dispassionate description kept him out of trouble.

And then there's Mr. Capitalism himself,[3] the Scotsman Adam Smith (1723–90). If you can identify only one rule in capitalism, I bet it's the idea that prices are determined by supply and demand. Aye, that's Adam Smith fir ya. He also explained the value of rational self-interest, division of labor, and competition. Like his Enlightenment brothers, he thought that people were good and that economic systems should enable individual freedom, in order to improve society. His main book, *The Wealth of Nations* (1776), described an "invisible hand" that would benefit people's lives if they all pursued their own interests. These ideas also challenged the broad assumption at this time that governments should control economic life (the system of mercantilism). Smith's ideas have proven to be some of the most far-reaching of the Enlightenment. Like our man Montesquieu, Smith described what he saw. Specifically, he drew conclusions by observing working factories in Scotland and northern England. He used reason and evidence to create ideas that would become the basis for capitalism. Montesquieu and Smith didn't just theorize about new ways to set up society. They built their ideas on observation and rational analysis.

2. New ideas challenge established religion and nobility

Pretty much all of Europe in the eighteenth century was ruled by an aristocracy—an elite with titles and privileges—usually with religious support. Sure, there were differences between kings and duchesses and counts and all that. But they all basically had the same sweet gig: they owned land that others worked, which paid them money; they were exempt from taxes; and they usually had their own (more lenient) laws. Protestant and Catholic religious leaders supported that hierarchy, in part because the set-up earned them privileges too. Now, as we saw with the Scientific Revolution, the Catholic Church defended their own special place in society more aggressively than Protestant leaders did. Still, the basic ideas of the Enlightenment—humans are good, rational and scientific thinking improves society, systems mess people up, basic human equality—all challenged a European society based on noble and religious privileges. Let's get ready to rumble.

Are you really surprised that Enlightenment thought angered religious authorities? I mean, if people are good and can fix their own problems, then what help can God offer, or religious leaders? Most Enlightenment thinkers didn't go so far as to reject Christianity or God's existence. They were largely Kinda Questioning Christians or perhaps Doubting Deists, although a few embraced atheism. They believed in some divine role in the universe—like God as watchmaker—but thought that organized religion, especially the

---

[3] To be fair, Smith's reputation as the Creator of Capitalism actually came later in the nineteenth century.

Catholic Church, was one of those systems that needed to be fixed. Enlightenment thought thus challenged the basic rules of a society dominated in many ways by Christianity. Likewise, their doubts about religion made Enlightenment philosophes wary of Islam, although some Enlightenment types respected the radical, egalitarian implications in Muslim theology. In Christian Europe, especially in France, Enlightenment thinkers hit the Church where it hurt by challenging the economic and legal privileges clerics received.

And nobles? Don't get me started. The feudal ideal assumed that those who fight (knights/lords/nobles/aristocrats, who were all rich white guys) were supposed to protect those who pray (clerics) and those who work (everyone else), so they should also be supported financially. Oh, and they deserved basically their own legal system, too. Now, Enlightenment thinkers came from a variety of backgrounds, including the nobility. And many of them benefitted from noble patronage, especially in France. But that didn't stop these well-dressed rebels in wigs from questioning the privileged position of nobles in European society. No one did it better than Voltaire.

François-Marie Arouet (1694–1778) wrote under the name "Voltaire." And like other one-name celebrities—Cher, Bono, Jesus, Zendaya—it's sometimes hard to distinguish claims about him from reality. But Voltaire really was all that. He was crazy productive: he wrote like 2,000 books and some 20,000 letters! He advocated some of the most salient and longest-lasting ideas of the Enlightenment: freedom of religion and speech; separation of church and state; and rational, critical individualism. Voltaire was hilarious

Figure 3.1 Voltaire.

and hung out with nobles all around Europe. So, if you're funny, publish non-stop, chill with the beautiful people, demand that claims be backed by evidence, and ridicule the Catholic Church, are you shocked when you wind up in prison? Voltaire spent almost a year in the infamous Bastille prison in Paris, which is one of the reasons revolutionaries would storm that place in 1789 and liberate prisoners. Probably his best-known work was the wickedly satirical novel *Candide*, in which Voltaire makes fun of just about everyone. He especially slams clerics and philosophers who used their vague ideas to convince average people that their sad lives were good enough. Basically, Voltaire held people to high standards of behavior. His perspective encapsulates one of the major Enlightenment critiques: leaders should make decisions based on what is best for everyone.

3. Laws and organization help regulate and improve human behavior

Enlightenment writers often praised natural law, but what even is that? Well, natural law is basically a way to make something that humans invent—like rules or rights or culture—seem to be a part of nature and therefore just the way things organically *are* (or should be). John Locke (1632–1704) crafted some of the basic ideas that prompted philosophes to focus on reason, rights, and freedom. He was like James Brown, the godfather of the Enlightenment. (No evidence available on how well Locke sang or danced.) And Locke wrote a lot about natural law. He said that in a state of nature, men are equal and free to do what they want. Locke believed that every man controlled himself and, by extension, controlled his own property. So, the ability to do what you want (as long as you don't harm others) and own property were the bases of Locke's ideas.

Locke was most concerned about how a government might limit those rights. He had lived through some tough events in England, where he saw that governments didn't always respect such property rights, even for rich guys like him. Locke believed that basic freedom and owning property were natural laws that should be enshrined in legal statues. The idea of natural law was super compelling in the eighteenth century because it drew inspiration from science, ancient thought, and even medieval religion. And besides, who wouldn't want to base rules and governments on natural laws? It appeals to reason and it *feels* right. Enlightenment thinkers wanted laws. But instead of limiting what people can do or protecting noble or religious privileges, the laws of an enlightened society should reflect natural laws. Such rules would free people to make their society better. The right kind of laws based on these ideals had the ability to challenge the status quo *and* ensure freedom, opportunity, and fairness. Right on!

Obviously, Enlightenment thinkers liked new and challenging ideas, but they also loved to organize things. Oh, yes! If you think about basic forms of writing—the novel, play, essay, poem, etc.—they all existed before the Enlightenment. But the Enlightenment gave us the encyclopedia: a bunch of info in a long series of books, nicely organized, distilled down to the important details, and ready to use. Oh, the encyclopedia, you say, very exciting. But just hold on, twenty-first century reader. I realize that this format—books on a shelf embodying important knowledge—seems rather cute and boring in our era of the internet and Wikipedia. It may also seem rather top-down controlling. I mean, a comprehensive set of printed books, especially one that tried to include "every branch of human knowledge," seems hard to imagine today.

But that's what Denis Diderot (1713–84) claimed about his *Encyclopedia, or A Systematic Dictionary of the Sciences, Arts, and Crafts*, which came out in installments from 1759 to 1772. The *Encyclopedia* project was kind of like the Enlightenment in a nutshell: a bunch of smart, amateur dudes wrote about everything they could think of. They wanted to improve people's lives in the process. They used evidence, assumed reason would make it work, and believed they had all the answers. And they pissed off authorities. Two of the governing principles of the encyclopedia collection—rational inquiry and the idea that states should serve people—challenged the bases of most European societies. Not surprisingly, French religious and political leaders hounded Diderot and the publishers for years, ultimately forcing the project to be completed outside France.

This collection of thousands of articles by hundreds of authors, including heavy-hitters like Voltaire, Jean-Jacques Rousseau (1712–78), and Montesquieu, tried to cover, well, all the knowledge in the world. Clearly there's some bias here. These guys wanted to know and share everything. But that's impossible, and they didn't recognize their own limited perspective. In fact, the *Encyclopedia* might have been more accurately called "A Collection of What a Bunch of Affluent, Rationally Educated White Guys from France Have Managed to Learn and (Sometimes Secretly) Write About the World." The project was so big that it helped define "knowledge" in a way that has privileged those perspectives ever since. Similarly, the *Encyclopedia* helped define two other important qualities of the Enlightenment: knowledge should be used, and it's important to identify and define things. That sounds pretty cool and scientific, but all that identifying and using gave a small minority of educated men the chief means for saying what everything was and how it should be used, including things they didn't really understand. Take the example of blackness.

White Enlightenment writers (wait, that's redundant) viewed race relations from their perspective of whiteness, even when they opposed slavery or praised universal human value. Enlightenment philosophes made race into something "scientific." They valued scientific differentiation over old-fashioned religious ideas about humans being the same. Perhaps that sounds like a good move for black folks. However, travel reports and even abolitionists (people working to end slavery) at the time like Nicolas de Condorcet (1743–94) thought that the best way for black people, especially slaves, to become good citizens was to become white folks. Huh? Georges-Louis Leclerc, Comte de Buffon (1707–88) wrote thirty-six encyclopedic volumes on natural history and paved the way for Charles Darwin's ideas of evolution. Yet he still thought that humans began as Caucasians, then *devolved* into other races, but could all return to being white!

Enlightenment thinkers used ideas about African bodies, along with thoughts from people in the slave trade, to define blackness. Also, their fascination with Muslim "Others"—as enemies, objects of curiosity, or inspiration—reinforced racial difference. This hot mess of ideas basically invented the myth that race as a thing, something "real" and rooted in observable science. However, race is actually a *social construct*, something that doesn't exist objectively but only in people's collective thinking.[4] Put simply, Enlightenment thinkers helped create the idea of race. And even the most generous among them said that black people had to get beyond their race to become fully human. Needless to say, they didn't say the same about white folks. White, it seems, was the new black. And, of course, these guys believed that such thinking was progress.

4. Society should be based on opportunity and merit (at least for some)

Yessir, things were looking up in the eighteenth century. Enlightenment ideas were going to empower individuals to think on their own and take down centuries-old privileges. They would make natural laws into real laws. They would give people the ability to advance based on what they did, not who their daddy was or where they were born or how they prayed. For John Locke and Adam Smith, this society of opportunity should, above all, be based on the ability to own and use property. Their ideas have helped us, ever since, realize that *economic* opportunity is one of the hallmarks of a free and progressive society. Sounds like capitalism, right? It turns out that protecting property rights has been one thing that governments since the Enlightenment have done pretty well. Property is tangible and easier to define than other rights. Owning property is also one of the things that all the Enlightenment thinkers and all their readers had in common, so it was one of their starting assumptions about how society should work. It's worth mentioning, though, one philosophe who had a slightly different take on opportunity, rights, and fairness.

Jean-Jacques Rousseau was pretty radical, even among Enlightenment thinkers. He was all over the place, literally and figuratively. He moved all around Europe, sometimes because governments opposed his ideas and sometimes because of romantic conflicts. He wrote about philosophy, government, laws, education, romance, history, child-rearing, music, and religion. Besides Locke's *Two Treatises*, probably no other book inspired the American and French revolutions more than Rousseau's 1762 *The Social Contract*. Rousseau certainly agreed with Locke and others that humans were good. He also believed in the natural law of human freedom and was generally cool with property rights. But Rousseau believed that the right to govern (political sovereignty) can come only from the *general will* of the whole population. On the one hand, this idea promoted hard-core, direct democracy. It placed Jean-Jacques atop the list of revolutionary ass kickers and got his book banned in France and elsewhere. At the same time, his ideas about popular sovereignty taking precedence over property meant that other rights might be more important than property ownership. Whoah! Most Enlightenment thinkers believed, like Locke, that democracy and private property reinforced each other. Rousseau pointed out that they might conflict with each other. As a result, his ideas expanded opportunities for those *without* property too. Like I said, Rousseau was a radical guy.

Generally, Enlightenment thought promised people the opportunity to succeed based on their effort, not birth, family, or faith. Basically, a meritocracy for educated white guys. The same people who had the resources (time, education, enough to eat, coffee) to think

---

[4]Other examples of social constructs: money, nations, teenage ideas about "popularity," class distinctions.

up these generous ideas would, not surprisingly, benefit most from them. To be fair, that perspective was radical back then and challenged the status quo in big ways. You can see that in the American and French Revolutions. But that perspective excluded most people in European society. First, we've already seen that many Enlightenment thinkers thought people of color were "noble savages" (Rousseau's term) and different from white people. Next, poor folks couldn't read this stuff, and without property, what stake did they have in society? Finally, where the women at?

Maybe you've been impressed before with noble-sounding language like "all men are created equal" or "he that has blah blah blah." Perhaps you thought, well, yeah, the author *meant* to include the ladies, but back in the day they just used "man" or "he" to mean everyone. And besides, it sounds old and cool. That still working for you? While some philosophes tried to treat women equally or considered some rights for them, by and large when these dudes were writing about "men" and "he," they meant guys only. Very few Enlightenment writers tackled directly the vastly inferior position of all women in European society.

The French Revolution would bring the issue up, especially when Olympe de Gouges (1748–93) totally roasted the 1789 "Declaration of the Rights of Man and Citizen" by penning her own "Declaration of the Rights of Woman and the Female Citizen" a couple of years later. The British author and activist Mary Wollstonecraft (1759–97), who also participated in the French Revolution, published the pathbreaking *Vindication of the Rights of Woman* in 1792, arguing especially for equal access to education for women and girls. To be sure, feminism of the nineteenth and twentieth centuries (and today) owes something to Enlightenment concepts of freedom, equality, and opportunity. But the fact that writers like de Gouges and Wollstonecraft are chiefly labelled "inspirations" should tell you that they had pretty much zero impact during their lifetime. "Inspiration" sounds better in the twenty-first century than they did for women in the eighteenth century.

5. *Progress is possible, maybe even inevitable*

You can thank science for this idea, as we discovered in the last chapter. Science is about change, challenge, and new knowledge. Put a political or social spin on it, and you've got a swell Enlightenment idea: things are not so great now, but history or fate or science or something is on our side, and things will improve. Eighteenth-century Enlightenment writers drew inspiration from the success of earlier scientists like Galileo, Copernicus, and Newton. Not only had those previous ideas yielded greater understanding of the universe; they had also created a scientific method that promised progressively more knowledge. And they showed everyone the value of freely exchanging ideas. Since Enlightenment thinkers employed similar approaches, they too promised progress.

The Scottish author David Hume (1711–76) exemplified the grounded optimism of Enlightenment thought. Like his kilted buddy Adam Smith,[5] Hume drew his ideas

---

[5]There is absolutely no evidence that either man wore a kilt, especially since kilt-wearing was an invented tradition of the nineteenth century, but that's another story. Anyway, sorry for the stereotype, but you have to admit that it's fun to imagine these two scholars earnestly conversing in kilts. Just saying.

from reason and observation. In particular Hume's 1742 essay "Of the Rise and Progress of the Arts and Sciences" argues that advances in science and the arts develop best in a republic and in turn help further that form of government. Uh-oh, Dave-o, your British monarchy might not like that republican talk. He didn't really get in trouble, though, because the British tolerated such stuff better than the French. Hume paired scientific and political progress in a way that may feel like some ideas we have today. Probably most of us assume that the free flow of scientific, economic, and political ideas all somehow depend upon each other and will, most likely, gradually make things better. That's Hume for you.

Together, the concepts that humans are (a) good and (b) able through learning to improve their lot meant that Enlightenment thinkers generally believed that life could be made better. They did not naively assume that the religious, political, and social systems that restricted human progress would just melt away. They called for real change, sometimes even revolution. And they believed that things were getting better and that their ideas would help improve living conditions for even more people. While their thoughts about freedom and equality were not meant for everyone, those concepts did in fact eventually support modern human rights movements like abolition, civil rights, women's emancipation, gay rights, and so on. Should we therefore give Enlightenment dudes the benefit of the doubt and assume that they, you know, *meant* these ideas to be for everyone, at least some day? Or do we take them at their word that they were writing to a very limited audience and could only imagine propertied white guys as the beneficiaries of these ideas of freedom? Depends on whether you think the glass is half full or half empty. Oddly enough, the answer may lie in opera.

Light vs. Dark

Mozart's 1791 opera *The Magic Flute* spells out pretty clearly the conflict at the heart of the Enlightenment: liberating, light Enlightenment vs. controlling, dark Enlightenment. I realize not everyone's into opera. But just search the "Queen of the Night Aria" from *The Magic Flute*, and you'll have to admit that it's some next-level stuff. Honestly, this opera has some great parts and is funny in places. But whether you dig it or not, Mozart's opera does epitomize the struggle between Enlightenment-for-everyone vs. just-for-white-guys.

Quick synopsis. Prince Tamino falls in love with the portrait of Princess Pamina, whom he thinks is being held against her will by the ruler Sarastro. Pamina's mother, the Queen of the Night, tells Tamino to go rescue her daughter and promises Pamina's hand in marriage if he succeeds. To help Tamino, the Queen sends him Papagano, a fun-loving bird catcher, and gives Tamino a magic flute. When Tamino and Papageno get to Sarastro's place, they find that he's actually pretty cool. It turns out Sarastro is Pamina's dad and the Queen's ex. He's basically the King of Light. He's always portrayed in bright colors and advocates calm, reason, wisdom, fairness, etc., so he's pretty much the opposite of the Queen of the Night. You getting the picture here? Queen of the Night, who demands loyalty and works with emotion, vs. Enlightenment Sarastro, who favors reason and gives the youngsters an opportunity to prove themselves.

Let's make the contrast shaper: Sarastro's slave, Monostatos, lusts for Pamina's "white skin," despite his being an "ugly" black man. Sarastro disapproves of Monostatos's feelings. However, he respects (rich white guy) Tamino's desire to win Pamina and promises to let them be together if he can pass difficult tests. But Sarastro's priests warn Tamino and Papageno against deceptive "idle women's talk," so he and Pamina can't communicate for a while. Pamina is sad, Tamino is resolute. Tamino leads Pamina through the tests successfully, with a little help from his magic flute, and they are brought together in a very, very bright ceremony at the end, presided over by Sarastro. Hurray! Oh, and Papageno gets a girl too, his new "little wife." Monostatos goes over to the Queen of the Night's side because she promises to give Pamina to him, if he helps challenge Sarastro. But in the end the Queen, Monostatos, and the Queen's ladies are defeated and sink into "eternal night."

There are two main ways to read this opera, either as promise for Enlightenment liberation or that the Enlightenment needs darkness to define light. Certainly, the opera was an allegory about the Enlightenment. Both Mozart and the guy who wrote the text were Freemasons in Vienna and supported Enlightenment ideals. Sarastro stands for the Enlightened Despot, a wise leader who can use his absolute power to promote Enlightenment ideals. Tamino controls his emotion and realizes the value of wisdom, reason, and generosity, in order to become a member of Sarastro's temple. In the end Pamina also gets to be part of this group, which includes women. So, the opera *could* be saying that women and perhaps everyone can earn Enlightenment freedom. The Queen of the Night and Monostatos represent emotion, blind desire for power, and unquestioned personal loyalty—not really Enlightenment qualities.

The other reading of this opera is less generous. Only the white men really get the goods. Pamina can join Club Enlightenment only because she's led there by a dude, and throughout the story she is basically the emotional damsel in distress. Plus, she's a princess, so at least she's got cash. Monostatos is defined by his "black skin" and lust for a white woman. Plus, the great Enlightened despot Sarastro keeps him as a slave. Awkward! The Queen of the Night of course represents all that the Enlightenment is not, and her minions literally worship her. The story wouldn't work without these "dark" characters. So, another reading of *The Magic Flute* is that you need darkness—dark ideas and unenlightened people—in order to recognize enlightenment. That reading implies that Enlightenment philosophes only aimed their liberating ideas at wealthy white men who could, in their minds, be enlightened like they were. This interpretation also means that the Enlightenment could be used to control people as much as to liberate them. This opera reflects, as well, the need to define people and their characteristics, usually at the expense of women and people of color. And hey, we've seen that's an Enlightenment quality too. After all, the great Encyclopedia promised to define and organize knowledge, so it would be easier to use—by those who could afford to buy all those books, which was almost exclusively wealthy white men.

We can therefore read *The Magic Flute* as evidence of the Enlightenment's tendency to liberate people *and* to define and control them. That point will shape much of what follows in European and world history. In fact, the Enlightenment has been appealing to lots of people precisely because it offers both the ability to liberate and control. I'll just mention one big example from the twentieth century. Enlightenment ideals helped free Jews from restrictive, unfair laws in Europe but also gave antisemites the ability to define Jews as unique and the opposite of what's good, with catastrophic results.

Enlightenment ideas in power

Our next chapter will address how Enlightenment ideas helped prompt significant political change in the French Revolution. Like, major, crazy change. While these ideas generally promised to blow the top off Europe's aristocratic and religious order, some of them nevertheless appealed to leaders in the eighteenth century. Austrian Emperor Joseph II (1741–90) was the inspiration for Sarastro in Mozart's *Magic Flute*. He used his enormous authority to push certain Enlightenment ideas into law. He rationalized and made more efficient Austria's bureaucracy and tax code. He also started universal elementary education (for boys) and abolished serfdom (which tied peasant farmers to the land, forced them to give most of what they harvest to their lord, and was only about one step better than slavery). Joseph II did not get rid of all the privileges for nobles or the Catholic Church, but he did create greater equity before the law and mandated religious tolerance, even for Jews. And he ended censorship of the press and theater. In short, this super-powerful monarch used his authority to pass Enlightenment-inspired reforms designed to help individuals and society. Needless to say, most other nobles hated this stuff, and his successors scaled back many of the changes. And there you see the implications of Enlightened Despotism: radical reform or soul-crushing reaction.

The Prussian[6] king Frederick the Great (1712–86) thought Enlightened Despotism was awesome. But even he admitted that monarchism could be the best or worst form of government, depending upon how it was administered. This guy, who wrote music and played a mean flute, also improved and rationalized his government and made the Prussian judicial system mega-efficient. He used Enlightenment ideals to enhance his country's economy, including opening new lands to immigrants and modernizing various industries.

Tsarina Catherine the Great (1729–96) in Russia also selectively used Enlightenment ideals. This tough gal married the future Russian tsar but eventually kicked him out, took control, and ruled for over thirty years. She reformed the Russian tax system and tried to create a national educational system for boys and girls. She granted some religious tolerance and used the wealth of the Russian Orthodox Church to help finance her state improvements. Both Frederick and Catherine were FOVs, Friends of Voltaire, which was like an official Badge of Enlightenment Approval. Catherine eventually soured a bit on

---

[6]Prussia vs. Russia? I was confused about the difference for a while. Russia you probably know, but Prussia was a German-speaking country in the northern part of what's today Germany and Poland. The German name, "Preussen" (pronounced "proi-sen") doesn't sound as much like "Russia," but translations make things interesting.

the Enlightenment, when heads started flying in the French Revolution. And really, don't think of these leaders as *too* Enlightened. After all, they were named "the Great" because they kicked military ass, not because they liberated anyone. And both of them, especially Freddy, used reason and science above all to strengthen his military.

In fact, all of these leaders used Enlightenment ideas for their own purposes. Their reforms may have helped some citizens, but the end result was to enhance the monarch's power. So, again, we see that Enlightenment conflict: these ideas could expand opportunities for people *and* give elites greater authority to control people. European thinkers and (some) leaders rightly celebrated Enlightenment ideas as a new civilization. As we'll see in the chapters that follow, they would use those concepts to remake governments, economies, social structures, and even families in Europe. Then they'd take them on the road and bring them, usually by force, to people around the world (see especially Chapter 7 on Imperialism). The inherently self-serving nature of Enlightenment thought, which we see clearly in the work of "enlightened despots," illustrates one of the main reasons Europeans took over the world in the modern era. Scientific and Enlightenment thought offered Europeans both the means and reasons for domination. At the heart of Enlightenment thinking lies the ethnocentric assumption that everyone would benefit from these concepts, even if they have to be forced to see that.

Where is all this happening?

Obviously, many Enlightenment ideas threatened the status quo, so people who talked about them had to make sure they were safe from government or Church spies. Enlightenment thinkers and their fans were often challenging traditional social organizations—state, Church, family—so they created new places to discuss these things. Official organizations like the *Académie Royale des Sciences* in Paris and the Royal Society of London for Improving Natural Knowledge offered scientists and mathematicians places to share new knowledge. But what if you wanted to talk about politics or social issues? That could get risky since most governments in Europe viewed such topics as dangerous. So, Enlightenment thinkers often retreated to private spaces, especially salons and secret societies.

Wealthy women in eighteenth-century Paris in particular opened their homes to men and women interested in learning about new ideas. They called these gatherings *salons*. They invited poets, philosophers, scientists, political theorists, and others to informal yet stimulating events. Kind of like book clubs today, people from a variety of backgrounds hung out in private homes. There might be a reading by an author or discussion of a new work or idea. Of course, there were entry fees: to be invited you had to know someone, be literate, and have good manners. So, salons certainly did not include everyone, like the poor or uneducated. But they did allow the middle class and nobility to mix, as well as men and women, on fairly equal ground. In some places influential Jews hosted salons. And the people who put these informal meetings together, the *salonnières*, were almost exclusively women. French salons were most famous, but these informal organizations popped up all around Europe. Enlightenment ideas spread through these gatherings, so the salons may be the most important way in which women shaped Enlightenment thinking. In this rare case, sexism actually benefitted women because authorities didn't take these gatherings organized by women so seriously. But in fact, women were helping to define a whole new public sphere, a place where people could consider ideas and policies as equals (well, sometimes).

Folks keen on Enlightenment ideas also met in secret societies. We may be entertained by books and movies about secret societies out to rule the world or protect dark secrets or guard huge treasures, but such groups mainly employed elaborate protections to stay out of jail. Take the Freemasons. This organization, which began with medieval stonecutters, largely embraced rational, secular ideas in the eighteenth century. The Illuminati, who seem super mysterious in block-buster films and conspiracy-theory websites, were similarly in favor of rational ideas, although they tried to merge that with some Catholic teachings. Masons and Illuminati and others weren't sitting around plotting the overthrow of governments, but they were talking about ideas—democracy, science, equal rights, limiting the Church's influence—that authorities didn't like.

These groups were run by well-connected men, which made them dangerous in the minds of government and religious officials. Leaders kept close tabs on such groups. But they were hard to infiltrate, due to their secret practices to protect their members and their work. These societies in Europe and North America gave Enlightenment supporters another space in which to consider and promote new ideas. Like salons, these clubs helped create a new public sphere for developing Enlightenment ideas and eventually putting them into action. During the French Revolution, the street and battlefield would become the most decisive parts of the public sphere. But places like salons and private clubs would continue to promote new ideas in the decades that followed.

A final word about humor

It's important to note that my very ability to use humor (or try) and irony to make some points stems partly from Enlightenment thought. Of course, folks had been funny and ironic for centuries. Renaissance writers particularly learned the value of humor from ancient texts. See, ancient Greek and Roman writers did not have a (relatively humorless) Bible to cite as authority, so they used humor and sarcasm as some of the many tools to make their works more appealing to readers. More than their predecessors, many Enlightenment writers used satire to make their arguments. For one thing, that style was entertaining. Plus, using humor or even ridicule to attack your opponents could also be safer: "oh no, your honor, of course I wasn't making fun of the king. My story about some pathetic monarch who destroys his country was clearly just a joke, not something that could ever happen here ..." So, here's another great legacy of the Enlightenment: our ability to use humor to challenge the powers that be.

So, yeah, the Enlightenment may free you or mess you up. Or both. It did both to a lot of people in the centuries that followed. Hopefully it's clear that these rational, scientific, human-oriented concepts had the potential to liberate people from restrictive rules. Enlightenment thinkers aimed to create governments to serve all citizens. Enlightenment ideas will help spawn all kinds of movements that will improve people's lives and free them from oppression. And they gave us a common, human standard for judging how well things are going. Above all, the Enlightenment promised progress. But there's also a storm coming, starting with what went down in 1789. Nationalism was definitely an Enlightenment idea that let people determine their own fate *and* prompted wars, oppression, and genocide. The ability to use these concepts to define things, people, goals, enemies, etc. can move us away from prejudice and assumption, but it can also give those in power new tools for controlling people. Welcome to the Janus-faced[7] world of the Enlightenment.

---

[7]Janus was a very old Roman god with faces looking two directions, symbolizing conflict, difference, etc. I guess this is a snooty way of saying "two-faced."

CHAPTER 4
NOW, *THAT'S* A REVOLUTION! (FRANCE, 1789)

I don't know how else to say it, but the French Revolution that started in 1789 was as big as it gets. It was an earth-shattering, society-breaking, head-chopping, new idea-exploding extravaganza. And it lasted for about twenty-five years. By the time it was over, many things were different, and we can start talking about "modern Europe." Well-heeled leaders afterwards would try to turn back the clock and pretend that concepts like nationalism, democracy, republicanism, and citizenship were just passing fads. Sorry, boys. In fact for the next two centuries and more, Europeans would be coming to terms with ideas that came busting out of the French Revolution.

Life for average people in Europe changed during this revolutionary period. For one thing, massive armies marching across your lands for twenty-five years and grabbing your sons tends to throw off normal life. The big ideas of the French Revolution also reshaped how people related to the state, and the French army kindly delivered these new approaches all over Europe. Feudalism ended in many places, as did lots of privileges that had guaranteed inequality. And people who got to be citizens instead of subjects (even briefly) rather liked it. It took a while, but gradually people's everyday lives shifted after the Revolution. And the changes were about more than just politics. The revolutionary ideas that occupied the minds of intellectuals, leaders, and wealthy people remade the lives of common people too in the form of new jobs, new countries, new clothes, new wars, new social relations, and new connections to the rest of the world. The French Revolution dramatically proved that Enlightenment ideas could rework human society and maybe even humans themselves.

Building the argument

The French Revolution was, in many ways, Enlightenment with guns. And of course you can get further with a kind word and a gun than you can with just a kind word.[1] Long-term economic, political, and social conditions created the conditions for a revolutionary explosion, and short-term desperation provided the spark for violent change. Eighteenth-century Enlightenment ideas provided the sustained motivation and rationale behind the major changes of the French Revolution. Enlightenment ideas—humans are good, reason and science and laws can improve things, merit should determine success, and progress is possible—all became government policies. This chapter will show what happens to bold ideas when people use them to destroy a government and then make a

---

[1] Often attributed apocryphally to Chicago gangster Al Capone.

new one. The Revolution also made clear the dual nature of Enlightenment ideas, sometimes liberating and sometimes controlling people. France remained a strong, centralized state, so both sides of those ideas hit citizens hard.

In this chapter we will explore, first, the causes of the Revolution. Next, we'll consider the very different phases of the Revolution. I mean, it's a long ways from a republic with universal male suffrage to an empire controlled mainly by one guy, Napoleon Bonaparte. It's worth asking if we're even talking about the same event. Did Napoleon continue or undermine the ideals of the revolution? Enlightenment ideas could be somewhat conservative or fairly radical. Our main aim in this chapter is to figure out what happens when those ideas become laws, policies, and new traditions. Then we'll be in good shape to consider their impact in subsequent chapters. Because in this book and in our world, those ideas aren't going anywhere.

Causes of the Revolution: the long, medium, and short of it

The French Revolution was a big event, a seismic shift that altered everything that followed. Take politics. Ever wondered why we talk about the "left" as more liberal, change-oriented, and willing to let government fix things? Well, when deputies during the Revolution sat in the National Assembly, the king happened to sit on the right. Deputies favoring less change sat closer to the king on the right, whereas those who wanted radical change sat as far from the king as possible on the left side. So, left = change, right = conserve status quo.

How about concepts of time? Revolutionaries changed the whole damn calendar and renamed every month and day and started a new era with the founding of the French Republic. Gender relations? The Revolution certainly didn't make men and women equal, but women did gain more freedoms at various points during this era. And the sustained attempt to create a more equitable society made women's rights into a permanent issue thereafter and began what we might call the first wave of feminism. I could go on: the welfare state, the metric system, national anthems, the idea of Germany. Like I said: big changes.

To understand such a mega-event, we need to consider the long-, medium-, and short-term causes. Some of the long-term causes of the Revolution we've already studied, like the tensions in feudalism, concepts of absolutism, and Enlightenment ideas. Medium-term causes were the events and changes of the twenty or thirty years before 1789. And the short-term causes tipped the situation into revolution. Let's look at each one.

Long-term causes

We've already hit the biggies. Chapter 2 talked about how French kings in the seventeenth century, especially Louis XIV, reversed the system of feudalism to enhance royal authority and create absolutism. Chapter 3 looked at Enlightenment ideas, many of which reacted to the experience of living under absolutism. Put simply, the way that absolutism worked and didn't work in France ultimately resulted in the 1789 revolution. France was a big, powerful country. In 1700, one-fifth of all Europeans lived there. So the stakes were high for its system to work.

But—too bad—the system was not working by the eighteenth century. The king wanted to bypass feudalism so he could control the military and taxation. At the same time, the king, nobles, and clerics all wanted to keep the social divisions of feudalism, a hierarchy they believed to have been created by God. This system divided society into three groups or Estates: those who pray (clerics, the First Estate), those who fight (nobles, Second Estate), and those who work (everybody else, the Third Estate). Each group was supposed to support the other two. Those who pray were supposed to do so for fighters and workers. Fighters were supposed to protect prayers and workers. Those who work raised the resources for the prayers and fighters. I bet you can guess which group got the shaft.

This mutual-reinforcing system of feudalism probably never really worked, but it sure as hell did not reflect reality in the eighteenth century. Major economic differences divided all three groups. A poor parish priest, for example, might not be living much better than the peasants he served, while an archbishop kicked it like a prince. Some nobles had fallen on hard times and clung to their privileges as the only thing holding them above other poor people. The vast majority of people in France, about 98 percent of the population, was in the Third Estate. They could be the wealthiest bankers financing the French state or face starvation every winter, but they all had the same limited rights. Clerics and nobles were defined by their privileges, especially having their own laws and paying no taxes.[2] Those privileges were tradition in France and bound the king, Church, and nobility together. Despite his centralized authority, the French king had to negotiate complex traditional privileges and an even more complicated tax system to keep his absolutist system working. As the king went deeper into debt in the eighteenth century, he had to accept more scrutiny about public finances and how the country was run. Traditional privileges were probably the thing that pissed off Enlightenment thinkers the most. They undermined human equality, preventing society from benefitting from everyone's ideas and labor. In pre-Revolution France, your corporate identity through your Estate, guild, religious order, town association, etc. defined your contribution to society, whereas Enlightenment thought valued *individual* effort.

Medium-term causes

Wars and other economic blows to the crown further messed up this bizarre, expensive, inefficient system. The French king could wage war, but that got more expensive than the

---

[2]Many readers will surely find it hard to believe that different rules may apply to wealthy people or that they don't pay much in taxes.

system could handle. By the middle of the eighteenth century, things were getting rough for King Louis XV, who ruled from 1715 to 1774. The Seven Years War (1756–63) put the entire economic basis of the French absolute monarchy at risk. The conflict raged in Europe, North America, West Africa, the Philippines, and India. War is always expensive, but a world war on five continents really costs a lot, especially when you get whipped! Defeated France had to surrender large portions of its North American colonies and some Caribbean islands to the British. Ouch. These losses came as a one-two punch to France. Like all the European powers, France had gone into massive debt to finance the war, and then it lost some of its imperial means to regain economic strength. After the Seven Years War, over half of the French government's income went to servicing debt! That situation simply couldn't last. France was just a step or two away from forcing major change, like (gasp!) taxing nobles and clerics or (bigger gasp!) giving the Third Estate greater power. The American Revolution, which grew in part from the Seven Years War (what Americans call the French and Indian War), pushed France closer to crisis.

France supported American independence to get back at the British and to create a new trading partner. The French bankrolled much of the colonists' fight against the British. Indeed, it's safe to say that the revolution would have failed without French military and financial assistance.[3] And while the French backed the winning horse this time, it was still an expensive bet that put the government further into debt. Fixing the situation would require two things. First, the King, nobles, clerics, and leading members of the Third Estate would have to play nice and find a way to revise tax responsibilities to pay for the crown's debt. Second, there would be no other crises. *Je suis désolé*; neither worked out, so here we go!

Short-term causes

Over-taxing the Third Estate while giving the wealthier First and Second Estates passes created a powder keg in France. Enlightenment thinkers had noted the unfairness and inefficiency of this system. French ministers knew it; they read our Enlightenment friends like Locke, Montesquieu, and Rousseau. Unhappy urban workers, by then a somewhat educated lot, were also familiar with Enlightenment critiques and were reading discussions of the economic crisis in newspapers. In the summer of 1788, the French government failed to make a debt payment, undermining trust in financial markets, which were of course tied directly to the state. The king realized he would have to call the ancient body of the Estates General, which brought all three Estates together, in order to renegotiate taxes to solve the government's financial crisis. This Estates General hadn't met since 1614. Almost all men in France could vote for representatives to the Estates General, so the whole country had a lot invested in this meeting. The swirl of ideas and anger about national finances, though, meant that the meeting in May 1789 would be ugly. On top of

---

[3]That's right, 'Muricans: no French support, no USA.

that, two bad harvests caused the price of bread to skyrocket. In fact, urban workers were paying like 80 percent of their salaries for bread alone!

So, tensions were high when the Estates General met in May 1789. The First and Second Estate reps made sure they could vote together to stop any reforms by the Third. Well, the clever Third Estate fellows knew they were the ones doing all the work. Forget you, they said, and left to form the National Assembly. They immediately demanded an end to the current tax system. Uh-oh. That's hitting the king where it hurt most. Some of the First and Second Estate guys agreed and joined them. On June 20, 1789, after being locked out of their chamber, they moved to the royal tennis court nearby and there swore an oath to stay together until they could forge a constitution. Advantage, National Assembly! The king waffled in his response. But by this point the King and his troops were no longer in control of the situation.

The French Revolution began on 14 July 1789 when a crowd in Paris of mostly artisans and workers stormed the Bastille prison and released the prisoners. That prison had held some political prisoners, including Voltaire seventy years earlier. The Bastille's quick fall shifted the country's mood dramatically. The king could no longer count on the loyalty of his soldiers. The Bastille's fall emboldened protestors across France (and in some other countries too) and scared the hell out of nobles around Europe. Revolutionaries knew they wanted to tear down the political system but found it much harder to rebuild something in its place. Enlightenment ideas offered some guidance but didn't always work out as planned, once they became laws and policies and were backed by cannons and bayonets.

Historians usually divide the revolutionary period into four main stages:

1. Moderate, 1789–91.
2. Radical, 1792–4.
3. Thermidorian Directory, 1794–9.
4. Napoleon, 1799–1815.

If you choose at any point to conclude that, well, *this* is the real end of the Revolution and what followed was something different, you will be in good company. Scholars have long debated what marks the end of the Revolution. I'm going with the big definition from 1789 to 1815 because it helps us see various ways Enlightenment ideas worked and failed. Treating the Revolution as a longer period also makes clear that no one group or person was ever really in control of events. It was a hot mess of ideas, popular will, elite opinion, violence, laws, warfare, tradition, guillotines, and change.

1. Moderate Phase, 1789–91

"Moderate" is a relative thing here. We're still talking about something unprecedented: the abrupt and definitive end to one of Europe's greatest kingdoms, an international empire and world power taken over by popular will. Rousseau and his gang would have been giddy. They might have been nervous too. Fundamentally, the Revolution showed that things could change, that social and political organization was not fixed. And it was a surprise. No one planned it or even anticipated it.

Events in the summer of 1789 began in Paris and nearby Versailles but spread quickly to the rest of the country. Paris was huge: population 750,000. It was bigger than the next nine cities in France combined. So, no surprise that it remained the center of revolution and that political bodies across the country quickly affirmed support for the National Assembly. Still, 80 percent of France's 28 million people lived and farmed in the countryside. Those folks were aware of events in Paris but were most concerned about nobles' control of land and the feudal laws that bound them to lords or the Church. Some of them took matters in their own hands and seized land from weakened nobles. Peasants feared that nobles would hire ruffians to restore order in the countryside, which only pushed the land grab further.[4] This "Great Fear" concerned everyone and drove the National Assembly to abolish feudal laws quickly.

So, suddenly on August 4, 1789 the National Assembly, now the main authority in France, ended the old regime. Just like that. In one night Assembly deputies got rid of all feudal privileges. You know, the rights and rules that had defined France and most European principalities for centuries. They swept away serfdom (tying peasants to lands and lords), special legal treatment for nobles and clerics, and noble privileges, as well as required donations to the Church. The Assembly made taxation equal and ended the myriad privileges of various corporate bodies across France. What a night! City folks rejoiced, peasants chilled. And so, France literally transformed from July 14 to August 5, 1789 into a totally different country. There had been violence, resentment, and elite resistance, yes. But previously opposed social groups had also cooperated with each other. The king, who was in shock like everyone else, didn't seem willing to oppose these swift changes. Needless to say, there was enormous work to be done to create something in place of what had been destroyed. But the summer of '89 was one to remember.

Followed by a hangover in the fall, when new leaders had to create a new regime. But French revolutionaries do not run from a challenge! And they came up with a whole new government, starting with a constitution. And you know they had some pretty good Enlightenment ideas to work with.

"The Declaration of the Rights of Man and Citizen" articulated important Enlightenment ideas like natural rights, equality before the law, human liberty, property rights, and representative government. In that heady summer of 1789, revolutionary celebs Abbé Sieyès (1748–1836) and the Marquis de Lafayette (1757–1834) pulled together Enlightenment ideals and consulted with Thomas Jefferson in the United States (which happened to be working out its own new constitution at the time). Unlike the American "Declaration of Independence," though, the French "Declaration" was a more abstract description of rights aimed at creating a new government that would work *with* the monarch. The "Declaration's" broad assertions were intended to be the pillars of a new government based on liberty, fraternity, and equality, the aims of the French

---

[4]They may be mean, but "ruffians" is a pretty fun word to use.

Revolution. This blueprint insisted that man is born free and that liberty is that which does not harm others; that social distinctions should be based on usefulness, not birth; and that taxes should be evenly distributed. Government, laws, and the military reflect the will of the people, and power should be divided across government. It promoted equality before the law and that people are innocent until proven guilty. It guaranteed freedom of speech and religion.

You can see our pals Locke, Rousseau, and Montesquieu here. The "Declaration" was adopted by the National Assembly on August 26, 1789, reflecting widespread agreement by leaders and many citizens on these ideals. The one exception was religion. Deputies and French people held a range of opinions about religion, from assuming Catholicism to be the official faith of the land to questioning religion all together. These opinions would divide views about the revolution for the next twenty-five years.

For two years thereafter the National Assembly—renamed the Constituent Assembly—worked on a constitution and basically redid, like, everything in France. Friends, here is where the Enlightenment rubber hit the political road. These folks took abstract ideas and made them real policies. For the biggest, most powerful country in Europe! They created voting rights for (white) men who owned some property (which was still more voting rights than almost anywhere else in the world), natural and civil rights for all French citizens, equality before the law, and a clergy selected by citizens. They completely reorganized the French state and abolished the political role of nobles. Busy! The constitution itself took longer and was often derailed by events like, say, the King's attempt to flee in June 1790. But they got it worked out and passed by September 1791, creating a constitutional monarchy in France. Good job, guys. Unfortunately the constitution didn't last a year.

That same month the playwright Olympe de Gouges (1748–93) wrote "The Declaration of the Rights of Woman and the Female Citizen." She used the high-minded ideas of "The Declaration of the Rights of Man" to highlight the limits of the Revolution and Enlightenment ideals. She revised the bold claims of the "Declaration of the Rights of Man" to include women. It was not well received. It's hard to say if revolutionary dudes were just not ready to include the ladies, or if they believed that women were fundamentally not capable of enlightenment and citizenship. Remember the *Magic Flute*? De Gouges actually took Enlightenment ideas even further. She attacked slavery, advocated new divorce laws, children's rights, and the need for state unemployment plans and a jury system. De Gouges made thinkers and leaders consider the limits of their grand ideas. Guess what happened to her. Guillotine, 1793. Revolutionary radicals didn't believe she supported the revolution fervently enough. Right, fellas. Another iconoclastic writer, British feminist and Revolution supporter Mary Wollstonecraft (1759–97), also highlighted the limits of Enlightened revolution in her 1792 *Vindication of the Rights of Women*. She narrowly escaped France with her head. Wollstonecraft was a little more moderate than De Gouges, arguing that failing to educate women had limited their ability to contribute to society.

Both of these women often get the label of "inspiration for later generations" that comes with banging your head against the wall. They articulated how far revolutionary ideas *could* go. They showed that even the most progressive revolutionary leaders reflected misogynist, racist assumptions. Women played prominent roles in all the events of the revolution, especially the important protests and struggles in the streets. There were even some short-lived, state-run knitting factories for women that promised a more economic definition of citizenship. Before, during, and after the Revolution, women ran the majority of French households and knew best how politics impacted the lives of average people. Most political leaders just didn't think that perspective merited representation in public political activities.

Even more dramatically, slave revolts in Caribbean islands in the French Empire revealed the limits and contradictions of revolutionary ideas. In several cases African slaves revolted during the first years of the Revolution. They heard all the talk of liberty, equality, and fraternity and thought, hey, that's for us too! Well, maybe. Revolts by African slaves in Caribbean colonies put abstract ideals of universal rights into action, creating a new colonial order based on universal, Enlightenment ideals. While most of these revolts ultimately failed, they paved the way for emancipation throughout the Americas in the nineteenth century. Slave revolts, even more than calls for women's emancipation, shined a harsh light on the contradictions of revolutionary ideals. The very fact of slaves winning emancipation and human rights challenged the property rights of former owners, both of which were enshrined in the "Declaration." Oops. Most (white) revolutionary leaders responded by arguing that slaves and people of color generally were not capable of understanding or holding such rights. Racism to the rescue! That's why good revolutionary republicans had to put down slave revolts. This action further reinforced the Enlightenment tendency to control and to assume that some folks just aren't cut out to be enlightened.

And speaking of how far revolutionary ideas should go, it's time to end this calm, moderate phase of the Revolution and get radical! I mean, there was plenty of excitement in the first two years of the revolution, but four things pushed events in France to the next level:

- A counter-revolutionary movement by dissatisfied nobles and clergy, with some popular support because of the new state's "attack" on religion.
- Unhappy urban poor people who felt like one rich group (the middle-class) was just taking the place of another (the nobles and clerics) and wanted instead a broader democratic republic.
- Fighting around the king in August 1792.
- War with Austria and Prussia.

2. The Radical Phase, 1792–4

I often joke with my students that the United States did not really come from a revolution, just a long tax revolt. Sometimes they get defensive about their revolution coming first, etc. But after we talk about all the mayhem during this radical phase, they usually decide they are proud of their little tax revolt. Hence the title of this chapter.

War made events in France more urgent and more tense. Revolutionary leaders had long suspected that angry nobles were plotting with aristocrats outside France to undermine the revolution. The royal family, as well, had not proven themselves to be super loyal to the Revolution. And there was in fact evidence that nobles and the king and queen had sought help from Austria and Prussia. The National Assembly in April 1792 overwhelmingly voted to declare war on Austria. The moderate 1791 constitution quickly fell apart, especially since many leaders and citizens alike now wanted a republic and an end to the monarchy.

King Louis XVI knew things were not looking good for him. In August 1792, opposition to the monarchy reached a peak, and, amid fighting in Paris around the king, the Assembly ended the monarchy and voted to create a republic. News of the Austrian army heading toward Paris freaked people out and resulted in popular massacres of over 1,200 prisoners, who were assumed to be anti-revolutionary nobles and priests. In fact maybe a quarter were "political" enemies of the revolution; the rest were ordinary criminals. This mob violence frightened anyone considering moderate solutions, further radicalizing the Revolution. Here we see another important tension in the French Revolution. Progressive leaders often sought to empower "the people" by creating new institutions based on Enlightenment ideals of equality. Yet violent mobs, driven by fear and thirst for revenge, sometimes limited options for the developing government. Some political organizations, especially the Jacobin Club, made use of popular violence to advance their radical agenda.

The shiny new French Republic faced a number of problems—war, angry citizens, bad harvest, fear, economic downturn, the usual. But above all, leaders had to figure out what to do about the king. They had ended the monarchy and nullified the constitution that gave him a place in political life. After much debate in December 1792, the Assembly found him guilty of crimes against France and sentenced him to death. On January 21, 1793 Louis XVI was executed by guillotine. The king's death simultaneously removed a symbol of those trying to restore the monarchy *and* empowered opposition to the Revolution, especially in rural areas. Queen Marie Antoinette was found guilty in October of treason and, tellingly for a misogynist Revolution, fabricated stories about her sexual appetites. She was guillotined October 16, 1793.

Things were not going well for the French Republic in 1793. The country was at war and increasingly divided over religion and the monarchy. Plus, there was no constitution to define the government. The Constitutional Convention set up a special court, the Revolutionary Tribunal, to try enemies of the Revolution. A new Committee on Public Safety took over more and more government functions. With popular Parisian support, the radical Jacobin Club—a sort of an early political party—purged the Convention of opponents and began attacking those they saw as enemies of the Revolution. Soon a few Jacobins were running a dictatorship. Starting fall 1793, the powerful Committee on Public Safety was led by Maximilien Robespierre (1758–94), a middle-class lawyer from north of Paris who saw himself as a disciple of Jean-Jacques Rousseau.[5] He and the Committee claimed to be the instruments to protect the

---

[5] Jean-Jacque rolls over in grave.

Figure 4.1 The guillotine, tool of Enlightenment.

Revolution. They banned free elections and basically made the legal system a weapon to attack perceived enemies. This "Reign of Terror" used revolutionary tribunals and quick executions to remove opposition to a radical revolution. In the next ten months or so, over 15,000 people were executed in "courts" that sometimes required as little as one witness to denounce and find the accused guilty. The Terror aimed to remove old First and Second Estate enemies, but those groups comprised maybe one-quarter of all victims.

The guillotine is pretty scary-looking, right? It certainly frightened people during the Terror since it was used about 500 times per month in the course of this violent spasm across France. But the guillotine was both literally and figuratively a tool of the Enlightenment. As an instrument of execution, it was far more efficient and less painful that other methods. In fact, some people complained during the Terror that guillotined victims didn't suffer enough. The guillotine was thus a more humane way to carry out death sentences. In the hands of Robespierre and his buddies, it became a tool for promoting revolutionary and Enlightenment ideals. The Terror and the guillotine also gave some average people the ability to use state power to settle differences, exact revenge, and carry out their own interpretation of the Revolution since denunciations were essential to the Terror's work. Remember my warning in Chapter 2 about what happens when you let people use state-sanctioned violence against each other? Just saying.

The most radical ideas from the French Revolution grew out of this period, often as aggressive attempts to promote reason and science. Perhaps the most wacky and fun was the new de-Christianized calendar. Revolutionary leaders humbly believed that a new era began with the creation of the French Republic on September 22, 1792, what came to be known as Year I. They created a ten-day week (which did not go over well with workers!) and named the days after crops, animals, and agricultural tools. Each month, which consisted of three ten-day weeks, got a new name. And why not? Month names were connected to seasons or weather: *Vendémiaire* (grape harvest) and *Brumaire* (fog) in the fall. *Messidor* (crops/harvest) and *Thermidor* (heat) in summer. There were new non-Christian holidays too, like Festivals of Reason and of the Supreme Being, both of which turned churches (including Notre Dame) into temples to reason and revolution.

The radicals in charge stripped the Catholic Church of much of its authority, including the right to marry people. Sometimes they used churches as warehouses! Radicals often blamed women for society's emotional connection to the Church, which partly explains why the new government didn't offer those grand Enlightenment ideas to the ladies. Such anti-Christian moves further divided France between those who respected traditions vs. those who repudiated them. Many radical reforms didn't last, although the spirit of anti-clericalism persisted. The creation of the metric system, based on math and science, has certainly been the most enduring new way the Revolution proposed to look at the world. So, the radical phase wasn't all heads rolling.

War against much of Europe and civil war inside France drove the Terror to a feverish pitch in 1794. Heads were flying! Eventually a group of moderate leaders seized the government in July 1794. And in one of the most poetically just moments of the French Revolution, Robespierre and his accomplices were themselves guillotined, ending the Reign of Terror. The political change came on 9 Thermidor II (July 27, 1794), which is why we call what followed the Thermidorian Directory. The radical phase shaped how most people at the time and since have viewed the revolution. Conservatives were of course appalled, but so were many liberal supporters of the Revolution. Even strong allies like Thomas Jefferson concluded that the revolution had gone too far too fast. Still, given the number of internal and external threats facing France in 1792, the revolution could have easily faltered without some dramatic way to continue revolutionary momentum. That's not to say a despotic regime that unleashed terror and violence on its citizens was the only answer. But it was an answer, and it did sort of work.

3. Thermidorian Directory, 1794–9

Squeezed between the manic violence of the radical phase and international warfare under Napoleon, the sweet, little Thermidorian Directory seems pretty unsexy. In 1794, the task facing the government—now led by a five-person Directory—was to heal the deep divisions caused by the Terror, while continuing revolutionary ideals. The enemies of the revolution remained much the same: exiled nobles, royalist supporters, priests unwilling to swear oaths to the revolution, plenty of peasant farmers, and maybe even some frustrated liberals and radicals, not to mention most of the kingdoms of Europe. And economic troubles did not go away. It's all the more impressive therefore that the Directory managed to consolidate and build upon the accomplishments from moderate revolution.

In many ways, the Directory faced similar problems that had stymied early revolutionaries: ineffective government and taxation systems, major debt, deep religious differences, and being at war with Austria, Prussia, and Britain. They also had to deal with great expectations and fears from the first six years of revolution. The Constitution of 1795 created a moderate democracy with strong separation of powers, direct and indirect elections that allowed fairly broad male voting, and an administration led by the Directory. The new system stabilized taxes and debt and created a professional bureaucracy. The government also restored some of the Catholic Church's authority as part of broad religious tolerance. However, deep divisions in France about the king, Church, and the Revolution made it impossible for the Directory to bring real political stability to France.

During this period the military—now a professional citizen army of 750,000 or more—expanded French borders to include Belgium and Holland, areas along the Rhine river, much of Italy, and portions of northern Egypt. It helped that France's enemies were not always united and that the French had some rocking good generals, including this one guy named Napoleon Bonaparte (1769–1821). The politically engaged, pro-revolution army exported the ideals and sometimes institutions of the French Revolution to other parts of Europe. Winning battle after battle, Bonaparte became France's leading general. He conquered large parts of Europe and then Egypt. Unfortunately, that victory on the Nile united the Ottoman and Russian empires against France, which ultimately didn't bode well for France. In 1799 Bonaparte used his Egyptian victory to return home with a plan to fix the ineffectual government. And when a super successful, ambitious general returns home with loyal troops to "fix" things, you better watch out.

The Directory welcomed Napoleon and asked him to join the government to help stabilize the country. Yeah, he was a pretty big deal by then, so we can start using his first name only. Napoleon saw himself as the consolidator of the Revolution. He clashed with Directory leaders about his role, though, and had to bring out the big guns. He used his military forces, and on the 18 Brumaire Year VIII (November 9, 1799), he easily took over the government. Napoleon wanted to change the government by legal means and only saw force as a last resort. Of course, that last resort was the resort he knew best! Napoleon and his allies created a new three-person Consulate, and by the end of the year, legislators had written a new constitution. Napoleon was First Consul[6] among three. The new government was kind of a constitutional oligarchy, in which a small number of guys controlled the state with some legal checks on their power. The new system still separated powers and guaranteed rights but was tilted more toward executive power. It focused more on stability than rights, liberty, or equality. Subsequent amendments gradually strengthened Napoleon's position, especially when he became First Consul for Life.[7] Previous changes to the government had usually prompted public celebrations and protest. Now, after ten years of revolutionary upheaval and seven years of war, most people in France just shrugged their shoulders at the change or welcomed its stability. However, with one of the best generals ever in charge, that stability wasn't going to last long.[8]

---

[6]The term used to describe the rulers of the ancient Roman Republic and Empire. Napoleon liked that.
[7]Which Napoleon really liked.
[8]Just like haters gonna hate, soldiers gonna soldier.

Figure 4.2 Napoleon Bonaparte.

4. Uh-oh, it's Napoleon 1799–1815

Napoleon Bonaparte was a lot of things, depending upon whom you asked during his lifetime. Hero, savior, anti-Christ, great general, liberator, oppressor, arrogant asshole, destroyer of Europe, architect of Europe, Enlightenment delivery boy, end to the French Revolution. He was certainly the precursor to twentieth-century dictator. He used the press to control opinions about him and a police state to enforce conformity. He appealed to and received the admiration of common people. Napoleon helped create modern nationalism, a blend of racial, cultural, and ideological identity. And he was for most of his career the greatest military leader of the time. The invasion of Russia kinda blew his reputation there, but we'll get to that shortly.

Austrian composer Ludwig van Beethoven (1770–1827) was a fan, at least initially. Fanboy Beethoven dedicated his Third Symphony to Napoleon in 1804. This piece actually blew people away. They came out of the debut performance holding their ears because it seemed so loud. And the piece marks the shift in Beethoven and the history of classical music to the more emotionally charged music of Romanticism. Anyway, Beethoven called it his "heroic symphony" and saw Napoleon as the heroic spirit of a new age informed by Enlightenment ideas. But then (spoiler alert!) when Napoleon became Emperor, Beethoven scratched out the dedication and rededicated the piece "to the memory of a once great man." Ouch. That reaction shows that Napoleon elicited dramatic and emotional responses from people across Europe.

Napoleon Bonaparte was born in 1769 to a minor noble family in Corsica, an island that was as much Italian as French, marking Bonaparte as an outsider in France. He was already an officer at age twenty when the Revolution began. He made use of France's new meritocracy (a system rewarding ability rather than birth) and its many international wars to become a general at age twenty-four. By the time he was thirty, he had led France's most successful campaigns in Europe and Egypt, defended the Revolution against royalist insurgents, and become First Consul, effectively the leader of France. His combination of liberty, opportunity, and authority from above continued some aspects of the Revolution and repudiated others. Plenty of historians see his 1799 takeover as the end of the Revolution because it more or less squashed any semblance of democracy. That's fair, but Napoleon also solidified important ideals of the Revolution and Enlightenment. And as we've seen already in this chapter and the previous one, these revolutionary ideals could be used to liberate *and* control. Considering Napoleon as part of the French Revolution therefore reveals the contradictory implications of this big event and the ideas behind it. Plus, Napoleon, most French citizens, and most Europeans considered Napoleon to be an extension of the Revolution. That's a major reason so many Europeans soured on the Revolution.

Napoleon did not introduce many new ideas in France but continued and firmly rooted some important aspects of the Revolution. He rationalized France's sprawling bureaucracy, making it an instrument to help poor and middle-class people. His government valued both meritocracy and titles, like Napoleon himself did. Birth no longer determined one's fate in France, a core value of the Enlightenment and the Revolution. At the same time Napoleon loved all the titles he gathered while conquering Europe and recognized a place for nobles in governing a complex society. His government also created a broad, secular public school system, an idea going back to the Renaissance that was part of early revolutionary aims. This school system promoted young men from all backgrounds, and it taught them how important Napoleon was in the history of, well, everything.

Probably the two most significant accomplishments of the Napoleonic era were reconciling the Church and Republic and creating a broad legal code. First, to say relations between the Revolution and Catholic Church had been tense is an understatement. Although plenty of folks in France resented clerics, the Republic's attacks on the Church had probably driven more people to oppose the Revolution than anything else. Napoleon understood that religion was the moral and social glue holding France together. A Concordat signed in 1801 with the Pope named Catholicism the "religion of the great majority of the French," though not the state religion, and guaranteed tolerance for non-Catholics. The Church gained more authority in appointing clerics, but priests still had to swear allegiance to the state and were paid by the state. And no lands confiscated during the Revolution went back to the Church. In short, the Concordat looked conservative compared to previous radical measured but really solidified the secular spirit of the Revolution.

Next, the Civil Code of 1804, which came to be known as the Code Napoleon in 1807, enshrined many of the basic ideas of the Revolution and Enlightenment, especially equality before the law, property ownership, and freedom of contract and careers. The Code helped create a new educated, professional elite in France and was the main method for exporting revolutionary ideas to all the fine places the French conquered during this time. A powerful combination of traditional Roman law[9] and Enlightenment concepts, the Code has remained the basis for French law ever since. The Code also reflected the Janus-faced nature of the Enlightenment and Revolution. While most male citizens benefitted, women were systematically denied many rights (property rights, divorce, public representation), including ones they had before the Code or even before the Revolution began. It's almost a perfect expression of the point I've been stressing about the Enlightenment. Proponents of the Code may have thought that women just weren't ready for these rights yet. Or they may have believed, like they did with French citizens of color, that women were fundamentally incapable of handling legal rights. Maybe they even thought that part of expanding revolutionary rights for men meant restricting them for women. The new educational system did the same thing: big win for men, loss of opportunity for women. Probably most of us don't look at rights as a zero-sum balancing act, but that seemed to have been part of French officials' calculations.

Napoleon was no democrat, yet he wanted popular support to undergird his regime. So he used plebiscites to indicate approval. A plebiscite is democracy lite. You vote as to whether you approve something or not: "do you like the job Napoleon is doing, yea or nay?" They pretty much guaranteed positive results, especially when soldiers with guns delivered them. In an 1802 referendum well over half the electorate supported making Napoleon First Counsul for life. The ever-confident Napoleon took the results as evidence that the populace wanted him to have even greater power. *Merci*! In 1804 he asked voters if they thought he should be emperor. And what do you know, over 99 percent said yes! Assassination attempts that year strengthened his position and resolve. On December 2, 1804 he crowned himself Emperor of the French, a neat trick that made clear that only Napoleon had the authority to crown Napoleon.

Napoleon was sometimes a good statesman and ruler, but he was, first and foremost, a hell of a general. He was very blunt about the fact that his power depended upon glory, which depended upon victories. He did pretty well there. Napoleon pioneered important advances in military strategy, including pushing his forces to move far faster than had been previously expected and using the press to confuse his enemies. From the mid-1790s until 1810 or so, Napoleon and the French army dominated Europe. By 1810, France had conquered or allied with basically every power on the continent. Now, these "alliances" often only lasted as long as it took European powers to find a new partner to attack France. France fought seven different coalitions from 1792 to 1815, various

---

[9]That is, from the government, not based on precedent like English common law.

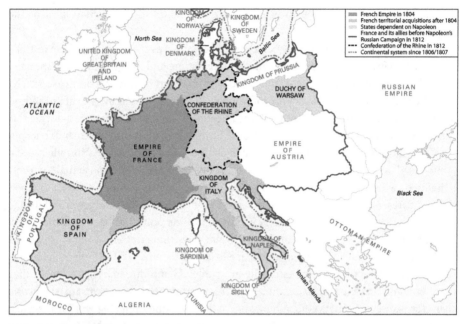

Map 4.1 Europe, 1812.

combinations of the great powers: United Kingdom,[10] Russia, Prussia, Austria, and Spain. While France wasn't always victorious, they pretty much had their way with European powers until about 1812. And Napoleon was a major reason.

The French Revolution created nationalism, both in France and elsewhere. More about all that next chapter. Modern nationalism, simply put, combines traditional love of place (culture, history, food, language, religion, geography, etc.) with ideology. France exported its culture and the ideology of the Revolution through war. Europeans had, um, mixed feelings. Many people outside France welcomed core revolutionary values like equality before the law, ending serfdom, meritocracy, and economic opportunity. But receiving them at the barrel of a gun didn't always go over well. Anger about French military dominance and resistance to French occupation undermined many of the splendid Enlightenment ideals the French "gave" to those it conquered. Such reactions often engendered nationalist feelings. Napoleon and his government also simplified the dizzying patchwork of European principalities, especially in central Europe. These mostly German-speaking lands were often pressed together for easier rule by French leaders, at which point they began to realize they had some things in common: (1) they hated the

---

[10]After uniting the "Kingdom of Great Britain" in 1707, they changed the name in 1801 to "United Kingdom of Britain and Ireland." The name changed again in 1922, when most of Ireland formed its own republic, to "United Kingdom of Britain and Northern Ireland." But for most of this book the *people* will be the "British," and sometimes I might use "Great Britain" instead of "United Kingdom."

French, (2) they spoke a common language, and (3) they really hated the French. So in a way, Napoleon and his boys also created German nationalism. Yeah, karma's rough.

After 1810 things began to unravel for our man Napoleon. In 1812 he reached for some serious glory by invading Russia. Well, he wasn't the first or last to forget that Russia is two things: big and cold.[11] France took the largest army ever assembled—over 600,000 soldiers, 200,000 animals, 20,000 vehicles—into Russia, but less than 100,000 men made it back to France. Russians were willing to burn crops and kill their livestock—so-called "scorched earth policy"—to combat the French.[12] This massive defeat ultimately led to Napoleon's downfall and abdication of the throne. He was exiled to Elba, a small island just south of Corsica. Turns out that you should not exile an Emperor of France to such a nearby place. While the allies—pretty much every other power in Europe—were toasting their victory in Vienna, Napoleon snuck back to France, rallied his troops, and marched to Paris. The grand coalition once again defeated him soundly at Waterloo. Cue the ABBA song. This time they exiled him to St. Helena island in the middle of the south Atlantic. Napoleon died there in May 1821. He was fifty-one years old.

Was Napoleon the maker or breaker of the French Revolution? Most historians see him as a breaker, someone who undermined the fundamental tenets of the Revolution, especially liberty, equality, and fraternity. He weakened civil rights and popular rule. The nineteenth-century liberal observer Alexis de Tocqueville (1805–59) regarded Napoleon as an authoritarian ruler more in line with old regime monarchs than revolutionary ideals of liberty. At the same time, his administration put into law and policy many of the ideals that previous revolutionary governments could not make reality. This very tension between different aspects of Napoleon's legacy, in my mind, is what makes him an important part of the revolutionary period.

And thus begins the "long nineteenth century"

Historians really don't obsess over dates. For us they are just a simple way to denote change over time. But we do get excited about periodization, that is, how you define historical eras. Like many other historians, I like the idea of a "long nineteenth century" from 1789 to about 1916, that is, from the start of the French Revolution until the middle of World War I. Considering this "long nineteenth century" as a single era helps us trace the broad impact of the big ideas we've studied from the Renaissance, Scientific Revolution, and Enlightenment.

In the French Revolution we see the start of modern Europe. The big ideas were there: nationalism, feminism, democracy, capitalism, republicanism, even socialism, communism, and fascism. So was the violence. The Revolution fundamentally redefined people's relationship with government. Now, it wasn't like everybody in Europe suddenly

---

[11]Yes, one of the classic blunders: getting involved in a land war in Asia.
[12]Foreshadowing: something similar will happen to another dude 129 years later who invaded Russia.

became citizens with rights and opportunities. But once a lot of people got the notion that they were citizens, not subjects, you couldn't put that idea back in the box. More than anything, the Revolution demonstrated to the world that things can change—even big, old, well-established things like monarchies or maps or marital relations. People in France and across Europe were tired of the whole mess by 1815. But the ideas, hopes, fears, dangers, and possibilities of the French Revolution would not rest.

CHAPTER 5
I'VE GOT A FEVER, AND THE ONLY
PRESCRIPTION IS MORE NATIONALISM!

By now you may be getting just the tinniest bit tired of France since much of what we've studied for the last couple of chapters has been centered there. French absolutism, French Enlightenment, French dressing, French Revolution, French military hats. Enough! Well, France was a big place in early modern Europe, literally and figuratively, and important concepts like the modern nation state, citizen, race, and equality before the law came out of there and reshaped Europe. Now it's time to consider the wider impact of those ideas and events.

Nationalism after the French Revolution notched some pretty dramatic results. Big nations helped create a modern, industrialized world. They fought some tremendous wars, especially in the twentieth century, and dabbled a bit in genocide. They created a vehicle for defining and protecting individual rights. And basically, they took over the world, injecting Western ideas into pretty much every corner of the planet. That's all.

Nationalism was arguably the most powerful force coming out of the Enlightenment and French Revolution. Some of the big political ideologies—capitalism, socialism, democracy—will of course also be terribly important in the nineteenth and twentieth centuries. But those ideas affected people in part because of the power of modern nation states. Nationalism helped create empires and nations. It ripped countries apart and regularly redrew Europe's map. Nationalism can be a process of formation or a sentiment. It's usually connected to a pre-modern idea of a population connected by shared myths, histories, culture, and geography.[1] Nationalism can give average people a voice or guarantee them rights, and it can brutally repress minorities. Above all, nationalism generates more nationalism. It's not a quiet, stay-at-home kind of concept. Nationalists usually want to show the world, often with violence, how great their country is. They naturally step on other people's toes, and those folks frequently say, hey, maybe we need our own nation too.

Today nationalism continues to serve as rallying cry for both unity and division. Think about the success that right-leaning nationalists have had in Hungary, France, Austria, the United Kingdom, the United States, Germany, and elsewhere recently by rejecting external authority and highlighting the impact of immigrants. Or look at independence movements in Scotland and Catalonia. Nationalism might in fact be stronger now than it has been since the 1990s. It remains one of the most powerful identities for people around the world. So we should probably figure out how we got here.

---

[1]Anthony D. Smith, *Nationalism* (Cambridge: Cambridge University Press, 2001).

Building the argument

Nationalism grew out of the French Revolution, an odd synthesis of early modern absolutism and Enlightenment ideas. The resulting tension between authority/control vs. freedom/opportunity has defined nationalism right up to the present day. While nationalism is an idea that can inspire people to do things, building nation states is more mundane, bureaucratic work. We saw that in the French Revolution: so much more fun to march, tear down, and proclaim than it is to deliver the mail or finance debt.

This chapter traces the history of nationalism over much of the nineteenth century. In the first half of the century, nationalism tended to be a bottom-up, liberating force, inspiring people to challenge the status quo, which was pretty similar to the status quo the French Revolution attacked. We'll look at some fine, failed revolutions of those decades. In the second half of the nineteenth century, nationalism increasingly became a tool for elite control. Of course, elites were usually in control (hence being *elites*). But many leaders who might have felt threatened by nationalism in, say, the 1820s or 1830s realized how it could enhance their authority in the 1860s and 1870s. The examples of Italy, Germany, and Russia will help demonstrate this process. We close by looking at increasingly racialized notions of nationalism, concepts that will be especially important for European imperialist expansion, the subject of Chapter 7. This chapter will also help us understand how powerful modern nations engendered industrial growth, the topic of Chapter 6. Really, given the power of states in the modern world, nationalism will weave its way through just about every subsequent chapter in this book.

1815 and beyond

Vienna in 1815 was a fine place to celebrate the end of a quarter century of revolution and warfare. The champagne flowed, and every night there were waltzes. The Austrian Emperor Francis I hosted a splendid event, a nine-month party and diplomatic settlement for the aristocratic elite of Europe there to deal with the aftermath of the French Revolution and Napoleonic Wars. The "Festivals Committee" had a hard time coming up with enough banquet menus and fun activities. This meeting, known as the Congress of Vienna, had far-reaching consequences for European relations and the history of nationalism.

Led by Russia, Prussia, Austria, and the United Kingdom, this Congress solved several pressing issues in 1815. Leaders of those countries wanted to create a new balance of power to prevent one nation from gaining dominance in Europe like France had. The victors treated France as both a defeated state and a great power. The allies had in 1814 reinstalled the French monarchy and put Louis XVIII (1755–1824) on the throne. He was the beheaded King Louis XVI's brother and had long assumed he should be King of France.[2]

---

[2]Louis XVII, King Louis XVI's son, had died in prison in 1795. Not sure where it's written that all French kings *had* to be named Louis.

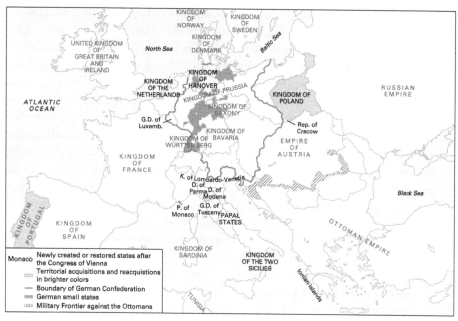

Map 5.1 Europe, 1815.

France was now a constitutional monarchy, a bit like the set-up from 1791. Pulling his collar up around his rather substantial neck, Louis XVIII readily agreed to the conditions of his return. Since land remained the chief source of wealth in these still mostly agrarian societies, the Congress of Vienna ironed out important territorial disputes. Like giving Poland to Russia: *do widzina*, Poland! Russia also took Finland for good measure. The Brits meanwhile pocketed colonies from France, Holland, and Denmark.

Most of the men settling up after revolution and war were backward-looking aristocrats. They wanted to return Europe to its previous state, where kings were kings, ladies were ladies, and peasants knew their place. The exception was the UK, which supported constitutional monarchy and, for idealistic and selfish reasons, promoted international free trade. Most of these guys at Vienna really wanted to get rid of democracy and nationalism. They disapproved of the secular forces that had motivated average French people to rise up, kill their king, and try to export their beliefs across Europe. We should avoid the temptation to view these nervous nobles as fools because, like the clerics who attacked Galileo, they wanted to hang on to their own power and stamp out compelling new ideas. Remember they were coming to terms with twenty-five years of fighting that had taken at least 3 million lives in Europe. With some justification, they blamed popular rule for this wave of destruction. They could temper notions of democracy, but nationalism was a wild force that could unify people into action. Most of these guys ruled over kingdoms comprising multiple ethnic groups, languages, and cultures. Nationalism, they rightly figured, could completely redraw Europe's map at their expense. In fact, that's exactly what happened, though it took a while.

Okay, French nationalism: we got that. Traditional love of place—check; ideology worth exporting to other places—check; military might as source of pride *and* to force others to listen—check. In the last chapter we also saw that French nationalism and occupation had helped create German nationalism. Well, it was a little more complicated than that, but French occupation brought German-speaking provinces together and gave them a common enemy. French repression in Spain had similar results, although Spain, unlike Germany, already existed as a nation. And Russian nationalism got a boost when their forces repelled the French in 1812. Polish nationalism had sidetracked Russia during the Napoleonic Wars. Groups of people, usually educated elites, in other places likewise began to dream about their own nation to embody their culture, language, and traditions. No matter who's fault it was, nationalism was out there, inspiring people to consider new political arrangements. The well-dressed folks in Vienna agreed on very little except that this kind of thinking had led to war and destruction and should be stopped.

Leaders at the Congress of Vienna created a system for working together to stamp out nationalism. Monarchs might mistrust each other, but they all recognized the need to prevent nationalist uprisings. This so-called "Congress System" grew from a common desire to keep regular tabs on France, but it became a tool for suppressing nationalism. Representatives from the four main victorious powers—Russia, Prussia, United Kingdom, and Austria—met occasionally thereafter and agreed to help each other stop surges of nationalism. They had their work cut out for them.

Liberal nationalism: enemy of conservatives

After the Napoleonic Wars, conservatives saw enemies everywhere. Enlightenment thought was no longer new. But the French Revolution had demonstrated that those bold ideas could actually change how people organized themselves, that the existing order was not permanent. Average people might get mad enough to take up weapons in the name of these ideas. The Revolution had also laid out a model for how to do revolution. Bad news for those wishing to conserve things.

Nationalism could particularly challenge the political status quo for three reasons. First, the French Revolution had turned subjects into citizens. There was plenty of debate thereafter about who deserved citizenship and what it meant, but the Revolution marked a fundamental shift in how people related to their government. I mean, really, what would *you* rather be, a subject or a citizen? Subjects connected to the *person* as head of state—their lord, king, duke, etc. Citizens, on the other hand, were part of a community defined by the state. Maybe they were still at the bottom of it, but they had a relationship with the institutions and ideas of the state.

Second, a nation-state assumed the existence of the "imagined community" of a *nation* and the actual political power of a *state*.[3] States had been around forever. They

---

[3]Benedict Anderson, *Imagined Communities* (London, New York: Verso, 1991).

told you what to do, protected you (hopefully), punished or rewarded you, taxed you, and sent you to war. But a nation was an imagined relationship between a bunch of people who didn't know each other yet agreed that some common idea—language, culture, history, geography, religion—united them.

That concept was very different from how previous states had worked. In feudal states your lord was your lord, either because he and his family always had been, or they rolled in with weapons and took over the place. Whatever the case, you owed him your allegiance and some portion of whatever you earned. The only thing you and your lord needed to have in common was Christian faith because religious leaders reminded you that states were ordained by God.[4] Aristocrats who spoke other languages or who lived very far away could be in charge. However, common people had seen how the French had moved beyond feudal, Christian ideas and united state and nation. They thought that sounded pretty cool: currency printed in the language I speak at home; common songs we all know! This basis for a state could really mess up multi-national empires like Russia or Austria. Modern nation-states, put simply, defined sovereignty (political authority) in ways that could negate existing states.

Finally, nationalism could serve as a progressive force challenging conservatives because liberals in the early nineteenth century rightly believed new nation-states could

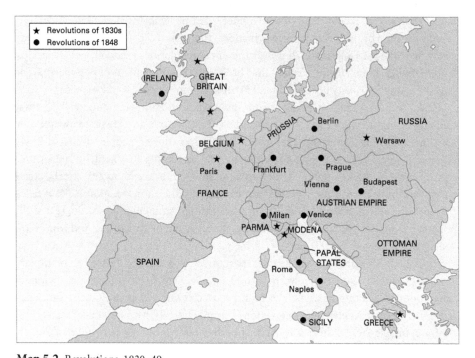

Map 5.2 Revolutions, 1830–49.

---

[4]Russia was a weird, important exception that I'll discuss below.

protect liberty better than old feudal regimes. As we've seen, old regimes were rooted in privilege, tradition, and control. People who believed in all kinds of liberty didn't have much faith that some hidebound system of privilege would promote liberty. And they had proof. These mainly educated middle class people had learned from the French Revolution (and the American Revolution) that modern nation states generally protected liberty better and gave citizens greater opportunities. In the United Kingdom, which was more liberal than most states in Europe, the middle class had greater freedoms and ways to advance. Still, Britain comprised a huge empire, and they had learned all too well how their splendid ideas about liberty might come back to bite them. See: American Revolution. All the leaders of Europe, including the king of France, therefore had very real reasons to suppress nationalism after 1815. They did a pretty good job of it but were kept rather busy for the next thirty years or so.

A hot mess of revolutions, 1820–49

Between 1820 and 1849, over forty revolutionary uprisings in Europe challenged existing governments, some small and brief, some large and deadly. Middle-class people often led groups of dissatisfied peasants or urban workers, so economic inequity definitely motivated some of these revolts. Almost all of them, though, sought to create liberal nation-states. Very few of these uprisings succeeded in achieving their goals. They were usually crushed by one or more major kingdoms that weren't keen on new liberal nation-states. See Map 5.2. Collectively, however, this era of revolutions gradually got rid of most feudal privileges and laws in Europe. They broadened some elements of popular rule and paved the way for subsequent successful nationalist movements.

First off, it was kind of France's fault, *naturellement*. You can't quite call all these uprising "copycat revolutions," but the great 1789 Revolution inspired people and gave them a model for revolt. The French Revolution allowed people to believe it was possible to replace their unjust government with something that actually represented them. Events of the Revolution sort of told you how to do it: rip up city streets, create barricades in the narrow passages of European cities, gather some weapons, take over the center of the capital city, proclaim a new, more just government, wait for the rest of the populace to rally to your cause, and pray that the army might sympathize and won't blow you away.

It's that last bit where things often fell apart. Armies usually *did* destroy revolutionary groups. The French Revolution wasn't a good a model here. In other places, the peasants, urban poor, and common soldiers were not as well connected as in France. Plus, when rebels in Sicily or Naples or Bologna, for example, called for a new Italian state, most common people there didn't really get it. They didn't *feel* Italian. More people felt French. Even rural peasants far from Paris quickly realized that a new national government could benefit them very directly. Remember how fast the National Assembly swept away most feudal obligations in 1789. So, France was an unrealistic model for most of these uprisings.

Most of these mini-revolutions, also unlike France, advocated political independence *from* some existing state and wanted to create *new* nation states. Um, dear leaders, please surrender sovereignty and let us create a new nation. Good luck with that. Waves of revolution in the 1820s, 1830, and 1848, for instance, on the Italian peninsula aimed to create a unified Italian nation-state. The powers that be—Italian-speaking principalities, the Papal States, France, Austria—all said *no, grazie* (or *non gratias tibi aget* or *non, merci,* or *nein, danke*). Really only a couple of the revolutions from this period succeeded. Greece gained independence from the Ottoman Empire (1821–32), and Belgium broke away from Holland (1830–9). In both cases, the project took a while and required the backing of other great powers, who saw self-interest in supporting these independence movements.[5] Otherwise, the major powers mostly agreed that any nationalism was bad nationalism, even when it weakened their enemy. Especially during the various uprisings of the 1820s and 1830s, the great powers (Austria, Russia, Prussia, France, and the UK) would either confer as a mini-Congress of Vienna or support each other's moves to stamp out nationalist movements.

A spate of revolutions in 1830 offered more serious challenges to old regimes in Europe than did the uprisings of the 1820s. Demands for new nations in Poland and Italy failed again, but a dozen uprisings across Europe did end feudal systems in many places. Oh, and they all got started in France, of course. The French Revolution of 1830 or "July Revolution" inspired other hotheads around Europe to take up arms against their oppressors.[6] Revolutionary leaders were often motivated by a combination of nationalism and desire to remedy social inequity. They pushed liberalism, republicanism, and even socialism as ways to make people's lives better, especially in the context of a new nation state. Once again, middle-class people often led poorer people in these revolts. The growing middle class in Europe—bankers, traders, doctors, business owners, bureaucrats, manufacturers, lawyers—normally reaped the most benefit from these movements. After all, poor folks—as usual—did most of the fighting and dying. Although aristocrats continued to hold power in most European states, revolutions and reforms in the 1820s and 1830s indicated that an expanding middle class was becoming more important in many places, especially in Western and Central Europe.

In 1848, as many as twenty-five violent uprisings ripped across Europe. As usual, the French kicked things off, chiefly because of ongoing conflicts that the *last* revolution (1830) had not solved. Unfortunately, the 1848 Revolution in France had a familiar-sounding storyline: popular uprising, overthrow the king, declare a republic, some craziness, a guy named Bonaparte gains popular support, and then there's a French Empire. Yes, Napoleon's nephew, who was nowhere near the commander or politician his

---

[5]Greek independence also got a boost from support by the hot, wild, open-shirted poet Lord Byron. His money for the Greek navy helped too. The Belgians had help from six great powers, who signed a document in 1839 guaranteeing Belgium's neutrality.

[6]For the record, this is the revolution Victor Hugo wrote about in *Les Misérables* (1862) and the one about which Marius and his buddies sang, "Do you hear the people sing, singing the songs of angry men?" in the 1980 musical of the same name.

uncle had been, managed to get elected French president. He then turned the Second French Republic into an Empire, which lasted for twenty years. He named himself Napoleon III since OG Napoleon's son and brother had died.

Still, people all over Europe took heart from the popular 1848 French uprising and believed they might similarly change things. As always, the conditions and aims of uprisings differed greatly. And once again they all failed, but gee, folks learned some swell lessons from those failures. More than previous revolts, these mid-century revolutions indicated that social and economic conditions had changed significantly in many places in Europe since the Napoleonic Wars. Industrialization was expanding unevenly, but it was quickly altering the economic elite and giving more and more poor people a shared working experience. More on that next chapter. It's no wonder that Karl Marx (1818–83) and Friedrich Engels (1820–95) wrote *The Communist Manifesto* (1848) during these events. Nervous leaders in big cities like Paris and Vienna concluded that they should rebuild their capitals, opening up the narrow medieval streets into broad boulevards that revolutionaries couldn't barricade anymore.

Nationalism was changing too. In many ways the failed revolutions of 1848 represented the last gasp of liberal nationalism, the last time revolutionary leaders tried to use popular revolt to create new liberal nations. The poor Italians revolted in at least six places, still hoping to create a unified Italian nation-state. But there just weren't enough people *feeling* Italian to defeat the powers controlling the peninsula.[7] Similarly, German nationalists almost got themselves a Germany at last. There was a flag, a parliament in Frankfurt, and uprisings in at least eight German-speaking places. In both cases middle-class intellectuals felt Italian or German and believed a liberal nation-state would make all "their people" super excited. However, most people in those places still identified with their region or town far more than some abstract nation. The Austrians said, Oh my God, we've got to put an end to this nationalism threatening to destroy our empire. The Prussians thought, hmm, maybe we can use this idea to our advantage. As the Prussian statesman Otto von Bismarck (1815–98) put it in 1862, "Not through speeches and majority decisions will the great questions of the day be decided—that was the great mistake of 1848 and 1849—but by iron and blood." And thus endeth liberal nationalism in Europe. Welcome to a new kind of tension.

Example 1. Italy: butter vs. olive oil

It's hard to believe there was no such thing as Italy in 1860. Today it seems so distinct and recognizable. Well, all those (failed) revolutions in the first half of the nineteenth century indicated that some folks believed that there was an Italian *nation* and that therefore there should be an Italian *state*. Italy was created through a synthesis of both kinds of

---

[7]This may surprise you, if you've ever met an Italian or someone from an Italian family or someone who ever had a family member who might have lived in Italy.

Map 5.3 Italian unification, 1860–71.

nineteenth-century nationalism: bottom-up, liberating nationalism *and* top-down, controlling nationalism.

After the Napoleonic Wars, the area we would today consider Italy—the Italian peninsula or "boot" and the Island of Sicily—consisted of several small kingdoms in the north, the Papal States (ruled by the Catholic Church) in the middle, and in the South the Kingdom of the Two Sicilies, which was ruled by the royal family of France. The French had united and ruled directly certain parts of Italy during the Napoleonic Wars, inadvertently nurturing Italian nationalism. In one way or another after 1815, they continued to play an important role in Italy, supporting the Papal States and the Two Sicilies. The Austrians also controlled some northern parts. Italian nationalists up and down the peninsula had revolted against this very feudal set up, but they had not possessed the popular support to create something new. Or the guns.

They had the ideas, though, and the swagger. Journalist and author Giuseppe Mazzini (1805–72), in particular, had been advocating for an Italian nation-state since the 1830s. He wanted an independent Italian republic. You may not be surprised that he spent plenty of time in exile for such ideas. He founded various organizations and publications devoted to Italian nationalism and even hooked up with like-minded nationalists from Germany and Poland who were all hanging out together, in exile, in Switzerland. Mazzini's ideas inspired the merchant navy captain and revolutionary hero Giuseppe Garibaldi (1807–82). You may wonder: how do you get the title "revolutionary hero"? Garibaldi aided revolutions in Brazil and Uruguay in the 1840s, after being exiled for participating in an 1833 uprising in Genoa. He and his followers in South America wore red shirts instead of uniforms. *Belli!*

When the 1848 revolutions broke out in Italy, Garibaldi and some of his "red shirts" high-tailed it back to Italy to join the fun. Well, that didn't work out, so Garibaldi got exiled again. He spent time pushing for Italian independence and looking good in red all over the world (South America, Australia, London, New York). By 1860 he was back in northern Italy to take part in more nationalist uprisings. These comings and goings prompted some serious eye rolling by elites. But Garibaldi was more than a globe-trotting troublemaker. He had his own small navy and a good number of armed supporters. He had the ideas and the guns, not to mention the red shirts. Garibaldi frustrated traditional elites, but at least some of them realized that he might be on to something. Here's where things get interesting in Italy.

In 1860, Italian nationalism was heading in two directions: the popular, revolutionary, red-shirted movement led by Garibaldi and the gradual expansion of power by the conservative northern Italian kingdom of Piedmont-Sardinia, under the direction of Count Cavour (1810–61). Not surprisingly, these two didn't get along. Garibaldi gathered a thousand of his followers and took over Sicily, kicking out rulers and gaining supporters everywhere he went. He then began moving up the peninsula toward Rome. He was winning supporters and convincing average people for the first time the value of creating an Italian nation. See Map 5.3. That really freaked out conservatives like Count Cavour and Napoleon III, who provided the military forces protecting the Papal States. The Church and internal and external leaders feared Garibaldi's successful popular insurrection. Cavour made them a deal. Look, he explained, there's going to be a unified Italian nation-state soon. Do you want it to be led by some rambunctious revolutionary hero in a red shirt or by my guy, King Victor Emmanuel, your type of monarchical conservative? They went with the King Vic[8] of course. Fortunately, so did the generous Garibaldi, who was willing to surrender his southern winnings for the sake of creating a unified Italy. The Kingdom of Italy was proclaimed in 1861, though it took some additional fighting and negotiating to incorporate the Papal States and secure Rome as the capital in 1871.

---

[8]You have to admit that sounds like a brand of malt liquor.

If you know much about Italian food, you probably know that most Italians cook with olive oil. But some northern Italians, including folks around Piedmont, cook with butter. Plenty of Italians see cooking with butter as basically *German*. Not a compliment. In the process of Italian unification, the southern Italians brought the popular, liberating revolutionary nationalism, and the olive oil. Garibaldi wasn't from southern Italy but harnessed or helped engender popular nationalism down there that pressured conservatives to the point of unification.[9] His liberating nationalism seriously threatened Italian elites. Ultimately, it was the butter-loving northern conservatives, especially Count Cavour, who managed to win.[10] Cavour's diplomacy and scare tactics harnessed nationalism and created an Italian kingdom for the first time.

Successful Italian nationalism was also tough-guy nationalism. The men who had imagined Italy through literature, music, and other cultural means earlier in the century just couldn't get the job done. In the nineteenth century plenty of Europeans saw Italians as strong on emotion yet weak on action. Unification proved those stereotypes wrong. Italian men could take up arms, march in line, sacrifice, and do what was necessary to create an Italian nation for the first time. When they did, they also overcame popular stereotypes of "feminine" Italy, that is, a place that exhibited traits commonly associated then with women: fragility, emotion, vanity, and moral weakness. The Enlightenment ideals behind nationalism—popular political representation, equality before the law, the nation as embodiment of general will—could all be applied to men and women. Of course, we've seen that pretty much only the guys benefited. Plus, men controlled the states that nationalists fought against. And men carried the guns on both sides.

The success of nationalism in Italy therefore reinforced the notion that nation-states were fundamentally "masculine," literally and figuratively. Just like Enlightenment thought needed darkness to define light, so too was masculine nationalism defined by the "feminine" Other. That Other could be women at home, in contrast to men in public politics. Or it could be the (dark) peoples that well-armed nations dominated through imperialism (Chapter 7). In Italy, unification demonstrated that modern nationalism was masculine: tough, unyielding, logical, unemotional, and ready for a fight. God knows that was the case in Germany.

Example 2. Forging Germany with blood and iron

If Italian nationalism was tough-guy brand, then German nationalism was tough-guy-on-steroids brand. It was 100 percent top-down. Lots of fighting, chest beating, spiked helmets, and bushy mustaches. Nationalism in Germany especially grew from the experience of Napoleonic occupation. German literature also inspired nationalists to imagine a single German-speaking country. In the many failed 1848 revolutions in Central Europe, these fair readers actually tried to create Germany. They even went so far

---

[9]Garibaldi was from Nice, which was in the north but usually cooks with olive oil.
[10]To be fair, the Piedmontese don't always use butter, but I can't quit this metaphor!

as to start a German parliament in Frankfurt. Liberal, revolutionary, and Romantic, these guys realized in defeat that, alas, average people didn't feel German they way they did. They also realized that feeling nationalist, reading poetry, and postulating a liberal nation state would not create one.

The composer Richard Wagner (1813–83) reflected the development of German nationalism around this time. In the 1840s, the young composer was involved in left-wing, nationalist groups in Dresden. He bought into all that Enlightenment business: equality, liberty, popular rule, nationalism, even socialism. After taking part in the failed 1848 nationalist uprising there, he fled to Switzerland. Disenchanted with liberal nationalism, Wagner began composing operas based on old Germanic stories and myths, above all, his four-part, sixteen-hour(!) *Ring* epic. Wagner believed those ancient stories could arouse greater support for a German nation than namby-pamby Enlightenment

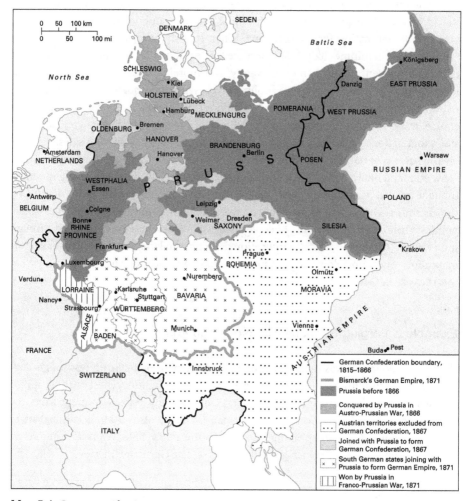

Map 5.4 German unification, 1860s–71.

ideals, which were, after all, mainly French. And he looked less to democracy than to great leaders for direction. Also, in the 1850s Wagner became increasingly antisemitic, maintaining that Jews represented a threat to German culture and people. This idea points to the fact that nationalists have tended to look for external and internal enemies to define their cause. Even today.

While the concept of "Germany" goes back to the Middle Ages, the nineteenth-century notion of *Deutschland*—a *Land* where *Deutsch* was spoken—had to do with which German-speakers to include and exclude. Even after Napoleon's consolidation of Central Europe, there were a lot of German-speaking countries. The real issue was Austria. Sure, the Austrian Empire was run by German-speakers, but over three-quarters of inhabitants spoke other languages: Czech, Magyar (Hungarian), Slovenian, Slovakian, Polish, Russian, Serbian, and a bunch of others. So, Austria was a powerful "German" country, but how can you create a nation-state based chiefly on the German language with all those other languages in there? Plus, the Prussians, the other major German-speaking power, wanted to control everything. No surprise. Like the Italians from Piedmont-Sardinia, the Prussians had concluded that bottom-up, revolutionary nationalism was silly and dangerous. But they figured they could use nationalism to unite and exclude their way into creating a big, ole German state that they could dominate. They did so by using war and economics, but mostly war.

The powerful and effective Prussian statesman Otto von Bismarck was the driving force behind German unification. Over the course of the 1860s, he used economic opportunities, the promise of military cooperation, common enemies, and calculated warfare to forge a German nation. After the Napoleonic Wars many of the German states—though not Austria—created a Customs Union to make trade and economic development better for all of them. This economic cooperation got them used to working together and, like back in the bad old days of French occupation, reminded them of common interests. But still there was Austria, wanting to join Club German, maybe wanting to run the club, thinking it was all that, and messing up Prussian plans. Bismarck had a great scheme for how to exclude the Austrians, though. It's very likely that he twirled his big mustache and laughed maniacally to himself at least two or three times during this process.

First, he coaxed the Austrians into a war against Denmark in 1864. That's right: the two greatest powers in Central Europe attacked Denmark over the areas called Schleswig and Holstein. Now, these parts of Denmark contained lots of German-speakers, and there had been tension surrounding them for at least twenty years. Not surprisingly, the Austrians and Prussians quickly whipped the Danes and took over these two hard-to-pronounce regions. Time to divide the spoils of war: one for you, one for me. You might look at Map 5.4 and wonder what the Austrians were going to do with a region way up north of their main territory. That was no problem in their minds because the Austrian monarchy was still more or less in feudal mode, where you built an empire all over the place and subjects had to give allegiance.

The clever Prussians knew that and refused to yield Holstein, as promised, to the Austrians. What are you going to do about it, Austria, go to war with Prussia? *Jawohl*!

Both sides gathered some allies, but the Seven-Week War, as it's sometimes called, in 1866 was pretty much a Prussian beat-down of Austria. Not only did the Austrians slink home in defeat, they had to face nationalist uprisings that forced them to change the country's name to The Austro-Hungarian Empire. Awkward! On top of that, several of the German states involved in the war joined Prussia in 1866 to make it even bigger. Bismarck stroked his fine mustache and thought: this is all going according to my dastardly plan.

But how could Prussia convince some hold-out German states, especially Bavaria, to join in making a German nation? The Bavarians knew the Prussians would take over whatever happened. Ah, but what one thing can bring together even bitter German enemies? Hating on the French of course! Bismarck knew he could goad Napoleon III into a fight and used a conflict over the potential Spanish king to make it happen. In July 1870, France declared war on Prussia. Bavaria and other German states swallowed their pride and joined Prussia in fighting France. While the conflict lasted several months, the main fighting resulted in swift and decisive Prussian victories. Especially when the Prussian-led army conquered Paris (oh, the shame), things fell apart rapidly in France: a revolution kicked out Napoleon III, then the French army put down a brief radical Commune, and the Third French Republic was proclaimed.

Meanwhile, the Prussians, or *Germans*, poured salt in France's war wounds. On January 1, 1871 they proclaimed the new German Empire (*Kaiserreich*) in the Hall of Mirrors in Versailles. Germans in Versailles! The Prussian King Wilhelm became the new German Kaiser (Emperor) Wilhelm I. That was a clever move if you think about it. If you bring a bunch of noble-led principalities together and make one guy king, what happens to everyone else. Do kings get demoted to princes? Do princes get demoted to dukes? No problem. Everyone could keep their titles with a German Emperor atop them all.

It was a long way from the literature-loving, liberal nationalists longing to create Germany in 1848 to the alliance-forging, ass-kicking Prussians that made the German Empire in 1871. Like Bismarck said, "iron and blood" got the job done, not ideas and democracy. Although the German Empire had its problems after 1871, this country of 41 million people quickly became the most powerful on the continent. In fact, the advent of a unified Germany terrified other countries and pretty much created a landslide of alliances that would set the stage for World War I in 1914. But let's not get ahead of ourselves. For now, let's remember that these two new nations, Italy and Germany, began with French Revolution-era liberating nationalism but actually came together as a result of elites using nationalism to their own ends. Russian leaders certainly forged their country from the top down too, but the truly enormous and complex example of their empire illustrates a very different path.

Example 3. Russia: messy and multi-ethnic across eleven time zones

It's probably not even right to talk about a Russian nation-state in the nineteenth century. An empire, absolutely, or a kingdom. But the very word "nation" in Russia made the Tsar

(Emperor) cringe. All those guys trying to stamp out nationalism at the Congress of Vienna in 1815 had their own reasons for wanting to do so, but the Russian empire had been working for a couple of centuries to make sure the many different groups within its borders remained loyal to the Tsar. In other words, they really worried about nationalism. Russia after the Napoleonic Wars was a vast, multiethnic empire in which at least 130 languages were spoken. I mean, when you're in St. Petersburg, which was for a while the Russian capital, you're only a little further from New York City than you are from the easternmost point of Russia! And the differences between nomadic hunters in Siberia, Asian fishermen in Vladivostok, Jewish doctors in Warsaw, and Muslim clerics in Kazan was far greater than any ethnic distinctions in, say, the Austrian Empire. In short, Russia presents a counter-example to the more ethnically similar nationalism we've seen thus far. But then Russia wasn't quite like the rest of Europe. In fact, most of Russia wasn't even *in* Europe.

We can trace the history of the Russian kingdom back to Ivan the Terrible in the sixteenth century or even back to the eleventh-century "lost kingdom" of Kievan Rus. See, while the rest of Europe was Renaissancing, Reformationing, and growing the concepts we studied in the first three chapters, various Russian kingdoms were trying to hold back the Mongolians. In 1552, though, the Russian army defeated the Mongols at Kazan and began pushing east into former Mongol territory and south into the various Islamic kingdoms. And because those places were just too warm, they then moved into Siberia, where even the Russians shivered. And hey, why not keep going east into Asia too. By 1639 there were Russian troops stationed on the Pacific Ocean, making a Russian Empire that spanned almost 3,500 miles (5,600 km)!

In the eighteenth century, Russian leaders attempted to come to terms with the implications of this giant, land-based empire *and* with Western ideas. It started with the big man, Tsar Peter the Great (1672–1725),[11] who was the first to call Russia an empire and further expanded its borders. He also shaved his beard, brought in foreign ideas, and tried generally to turn Russia into a European country. A real Enlightened Despot, he reflected the contradictions in such a concept. On the one hand, he used Western ideas to liberate nobles and women to a certain extent, to create more humane laws for all subjects, and to build new industries to advance Russia. On the other hand, he deepened divisions in society by expanding serfdom, tightly controlling new industries, and repressing ethnic and religious self-expression. Later in the eighteenth century, Tsarina Catherine the Great also grew the empire. We saw back in Chapter 3 that she used French Enlightenment ideas to write new laws, promote tolerance, modernize taxation, expand education, and dial back efforts to convert people to the Russian Orthodox faith. Yet she too strengthened Russian autocracy and implemented more absolutism.

Catherine's reign (1763–96) also began a very different kind of relationship between Christians and Muslims. Islamic armies had been pressing into parts of southern Europe since the Middle Ages. By the late 1600s, the Ottoman Empire particularly controlled

---

[11]Legitimately big: he was six-foot eight-inches (over 2 meters) tall!

much of southeastern Europe, nearly taking over Vienna in 1683. The Russians developed a very different relationship with Islamic groups in the southern parts of their empire. They fought and conquered Islamic regimes in central Asia but then used religion to integrate Islamic subjects into the regime. Russian leaders didn't just let Muslims do their thing without interference. Instead, Russian officials got right in there and actually helped Muslims practice their faith better and keep their own laws.

This bizarre mixture of Enlightenment religious tolerance and invasive bureaucracy turned out to be a very effective policy. By the late nineteenth century, Muslims were the second-largest religious group in Russia, right behind Russian Orthodox believers. Instead of calling Russia a multi-ethnic empire, we might in fact understand it better as a multi-religious empire since all subjects had to declare a religious affinity. Defining people by their faith in the eighteenth and nineteenth centuries might sound old fashioned but using an invasive state bureaucracy to control folks was definitely a hallmark of how all modern states have functioned. And it worked. This approach helped hold an insanely diverse empire together for, like, 300 years! Muslims didn't leave the Russian empire en masse until 1991.

The Russians practiced this kind of old and new control across their empire in the nineteenth century. But especially in their European parts, nationalism represented an existential threat. Ideas about ethnic or cultural self-determination threatened to tear the empire apart. And any kind of nationalist agitation that aimed to unify the empire based on common culture or ideology ran squarely into 400 years of Russian history that had crafted a state intentionally *not* based on national unity.

That's why Tsar Alexander I was the most adamant at the 1815 Congress of Vienna that everyone agree on how bad nationalism was. The Poles, for example, represented a particularly annoying thorn in the Russian side throughout the nineteenth century. Austria, Prussia, and especially Russia used the Napoleonic wars to gobble up Poland. Polish intellectuals and some middle-class leaders rebelled against Russia in 1830, in a bid for national independence. Russia squashed that idea like a pierogi. For all intents and purposes, Poland would remain part of the Russian Empire until 1989. The independent Polish state between World War I and World War II was a short-lived anomaly. Repressed nationalist sentiments in Poland and elsewhere point to one of the reasons the Soviet empire would fall apart at the end of the twentieth century and why nationalism has continued to animate Eastern European politics in dramatic ways.

Russia's multi-ethnic and multi-religious character clearly shaped ideas about nationalism there, for both the centralized tsarist government and any doomed advocates of national self-determination. You can see how the Russian state used nationalism in composer Peter Tchaikovsky's (1840–93) rousing *1812 Overture*, written in 1880 to commemorate the Russian defeat of Napoleon's forces. This very loud tone poem features Russian folk songs, horns blowing "La Marseillaise" to represent the French invasion, a couple of battles, complete with cannons, and ultimate Russian victory. Tchaikovsky uses music from traditional Russian Orthodox hymns like "O, Lord, Save Thy People" to represent Russia, and he concludes the piece with a stirring version of "God Save the Tsar" while victory bells toll. This piece thus rejects French nationalism, with its

Enlightenment ideals carried by Napoleon's armies. Instead the overture promotes Russian nationalism based on religion, traditional folk songs, and loyalty to the tsar. I really encourage you to check this piece out, especially the last four minutes because it's just one hell of an ending to anything, including this section of the chapter. Baton dropped.

Nationalism's long and violent history

Okay, let's wrap up with some general thoughts about the lasting impact of nationalism. Short version: it's going to get a lot worse before it gets better.[12] First, nationalism begets nationalism. It's not a thoughtful, inclusive idea. Nationalism doesn't affirm others; it defines others and then beats them. Pretty much every conflict in the West that we're going to study was caused in some way by nationalism. It's pretty hard to conclude that your culture, your home, your peeps, your faith, your form of government are the best and *not* oppress other people. Just look at the story of this chapter. French nationalism begat German and Italian nationalism. German nationalism begat Austrian nationalism, which in turn begat Hungarian nationalism. And then Hungarian nationalism, wouldn't you know it, begat Transylvanian and Slovakian nationalism. And so on. In each case "begat" is short-hand for "defined, oppressed, woke, and fought." (And it's a fun archaic word you don't get to use much outside the King James version of the Bible.) Nation-states *can* respect and cooperate with each other of course. The growing tendency in nineteenth-century Europe for countries to trade fairly with each other and respect alliances, for example, testified to the fact that nationalism wasn't solely destructive. Nevertheless, this idea's aggressive confidence enabled large and small nations alike in the nineteenth century to believe that their people's hope and survival lay in this relatively new form of state. As a result, the nation will become, especially in the twentieth century, a major source for many Europeans' identity.

Nationalism also begets empire. As we will learn in Chapter 7, nationalist conflicts in Europe drove European powers to take over more and more parts of the world in the nineteenth century. They did so because they thought they were all that. I mean, they were willing to fight and kill other white Europeans who worshipped the same God, so no surprise that Europeans would use force on "uncivilized" people in Africa, Asia, and the Middle East. Their fine Enlightenment ideas reinforced this process of Othering. European powers also competed with each other by amassing colonial holdings. Yes, nationalism was also a pissing contest.

One of the strangest and most dangerous implications for nationalism in the late nineteenth century was the way it merged with notions of science—or at least pseudo-science—to support racist views of the world. We've already seen how the Enlightenment created the notion of race. The concept of Social Darwinism reinforced racism. In 1859

---

[12]And it's hard to say if it's gotten any better, even today.

Charles Darwin (1809–82) published his revolutionary *On the Origin of Species*, which detailed his theory of evolution and supported it with evidence. Darwin's ideas rocked many people's worlds for scientific, religious, and cultural reasons.

Some people used his concept of the survival of the fittest to justify their own assumptions about a hierarchy of races and nations. In his book, Darwin discussed neither nation nor race (though he reveals his prejudices in some sections). But proponents of Social Darwinism used his thoughts about why some species dominate others to explain how nations and races should treat each other. This concept employed something that *seemed* like science to support prejudice, racism, and plans to exploit other nations. Good news for rich and powerful white folks! Similarly, the idea of eugenics, which grew from Social Darwinism, argued that humans should practice selective breeding, in order to improve racial or national populations. You know, like breeding horses or dogs. Uh, Nazi much? These two ideas informed twentieth-century racist policies in the United States and across Europe, especially in Nazi Germany. In sum:

$$\frac{\text{Prejudice} + \text{Nationalism}}{\text{Science}} = \text{Bad News.}$$

Finally, the history of nationalism came full circle at the end of the nineteenth century. Bottom-up nationalism in the first half of the century often challenged existing traditional elites by promising self-determination. In the second half of the nineteenth century, traditional aristocratic elites used top-down nationalism for their own purposes, to control populations rather than free them. But in some countries in the 1890s, popular nationalist movements again pushed governments further than they would have liked. That happened in Germany, for example. In the years before World War I, nationalists across Europe demanded that their government promote their nation at all costs. As we will see in Chapter 9, that cost will be high indeed.

CHAPTER 6
INDUSTRIALIZATION, OR: WELCOME TO THE MACHINE

And did those feet in ancient time,
Walk upon Englands mountains green:
And was the Holy Lamb of God,
On Englands pleasant pastures seen!

And did the Countenance Divine,
Shine forth upon our clouded hills?
And was Jerusalem builded here,
Amongst these dark Satanic Mills?

Bring me my Bow of burning gold:
Bring me my Arrows of desire:
Bring me my Spear: O clouds unfold.
Bring me my Chariot of Fire!

I will not cease from Mental Fight
Nor shall my Sword sleep in my hand:
Till we have built Jerusalem,
In Englands green & pleasant land.

William Blake, from *Milton*, 1804[1]

Sure, it's a famous poem, but it kinda looks like a series of texting errors: "Englands" instead of "England's," exclamation point instead of question mark, random capitalizations, "builded."[2] Well, Blake (1757–1827) could get away with that. But what did he mean? Was this poem radical or conservative? Blake was clearly attacking the "dark Satanic Mills" of industrialization. But was he a socialist advocating for workers' rights or a conservative angry about how industrialization had ruined an idyllic rural world? In 1916, Hubert Parry set the lyrics to hymn-like music. That song has been used variously to support women's rights, British patriotism, trade unions, cricket, and rugby. You should check it out. Debate over the meaning of the poem and the song tell us something about the subject of this chapter. Industrialization *was* radical and conservative. It changed

---

[1] Blake "Jerusalem" in A.G.B. Russell and E.R.D. Maclagan, eds., *The Prophetic Books of William Blake: Jerusalem* (London: A.H. Bullen, 1907), 2.
[2] At least that's how Blake wrote it in the original, beautifully illustrated 1804 version.

everything and pushed the world forward but also helped update and make permanent some of the inequities and prejudices of pre-modern times.

The historian E.J. Hobsbawm insists that the Industrial Revolution "marks the most fundamental transformation of human life in the history of the world recorded in written documents."[3] Wow, E.J., even more than smart phones? Even more than the internet?! While not all historians agree (of course), it's pretty hard to argue against the massive impact of industrialization. Just look around: can you can find one thing that wasn't produced in some sort of industrial factory? Didn't think so. The Industrial Revolution, as these deep changes are often called, made big ideas like capitalism, socialism, and imperialism into real experiences. Industrialization especially connected Europeans with the wealth and violence of international empire. Also, industrialization basically set the terms for all work that we do, from that coffee shop gig you're doing now to the important and well-paying professional job you plan to have after you graduate.

Building the argument

Industrialization grew out of ideas from the Enlightenment and Scientific Revolution. This process got rolling around the 1760s and took a good century or more to impact most people in Europe. It was uneven. Lots of places in Europe weren't fully industrialized until well into the twentieth century. We saw back in Chapter 2 that the study of science began with practical application. The scientific method and Enlightenment thought promised ways to control nature and allow humans to fix the world in which they lived. Capitalist champs like Locke and especially Smith emphasized that *capital*, not human labor, was the driving force for economic development. And of course, the dudes implementing these ideas liked that: they already had themselves some capital and were anxious to figure out how to use it to make more. Socialism also grew out of the Enlightenment. You can see hints of it especially in radical egalitarian types like Rousseau. Socialism, above all Karl Marx's version of it, will offer the most radical response to capitalist development. In fact, that conflict—capitalism vs. socialism or communism— will rock Europe from the late nineteenth until the late twentieth century. Democracy will occupy an uneasy place between these two economic big boys.

Like a lot of big ideas, industrialization certainly helped liberate and improve average people's lives. But the impulse to create industrial factories and produce more goods came from people who already owned and controlled property. Especially in the early years of industrialization, this process benefitted owners at the expense of workers. In other words, the new concept of industrialization was built upon old ways of power, ownership, and control. That very typical Enlightenment tension between liberation and

---

[3] Hobsbawm, *Industry and Empire* (Harmondsworth: Penguin, 1969), 13.

control shaped how new industries developed, the social impact of that development, and the legacy of industrialization.

In this chapter we will look at the origins of industrialization and how it grew first in Great Britain and then elsewhere in Europe. The Industrial Revolution impacted Europeans in waves, and we'll talk about the different ways that happened over the course of the nineteenth century. Industrialization ultimately benefitted most people in the West, but it sure did suck for a while for workers. We'll consider their experiences and why the ideas of Marx held great appeal for fixing or throwing out industrial relations. Industrialization also helps us understand expanding European empires (Chapter 7): the need for guns helped push industrialization and further empowered Europeans to take over the world.

So, what was industrialization?

You probably already have an idea. You know that machines improve our lives, make things easier, enhance communication and transportation, and give us lots of cool stuff. They allow a smaller number of people to do more powerful things. Put simply, industrialization was about using machines and new sources of power to produce goods. To build these new machines and harness sources of power, like water or coal, you need some extra coin. So, where you gonna get that additional money in a boring, old agrarian society? Time to innovate! The first step was to squeeze more capital out of traditional agriculture. Nobles had been doing that for a while. That's where they got all their fancy palaces, gardens, wigs, waistcoats, and wars after all. But a few creative, ambitious landowners figured out ways to earn more from farming. Then they used that extra capital to build factories, dig up coal and iron, develop other natural resources, ship things around the world to sell. And pay for more wars and waistcoats.

Initially, these new factories were basically just souped-up versions of what people had done before. For instance, women had been spinning and weaving cloth at home to sell for centuries. Early factories did that on a larger scale, creating massive looms to weave large pieces of cloth. Textiles were some of the first products from the Industrial Revolution because folks decided, you know what, it's time to have some underwear, and maybe more than one pair. That's right: underwear caused the Industrial Revolution. Or something like that.

Or you could say that guns caused the Industrial Revolution. Great Britain was at war for much of the eighteenth century and building an international empire. Massive government demand for all kinds of weapons, ammo, and transportation helped turn old-fashioned gun- and metal-smith artisan shops into big-ass factories. If you know anything about supply and demand, you'll realize what followed was a chicken-and-egg game. Once manufacturers started producing lots of weapons, they *needed* the demand— i.e., the wars and imperial expansion—to continue. More on that in the next chapter.

Now, how do you power the machines making all this stuff? One familiar source of power was water. People throughout Europe had for centuries used running water

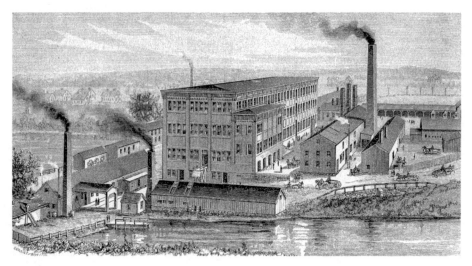

Figure 6.1 Nineteenth-century factory.

(streams, rivers) to power mills to grind wheat into flour. Early factories did some of that but often needed more power than water could provide or didn't want to rely upon rainfall for production. James Watt (1736–1819) created the coal-burning steam engine in 1776 to enable factories to run continuously and at greater capacity. It's pretty expensive to build a factory, ensure a steady source of energy, maintain machines, get raw materials, hire workers, make cool things, and then ship them off to sell. Not all these factories worked. It was risky. So, owners wanted to make sure they earned enough profit to make it worthwhile. Plus, owners often had to repay investors who had helped fund the factory. And as more factories popped up, owners often had to expand to stay successful. The need for profit and for growth drove owners to squeeze as much as they could out of factories and the people who worked there.

And it all started in Great Britain[4]

Unlike the French Revolution, there's no official starting date of the Industrial Revolution. But we can say that by the mid-1700s people in Britain were beginning to use machines to produce more and more goods by harnessing sources of power. Why Great Britain? Basically, that place in the eighteenth century had the right systems, people, and stuff to do it. First, the systems. The British government boasted a stable constitutional monarchy after 1688, controlled by Parliamentary land-owners who supported agricultural innovation and the protection of private property. There were fewer old-fashioned guild restrictions in Britain, especially up north, where the first factories mostly got going.

---

[4]A.k.a. after 1801 the United Kingdom.

British law built upon past master/servant relations to give owners great power and potential profits. More than most European nations, Britain's wealth and power came from international trade, especially the slave-based cotton and tobacco trade with North America. Even after losing the American colonies in 1783, Britain's international trade continued to grow. Perfect Enlightenment conditions right there: political and economic opportunities supported by elite property ownership and slavery. A big empire and fighting lots of wars demanded guns and transportation. Improvements in agriculture helped support growing populations and allowed fewer farmers to produce more food, which would in turn freed up folks to go work in factories.

Next, the people. Great Britain's population grew throughout the eighteenth century. More people chasing after the same resources meant that wages were falling. Falling agricultural wages meant that agricultural workers saw new factory jobs as potentially beneficial. And wealthy British people were willing to take risks. The British aristocracy and growing middle class found new ways to make money. As we saw in Chapter 2, that didn't happen as much in other countries. Individuals with some means and new ideas made good money in Britain, and that encouraged more entrepreneurship. British Puritanism, which frowned on conspicuous consumption, may have also encouraged more investment in industry.

Finally, you gotta have the goods to get industrialization going. That "green & pleasant land" turned out to have the raw materials that industry needed: coal to power new factories and iron to make machines and railroads and all that mechanical stuff. Britain also had plenty of materials to make textiles, like wool from splendid British sheep and cotton from a massive empire. Plus, that empire meant the Brits understood long-distance shipping and helped create a ready-made market for British goods. They were also the first to build railroads and use steam engines on ships, both of which further empowered Britain's military and imperial reach.

The British dominated industrialization until the late nineteenth century. The country was known as the "workshop of the world." Especially after the Napoleonic Wars, new British technology lead to more innovations, increased exports, and greater economic expansion. The government passed laws that supported industrialization and paid handsomely for the many industrial products necessary to wage war and grow an empire. But, as Adam Smith had hoped, the British government did not regulate industrialists too much. That "hands-off" approach had some pretty dire consequences for workers in these new industries, at least until the middle of the nineteenth century. And this approach did not always work in other countries.

Yeah, but was it a revolution?

You bet it was. Okay, maybe it's a little weird to call something that lasted from like the 1760s to the 1890s or even the 1950s a "revolution" because there's no clear start or stop. You could even say this revolution is still going. But industrialization changed everything! Besides, the Neolithic Agricultural Revolution, when hunting-and-gathering people settled down and began farming about 12,000 years ago, lasted a couple thousand years. So, yeah, the Industrial Revolution, baby!

And the further it spread, the more revolutionary things got. We could measure industrialization's impact in the amount of iron produced or railroad tracks laid or number of people who moved to cities. All big numbers by the way. But perhaps the most revolutionary thing about industrialization was the fact that it altered how people organized themselves and how they related to the material world. It even altered hairstyles. Families changed and gender relations changed because the ways that individuals and families earned money, found housing, and put food on the table shifted. In many cases existing inequities continued or were strengthened.

Take the case of women's work. Almost all women had always worked in and out of the home. Some factory owners gladly hired women to work and paid them less since no one saw them as the primary breadwinner (sexism). But in those circumstances, they sometimes *did* bring in the majority of the household income, so families suffered financially. And many men had to adjust to a new role. Sometimes women earned less than men because many jobs, especially in the early decades of industrialization, required greater physical strength and because women entered and left the workforce more often to have children. Gender inequity thus got built into this new system of work. And when male workers began organizing into unions and other groups to protect their interests, they excluded women to protect their own economic interests. Overall, industrialization weakened women's ability to contribute economically to society. And the gendered assumption that women's work was secondary to that of the male family breadwinner ensured that "women's jobs" (domestic work, child-care, education, nursing) from then on would pay poorly. Thankfully women in all Western societies would eventually have the same work opportunities and earn the same pay as men. Oh, wait, that still hasn't happened.

Anyway, industrialization also sharpened the division between home and work. As more and more people took factory jobs that were outside the home, the difference between home and work intensified. Men became the primary income earner in most industrial societies, but they weren't the only ones working. Even when they didn't hold full-time factory jobs, most women worked at home, either paid or unpaid. Especially in the first period of industrialization, these families usually moved to urban centers, far from their traditional village extended support network. Women (and sometimes men) at home had to work hard to maintain the family household—care for children, pay for and prepare food, manage housing, attend to laundry, etc. Wealthier women in the growing middle class could, for the first time, define the home as their sphere of influence. There they raised and educated children and created a domestic haven away from the pressures of work for their hard-working man. They usually had help from poorer women as domestic servants.

Working-class children also worked in factories. Of course, children had always worked in agrarian societies with their families. The Industrial Revolution marked the first time, though, that children worked in large numbers under the supervision of someone outside their family. And as individuals' economic value became more defined by their ability to contribute wages, even the role of elderly people changed. Their accumulation of wisdom about farming, the weather, medicine, child rearing, and other traditions passed down orally meant less in an increasingly mechanized and scientific world. Sorry, gramps.

The Industrial Revolution also made people think differently about the material world in three important ways. First, they started to have more stuff. Wealthy people were really rolling in the goods. But mass production produces for the masses—like millions of pairs of underwear. So average folks too accumulated more material objects in their lives. Second, machines extended humans' hands dramatically, allowing factories to produce in days what individuals had created before in months or years. Not everyone liked that. Initially, for example, some individual weavers destroyed machines in the textile industry to try to reassert their value. They sometimes left mysterious notes that "Ned Ludd" had done it, which eventually coined the term "Luddite," meaning someone who opposes new technology. That's a fun word to use. Early machines were of course too huge and expensive for individual people to own, but they began to be a part of people's lives at work. By the twentieth century, machines were increasingly common. In fact, lots and lots of Europeans would have the chance to get killed by machines in World War I.

Third, industrialization spawned big ideas about how material reality *should* be organized. Capitalists assumed that laws of supply and demand and property should determine how everything economic worked, including what wages workers should earn. And they thought that, if everyone pursued their own self-interest in that context, the world would become a better place. Thanks, John Locke and Adam Smith. Other free-trade economists like Robert Malthus (1766–1834) and David Ricardo (1772–1823) took Smith's laws further and argued that poor people's suffering was part of a natural rhythm of capitalist development. Yeah, everyone had posters of *those* guys on their walls. Socialists, on the other hand, believed that private property and competition perpetuated inequality. They proposed instead that *cooperative* working relations would make things better for everyone. Neither capitalism nor socialism was ever practiced perfectly. But for sure many people—not just intellectuals—began to believe that these concepts should influence how humans behave.

Looking like a revolution yet? Well, how about this: industrialization gradually created a new, urban society. More efficient farming allowed a massive workforce to migrate toward factory jobs. Owners often built factories in areas near natural resources (coal, iron, cotton, wool, waterpower) and shipping avenues (ocean ports, rivers, canals), so large numbers of people moved there, creating new, rapidly growing cities. For instance, Manchester, which was the center of British cotton manufacturing, grew from a town of 25,000 in 1772 to a city of 367,000 in 1851. London, the largest city in the world at the time, ballooned from a population of 575,000 in 1700 to almost 1 million by 1800. By 1871, almost two-thirds of people in the United Kingdom lived in towns and cities, nearly double the number elsewhere. As other countries industrialized in the nineteenth century, their numbers of large cities also went up. Urban societies spawned new forms of culture, entertainment, and free-time activities, as well as new forms of social interaction like clubs and mutual aid organizations.

Industrialization also began a long process of tearing up the planet. Those "dark Satanic Mills" did a number on the "green & pleasant land." That's still happening. Most Westerners today recognize that industrial living has majorly impacted our ecosystem. But back then the Industrial Revolution convinced Europeans to think that nature was, above all, a resource to be tamed and used. And living in close proximity to a bunch of other people was just straight up new and weird and stinky. For like 12,000 years or so humans had mostly lived in small, rural farming communities. During the nineteenth century, most Western Europeans moved to cities. Eventually better housing, sanitation, lighting, medical care, and food production would make cities healthier places to live. And the restaurants were better. But for a while industrial cities kinda sucked to live in.

M&Ms, clocks, and potatoes: The impact on workers

Hopefully it's clear that industrialization impacted everyone in Europe, especially workers. Industrialization provided great opportunity for middle-class inventors, financiers, engineers, managers, and others who helped build factories and make them run, not to mention many professionals (doctors, lawyers, accountants, educators) who served this new middle class. By the twentieth century, industrialization benefitted the lives of almost everyone in Western societies, and there were new opportunities for improvement, even for workers. But especially during the first decades of industrialization, workers who left rural villages to work in urban factories bore the brunt of the hard transition to an industrial society.

A lot of people in the Western world believe that capitalism allows people to work hard and get ahead, even to "pull themselves up by their bootstraps." If you happen to have bootstraps, you should try that and see how it goes. Still, capitalist systems did eventually give people opportunities to improve their lives. In the early days of industrialization, however, that was just about impossible. I like to do an exercise with my students to help them think about how hard it was for early industrial workers to improve their lives.

I split the class and send half of them to wait out in the hall. From the remaining half (fifteen or so students), I pick three to serve as factory owners with me. The rest are workers. We owners have a big bowl of M&Ms (ideally dark chocolate, so you get some anti-oxidants!) that represents all the property. We munch on some because we own the property and can do whatever we want with it. We explain to the workers that they need 100 M&Ms to have enough property to earn the right to vote. To earn property they must do work for us, like write papers or do assignments for class. Who's willing, we owners ask, to make an offer for that work?

The workers start making offers, to which we reply that we're looking to spend less. Soon enough someone's making some crazy cheap deal that only earns them ten or fifteen M&Ms for a bunch of work, or less. Some of the workers will get creative and talk about their specialized skills—history major, writing major, high GPA, whatever—that makes them better suited to do the job. We don't care; we just need some basic assignments done. Occasionally some worker gets uppity and says to the rest, hey, let's all agree that we'll only do the work for a certain price. If that happens, we just send them right out into the hall and bring in the other workers and repeat the exercise. Union busted! I mention that I know the head of campus security personally and can get him over here, if there's any trouble. When it's all over, this simple exercise shows students that it was almost impossible for unskilled workers to improve their lives by working harder. Then we share the M&Ms with everyone—sort of like what happened later in the twentieth century.

Most workers in the early phase of industrialization were relatively unskilled. Industrialization built upon specialization: you do your job over and over, while someone else does a different job repeatedly. As machinery and industrial processes became more sophisticated, jobs became more complex and required training. When factory owners started to need specific skills, workers were then able to negotiate better pay, fewer hours, and better conditions. And eventually factory owners and politicians realized that educating future workers would benefit their society. But for a while in Great Britain and other industrializing countries, life was not good for workers.

Clocks stood as the great oppressors. Well, one of them. Maybe that situation makes sense to you, as many of us often feel rushed or don't have enough time to do things (like finish this reading or a written exam!). Well, imagine you'd never owned a clock. That's how most people in agrarian societies lived. Yes, there were church bells that would ring at various points in the day that might tell you approximately when you should do some things. But mostly you woke up when it got light. You worked until a mid-day break and then again until it started getting dark. You did different jobs over the course of the year, all of which were mainly determined by weather, crops, and sunlight. If you were sick or hung-over one day and started work a little later, no big deal. All that changed with factory work. You had to be there at 7:00 a.m., or you got locked out and lost pay. You worked until the quitting time whistle at 6:00 or 7:00 p.m. Your work and your short breaks were regulated, often by means of clocks, to make production more efficient. That kind of regulation was new and often painful to workers, literally.

Yes, industrialization eventually benefitted everyone in Western societies. Birth rates went up, mortality rates went down. Average people were eventually able to consume more calories, secure better housing and health care, and access greater opportunities to change and improve their lives. But the transition seemed really tough on workers. Look at potatoes. Yes, potatoes. In the early nineteenth century, British factory owners used potatoes as a more efficient way to feed workers in concentrated urban centers. Potatoes provided more calories and nutrients, which improved workers' health. But British workers at this time, who had not traditionally farmed potatoes, saw them as something the Irish ate. And in their prejudiced view, having to eat potatoes was thus insulting. Factory owners rightly concluded that potatoes would improve workers' health (and thus their productivity), but that process made workers in the short run feel even worse. That pretty much sums up the early phases of industrialization.

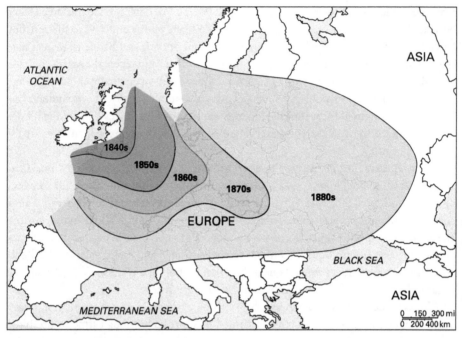

Map 6.1 Spread of industrialization.

Who wants to be like the Brits? The second wave of industrialization

The British ruled industrialization for the better part of a century, from the late eighteenth to the late nineteenth century. But other countries began to see the advantages of an industrial economy. Factories made Britain rich and powerful. The enormous British empire helped fuel industrialization *and* got bigger because of industrial tools (steamships, railroads, guns). By the 1820s, the United Kingdom had become the most powerful nation on the planet. Who wouldn't want some of that?

The UK's nearest neighbors, France, Belgium, and the Netherlands, certainly wanted in on that action, so they copied the hell out of the Brits. They imported British technology, British processes, and British advisors. Unfortunately, they didn't have some of the British natural resources, especially coal. But they used their significant resources from long traditions of banking, trade, and farming to finance factories starting in the 1830s. As in the UK, these governments encouraged industrialization but mainly let private industry build the mechanized economy. Industrialization in France, Belgium, and the Netherlands slowly grew over the nineteenth century.

Other countries, like Germany and Russia, came late to the game and were like, no way we're doing this at some slow, splendid, British pace; let's get moving! Starting in the 1870s, the German state directly assisted industrialization by financing and helping to create large companies and cartels that produced many related products. This form of industrialization was still rooted in capitalist competition and private enterprise. But through more directed efforts, Germany managed to accomplish in about twenty years what had taken the British a century. Indeed by 1890, the very young German industrial economy surpassed old man Britain in industrial output.[5] *Achtung!*

This rapid growth also produced a German working class in short order, all of whom shared similar, largely unpleasant experiences. Socialist ideas about fixing things quickly took hold. But the German government, instead of resisting reform like politicians mostly did in Britain, actually gave workers what they wanted: unemployment insurance, health care, retirement programs, and other assistance. Yep, real welfare programs from bushy-mustached Germans. Bet you didn't see that coming. Neither did German workers, and those moves went a long way to minimizing worker discontent there.

In Russia, needless to say, the government was not so generous. Russia too used major government financing to jump start industrialization. All European countries had their own jealous reasons for pushing industrialization, but Russia especially wanted a stronger military to stand up to the mighty British Empire. The Russians actually got whipped by the Brits (and others) in the Crimean War in 1856. That defeat turned out to be a wake-up call that it was time to move out of the Middle Ages. Russia freed its serfs in 1861 and embarked on a program to modernize its economy and military, although the tsar definitely said *nyet* to any political or social reform.

Official support for industrialization in late nineteenth-century Russia enabled the government to control industrialization and modernization. Of course, Russia was the only country in Europe to experience a massive communist revolution (in 1917), so their plans didn't work out so well. Anyhoo, the Russians also caught up to the Brits in terms of industrial output pretty fast. Their reforms also produced rapid population growth: Russia grew from 68 million people in 1858 to 163 million in 1914, including a new and expanding working class. Unlike in Western Europe, though, there were no outlets like political parties, organizations, reform movements, or even publications to discuss their plight. Aha! That may be one reason for that whole 1917 communist revolution thing.

Across Europe in the last third of the nineteenth century, a "second wave" of industrialization further transformed people's experiences. As industrial techniques became more sophisticated, workers could use their increasing specialization to earn more and secure more safety and security. Governments also saw, to varying degrees, good reasons to provide public education, which gave workers greater opportunities. Industrialization in fact generally brought governments even more into average people's lives. They promoted factory growth and protected the private property on which industrialization rested everywhere. A few states provided social welfare programs or passed reforms to improve workers' experiences.

Technological advances also enhanced Europeans' ability to take over and dominate other parts of the world, as we'll see in the next chapter. A mechanized military enabled fewer European soldiers to control more people. Although Enlightenment thinkers

---

[5]Which gave the British, French, and Russians more reasons to worry about Germany and start forming alliances.

waxed eloquent about equality, they also reinforced who was enlightened and who was in the dark. Most European nations abolished slavery in the early nineteenth century. Still, they had long made *beaucoup* dough from this most unequal and racist form of labor, and that perspective informed their economic assumptions about the world. Industrialization encouraged Westerners to view their supremacy increasingly through technology. Ironically, Europeans also saw their technological might as a generous gift to share with the same peoples they were conquering and exploiting. You're welcome!

In fact, ideas about race influenced industrialization right from the start. Slavery had given colonial powers like the Great Britain, France, and Holland greater resources to convert to factories. And unequal trading with non-white people encouraged European industrialists to use similarly uneven work agreements with factory workers. Imperial expansion pushed industrial growth, which further pushed imperial expansion. And these economic benefits fit nicely with Europeans' assumptions that their industrial strength reflected their racial superiority.

Responses: reform, unions, revolution

Let's review: (1) industrialization changed daily activities and relationships for lots of Europeans; (2) it kinda blew for workers. Especially in the first phase of industrialization, the profound changes grew out of established inequities. Getting capital in a capitalist society was not easy for folks at the bottom. The combination of capital's control of labor, the laws of supply and demand, and the profit motive encouraged owners to pay workers as little as possible. Okay, a few crazy dudes like Robert Owen (1771–1858) set up factories in Britain and the USA with free education, health care, and opportunities for male and female workers. But then, he was basically a socialist, so what do you expect? Weirdo. Most workers had three options for how to respond to harsh industrial conditions: push for political reform, form unions, or revolution. And plenty of them drank heavily too.

The United Kingdom in the first half of the nineteenth century was sort of a democracy. Before 1832, only like 3 percent of British citizens could vote, but the Reform Act of 1832 expanded the franchise to about 20 percent of men. (That increased further in 1867 and 1884, by which time about 60 percent of men could vote.) Since voters had to own property, workers almost never qualified. See: M&Ms! But they did pressure Parliamentary representatives to pass reforms in the 1830s that modestly benefitted workers, including the 1833 Factory Acts, which limited child labor a little. Poor children didn't have the chance to go to school regularly until around 1870.

Workers' biggest push for political reform was a movement in the 1830s and 1840s known as Chartism. Reformers drafted a "People's Charter" that demanded fair, open elections and basically universal male suffrage. Workers hoped to elect Parliamentary representatives who would pass laws to improve working conditions. They brought "Charters" as official petitions to Parliament in 1838, 1842, and 1848 that were signed by millions of people in the United Kingdom. In 1848 there were mass demonstrations, too.

British politicians patted themselves on the back for restrained British reform during that year of Europe-wide revolution. But like those continental revolutions, British reforms ultimately came to very little, notifying workers that they'd have to find other ways to fix their conditions.

So, workers looked to unions as a DIY solution. Labor unions in the UK were legalized in 1824. Local organizations grew in the 1830s, and some workers even attempted to develop national unions. After the Chartism movement failed, workers in the 1850s and 1860s increasingly organized into effective unions at local factories, across trades, and even nationally. It helped that factory work was becoming more specialized in the second half of the nineteenth century, so some workers had greater leverage for improving their conditions. Unions helped workers bargain for better pay and protections. Unions and other organizations like mutual aid societies pooled money to help workers who got injured on the job or were laid off or faced health crises. In the long run, unions offered the best protection until governments in the twentieth century finally enacted laws to protect workers and improve their lot.

So, that leaves revolution. Some of the failed revolutions of the 1830s and 1840s were motivated by economic desires, including the urge to improve workers' lives. You saw how those turned out in the last chapter. Even later in the nineteenth century, revolution sounded good but was not much of an option really. We need to hear about that from Mr. Socialist Revolution himself, Karl Marx.

Karl Marx, socialist revolutionary and Enlightenment thinker

Let's be fair: Marx was more than a socialist revolutionary champ. He also had a great beard. And he offered a completely new perspective on history and human society. Like his Enlightenment amigos, he wanted to discover the rules that determined how things worked. He talked a lot about the scientific laws of history. And also like other Enlightenment thinkers, Marx believed that fixing the system and unleashing people's goodness would make the world a better place. He thought that all human history and relations were shaped by class conflict. Today most people look at Marxism as a concept that has failed in places like the Soviet Union, China, North Korea, and Cuba. In subsequent chapters we'll see that communism in the Soviet Union and elsewhere really wasn't very Marxist. Nevertheless, a lot of blood was spilled in the twentieth century in the name of Marxism, so it's important to understand why Marx's ideals were so powerful and appealing. Time for some dialectical materialism, which was at the heart of Marx's ideas.

German philosopher Georg Wilhelm Friedrich Hegel (1770–1831) created the idea of a *dialectic*, of progress based on conflict. Hegel believed that human history and human progress moved this way: An established idea or way of thinking—the *thesis*—was challenged by a new idea or way of thinking—the *antithesis*. The conflict between the two created something new, a *synthesis*. That new concept then became the new, dominant *thesis*, and the process would begin again. Like this:

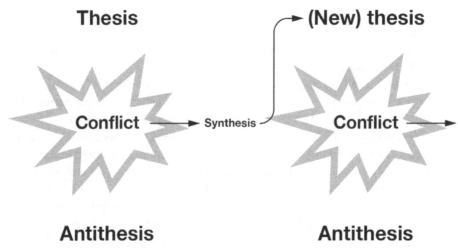

Figure 6.2 Fairly lame rendering of dialectic.

This progressive concept assumes things *will* change and improve. Very Enlightenment, very scientific.

Very attractive to Marx, but he had a major disagreement with his boy Hegel. See, Hegel believed that these conflicts were about *ideas* and that those ideas then shaped material reality. Marx turned Hegel on his head, as it's often described, and said instead that *material* conflicts matter most and they in turn shape ideas. Marx insisted that the thesis and the antithesis were always about who had the money, or who *controlled the means of production*. He used that phrase because how you stayed rich and powerful changed throughout human history. Sometimes what mattered was owning and controlling land, sometimes it was about controlling people, sometimes it was about having capital. Whatever the case, Marx thought that class conflicts about *material* or economic differences drove history. Hence, *dialectical materialism*.

Marx explained all of human history and indeed all of human interactions this way. That's one of the reasons Marxism has mattered. Scholars still use his ideas to explain many things that people have done. He also offered a handy, compelling way to look at history. He simplified the issue of controlling the means of production into two classes of those control the means of production (the Haves) and those who do not (the Have Nots). See Figure 6.3, another highly simplified chart.

In each case a conflict between the Haves (the thesis) and Have Nots (antithesis) produced a new economic system and divided Europe again between those who controlled the means of production and those who did most of the producing.

Marx called these class conflicts the fundamental *structure* of every society, the thing that matters most. Everything else in a society—state, religion, culture, gender relations, concepts of race—all exist only to reinforce the structural differences between classes.

Haves (thesis)	Ancient World (esp Greece and Rome)		Feudal Europe		Capitalist Industrial World	Welcome to Communism!
	Slave/Land Owners	Conflict around fall of Roman Empire	Lords	Conflict around French Revolution	Bourgeoise (middle-class factory owners)	(the end of class conflict and therefore all this tedious history business)
Have Nots (antithesis)	Slaves		Serfs		Proletariat (factory workers)	

Figure 6.3 Marx's vision of European history.

Marx called those things *superstructure*. For example, Marx argued that Catholicism in feudal Europe kept serfs from asking how they could make things more fair because it pushed them to worry about the afterlife more than this life. Similarly, Marx thought that concepts of liberty or democracy in a modern industrial society helped keep the middle class in charge of the means of production. Above all, Marx railed against private property—and laws protecting it—as the main thing that maintained inequality in a modern industrial society.

Marx believed that some day, probably in his lifetime, the working class around the world would realize that they were the ones doing everything and would rise up and overthrow the capitalist system. In the second half of the nineteenth century, Marx looked around Europe and saw more and more workers. He predicted that the next conflict between the Haves and Have Nots would result in *communism* or an end to class conflict. That's what he called his vision of socialism, where cooperation replaces competition and there are no more classes. Without private property making everyone crazy acquisitive, folks could do what they wanted and were best at. And, guess what, there'd be no need for states or religion to keep the class structure together. Sounds like that John Lennon song, "Imagine," doesn't it? You may say Marx is a dreamer, but he's not the only one.

Now, people back then and ever since have pointed out plenty of holes in this theory and criticized it for simplifying or assuming too much. But workers in the nineteenth century found these basic ideas incredibly appealing. So did some intellectuals. After all, Marxism offered a secular total explanation of human behavior and history. And Marx said progress was inevitable, according the laws of history. Sign up now for the winning side of history! He imagined a world in which your *labor* mattered, not what capital you controlled. And since workers had little capital and were usually on the losing end of a society based on property, Marx offered a way to change that.

Unfortunately, our buddy Karl didn't give many directions on how a spontaneous, overwhelming, international communist revolution would just … happen. Nor did he say much about how a post-revolutionary, classless, communist society would work. He did say that there would be a brief "dictatorship of the proletariat" after the revolution to get rid of the few elites who resisted the shift to communism. Um-hm. Just like with Jesus, Muhammed, and other prophetic thinkers of the past, ambitious people definitely filled in their own ideas about what *that* meant. Basically, the Soviet Union and other "communist" societies got stuck at that "dictatorship" phase and never moved on to the state withering away and the bliss of a classless society.

So, really Marx did *not* provide a clear way to solve the problems of industrialization with revolution. He simply promised that it would happen. Marx's ideas did explain, though, why an industrial society was unequal and gave people ways to challenge that system. In order to minimize the inequalities in industrial society, some socialists took advantage of limited democracy to push laws through the state. Others used unions to lessen the impact of industrialization on workers. Those folks were called *evolutionary* socialists, and they would fight a lot in the twentieth century with *revolutionary* socialists. Still, all socialists took from Marx a thorough and compelling explanation for industrialization and the burning desire to fix it.

Feminism: One idea that people did not kill and die for

By the nineteenth century people were starting to kill each other over ideas. They would perfect that action in the twentieth century. Like the Enlightenment ideas we've discussed so far—capitalism, nationalism, socialism, communism—feminism prompted conflict, too, and people, especially women, got hurt promoting it. But unlike these other "isms," feminism was not an ideal for which people went to war.

Really, the Enlightenment was rather cruel to women. Those grand ideas of equality and freedom seemed to have been written directly *for* women. A few eighteen-century feminists tried to make good on those promises. Yet the prejudices of that era were baked into Enlightenment thought, and they may have actually made things *worse* for women by defining them as the "dark" that opposed enlightenment. We've seen, for example, that industrial work offered women some new opportunities but often paid them less than men. Even union activities aimed at improving poor workers' lives often excluded women as a way to strengthen male workers' place in society. Ah, there it is again: that double-standard, that one-step-forward-and-two-steps-back kind of progress.

In 1848, a number of women's rights advocates met in Seneca Falls, New York in the United States to articulate how women might take advantage of Enlightenment ideals. Their "Declaration of Sentiments," which was modeled on the US "Declaration of Independence," proposed that women have the right to own property, divorce, work, and vote. They didn't really have any means to put these things into effect, but they created a broad framework for women's rights that would continue to be relevant right up to today. Twenty years later in the United Kingdom, the philosopher and politician John Stuart Mill (1806–73) published his sweeping book *The Subjection of Women*. He used big Enlightenment ideas to argue that granting women rights and equality would make everyone happier. And yet, the number of real legal changes for women in Europe were . . . yeah, pretty much none.

At the start of the twentieth century women's rights groups were divided about whether economic or political rights mattered more for women. Should women be able to work and earn the same as men, or should they get the vote? Especially in Britain, this issue divided progressive organizations. In 1896 the author and civil servant Beatrice Webb (1858–1943) argued that women and the whole British economy would benefit from laws guaranteeing equal pay and work opportunities to women. Webb of course wanted women to be able to vote too. But she reasoned that male politicians and employers might *first* see the enlightened self-interest in giving women economic opportunity. Plus, she was a democratic socialist and prioritized economic change.

Around this same time influential, middle-class organizations advocated for women's right to vote. Sylvia Pankhust (1882–1960) led one of several groups in the UK pushing for women's suffrage. She was arrested fifteen times, force fed in prison, and regularly suffered physical abuse for her advocacy. Like most Western democracies, the United Kingdom gave women the vote after World War I, whereas fights for women to earn the same as men continue to this day. So, maybe Marx was right about the importance of economic power.

The politics of industrial history

Look, writing history is political. I suspect that's one reason not everyone likes it. But as I discussed in this book's introduction, any time you tell a story you are being political: deciding what to put in and what to leave out, figuring out how to convince your audience, and trying to make a point. This chapter's topic about industrialization and its impact on workers and the world seems particularly politically important. People who had all the money came up with brilliant ways to use that money to make factories and ultimately help people live better. They also solidified their ability to control how people work.

Yes, just as democracy was spreading in some places and bringing more people into the process of ruling, industrialization pretty much guaranteed that there would be no democracy at work. Think about that for a moment. You live in a society that *requires* your participation in a democracy to function (even if it doesn't always work out as planned). But when you go to work, you function under a very different set of relations that are mostly not democratic. Sure, there may be laws to protect you and ways that you can hold employers accountable. But by and large working relations are hierarchical and not democratic. That's one of the most profound yet unseen results of the Industrial Revolution.

I'm bringing this up because it's implied in this chapter, and I wanted to be transparent about one of the reasons you should understand this big process of industrialization. You don't have to go out and overthrow that system. Frankly, you wouldn't be the first to try and fail and usually end up in jail or dead. So, yeah, not the best idea. Still, it's worth understanding why working relationships, which will shape the rest of your life, are how they are. Lots of historians have tried to tell us about the average people who sacrificed for our fabulous society filled with computers, closets full of clothes, and inexpensive coffee. They have tried to help us realize where current work relations came from and why. We owe it to people of the past not to look down on them, in part because we don't want historians doing the same thing to us in the future! Hopefully learning about how our insanely wealthy, modern material society developed demonstrates that great things in history almost always come at a price for someone. Maybe knowing that price will make us all more thoughtful about minimizing suffering in the future. Thank you, sisters and brothers, for tuning into today's sermon!

CHAPTER 7
ON THE ROAD AGAIN: THE IDEAS AND VIOLENCE OF WESTERN IMPERIALISM

So, yeah, that happened. This 1899 advertisement (Figure 7.1) used themes in a poem from the same year by Rudyard Kipling (1865–1936). Kipling encouraged the British and Americans to "Take up the White Man's burden/Send forth the best ye breed/Go send your sons to exile/To serve your captives' need."[1] And the folks at Pears' Soap figured the best way to do their duty to civilize natives whose land and resources white men were stealing was to give those poor people some soap. It makes me wonder if I shouldn't revise this entire book. I mean, it says here that that soap holds "the highest place . . .amongst

The first step towards lightening

The White Man's Burden

is through teaching the virtues of cleanliness.

Pears' Soap

is a potent factor in brightening the dark corners of the earth as civilization advances, while amongst the cultured of all nations it holds the highest place—it is the ideal toilet soap.

Figure 7.1 Pears', the soap of the white man.

---

[1]Kipling, "White Man's Burden," in *Rudyard Kipling's Verse: Definitive Edition* (Garden City, New York: Doubleday, 1929), originally published in *The Times* (London), February 4, 1899.

the cultured of all nations." And here I thought it might be Enlightenment notions of freedom or equality or some such. Wash out your mouth, Immanuel Kant! It's *soap* that enlightens "the dark corners of the earth."

This advertisement lays out well the issues at stake in this chapter on imperialism. Sure, imperialism was about selling stuff. Everyone knew this was an ad for soap. It also featured cool technology—a steam-powered gunboat with a bathroom offering running water and lights—that allowed the White Man to go and make people captives. But that same desire to conquer and sell was wrapped up with assumptions that Westerners were bringing superior civilization to share with non-Westerners. And like some Enlightenment ideas about race, Pears' Soap even implied their product might make dark people white.[2]

Kipling and others recognized that imperialism would benefit the home country, but it was also the *duty* of white men to capture and force their superior civilization on these "dark" areas and people. Put simply, those motivations—making money, using technology, and civilizing the world—drove Europe's dramatic expansion in the late nineteenth and early twentieth centuries. It was a tough job, but the White Man had to do it.

Building the argument

Like industrialization, the process of imperialism built upon a combination of established prejudices and (you guessed it) Enlightenment ideals. We've already seen that Western powers have used powerful technology and assumptions about Others to take over parts of the world. Really that had been going on for thousands of years around the world. Empires were nothing new. But the scope of what Europeans did in the late nineteenth and early twentieth centuries was just crazy. By 1914, when World War I started, European powers controlled large portions of the world. So, if you want to understand the interdependent and international world today, you've got to understand imperialism. How did we get addicted to good coffee, cheap televisions, and oil from thousands of miles away? How did immigration become an explosive political issue? Why do mostly white folks in the northern hemisphere control the majority of the world's resources? Why, imperialism of course.

The genealogy of imperialism is fairly simple. It builds upon most of the ideas we've studied thus far: religious conflict, science, nationalism, and industrialization. Based on old prejudices, often stemming from religious conflicts, Europeans thought they were better than everyone else in the world, and they had few qualms about using violence to prove it. Thanks to modern industry, Europeans had access to more powerful technologies, like guns and steamships. Nationalist European states competed with each other for economic resources and ways to show who was most powerful. Informed by Social Darwinism, many

---

[2]Seriously. Pears' ran an advertisement around this time in which a white baby gives soap to a black baby. After bathing, the black baby's body—but not head—turns white! Another Pears' ad shows some native type (dark, scantily clad, feather in hair, holding a spear) admiring soap that has washed up on the shore with the heading "the birth of civilization." Yet another entitled "Sambo's Testimonial" shows a winking Black man saying "matchless for um komplekshun." You can't make this stuff up.

Europeans expected conflicts between groups, and they believed that strong peoples would dominate weak ones. We can really see the dual nature of the Enlightenment here. These means to expand, control, and dominate come from Enlightenment thought, but so did Europeans' urges to liberate and improve the world. Napoleon brought Enlightenment ideals to Europe with guns. Likewise, Europeans believed they were bringing the fruits of Enlightenment and science to the rest of the world on steamships and gunboats.

This chapter will first present a short history of imperialism and the reasons behind the expansion in the late nineteenth and early twentieth centuries that basically gave Europeans control of the globe. We then study the specific cases of Europeans going into Asia and Africa, the two main areas of expansion during this time. Comparing Kipling's ideas with those of author George Orwell (1903–50) will help us understand better this bizarre concept of the "white man's burden."

I need to state clearly that this chapter, like this book, is about European history. This chapter mainly focuses on how Europeans expanded into the world and what that process did to European society. To say that imperialism impacted colonized subjects is a major understatement. And I recognize that my featuring European experiences and perspectives kind of reproduces imperialism. Non-Western voices are essential to explain the full extent of imperialism, and we will explore some of those. Nevertheless, for this book it's valuable to dig deeply into Europeans' motivations and experiences of imperialism in order to unpack the ways they continue to shape Western and the world.

Imperialism, colonialism: what's the difference?

These are similar, overlapping concepts, but the difference helps us understand what happened during this time period. Imperialism is the expansion of one state by military means into another territory, using its power to control people and places beyond its borders. Colonialism is when one group settles another area, when one state enables a large number of its people to move into someone else's territory. Colonial expansion relies upon military might, too: you have to conquer a place before you can move in there. In fact, colonialism always starts with imperialism. In both cases one group violently moves into the area of another group.

The major difference between imperialism and colonialism is degree. While imperialist expansion definitely involves people conquering and moving into someone else's territory, the numbers tended to be smaller. In British India, for example, about 250,000 Britons ruled close to 300 million native people. The ratio of Europeans to non-Europeans was even lower in other places, especially Africa. On the other hand, many more Europeans moved to the *colonies* they established. The North American colonies that Great Britain set up in the seventeenth and eighteenth centuries are the most obvious examples. French people similarly eventually made up 17 percent of the population in Algeria in North Africa. To make things more confusing, the process in this chapter was *imperialism*, but when Europeans pull out of these places (the subject of Chapter 13), we call that *decolonization*, not de-imperialization. Sorry.

This chapter mainly deals with European imperialism in the nineteenth and twentieth centuries. Some European powers—the UK, France, Holland—had been *colonial* rulers before, and those experiences shaped the ways they expanded their empires in this more recent period. In each case European expansion disrupted those places, to say the least. Even small numbers of European troops or officials had massive economic and cultural impact on the conquered places. That's the main point here. Imperialist expansion exploited and reshaped the places Europeans conquered, no matter how many white folks moved in there. And those experiences in turn altered life back in the European countries too.

Just a little history of imperialism

In the modern world there were two main periods of European imperialism. First, Europeans took over and colonized the Americas, starting with big Christopher Columbus sailing across the ocean blue in fourteen hundred and ninety-two. That murderous conquest (and colonization) lasted until the 1830s or so, by which time a bunch of revolts in North and South America had mostly ended European direct rule there. For Round Two, Europeans started moving into Asia, Africa, the Middle East, and places in the Pacific Ocean. That expansion began around 1700, gradually grew over the next two centuries, then blew up at the end of the nineteenth century and didn't end until the late twentieth century. It's this second phase of imperialism, especially the blowing up part, that concerns us here.

That first spate of colonial expansions continued some of the traditions and assumptions from ancient empires. Jeez, how many times will modern Europeans keep thinking they were like the Romans? The Romans certainly came barreling into various parts of Europe, but they were not doing it across a damn ocean! That massive distance between the home and colonized countries made the modern process more complicated. For one thing, when Europeans landed in what turned out to be the Americas,[3] there were a lot of very different looking and acting people everywhere. However, most of these natives politely died after Europeans arrived, seeming to beckon Europeans into virgin wilderness. Columbus landed in October 1492 in what's today the Bahamas. Over the next century or so, about 90 percent of the population in North and South America died, mainly from diseases the Europeans brought over. The Europeans thought they were pretty bad ass with their guns and armor and ships and stuff. But really it was their diseases that made it easy for them to conquer the Americas—diseases to which people in the Americas had not been exposed for like 35,000 years. (See Chapter Negative 22 on the Ice Age.)

Anyway, all this easy conquest made the Europeans feel really tough. And just about the time when Europeans figured out that they could make good money selling

---

[3]Of course, Columbus and others initially thought they had landed in India, which is why they first called folks they encountered "Indians." Still plenty of debate about that term today.

awesomely addictive sugar and tobacco back home, they looked around and saw no workers in the Americas. So, they brought slaves from Africa. That cruel and ultimately inefficient form of labor made plenty of European settlers rich yet sowed the seeds of independence movements that would consume the Americas for much of the nineteenth centuries. It also taught Europeans that this system of colonial rule did not really work. The folks who remained in charge in North and South America after various revolutions were almost exclusively European descendants. The legacy of racial tension between European immigrants, forced African immigrants (slaves), and native peoples has continued to shape the politics and social lives of people in pretty much every country in North and South America right up to the present day.

Now, you might think that these lessons, coupled with all that wonderful Enlightenment thought, would convince Europeans that they should treat people around the world fairly. Or at least leave them alone and not conquer them. Plus, many of the European nations we're considering—the United Kingdom, France, Holland, even Germany—were becoming a little more democratic in this period. Please. Surely you haven't forgotten that it was the Enlightenment that taught Europeans to think in terms of race, to label people, and to define themselves in part against the "dark" peoples of the earth. Recall that the Enlightenment natural history "expert" Buffon (love that name!) thought that all people had started out white! Plus, the desire to share God's word still motivated plenty of Europeans. So, Europeans learned some lessons from colonizing the Americas, but assumptions of superiority still trumped concepts of universal equality.

Here's a great irony of that first wave of imperialism. If early modern colonizers had been a little less powerful and maybe carried fewer diseases, they would have been forced to trade with indigenous people in the Americas more fairly. Or, had they been a little more attuned to Enlightenment ideas of equality, they might not have conquered and settled so many places. But alas . . .

A variety of motives, especially economic, inspired the second wave of imperialism. Many European powers believed that commercial relations with other parts of the world would benefit them *and* the people in those places. But, you know, sometimes you gotta convince people to trade, and guns and superior technology sure can help with that. People advancing their own commercial interests in new places often did what they had to in order to open trading routes, usually inviting governments to follow them. A compelling mix of commercial, Christian, and civilizing motives drove modern imperialism. It was a heady combo that, along with great technology, allowed Europeans to take over the globe in a way not seen before, and one that continues to define our society today.

Why "send forth the best ye breed"? Imperialist motives

So, we've seen the big reasons Europeans just kept taking over the world: Enlightenment ideas, religious self-righteousness, greed. The usual. Now let's dig a little deeper into these motives. You may think I sound like a broken record . . . wait, who even knows what a "broken record" means these days?[4] Anyway, imperialism often used newer Enlightenment ideas (free-market capitalism, bringing light to dark places, even notions of democracy) to justify older ideas (religious, cultural, racial superiority, absolutism, etc.). What were some of the specific ways this synthesis of old and new motivated Europeans starting in the late nineteenth century to expand into more and more parts of the world?

Economics

Access to potentially valuable resources (petroleum, gold, rubber, cotton, ivory, spices, lumber) certainly motivated Europeans to move into many parts of the world. Private and state enterprises gained raw materials in order to manufacture more products. And European companies forcibly created new markets by taking over other places. You didn't think the makers of Pears' Soap were just going to give their product away, did you? Imperialism helped European companies and countries make money. Eventually those European (and American) companies would realize that empires were costly and they could still make plenty of money from unequal trade relationships with former colonies. We'll get to that in Chapter 13.

Aggressive capitalism

If a capitalist economy ain't growing, it ain't working. So, let's look at three ways that capitalist expansion fueled imperialism. First, capitalists of all kinds concluded that they needed to move into unknown parts of Africa and Asia because there *might* be good stuff there. If you don't get in there, you won't have access to what could be there. We see this kind of thing all the time today with tech firms. Some start-up creates an app or a piece of software or hardware, and then Google, Apple, or Microsoft buys them up. Those tech giants don't know if what they purchased will be the next big thing or not. But if one out of every ten purchases pays off, they still make bank. And of course, they need to make sure their competitors don't get hold of it first. Same with imperialist nations: grab the land, so you might benefit from it and your competitor will not. Second, a lot of expanding, especially in Africa, amounted to private individuals or groups with their own armed forces taking over places and then asking their government to sanction their conquest by planting their flag. For example, in the 1890s Cecil Rhodes (1853–1902) pushed the interests of the mining British South Africa Company into the area that eventually became the British colony Rhodesia (and then the free country of Zimbabwe in the 1960s).[5] The British military, administration, and flag followed, sometimes reluctantly.

---

[4]Someone working in a museum? Hipsters in Brooklyn or Hackney?
[5]Rhodes basically created a monopoly on diamond mining in South Africa, which made him super rich. He eventually used some of his money to found the Rhodes Scholarship. Rhodes was by the way a major white supremist, believing that non-white people were better off ruled by the British. It's kind of ironic that his Scholarship has, especially since World War II, helped foster international cooperation.

The third point about aggressive capitalism comes from Vladimir Lenin (1870–1924) in a book he wrote in 1916 before leading the Russian Revolution. In *Imperialism, the Highest Stage of Capitalism*, Lenin explained that capitalism had managed to survive its natural boom-and-bust cycle by expanding into other parts of the world, where capitalists could find cheap raw materials and labor and where they could create new markets. As a Marxist, Lenin believed capitalism's life extension through imperialism would eventually run out, when there were no more new markets to conquer. Then it's revolution time. You don't have to be a socialist revolutionary to see some sense in Lenin's argument. Think about tobacco companies. They would have gone bankrupt long ago, were it not for new markets of smokers in China especially. Capitalist economies always have to grow, and imperialism helped them do that in ways that might have released some of the pressures in the late nineteenth century that workers felt. Of course, Lenin's predictions didn't quite come true. Still, it's hard to imagine the success of many Western companies today without the cheap materials and labor that grew from imperialism, not to mention the expanding markets for their products.

Industrial Revolution

Maybe this is obvious. The Industrial Revolution made possible the communications and transportation necessary to command a world empire. It gave Westerners superior technology to overwhelm populations in Asia and Africa (and let Europeans believe that toting better guns made them better people). For example, the Gatling gun, an early machine gun, saw plenty of use in imperialist conflicts. It allowed one shooter to fire hundreds of rounds per minute, effectively doing the work of dozens of soldiers. The Industrial Revolution also created its own needs for goods and for international markets. The ability to produce a bunch of stuff required manufacturers to expand their resources and markets constantly.

Nationalism

Remember back in Chapter 5 when I said that much of what happened in the nineteenth and twentieth centuries was due to nationalism? Well, nationalism worked in a couple of ways to encourage imperialism. First, European powers competed with each other. In some ways the unification of Germany in 1871 pushed other European powers to build their powerbase elsewhere, like in Asia and Africa. Conflicts over empires will mean even more when we consider how World War I started. (In fact, imperialism helped put the "world" in "World War I.")

Above all, though, everyone was trying to catch up to the British. Such Brit envy! They had the biggest navy, the largest empire, the best industry, the most enthusiastic poetry, and the whitest soap. Other European powers started grabbing more colonies to thwart further British growth and to show the world that, doggone it, they were real, live colonial powers too! More than once at the end of nineteenth century, these tensions almost boiled over into war. Imperialism was, in other words, sometimes nationalism by other means. And if these people with so many similarities—white, big mustaches, Christian, capitalist, supremely confident—were willing to fight each other, then imagine what they were willing to do to very different people they found in Africa, Asia, and elsewhere!

Racism

Racism in Europe was nothing new. Europeans had long thought they were better than people from Africa, the Middle East, Asia, and the Americas. Some of those assumptions stemmed from colonial contact going back to the fifteenth century. Enlightenment ideas helped Europeans divide people according to race and figure out who was "dark" and in need of enlightenment. Still, European imperialism starting in the late nineteenth century employed racism differently because these white folks *took action* against their so-called inferiors. They invaded, took places over, and justified their actions with the belief that they were superior to the people they conquered. In Chapter 5 we saw how Social Darwinism sharpened nationalist conflicts in the nineteenth century in Europe. The basic assumptions of Social Darwinism—the strong *must* dominate the weak, racial conflict will help humans evolve, and scientific evidence supports racial hierarchies—were some of the most potent motivations for Europeans supporting imperialism.

Christianity

Christianity offered Europeans yet another reason to feel superior to other people in the world *and* to want to go out and help them. Are you noticing a pattern here? Missionaries wanted to take the good news of Christianity to the heathens of the world, and, boy, there were a lot of heathens in Africa and Asia. The notion that Europeans were bringing salvation to those unfamiliar with Christianity inspired missionaries and mercenaries alike. Even if their aims were a little presumptuous, missionaries deserve credit for preserving hundreds of previously unwritten languages right up to the present day. They also found ways to understand the people they visited, not just exploit them. And eventually missionaries' universalist message would help challenge some aspects of imperialism. Yet missionaries, like all imperialists, brought themselves and their assumptions about civilization to the places they visited.

Civilization

So many of the reasons above—commerce, Christianity, industrial technology, nationalist culture—all got wrapped into the goal of bringing Western "civilization" to the rest of the world. Most Westerners believed that civilization was linear, that there was a continuum from less to more civilized. Guess who was more civilized? Modern Western definitions of civilization have usually been material: having communication and transportation facilities, ways to control nature, technology to make life easier, pairs of underwear, machines to extend human reach, medicine. Or they were rooted in assumptions about what social systems maximize human ability. All those ideas convinced most Europeans that they lived best and that others should know about their fine ways.

Consider the soap example again. If you're honest, you probably value cleanliness: it prevents disease, it looks good, it makes devices work better, etc. So, as awfully racist as that Pears' Soap ad was, it conveys a set of assumptions about how one group of people can help another. Those motives are similar to the aims of organizations like Charity: Water, Doctors without Borders, the US Peace Corps, UN Volunteers, and others. These mainly Western groups today help people in many of the same places Europeans colonized in the late nineteenth century. Of course, European imperialists brought civilization with guns, not Birkenstocks.

Now we come to the dark and probably not surprising realization that imperialism revealed some of the worst, most violent elements of Enlightenment thought. Imperialists probably believed in positive, liberating ideas like rational thought, universal liberalism, free trade, and progress. And they certainly acted on the exclusive and exclusionary implications of the Enlightenment. Imperialism also helped fuel the massive economic growth that tore into the undeveloped world, enriching Western powers and deepening the gulf between rich and poor people in the world. And since these developments would shape the history of the twentieth century, imperialism acts as a bridge between the nineteenth and twentieth centuries.

Imperialism went down differently in Asia and Africa, yet the main contours were the same. Europeans used superior technology, demands for advantageous trade, and

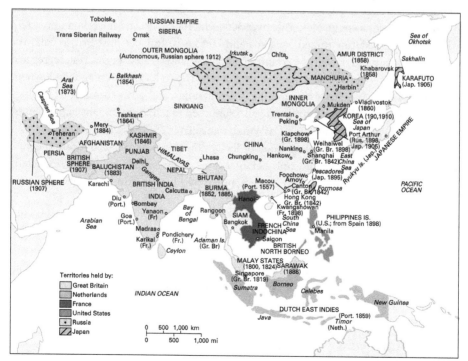

Map 7.1 Imperialism in Asia.

assumptions about their civilization to open up and take over portions of these places. They sent relatively few colonists there, so they had to work out how to get the most economic and strategic benefit from new colonies.

Dreams of the Orient: opening Asia

"The Orient," in case you're wondering, is an old term that just means "the east." It is the opposite of "the Occident," or "the west."[6] By the nineteenth century, "the Orient" in Europe referred broadly to pretty much all of Asia, including the Middle East and India. Europeans were often more fascinated by "the Orient" than remotely informed about it.[7] Together with some major commercial interests, that curiosity and cluelessness helped motivate Europeans to expand further into Asia. Europeans had been trading with the powerful kingdoms of India, China, and Japan since the fifteenth centuries. For most of that time, the Europeans were the weaklings. The technologically, militarily, and culturally stronger Asians called the shots. However, that balance began to shift in the eighteenth century.

India

British traders and their private military forces moved into India in the 1730s, when the place was being torn apart by religious warfare between Muslims, Hindus, and Sikhs. The private British East India Company initially ruled India indirectly. Yes, the commercial-minded Brits sent a company to rule over 300 million people. And it worked until 1857, when the Sepoy Mutiny united Muslims and Hindus in India against British rule. The UK sent in troops, took over the country completely, and created a powerful, segregated state under British direct rule, though they still relied upon local leaders and landowners. British leaders built railroads, communications systems, and other forms of technology to make trade easier. These moves were also supposed to make the Indians happy. But by the 1880s educated Indians like Dadabhai Naoroji (1825–1917) had concluded that British imperialism was draining India of its wealth. Naoroji's so-called "drain theory"[8] would ultimately inform many anti-colonial movements around the world, especially the post-World War II nationalist movement led by Mahatma Gandhi that would free India from British rule.

China

For about 3,000 years, the Chinese had considered their home to be the Middle Kingdom between heaven and the barbarians on earth. So, even when Europeans with cool names

---

[6]Brief Professor Moment. Both words come from Latin; "Orient" refers to east, where the sun rises and "Occident" refers to west, where the sun sets. I like how that works.
[7]That's the main point of Edward W. Saïd's *Orientalism* (New York: Pantheon Books, 1978).
[8]He considered other names first: "exploit-like-hell theory," "suck-'em-dry theory."

like Marco Polo rolled in during the 1300s, they were not impressed. Thus spoke the Chinese: yes, barbarians, we have better weapons, pottery, palaces, hygiene, and hairstyles than you. And of course, the Chinese had their own massive empire under the Qing Dynasty, which ruled from 1644 to 1911. Like European imperialists, the Qing assumed their ways were superior to other groups and that they were doing people a favor by conquering them. But the Chinese controlled a land-based empire, which made it easier to move troops and people into new places and meant that the groups in question had for many centuries had at least some contact with each other. European imperialists in the nineteenth century, by contrast, expanded somewhat abruptly into places accessible only by sea and into cultures that Europeans knew very little about.

Initially in the nineteenth century, the Chinese kept chuckling to themselves about the barbarian Europeans, and they restricted trade as a way to protect their kingdom, culture, and religious traditions. That was working fine until Chinese leaders had to acknowledge in the Opium War (1839–42) that the British had gone and grown up big and strong. Afterwards, China had to allow more merchants and supporters to live there. So, yeah, China could still consider itself more or less the Middle Kingdom. Until Jesus Christ's brother came to town.

In 1850, Hong Xiuquan, from the Hakka ethnic group, claimed to be the brother of Jesus[9] and led the Taiping Rebellion for fourteen years against the Chinese emperor. Millions of Chinese died, especially because of disease and famine. The emperor, to his great shame, had to rely upon help from the barbarian Europeans to reassert control. Of course, the Europeans, who had no qualms about kicking a semi-heavenly empire when it was down, used the opportunity to demand more trading and settling concessions. British and French businessmen, with military support, set up shop at all of China's important ports.

Then China lost a war in 1895 to Japan. More shame, more concessions, more barbarians moving in. This time Russia and Germany joined the UK and France in carving up larger portions beyond the coasts, creating spheres of influence and protectorates where Chinese authority no longer mattered. We'll see below that in Africa, Europeans used such costal trading outposts to take over almost that whole continent. However, in China the blustering U.S. of A. insisted in 1899 on an "Open Door Policy" to respect Chinese territory and maximize trading possibilities for everyone. Chinese traditionalists and Western-inspired nationalists resented the deep Western incursions into their territory and began fighting Westerners, eventually declaring a Republic in 1911. Unfortunately, civil war continued for almost forty more years between various factions in China, especially nationalists and communists, until the Communists declared the People's Republic of China in 1949.

Japan

Japan took a very different path when the Westerners showed up (with guns) for business. In 1853, the American navy sailed into Tokyo Bay with gunboats and demanded that

---

[9]Second son of God? Step-son of God? You know how complicated family can be.

Westerners be granted special access to Japanese trade. Japanese leaders understood they were beaten and signed humiliating treaties that gave Westerners some territorial rights in Japan and major control over trade. When some noble (samurai) leaders retaliated, the Americans destroyed important Japanese fortresses, prompting civil war in Japan. In 1867 forces loyal to the Japanese emperor put him back in change, suppressing the samurai aristocracy. The emperor and his government quickly reversed course and began to emulate the West.

They modernized and centralized the state, created new forms of government, and, most importantly, began to industrialize. Like in Germany and Russia, the Japanese state contributed significantly to industrialization. By 1900, Japan had become one of the top ten industrial nations in the world. They tore up those unequal treaties with the West and embarked on creating their own empire. See, they had gunboats too! They beat China handily in 1895 and then whipped Russia in 1905. For Russia the defeat dealt a major blow to the Tsar's authority and caused a brief revolution that was an important precursor to the massive 1917 revolution that would end the Russian Empire. The Japanese used their victory to expand their empire into Korea and parts of Russia and China. Japan's roasting of Russia also made clear that Europeans were not invincible, giving hope to colonized people around the world.

Southeast Asia

Finally, in Southeast Asia, Europeans expanded their holdings in the nineteenth century. The British, French, and Dutch had built trading empires in this region in the late sixteenth century and used those positions to grow or tighten control of colonies in the nineteenth century. France, for instance, went to war with China in the 1880s to take control of areas that are today Vietnam, Laos, and Cambodia. The Germans tried to squeeze into this region, but Britain and France cooperated to thwart them. The Dutch probably thought their control of the Indonesian spice trade was pretty awesome in the early modern period. But having to manage a diverse colony of 17,000 islands posed some challenges, especially when it came to religion.

The Dutch and the *hajj*: Islam and international empire

See, big European empires sometimes ran into *other* international organizations, like, say Islam. Europeans often wisely figured out how to work with local leaders and local religions in places they took over. The Muslim faith, though, connected local power bases to a large international network. Colonized subjects used Islam as a way both to cooperate with *and* resist European imperialism. One telling example was the various ways Dutch colonizers worked with Muslims in Indonesia to help them travel to Mecca as religious pilgrims.

The *hajj* is a pilgrimage to Mecca that all Muslims (who are able) are required to do in their life, as part of the Five Pillars of Islam. That trip was never easy, but it was especially tough for Indonesian Muslims, who were 7,000 miles (11,000 km) from Arabia! Nevertheless, many of them regularly made the massive trek. When the Dutch took over this area (the East Indies) in the late sixteenth century, they pretty quickly clued into how important this trip was for many of their subjects. Locals who had made the pilgrimage were respected as "hajjis." One late seventeenth-century leader even called himself "Sultan Haji."

Dutch colonizers recognized various reasons to help Muslim pilgrims. Dutch shipping companies could make money hauling pilgrims to and from Arabia. Plenty of poorer people served as indentured servants for years on colonial plantations to pay for their passage. Dutch leaders tightly controlled traffic to and from Mecca, in order to minimize the spread of diseases along this lengthy passage. Plus, Dutch colonizers genuinely wanted to help their subjects and be seen as supportive of all kinds of religion. At the same time, Dutch leaders recognized the potential threat that Islam posed to their control of Indonesia. Especially starting in the late nineteenth century, pilgrims sometimes brought back radical, anti-colonial visions of Islam, perspectives that reinforced nationalist movements in Indonesia. The complexities of Islamic pilgrimage illustrated how European imperial powers had to work with local customs and leaders, even as they expanded their control over new territories.

The scramble for Africa

Rarely have two maps explained so much, so clearly. In Map 7.2, the small map details Europeans' very limited colonial holdings in Africa in 1878—mainly footholds around the edges developed for trade. Then the larger map shows how much of Africa Europeans controlled by 1914. In just thirty-six years Europeans had taken over almost the entire continent! Only the small West African nation of Liberia and the strong eastern kingdom of Ethiopia remained independent. Certainly, the British and the French held the lion's share of African colonies,[10] but Germany and Portugal had gotten in on the action too. The Belgians, Italians, and Spanish were also repping.

We call this expansion the "scramble for Africa" because it happened so fast and aggressively. You know how kids dive and fight for candy that's been knocked out of a piñata? That's kind of what I imagine European nations doing during those thirty-six years: I don't care what it is, just gimme some of that African candy! This manic drive to grab colonies seemed to be almost for the sheer sake of having colonies or—even better— making sure rivals didn't get them. It may not surprise you therefore to know that some of the worst abuses of imperialism occurred in these colonies and that this scramble left some of the most problematic legacies, as we'll discover in Chapter 13. More immediately this mad grab for colonies ratcheted up tension between European powers, which partially led to World War I. The major conflict in Africa was between the imperialist big boys, France and the United Kingdom.

---

[10]See how I did that?

So, About Modern Europe …

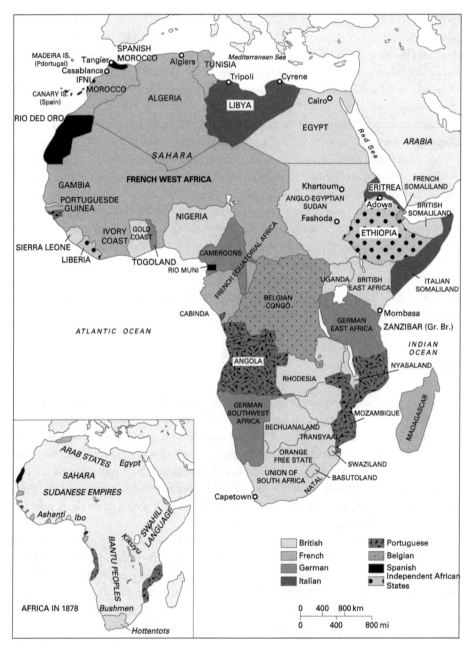

Map 7.2 European colonies in Africa, 1878 vs. 1914.

Both France and Britain had a fairly tortured history of imperialism *and* colonialism going back to the seventeenth century, and they didn't always get along. So maybe it wasn't the best idea for these two countries to build a canal together through Egypt connecting the Mediterranean and Red Seas. (Sure saved a lot of time, though, when you didn't have to sail around Africa to get to India or Southeast Asia!) The Suez Canal opened in 1869 under French control, but the Brits remained close at hand in Egypt. And when some local folks got a little uppity in the 1880s, the British military took control of the canal and the surrounding area. Eventually, the UK just decided they needed to take over all of Egypt for good measure. They were busy chasing down and slaughtering resistance fighters into Sudan when they bumped into the French again.

On that map you'll notice that the French seemed to control much of Africa going from the west coast to the east coast. And the British had a big swath running from north to south. British imperialists like Cecil Rhodes were super excited about seeing the British Empire stretch "from Cairo to Cape Town." The French had similar east-west dreams. Unfortunately, these two grand plans were still in the works in 1898 when the south-moving Brits ran into the east-moving French in Fashoda in what's today Sudan. The two countries almost went to war over who would get to have a big ole corridor along Africa. Git yer guns; it's the Showdown at Fashoda![11] Did they care about Fashoda? Had they even heard of Fashoda? Of course not, but, damn it, they wanted that corridor across Africa! Eventually, the French backed down. But the British didn't get what they wanted either, because the Germans squeezed into their north-south corridor with German East Africa. *Ach,* snap!

Initially, Germany didn't care too much about colonies. Just as the "scramble" was getting started in 1884, Bismarck invited current and would-be colonial powers to Berlin to lay some ground rules for taking colonies in Africa. Right. Whatever "rules" these folks agreed to didn't last long. The Berlin Conference chiefly seemed to sanction European powers' rapid takeover of Africa. Germany had already moved into parts of Africa and the Pacific islands near New Guinea when the new Kaiser Wilhelm II (1859–1941) came to power in 1888. He wanted Germany to have its "place in the sun" and pushed Germany further into the "scramble." Individuals like Rhodes or French-Italian explorer Pierre Savorgnan de Brazza (1852–1905) helped open and explore many parts of Africa as much as states did. Similarly, the Belgian King Leopold II (1835–1909) used hired mercenaries to carve out his own personal fiefdom in central Africa, where as many as 10 million people died in one of the most brutal experiences of imperialism. Workers, including children, sometimes had a hand or foot amputated when they failed to produce enough rubber.

In Europe, the cost of this colonial grab was deteriorating relations between powers. Not that European nations got along before they all ran headlong into Africa. But international empires meant that most European countries had more ways to come into

---

[11]Historians usually call it the "Fashoda Incident," but that sounds like a lame spy movie rather than an exciting, shoot-'em-up Western.

conflict with each other, more to fight about, and more resources to throw at each other. Maybe the scramble for Africa delayed an inevitable war. I'm not usually a fan of alternate history, but here's an interesting idea. What if European powers had *not* carved up Africa? We know that would have helped folks in Africa. Europeans might have gone to war with each other earlier—'cause, dumb as it was, there was definitely *going* to be a war. But a Great War in, say, 1895 or 1902 would have had lower stakes. Weapons would not have been quite as advanced. The fighting would have been pretty much in Europe only. Maybe they would have decided they had less to fight about. And perhaps the aftermath would have been less drastic. Anyhoo, back to reality.

Gradually, Europeans worked out various ways to administer African colonies. Because small numbers of European settlers moved there, administrators had to rely heavily on local leaders, translators, and workers. British leaders often chartered private companies, like Rhodes' South Africa Company, to do much of the initial opening-up work in Africa and allowed them to reap much of the profit. Other imperial powers often used mercenaries and paid private individuals to administer colonies. France tended to administer more directly the political and economic activities in their colonies. Needless to say, these guys who took personal economic risks to colonize unknown places in Africa were driven above all by profit motives. And even when government officials moved in, the mercenaries' brutal, racist methods frequently continued.

Still, some colonized subjects found ways to work within this system. These unequal relationships always advantaged the colonists but did offer some Africans, especially more educated ones, opportunities to advance and shape colonial rule. Colonial rule was always somewhat makeshift in Africa, especially in the sub-Saharan region. After World War I colonial rule became both more firm and more tenuous. On the one hand, Europeans worked out better administrative controls when there was no more "scrambling." Yet the expense and moral weight of Empire began to weigh upon most European powers. And their own internal conflicts and economic problems lessened some public resolve for imperialism. We will deal with the process of decolonization in Chapter 13. Suffice it to say here that the European empires sowed the seeds of their own destruction. Their often brutal policies enraged colonial subjects. And the clerks, workers, teachers, translators, and others whom Europeans had to rely upon also began to figure out how to mix local and European ideas to challenge imperial authorities.

Genocide in the sun: the massacre of the Herero and Nama

The Germans might have come a little late to imperialism, but they made up for it in terms of their violence and the shadow that imperialism cast over the rest of German history. And let's face it, friends, when you say, "the rest of German history," you're definitely talking about Nazis. Imperialism warped the histories of all the European powers involved and, even more dramatically, those of the colonized peoples. German settlers used racial science to support their assumptions that they could treat native populations however they wished in German Southwest Africa (today: Namibia).

Small numbers of Germans had been active in Southwest Africa before it became an official protectorate in 1884. This colony was the largest German holding and had the highest percentage of whites living there compared to other German colonies. Most of the native people living there engaged in cattle ranching, usually as nomads, which the very settled Germans didn't appreciate. Similar to United States policies toward Native Americans in the nineteenth century, the Germans in Southwest Africa tried to restrict the Herero and Nama people to less and less land, and to run railroads through their land. They even talked about putting them on reservations. And like the Americans, the Germans signed and then ignored treaties. German settlers kept pushing and sometimes abused (or killed) their local servants, increasing public and private tension.

Finally, in 1904 the Herero, led by Samuel Maherero (1856–1923), and the Nama, led by Captain Hendrik Witbooi (1830–1905), rebelled against the German colonists. They killed over a hundred Europeans, mostly male German farmers. This move gave aggressive German leaders like General Adrian von Trotha (1848–1920) the excuse they needed to attack and exterminate the Herero and Nama. This brutal general led his enthusiastic troops to slaughter men and drive women and children into the desert, where they died of dehydration, starvation, and exposure. Or sometimes he and his men just killed everyone or poisoned their water sources. Trotha made clear that he wanted to wipe out the Herero people. By 1906 Germans had killed three-fourths of the Herero people in Southwest Africa and by 1907 had "pacified" the Nama. Many of the few survivors then died in concentration camps.

Germans wanted to use the land differently and viewed the Herero and Nama as a threat to their economic plans. We can discern some Enlightenment thought at work in the motives of this genocide. Trotha believed that annihilating these native populations— cleansing Southwest Africa—would create a new, better society. Mass murder may conflict with Enlightenment ideals of valuing humans and their contributions to society. But the urge to label what's wrong and fix it in order to create a better system certainly has roots in Enlightenment thought. And of course, the light-dark metaphor has a scary implication here: light can also get rid of dark. This experience, which Germans debated in national politics, helped presage the Holocaust.

Kipling vs. Orwell

Rudyard Kipling and George Orwell (the pen name of Eric Blair) didn't have a lot in common. Kipling was a proud imperialist and white supremacist who believed in the "White Man's Burden" and that all people were better off being ruled by the British (or Americans[12]) than being independent. Orwell, whom you may know from his anti-totalitarian books *Animal Farm* and *Nineteen Eighty-Four*, was a democratic socialist. He

---

[12]Kipling actually wrote "The White Man's Burden" to encourage Americans in 1899 to take over the Philippines. The Americans did.

more or less agreed with Lenin's idea that imperialism was capitalism on steroids or at least desperate capitalism. But both men worked in the British Empire. Kipling, who was born in India but educated in England, worked for a Bombay newspaper as young man. Orwell, who was born and raised in England, worked for five years as a police officer in Burma. They both wrote about imperialism from up close, observing the everyday life in British colonies. We've seen that Kipling's "White Man's Burden" poem reflected many of the impulses that motivated imperial expansion.

Orwell published a short story in 1936 called "Shooting an Elephant," and you'd be hard pressed to find a more insightful and honest portrayal of how imperialists felt—even imperialists who were ashamed of imperialism, like Orwell was. He writes that in Burma "I was hated by large numbers of people—the only time in my life that I have been important enough for this to happen to me."

He describes an incident when he was called in to shoot an elephant that had gone on a rampage, ruined some crops, knocked down some structures, and killed a cow and a native man. Orwell was sent to shoot the wild elephant, but when he arrived the beast was calm, and Orwell saw no need to shoot it. But of course, he was the white imperial officer with the gun. Everyone *expected* him to shoot the elephant. The fact that he, the one in charge, felt compelled to do something came as a great realization:

> And it was at this moment, as I stood there with the rifle in my hands, that I first grasped the hollowness, the futility of the white man's dominion in the East. Here was I, the white man with his gun, standing in front of the unarmed native crowd—seemingly the leading actor of the piece; but in reality I was only an absurd puppet pushed to and fro by the will of those yellow faces behind. I perceived in this moment that when the white man turns tyrant it is his own freedom that he destroys.[13]

So that's one more thing Kipling and Orwell had in common.

In a way, Orwell was talking about a very different "white man's burden," one in which the system of imperialism *forced* the oppressor to oppress. Kipling saw that obligation as a worthy duty, that the white man would "reap his old reward:/The blame of those ye better,/The hate of those ye guard." Orwell thought it was absurd. And of course, Orwell recognized, above all, that imperialism was awful to colonial peoples, not some civilizing mission to help them. And, yes, Orwell did shoot the elephant, but he felt guilty about it for many years thereafter. He wasn't the only one.

---

[13]Orwell, "Shooting an Elephant." *New Writing* 2 (1936).

CHAPTER 8
LOOK, WE'VE GOT TO TALK ABOUT THE ENLIGHTENMENT

Okay, major spoiler alert. There's no such thing as Santa Claus, no Father Christmas. Presumably you knew that already. Do you remember, though, when you learned that sad truth? I realize that's a rather Christian-centric question; plenty of people in the English-speaking world celebrate other religious holidays or none at all. Still, Santa Claus is a cultural icon, and it was probably a big deal when you learned he didn't exist. I've asked my students this question and heard a wide range of answers. First, there are some good stories about how it happened: recognizing a parent's handwriting on gifts from Santa, hearing older kids on the school bus, a mean sibling breaking the news to make you mad, logical parents deciding you were old enough to know, or discovering a hidden cache of gifts before Christmas that turned out to come from Santa. Then, people experience a range of emotions: sadness at losing a childhood belief, anger at having been lied to, fear that they'll get no more presents, smug vindication, disappointment, and so on. But even when you got over it, you may have been asked by family members to keep up the ruse for a sibling or cousin or someone else young who still believed. And even if you felt angry or sad, you probably figured that you were in on the joke now and had a responsibility to work hard to maintain it. You might have even looked around and thought, wow, almost *everyone* is in on the joke. And given that Christmas decorations seem to appear each year earlier and earlier, it takes up months of our time.

Something similar happened in the late nineteenth century, when intellectuals began to realize that the Enlightenment was not all it was cracked up to be. It felt like the rug had been pulled out from beneath them or that someone had been fooling them. Big, mostly positive Enlightenment ideas had shaped people's lives and seemed to promise that things would keep getting better. Great notions of equality, democracy, capitalism, feminism, and socialism all indicated that human reason and goodness were working. Even nationalism, which often generated conflict, was generally a source of pride and unity. And even if imperialism was similarly imperfect, most Europeans thought it was mostly positive for their society and the ones taken over. In short, things were looking up, thanks to science, reason, and the Enlightenment.

But a few thinkers questioned these massive positive assumptions. As we'll see below, they concluded that humans were *not* rational, good, and able to fix things. They looked inside humans' hearts and minds and saw something darker and less rational than Enlightenment thinkers had supposed. For many of these intellectuals, this discovery was saddening, disappointing, and scary—a little like learning there's no Santa Claus. Some of them, like that mean sibling or cynical kid on the school bus, tried to share their realization. Others proposed that we had to keep up the ruse and convince everyone that humans *were* good, dammit, and our fine systems were improving lives, that Santa was as real as the spirit of Christmas!

Building the argument

This chapter traces that realization that the Enlightenment was not so positive or perhaps not so relevant. Some intellectuals at this time began to question the most basic truths in Western society—progress, science, reason, even God. This chapter focuses mainly on intellectuals. We'll meet some philosophers with hard to pronounce names like Schopenhauer and Nietzsche that most people had never heard of at the time but whose ideas became important later. Enlightenment thought may have come especially from France and Britain, but it was everywhere in Europe by the late nineteenth century. And if you note where the people mentioned in this chapter are from, you'll see that challenges to the Enlightenment came from many corners of Europe.

Toward the end of the nineteenth century, thinkers and artists realized that all those great ideals on which their society was built had also created major problems: greater inequality, industrial destruction, the threat of mechanized war, imperialist abuse of people around the world, etc. The positive, liberating side of the Enlightenment did not necessarily outweigh the negative, controlling side. Some thinkers proposed different ways to solve human problems, which focused more on internal, emotional issues than the big systems Enlightenment thinkers suggested. While some intellectuals mistrusted Enlightenment assumptions that humans were good and rational, they did not necessarily revert back to pre-Enlightenment, faith-based morality. Instead, they created new ways of viewing the world that rejected aspects of the Enlightenment and increasingly ignored religion. You might call it a new, more intense form of individualism. These thinkers concluded that no common idea, faith, or experience united Western culture any more. Judeo-Christian ideals didn't work for everyone. The Enlightenment didn't work for everyone. So they proposed some new ways of considering how individuals come to terms with their place in the world.

In 1924 the British writer Virginia Woolf pinpointed this shift:

On or about December 1910, human character changed. I am not saying that one went out, as one might into a garden, and there saw a rose that had flowered, or a hen that had laid an egg. The change was not sudden and definite like that. But a change there was nevertheless; and since one must be arbitrary, let us date it to about the year 1910.[1]

Intellectuals had discovered that Santa Claus didn't exist and had to figure out something new. These thinkers laid the groundwork for what we'll call *modernism*. We will see in

---

[1]*Mr. Bennet and Mrs. Brown* (London: Hogarth, 1924), 4.

this chapter that they came up with new ways to consider the human condition and our social organization, as well as new ways to write and make art and music. Their ideas shaped the twentieth century. And don't worry, average people will get to know these ideas too—all too well, especially in the bloodbath of World War I and its aftermath.

Now wait, you say, I'm pretty sure that big Enlightenment ideas continued into the twentieth century and are in fact still important today. Isn't that, like, this book's basic argument? True enough, but not everyone could accept what these idea-slaying intellectuals said. Sometimes ideas became *more* important when people realized they weren't exactly true. After all, we work really hard to maintain the myth of Santa Claus. In fact we work way harder to keep up that lie than we did to believe in it. So this chapter will also point to the rise of absolutely certain ideologies, concepts like fascism, capitalism, racism, and communism that people were willing to kill and die for in the twentieth century. Perhaps these ideas meant even more as myths. Perhaps they were more inspiring after intellectuals had tried to disprove them. Welcome to the modern condition: it's that unsettled feeling of advocating strongly for something that maybe deep down you don't fully believe in. Like telling kids that Santa Claus is real.

Irrationalism

Irrationalism sounds like a philosophy of being obnoxious or stubborn, right? Most of the time when we call someone irrational or unreasonable, we mean they won't consider *our* reasons or evidence. Well, that's not too far off from what I'm talking about here. Being irrational means you trust emotions or your desires to figure things out, not only reason. You could also call this way of thinking *non-rational*. As a philosophy, irrationalism represents a major shift from the weight given to reason since the Enlightenment or even the Renaissance. One of the main qualities of Enlightenment thought was reason. Enlightenment thinkers believed that people were fundamentally reasonable and that creating reasonable systems would maximize human goodness. Irrationalist thinking assumed, on the other hand, that we might learn more about who we are by considering our non-rational ways of relating to the world and other people.

There's of course a long history of people not being reasonable. Enlightenment thinkers would say, well, of course, that's *mostly* how people have been! But some philosophers have actually come up with whole perspectives based on irrationalism. Some ancient Greek thinkers, for instance, proposed that we should be skeptical about everything, including things we've learned through reason. The Greeks even had their own god of irrationalism—off-the-chain Dionysus. Medieval thought may not have been intentionally irrational, but it was rooted in faith, which was certainly different than reason. That's one of the main things that drove Enlightenment types crazy. Enlightenment thinkers tried to use reason to move away from faith-based thinking, or at least use reason to temper assumptions about faith.

Maybe another way of thinking about irrationalism is to see it as rejecting the assumption that *thinking* is the most important thing humans do. We met René Descartes in Chapter 2, and he claimed that the basis of his whole world view (and hairstyle) was "I think, therefore I am." Irratioinalists might say, "I feel, therefore I am" or "I intuit, therefore I am" or "I want, therefore I am." In other words, irrationalism assumes that we are more than just brains that think. Now, it's not like those super-reasonable Enlightenment guys never felt anything. They just wanted us to rely more on reason to understand the world and figure out how best to live in it. Irrationalists, on the other hand, said we should celebrate and use feelings, desires, and intuitions.

A couple of guys with long names are worth mentioning. Søren Kierkegaard (1813–55), a Danish philosopher and theologian, rejected reason as the only way to understand the individual's function in society. He struggled his whole life to figure out how God worked in society and was usually at odds with religious leaders. But Kierkegaard thought that faith mattered because it showed that humans were capable of doing something that was not based on reason. Kirkegaard didn't demand justification for belief in God or look for "proof" of God's existence. In fact, he thought it was more important that people chose to believe in God based on intuition, even emotion—*not* reason. OMG, thought Enlightenment supporters, this is just the kind of nonsense we've been fighting against! But wait: Kierkegaard was not saying therefore that The Church should rule people's lives and society. The emotional *choice* to believe was most important for him, that an individual used feelings to make such an important decision.

Another irrational fella, the German philosopher Arthur Schopenhauer (1788–1860), kind of agreed. He challenged Enlightenment thought and concluded that human *will* motivates us more than reason. Our will drives us to survive, to succeed, love, hate, or understand anything. Unlike Kierkegaard, Schopenhauer didn't see any space or need for God or belief. In fact he took more cues from Indian than Western religious thought. He also didn't see any meaning to life. That may explain why he looks so unhappy in photographs.[2] Schopenhauer's ideas about will influenced Nietzsche, as we'll see shortly.

Irrationalism, in short, offered a thoughtful response to the Enlightenment celebration of reason. The Enlightenment's focus on reason, evidence, and objectivity had not adequately explained human behavior. Above all, irrationalism emphasized *subjective* and *individual* ways of engaging with the world. The Enlightenment respected individuals, but mainly because they contributed to a larger system. Irrationalism emphasized a more radical individualism. Each individual actually experienced the world differently. Folks like Freud and Nietzsche couldn't agree more.

Are Freud and Nietzsche going to wreck the world or just make us self-absorbed?

Sigmund Freud (1856–1939) and Friedrich Nietzsche (1844–1900) are the two Irrationalist thinkers of this time who have probably had the biggest influence on

---

[2]Or maybe that's because he had to sit perfectly still for a long time, something that even his will couldn't change!

Western thought. It's worth, therefore, pronouncing their names correctly. (It will make you sound smart.) You say "froid" and "NEE-cheh." Even if you don't know much about them, you probably are familiar with some of their basic ideas. The assumption that psychological counselling has to dig into your past or deeper assumptions to help you: that's Freud. And the fact that we joke about sexual matters, sometimes unintentionally, was also an idea that Freud came up with.[3] Freud used scientific methods to study the unconscious and conclude that we are, deep down, irrational creatures. Nietzsche agreed, although he didn't need no science to tell him that. You've probably also heard one of Nietzsche's most famous quotes: what doesn't kill me makes me stronger.

Freud and Nietzsche challenged basic Enlightenment assumptions, ideas that had increasingly come to underpin how many Europeans looked at the world. And those ideas, frankly, made most Europeans at this time feel pretty good about themselves. Just look around at all the cool stuff we've created, Europeans thought, the fact people are living longer, that more people have rights; see how easily we have taken over the world and brought our fine things and superior lifestyles to everyone else. That cocky, collective back-patting came especially from belief in three main Enlightenment notions: people are good, reason is our greatest tool, and progress is inevitable.

Freud and Nietzsche spent their careers poking holes in these assumptions and trying to figure out how best to live as a result. Freud concluded that the irrational subconscious mind is just as important for decision-making as our rational conscious mind is. We are driven by desires and needs that mean that we're not fundamentally rational. Nietzsche likewise believed that our will was more important than reason for how we behave. He didn't think we are good or evil, but worrying about that distinction has restricted human ability. Nietzsche believed that humanity had in the modern world *regressed* significantly.

Both Freud and Nietzsche also blamed religion for some modern woes. Freud believed that Judeo-Christian rules had forced Westerners to feel guilty and anxious about their base desires. He said that religion had restricted scientific inquiry and human advancement. Nietzsche went further. Really, Nietzsche just went off. He thought that religion, especially Christianity, was the single worst thing that had ever happened to humanity. He believed that the Christian ideas of service, equality, and the afterlife had ruined individual human drive and potential. Nietzsche saw modern European political ideologies like democracy, liberalism, and socialism as terrible secular outgrowths of Christian morality. He wanted to smash the whole system and start anew. Freud was not so much into the smashing of everything. He thought we should acknowledge our deep desires and not let religious morality limit us, but he believed that reason and science should define our social organization. So, Freud and Nietzsche agreed that humans were irrational and oppressed by religion but disagreed on how science and reason might help us.

Freud and Nietzsche also agreed that solutions to human problems lay within us. Here, too, they challenged ye olde Enlightenment. Our Enlightenment amigos believed humans were fundamentally good but that various *systems* messed us up—unfair politics

---

[3]Accidentally saying something inappropriate that might reveal what's really on your mind is called a parapraxis or "Freudian slip."

based on aristocratic privilege, economic arrangements controlled by governments, radio stations playing smooth jazz, unequal social organization that gave one group greater authority than others, etc. Those systems prevented humans from maximizing their goodness. And in one way or another the big Enlightenment concepts we've been studying all aim to unleash human goodness and creativity to improve things for everyone. Well, we've seen that these fabulous ideas did not always work in practice and that the Enlightenment could also be controlling, prejudiced, and violent. But the main thrust of Enlightenment thought is that you can fix people by fixing the system of which they're a part. Freud and Nietzsche disagreed. They thought that people needed to look *inside* to fix their problems, that no wonderful external system was going to make people better.

In fact, they both maintained that external systems messed people up, including Enlightenment social organization. Freud was down with a society using basic Enlightenment ideas of fairness and opportunity, but he recognized that the rules necessary to live in a just society would impose limits on our desires. That tension between what we *want* to do and what we *should* do causes us to be neurotic. Nietzsche, on the other hand, was like: screw all that! We *are* our desires and our wills, so let's run with that. In his mind Western society spent a couple thousand years living with rules that forced everyone to focus on the average, mediocrity, or the "herd." He felt that we'd be better off letting individuals decide their own values and then seeing what society came from doing so. Despite their differences, both Freud and Nietzsche wanted people to look inside themselves—not to religion or politics or social organization—for ways to improve themselves.

Sigmund Freud

So, you gotta understand Freud because he's had a major impact on modern thinking. But he also helps us understand some jokes better. Lots of jokes about sex, moms, or accidentally saying the wrong things all originate in Freud's ideas. The dude even wrote a book about jokes.[4] The fact that there are lots of great, often inappropriate jokes and memes out there about Freud says something about how wide his ideas have reached. He was a big thinker like Marx, whose ideas seem to have one major application (psychotherapy) but have in fact ended up shaping intellectual discourse more generally. Freud demonstrated that we can understand what people do and want by studying their unconscious minds. He especially did that by analyzing dreams, starting with *The Interpretation of Dreams* (1900). But he also used other methods like hypnosis and stream-of-conscious writing to get at unconscious thought. Unlike previous work on the mind and dreams, Freud applied more systematic, scientific analysis to the study of this hard-to-reach part of human thought.

---

[4] *Jokes and Their Relation to the Unconscious* (1905). Of course, a 200-page book explaining humor might kill the joke a little bit.

Freud's most important ideas boil down to his explanation of different parts of the human mind. Basically, you got your *id, ego,* and *superego.* The id (Latin for "it") is our most basic, instinctual self. This bad boy is especially driven by sexual and instinctual desires; it's aggressive and wants immediate gratification. The id doesn't care about logic or morality or social stuff. Biologically, the id reflects our selfish drives to survive and be satisfied, regardless of others. The id is important yet unconscious, so it's tricky to access. Next, the ego is our (mostly) conscious daily way of dealing with everyday life and others. The ego can delay satisfaction for another day or for the sake of others. Ego tries to direct and control the id's wants. Imagine Ego as a rider on a horse called Id. Freud recognized that the ego-id tension creates anxiety and frustration, or what he called "neuroses." Finally, there's the superego, which is not an ego who can fly or teleport. The superego is your morality, your social values that you've learned from others—family, religion, school, reruns of *The Office,* etc. It shows up in your conscious and subconscious thought. Señor Superego can set pretty high standards for how Ego and Id should behave, and that can mess you up too, as you might imagine.

So, Freud used Enlightenment tools (science, reason, evidence) to conclude that, deep down, humans are *not* like Enlightenment thinkers said. Yet, Freud believed that we need Enlightenment-like social and political organization (ego and superego) to check irrational Mr. Id. That's modern life, according to Siggy Freud. It's full of tension, and altering your social, political, or economic set-up won't fix you. In fact, those external systems suppress our deepest desires. We have to look inside ourselves to deal with the frustration of social rules that inhibit what we really want. Freud called that psychotherapy. It's a lot to take in, I know: tension, frustration, Enlightenment, irrationalism, freaking out. If you're feeling a little confused and conflicted, then that's the point. Freud understood his ideas as a blow to human arrogance: our reason can't make us masters of everything. After all, we can't even use reason to be masters of our own mind!

Some of Freud's ideas about psychoanalysis have become less popular. Psychologists and philosophers have since decided that all Freud's focus on moms and penises and sex might reflect his own personal, male, even misogynist perspective. However, like Marx, his general ideas continue to help scholars understand the world. Indeed, some of the most fruitful analyses of literature, movies, music, and other forms of expression have come from psychological readings of these works. Historians sometimes get into this stuff too, although most of us agree that psychoanalyzing people from the past is difficult and usually way too speculative.[5] Still, Freud reminds historians that we need to take seriously the motives and actions of people in the past, even when they seem a little wacky. Maybe especially when they seem wacky. In short, Freud's ideas extend way beyond the psychotherapy he founded. All of us probably think a little like Freud. We love science and reason and big ideas, but deep down we are irrational creatures. That conflict helps explain why modern life is often tense. Freud identified that most clearly. But Nietzsche's got a solution.

---

[5] And God help me if I have to read one more biography of Hitler that focuses on his celibacy or single testicle or relationship with his father or some other speculative business!

Figure 8.1 Freddy Nietzsche and his very large moustache.

Friedrich Nietzsche

I'm just gonna say it: I've often wondered how Nietzsche could get away with what he did. I mean, the mustache! That thing extended a couple of inches beyond his face. Am I the only one who wonders how he ate? Nietzsche was like that snarky person at a party who's fun to sit next to and slam everyone there. He certainly had plenty of venom for just about everyone during his day. He proposed a lot of tearing down but didn't give details on building up. Nietzsche also wrote in a very unique style—not the kind of logical, evidence-based, argument-driven way most philosophers (and other academics) tend to write (and you should too!). He wrote lots of short chapters that don't always seem to fit together, and also poetry, sketches, and 2,650 short "sayings" called aphorisms. He used a lot of exclamation marks and ironic quotation marks. Sounds a bit like Twitter. In fact Nietzsche probably would have done well on Twitter.[6] This all-over-the-place style has made it hard to summarize Nietzsche's ideas and has certainly made his work open to all kinds of appropriation. Unfortunately, he died in an asylum in 1900 (suffering from dementia and brain cancer), which lends some credence to the thought that he was crazy. Perhaps at the end he ran into some demons even his will couldn't defeat. But for much

---

[6]You might check out @NeinQuarterly for what seems like twenty-first century Nietzchean wit.

of his life, Nietzsche railed and hollered and generally wrote things that made people think twice about a lot of things.

You've probably heard one of Nietzsche's best-known claims, that "God is dead."[7] But the full quote coming from the mouth of a madman in his 1882 book *The Gay Science* is actually more revealing:

God is dead! God will stay dead! And we have killed him! How do we console ourselves, the murderers of all murderers? The holiest and mightiest the world has ever known has bled to death against our knives—who will wipe the blood off? Where is the water to cleanse ourselves? What sort of rituals of atonement, what sort of sacred games, will we have to come up with now? Isn't the greatness of this deed too great for us? Don't we have to become gods ourselves simply to appear worthy of it? There has never been a greater deed, and whoever will be born after us will belong to a history greater than any history up to now![8]

All right, then. It's not enough for Nietzsche to state there is no God. He wants modern society to own the fact that we've killed the idea of God. Nietzsche spilled a lot of ink[9] attacking Christianity. He faulted it for focusing on the weak and for denouncing life rather than encouraging it. He thought Christianity rewarded suffering. He said Christianity was the first religion to make people hate themselves. Ouch. Unlike Freud, Nietzsche didn't think the solution was to replace religion with science. And Nietzsche believed Enlightenment thought was basically just secular Christianity. Nietzsche saw democracy, liberalism, and socialism as more of the same celebration of weakness and mediocrity. Hell, he called the French Revolution "the last great slave rebellion" of the powerless. You cut me deep, Fred.

So, Nietzsche knocked down Christianity, the Enlightenment, and science, which had been pretty much the major ways most folks in Europe understood the world. Small wonder, therefore, he went on to challenge the arrogant assumption that the Western world of the late nineteenth century represented the pinnacle of human achievement. Nietzsche, of course, thought the opposite. He lambasted the "herd mentality" he saw everywhere in Europe, whether it was socialists calling for revolution to fix social inequality or nationalists puffing their chests at how powerful they were or Christians serving others. Even liberals, who promoted individual freedom, seemed too interested in guaranteeing rights. Nietzsche was pretty much alone in slamming absolutely everything going on around him as weakness, failure, and a sign of how bad things had gotten.

But Nietzsche admired the ancient Greeks. A lot. Nietzsche embraced *all* of their ideas, especially their polytheistic (many gods) concept of religion and morality.

---

[7]And you've likely seen the various t-shirts and memes out there using this quote. Stuff like: "'God is dead'— Nietzsche / 'Nietzsche is dead.'—God." Or: "'God is dead'—Nietzsche / 'God is dad.'—Freud."

[8]From Peter Fritzsche, ed. and trans. *Nietzsche and the Death of God: Selected Writings* (Boston, MA: Bedford/ St. Martin, 2007), section 125.

[9]Another old-fashioned metaphor, like "broken record."

Nietzsche celebrated both the logic of Apollo and the emotion of Dionysus. Above all, he appreciated that the many Greek gods presented a bunch of different norms and morals. Nietzsche wanted European society to return to the ancient Greek notion of good vs. bad, not the Christian idea of good vs. evil. Whether a decision is good or bad depends upon its *effect*, whereas assessing if something is good or evil requires us to know the *intent* of the actor.

Greek gods could be good or bad, too, thus inspiring and empowering all of human behavior. Concluding something was evil, however, requires an objective set of morals on which everyone agrees. Nietzsche thought that monotheistic (single supreme god) Jewish and especially Christian law had imposed that set of morals on people in order to limit the strong and lift up the weak. Getting rid of objective definitions of good and evil would enable individuals to create their own morality based on what advances them and thus what advances humans. Killing God and getting rid of Christian morality thus makes humans godlike and thus capable of anything.

This new human Nietzsche called the *Übermensch*, which has been translated as "Overman" or "Superman." The superman can make his own rules and thus figure out what it means to be human. And anyone can be a superman; it's only masculine in English. The literal translation of "Übermensch" is "Overperson," which definitely does not work well as the name of a superhero.[10] In German it's a gender-neutral term, so anyone could be an *Übermensch*—man, women, or nonbinary. It's highly individual, about using your own morals, feelings, and will to look at the world. But some folks tried to use the superman concept to support ideologies in which one group controlled another, like nationalism, imperialism, Social Darwinism, racism, or, later, Nazism. Nietzsche wasn't having any of that. He disapproved of any kind of group think or action and wanted his ideas only to inspire individuals.

Nietzsche believed so much in the individual that he rejected the idea that there was an objective "real world" out there that everyone experienced the same way. All we can know, he argued, is what we can articulate and communicate through language. The words we have to describe reality present the only truth we can know. And since each of us has our own understanding of every word and experience, our individual visions of reality are all slightly different. Nietzsche doesn't think science can come waltzing in and present some objective reality to us, because even scientific concepts and discoveries can only be understood individually through language. So, there's no objective truth or reality for Nietzsche, just like there's no objective morality.

This (epistemological) idea about language and reality had far-reaching implications, laying the foundation for post-modern and post-structuralist thought. More generally, Nietzsche encouraged people to consider that life has only the meaning we give to it. That thought led to nihilism and eventually existentialism, both of which deny that life has any meaning. Some folks find that depressing. Nietzsche found it exciting and liberating to empower individuals to make their own meaning and fate. Hoo-wah!

---

[10]Look, somewhere over there: it's a cow, it's a slow-moving carriage; it's Overperson! See what I mean?

And now a word from sociology

Freud and Nietzsche weren't the only ones thinking about this stuff. At the end of the nineteenth century, the relatively new discipline of sociology offered useful perspectives on human action and social organization. Sociologists believe that our social surroundings shape how we behave. Three broad trends in European history helped create sociology as a discipline. First, we can call many Enlightenment thinkers early "social scientists" because they used scientific approaches (logic, hypotheses, experiments, evidence) to study social organization and suggest ways to improve it. Second, industrialization thoroughly altered daily life for millions of Europeans, and sociology studied those changes. Marx, for example, was kind of a sociologist. Third, imperialist expansion put Europeans in contact with more and more societies with very different cultures and ways of living. Comparing cultures could teach Europeans about their own societies. By the end of the nineteenth century, some thinkers were bringing these developments together to create a different perspective—sociology—to explain human organization and behavior.

French sociologist Émile Durkheim (1858–1917), who helped establish sociology as a legitimate academic discipline, wrote extensively about how social integration works. He said that people in modern Western society often suffer from *anomie*, the fact that there's no common set of values to which we all agree. Durkheim argued that *anomie* can cause despair and problems in people's lives. Modern Western society, he claimed, fails to provide something important that all people seem to need, namely a sense of belonging and common purpose. German sociologist Max Weber (1864–1920) also worried about the "disenchantment" he identified as a major characteristic of industrialized, rationalized, secularized modern European society. Weber cautioned modern societies to watch out for a *charismatic leader*. That kind of leader appeals to emotions and non-rational connections with people to convince followers to do things. Charismatic leadership could offer people a new sense of purpose. Weber died in 1920 before charismatic leaders like Mussolini, Hitler, Stalin, and others began to wreak havoc on Europe, but he saw the danger in letting such men give people meaning. Italian sociologist and economist Vilfredo Pareto (1848–1923) similarly recognized this important potential in leadership but didn't see a strong leader as bad.[11]

Both Weber and Pareto understood that a charismatic leader could convince people to sacrifice for a cause, especially nationalism. Pareto lived long enough to see Mussolini take over Italy but not to see the mayhem caused partly by him and other dictators.

In sum, sociologists Durkheim, Weber, and Pareto all recognized that modern Western society lacked a common set of values, traditions, and rituals—something Judeo-Christian beliefs had long supplied. Enlightenment thought had provided something similar for a couple hundred years. Like Freud and Nietzsche, these sociologists could no longer trust established religious, philosophical, or political ideas to connect

---

[11]Pareto became better known for his 80/20 Rule—that you spend 80 percent of your time on 20 percent of your problems or that 20 percent of your clients provide 80 percent of your revenue. It works in a lot of ways.

everyone in Europe. Durkheim and especially Weber worried about what or who might fill this void, while Pareto was cool with the idea that some strong man might do the job. That leader might sound like Superman, but it wasn't necessarily Nietzsche's Superman.

Who you got, Newton or Einstein?

People at this time lived a Newtonian universe. They considered scientific rules to be absolute. A formula for the density of gas worked just the same by the seaside, on a mountain, on Mars, or inside a star. Yes, science developed, but rules, once established, were universal, literally. But that was before Al came to town. German-born Albert Einstein (1879–1955) remains to this day probably the best-known scientist in the Western world, and not just because of his hair. His theory of relativity helped define modern physics and reshaped how we understand the universe. He challenged the basic laws and assumptions from Sir Isaac Newton. Maybe it was time. Newton's laws had been the bomb for well over 200 years, and that's a long time in science.

You may know that Einstein was toiling away in the Swiss Patent Office when he, well, changed the world. He later called 1905 his "miracle year." During that year he published four papers on, you know, just some basic stuff that the guys down at the Patent Office debated at the water cooler. The first was on the photoelectric effect, which helped kick start a little thing called quantum theory (whole new view of the atomic world); another was on Brownian motion and began to undermine established laws of thermodynamics by giving evidence for subatomic theories. Number three created the special theory of relativity, which explained that space and time were actually united and illustrated that many phenomenon change when approaching the speed of light. His last paper that year introduced the world a formula we all know (even if we don't understand): $E = mc^2$, which offered a new relationship between energy and matter and demonstrated that gravity could bend light. Einstein elaborated on all of these discoveries (and more) for the next fifty years, got the Nobel Prize, hung out with celebs, advised presidents, and blah blah blah. He continued to break new ground his whole life, but 1905 was a pretty special year for him. He was twenty-six. Oh, and he earned a PhD from the University of Zürich that year too.

I don't know about you, but I don't get to spend much time cruising near the speed of light (about 300 million meters or 186,000 miles per second), nor am I big enough for my gravity to bend light. Basically, we all still operate within Newton's laws of physics and can just pretend they always apply. But Einstein demonstrated that even scientific laws are relative and change depending upon the context. And if science is relative, then couldn't anything be relative? Clearly Einstein was not trying to undermine scientific inquiry. But like other thinkers in this chapter, he demonstrated that established rules didn't always work and that we were fooling ourselves if we continue to believe in them whole heartedly. Some people at this time pushed the boundaries of "science" even further.

Subject	Celebrate Irrationality	Promote Cautious Rationality
Philosophy, psychology	Nietzsche	Freud
Social organization, Sociology	Pareto	Durkheim, Weber
Science	Social Darwinist	Einstein

Figure 8.2 Irrational vs. cautiously rational in a super-basic chart.

Social Darwinists used Darwin's ideas about evolution and survival of the fittest to justify their prejudiced view of the world. Darwin's ideas stop at the species level; there is no biological subsection of the human species. But Social Darwinists used them to explain the behavior of races and nations. Some Social Darwinists tried to support their "scientific" views with measurements of human features as evidence of racial hierarchies. That's way beyond Einstein qualifying Newton a little bit. But the bigger point here is that some people began to question science as the absolute marker of truth.

Modernism in the arts: bring on the emotion!![12]

Digging into individual experiences and emotions seemed like a good source for artists too. Starting in the 1860s, European painters began to move away from realistic portrayals of things. They did so in part because the relatively new technology of photography could capture reality much more efficiently than a painting, thus freeing artists to get more creative. Artists in Europe followed the lead of irrational thinkers to consider their own perceptions of the world. Pioneering French painters like Claude Monet (1840–1926), Pierre-August Renoir (1841–1919), and Paul Cézanne (1839–1906) rejected the conservative standards of academic training and created their own association to show their work.

They eventually adopted the term *Impressionism* to describe their images because they strove to give an *impression* of the world, not necessarily an accurate representation. They used light, visible brush strokes to show that, yo, an *artist* had painted this picture. They often paid more attention to light and color than to the actual subject matter. And like modernist thinkers, they stressed that the artist's perspective mattered, something we can see in the American-born Impressionist Mary Cassatt (1844–1926), one of the few female painters among the French Impressionists. Her work also features color and light and illustrates her particular ability to portray women and children differently than her male colleagues.

Subsequent painters—often called Post-Impressionists and Expressionists—went further to use emotion to make art. Dutch painter Vincent Van Gogh (1853–90) painted with dramatic brush strokes and thickly layered colors to render the emotion of an image. Take, for example, his 1889 *Starry Night* (Figure 8.4). Now, the only way a starry night over a village looks like that is if you're on some powerful drugs or your contacts

---

[12]Double exclamation points = super, mega-strong emotion in academic writing.

Figure 8.3 Impressionism: *Bal du Moulin de la Galette* by Renoir.

Figure 8.4 Post-Impressionism: *Starry Night* by Van Gogh.

Figure 8.5 Expressionism: *The Scream* by Munch.

are really blurry. Van Gogh, though, is trying to share the feeling of viewing a star-filled night in rural France. Painting the reality—a lot of black with a few dots of light—would probably be pretty boring. Van Gogh captures the way stars can fill up a night sky and alter your perception. Norwegian artist Edward Munch (1863–1944) went further, as we can see in his 1895 *The Scream* (Figure 8.5). The point of this painting is to portray the way strong emotion can alter our reality. Learning terrible news or feeling despondent or suffering from depression doesn't actually make the sky turn different colors and wavy, but major emotional blows can make us see the world very differently, even believe that reality has changed.

Modernist artists often invoked the idea of *l'art pour l'art* or "art for art's sake" to insist that their work could just be art, that it did not need to fulfill some purpose from an external source like supporting a patron or the Church or civic celebration, as art often had done previously. Yet modernist art was only possible because artists could sell their work in a consumer capitalist economy. In this chapter we've mostly focused on a fairly small intellectual elite moving away from Enlightenment thought. But that good ole Enlightenment-inspired capitalist market continued to work just fine, which is why these painters could do what they did.

Writers during this time also found inspiration in their emotions, wills, desires, and even internal confusion. Russian writer Fyodor Dostoevsky (1821–81) created psychologically driven, morally ambivalent, and intensely unique characters that influenced the irrational thinkers we've considered here. In fact, Freud, Nietzsche, and Virginia Woolf all cited Dostoevsky's work as inspiration for their own. Perhaps no writer better captured the tension of modern life than Franz Kafka (1883–1924). Born in Prague in what was then the Austro-Hungarian Empire, Kafka grew up speaking Yiddish at home, Czech in public, and writing in German. His style combined intense realism and weird fantasy. In his short story "The Metamorphosis," for instance, the main character wakes up one day as a cockroach, and he and his family struggle to come to terms with this transformation. Uh, yeah. Kafka was a master at creating a totally bizarre situation and characters that accept these conditions yet yearn intensely for some normalcy. As a result, subsequent authors have increasingly used fiction to explore humans' psychological depths and the tensions in modern life.

Musical composers also used intellectual tension and irrationalism for inspiration. Richard Strauss (Germany, 1864–1949) even wrote a piece based on one of Nietzsche's books.[13] Romantic composers, starting with Beethoven in the early nineteenth century, had invested more emotion in their music, using dramatic changes in dynamics, tempo, and melody to approximate psychological mood swings. Late nineteenth-century composers went further and structured compositions around their emotions and unique experiences. Like his painting pals, French composer Claude Debussy (1862–1918) used music to express his impressions of the world. Debussy also took cues from non-Western music coming from French colonies. His *Prelude to the Afternoon of a Faun* (1894) followed a poem about a faun to consider dreams and desires. His 1908 *Children's Corner* suite of piano pieces weaves together inspirations from Africa, Asia, and Europe into playful melodies. In the early twentieth century, the popular American genre of *ragtime* music similarly drew from African rhythms for its syncopated or "ragged" left-hand bass line. African-American composer Scott Joplin (1868–1917) helped make this music popular throughout the Western world, laying the foundations for jazz, boogie-woogie, and other popular forms of music.[14] And of course the fact that all these forms of music, like modernist art, worked as consumer products illustrates the changing role of culture in European society.

Political implications of irrationalism

Okay, let's see where we're at: Newton's wrong, God is dead, and Santa's not real. Downer chapter, dude. Yes, and many of the ideas here get blamed for much of the badness in the

---

[13]Specifically Nietzsche's *Thus Spoke Zarathustra*. I guarantee that you know the first movement; it's one of the most famous pieces of music ever. Check out "Introduction" to the 1896 *Also Sprach Zarathustra*.

[14]I bet you've heard his piece *The Entertainer* (1902) or *Maple Leaf Rag* (1899).

twentieth century. In 1919 Irish poet W.B. Yeats (1865–1939) shared his own ringing endorsement of his times:

Things fall apart; the centre cannot hold;
Mere anarchy is loosed upon the world, . . .
The best lack all convictions, while the worst
Are full of passionate intensity.[15]

These four lines sum up the twentieth century pretty well. We've seen in this chapter how intellectuals identified the lack of a "centre" in European life. Some of them lamented that fact, while others celebrated it. Westerners would try to fill that "centre" with lots of things in the twentieth century: aggressive ideologies, awkward hairstyles, powerful states, consumerism, entertainment, drugs, and identity politics, among others. Some of them satisfied for a while, but some "loosed" anarchy and violence on Europe.

The "best" for Yeats were honest people who recognized there were no common values, so they could therefore no longer hold firm convictions. The "worst," on the other hand, couldn't admit the "centre" was gone and pushed their ideas forward with "passionate intensity," until those ideas became myth. They fervently believed their ideas in part *because* they were myth. Very often they were ready to die for those ideas or kill you if you disagreed. Perception, belief, and conviction thus became more important than reality. Just like with Santa.

Now, if you're trying to create a better political system, basing it on perception and myth might not turn out so well. Plenty of observers have faulted these Irrationalist types for removing Enlightenment, objective truth as a way to measure the behavior of individuals or government and for favoring emotion over reason. Some critics have argued that irrationalism led to Nazism and other twentieth-century disasters, and they often blame Nietzsche and his pals for encouraging people to focus more on their individual desires, will, and perceptions than on objective reality. One book that really hit this nail on the head was Max Horkheimer and Theodore Adorno's *Dialectic of Enlightenment* (1944).[16] Horkheimer and Adorno agree that irrationalism gave people some bad ideas, but they said that the issue is more than just the good Enlightenment vs. bad irrationalism.

Here's the truly big reveal of this book (at least for me). Horkheimer and Adorno identify the key to this whole book you're reading: the Enlightenment didn't have to get whacked by Irrationalist thugs, because it already contained the seeds of its own destruction. Enlightenment thought first replaced religion and myth with reason, science, and the assumption that humans are good. But then those ideas, by the start of the twentieth century, had themselves become myth and been used to dominate other people. Remember in the Introduction I said, "Very important: Enlightenment = good and bad." I've been making that point ever since.

---

[15]Yeats, "The Second Coming," in *Michael Robartes and the Dancer* (Churchtown: Cuala Press, 1920).
[16]Yep, more big, hard-to-pronounce German names. In grad school, we called these guys "Horky-Dorky."

The ideas in this chapter certainly helped cause some of the horrors of the twentieth century. German soldiers, for example, in World War I went to war carrying copies of Nietzsche's books in their knapsacks the Imperial German government had given them.[17] The idea that individuals, not some objective deity or process, determined truth and morality made it easier for strong men to direct people. Appealing to humans' darker desires, fears, and aggression could support violent ideologies and war-mongering. And the notion that we should build a system to allow better people to rise above inferior ones might justify genocide. Irrationalism thus deserves some blame for the destructive twentieth century. But so does the Enlightenment. In fact, all of the ideas that prompted such a violent century—nationalism, fascism, democracy, communism, consumer capitalism, imperialism—came from the Enlightenment. So did the rapid development of technology that armed these ideas with awesome weapons. In a post-Santa Claus world, those ideas could become myth and therefore absolutes. It's our job to understand how that happened and maybe to stop it from happening in the future.

---

[17]Nietzsche rolls over in grave. Of course, who knows how many of them read the stuff.

CHAPTER 9
WORLD WAR I: THE WAR THAT DID NOTHING BUT CHANGED EVERYTHING

Of course, no one called it "The First World War" or "World War I" when it started. Everyone just called "the war," and soon "The Great War" because of the totally awesome aspirations people had for it and the totally insane death toll it produced. You need a World War *Two* before you can have a World War *One*. Still to this day many people in Europe refer to it as the Great War. Sixty-eight million soldiers fought—literally a generation of men from every country in Europe and many other parts of the world. The conflict therefore impacted almost everyone in Europe to some degree. Mostly badly.

How then could it be the war that did nothing but changed everything? It did nothing because leaders' goals were ridiculous and failed big time. Heads of state, generals, and strategists could not imagine how war would be fought in the early twentieth century. Their main plan, and the only one that really worked, was to go through as many bodies and as much material resources as possible. They did just fine on that goal. Yet the Great War changed everything in part *because* of its massive destruction, waste, and output from states. The whole map of Europe changed: compare maps 9.1 and 9.2 below. Gender relations shifted. Citizens forged new relationships with states. Dogs and cats became friends. Almost every major event or development in the twentieth-century Western world originated in some way from the Great War: World War II, the Cold War, human rights, genocide, identity politics, jazz, massive welfare states, mass culture, and propaganda. The war tested all the big ideas we've been studying. On the one hand the war revealed the absurdity of fabulous Enlightenment-inspired ideas. On the other hand, the war cost so much that many Europeans felt that they *had* to double down on those ideas. And that's why World War I marked the real start of the twentieth century.

Building the argument

The war in fact bridged the "long nineteenth" and the "short twentieth" centuries. The "long nineteenth century" began with the French Revolution and, as I mentioned in Chapter 4, ended around 1916. Why 1916? That year was probably the darkest of the Great War, with the most futile death count. The idea of the "long nineteenth century" organizes this book by revealing the powerful positive and negative impacts of Enlightenment ideas on Europeans' daily lives. Many of those same concepts, made stronger and even mythical in World War I, defined the twentieth century. Those ideological conflicts ended around 1989 (Chapter 14). That's why we call it the "short twentieth century."

This chapter shows the real, bloody impact of the Scientific Revolution and Enlightenment. The Great War also marked the moment that many Europeans realized some of the things that intellectuals in the last chapter discussed, sometimes just before their heads got blown off. Human character may have changed for Virginia Woolf in December 1910, but for most Europeans that realization came during the First World War. Millions of people understood in one way or another that Enlightenment ideals of human goodness, scientific promises of progress, and the belief that humans were rational were a load of crap.

This chapter studies the long- and short-term causes of the war. We will follow some of the important aspects of the fighting. The Great War toppled several empires, but the 1917 Russian Revolutions—yes, two of them—especially altered Western history. The 1919 Treaty of Versailles, which formalized the war's end and the "peace" that followed, helped create the conflicts we'll be dealing with in the next two chapters. Remember that it was right after the Great War that Yeats wrote that "the best lack all convictions/While the worst are full of passionate intensity." Buckle up.

How bad was it? Numbers don't lie

Short answer: real bad, way worse than anyone could have imagined. War always kills and maims soldiers; it always wrecks and alters lives at home. But the Great War did more damage to more soldiers than the world had ever seen. Lots of people, especially Americans, tend to look at World War II as the big one. We'll see in Chapter 11 how bad that conflict was, especially for civilians. But for soldiers the Great War was much worse. Let's check out some numbers to get a sense of the scope:

- Estimated price tag: $330 billion ($180 billion in direct costs, $150 billion indirect costs).
- 4 European empires fell as a result of the war: Austria-Hungary, Germany, Ottoman, Russia.
- 10 new nations created in Europe: Austria, Czechoslovakia, Estonia, Finland, Hungary, Latvia, Lithuanian, Poland, Turkey, and Yugoslavia.
- 68 million soldiers mobilized.
- 10 million dead (8 million killed and 2 million died from disease and malnourishment).
- 21 million wounded.
- 46 percent of all soldiers involved were casualties, that is, either killed or wounded.
- 8 million prisoners of war or missing soldiers.
- 75 percent of the men in the French and Russian armies were killed or wounded.

Map 9.1 Europe, 1914.

- 1 million casualties each in the Battle of Verdun (February to December 1916) and the Somme (July to November 1916).[1]
- 6.6 million civilians died.

In short, the war radically altered European demographics. It's no exaggeration to state that a generation was more or less lost. And the conflict completely redrew the European map.

Causes of the Great War: big-time, long-term, and all-too familiar

The long-term causes will sound familiar. If you've kept up with your reading so far, then it should come as no surprise that the Europeans didn't learn from their mistakes. Above all, *nationalism* caused this conflict. It was alive and strong in every nation in Europe at the start of the twentieth century. Recall from Chapter 5 that nationalism started out as a popular movement in the first half of the nineteenth century, but elites eventually took charge of it. Well, by the start of the twentieth century, rulers had made

---

[1] These battles were truly awful. The United Kingdom, for example, lost more men in just a couple of months in the Battle of the Somme than they did during all of World War II. In fact, the UK suffered as many casualties in the month of July 1916 alone, during the Battle of the Somme, as the United States did during the whole war.

Map 9.2 Europe, 1919.

such good use of nationalism that they had sometimes made their populations *more* nationalist than the government. Large popular associations in Germany, for instance, such as the Pan-German League and Navy League, advocated for greater nationalist and imperialist expansion than even the sabre-rattling German Empire wanted. And that's saying something!

Imperialism was often European nationalism on another continent. As we saw in Chapter 7, imperialism intensified competition between European nations. They went after as much land as they could because they didn't know what might be there. Basically, imperial FOMO. Europeans grabbed up natural resources in Africa and Asia like oil and rubber, which strengthened their military capability, as did the native workforce. And Europeans first tried out new, deadly weapons on native populations. Colonial subjects also increased the number of bodies imperial powers could throw into a prolonged war. Eventually several million men fought for or aided imperial powers. Plus, imperialism made the Great War a world war. Fighting in Africa, Asia, the Middle East, and South America only minimally affected the war's outcome, but protecting and gaining colonies were important war aims for the main European combatant nations. Imperialism thus raised the stakes for any conflict between European countries.

European nations mistrusted each other, so they built bigger military forces and better weapons to protect themselves. Isn't that what everyone does who mistrusts someone else? This *arms race* both reflected and fueled nationalist competition. It also demonstrated the importance of *competitive capitalism*, especially during this exciting age of invention. European military leaders and arms manufacturers worked closely with each other to create more effective tools for killing humans (a.k.a. weapons). And if you make things that countries use in war, well, it stands to reason that war will allow you to sell more of your things. Nice. The weapons used in World War I were exceptionally efficient killing machines. Smells like the twentieth century!

Similarly, advances of *technology* and *industry* also helped cause the Great War. The same developments in communication and transportation that allowed Western powers to command empires around the globe empowered them to field millions of troops in a world war. A number of general technological advances greatly expanded the potential scope of war: tins for food storage, gas-powered vehicles to move men and material quickly, condoms,[2] machines to build and tear down fortifications, water purification, mass-production chemistry, medical advances, non-smoking gun powder, telephone and radio, and electricity. I'm not saying that condoms or radios caused World War I, but these advances, like those in weaponry, needed markets, and war provided some pretty great markets. Plus, a number of these advances allowed Europeans to feel both more powerful and more removed from physical harm. Mechanized weapons did the same thing—unless you were on the receiving end.

Expanding state authority also helped create conditions for a big ole war in several important ways. States throughout the nineteenth century were increasingly involved in people's economic and political lives. Engaged states could use and direct citizens' growing resources. Some countries, like France and Germany, actually used social welfare plans to help their citizens. In each case, the state became more closely entwined with people's lives. That closer connection generally bolstered nationalism and thus support for war in the twentieth century. Most Europeans were already used to their state shaping aspects of their daily lives and their opinions These conditions would in turn allow states during the Great War to direct soldiers and and direct civilians' views of the war.

European society by the turn of the twentieth century was rooted in *faith in science and progress* (and Santa Claus). Science undergirded many advances in Europe, especially in industry, technology, and state authority. The very nature of science assumed progress and offered people new tools to improve their lives. Likewise, Enlightenment thought sought to maximize human ability to do good, which would improve everyone's lives. Due to such beliefs, many Europeans actually thought the outbreak of war was a progressive opportunity for change. Yeah, right. Clearly someone had skipped their Nietzsche and Freud readings.

Finally, a general *intellectual malaise* and *irrationalism* helped cause the Great War. Especially for young people, who in the early twentieth century had grown up in relative peace, war could seem like a great test or opportunity for excitement or release of

---

[2] Seriously. The German military began promoting their use in the late nineteenth century. After all, rubber has many uses.

boredom. Boredom? People started the greatest slaughter of human life to date because they were *bored*? Yes, lots of people thought that war was adventurous and a chance for glory. Oops. We saw last chapter that some thinkers had already discovered that people were kinda bad. Irrationalists believed that people were more driven by their desires, fears, and aggression than by reason and goodness. Yeah, well, that take on humanity at the turn of the twentieth century did not bode well, especially as many Europeans continued to pat themselves on the back for being so awesome. In the end, everyone was wrong—or everyone was right. Both highly rational and progressive Enlightenment ideas and aggressive and selfish irrationalism helped produce war.

Medium-term causes: alliances rock, alliances suck

So, big, bad, unified Germany scared the hell out of everyone, especially the French and Russians. German unification in 1871 threw off the balance of power in Europe that had been in place since the Napoleonic Wars. France and Russia had actually very little in common at the end of the nineteenth century. One was a liberal republic with progressive culture and ideas. One was the most backward and autocratic regime in Europe. But they both hated themselves some Germany. In 1894 they signed a treaty to support each other militarily, especially against you-know-who.

The blustering, well-mustached Germans did not like to admit it in public, but they too had their moments of self-doubt as a world power. They pretty quickly made peace with the Austro-Hungarians, who had too many problems to stay mad at their German bros for long. Germany also allied with the Ottoman Empire in order to limit what Russia and Britain could do in the Mediterranean and Middle East.

And then there's the British. Oh, the British. Are they splendidly isolated? Are they nervous about Germany too? Do they only care about their empire? Will they fight? In 1904 they signed a semi-treaty with France and Russia. It mainly worked out conflicts in Africa and Asia but sort of brought the UK into alliance with Russia and France. "Sort of" meant that the United Kingdom didn't give its actual answer about allegiance until fighting began in 1914. And there it is: the United Kingdom as the Great Procrastinator.

Alliances are supposed to serve primarily as defensive measures or as deterrents. If you mess with one member of an alliance, you've got to deal with them all, so you keep the peace. However, the European alliance system that developed by the start of the twentieth century ended up promoting rather than preventing war. It emboldened some states to act more aggressively since they knew someone had their back. By the early 1900s, France and Russia had Germany and Austria surrounded, so any big war would force Germany to fight on two fronts. Unfortunately, a surrounded yet planning Germany, which was allied with anxious yet ambitious Austria-Hungary, made for a jumpy central Europe. Likewise, massive international empires—France, UK, and Russia—were often too distracted to realize they were giving wimps (smaller countries) the ability to act like bullies. Really, for all the confidence, might, wealth, and technological power these

Map 9.3 European alliances, 1914.

European countries had, it's kind of funny how much they acted on fear, mistrust, and insecurity. At least, it would have been funny, if 17 million people hadn't died.

Now, let's get this party started!

How the Great War began is a complicated nerd-fest for historians. We won't go into all of it, but you need to understand a few details, especially since the start of all this business determined the peace treaty that eventually ended it. And that peace treaty set the stage for World War II and subsequent conflicts. But first let's get to Kosovo and Belgium. Yes, those two small places played important roles in the outbreak of war.

I would describe most European powers around this time as bellicose idiots.[3] Europeans had not seen a major war on the continent since 1815, though God knows they'd been involved in plenty of smaller fights in Europe and in their colonies. Political and military leaders had also failed to learn lessons from a couple of nasty modern conflicts, the US Civil War (1861–5) and the Boer War in South Africa (1899–1902). Those wars featured long sieges, slow-moving military forces, efficient weaponry, significant state resources, and civilians as victims. In the early twentieth century European nations were already at each other's throats. France and Germany nearly went to war in 1905 and 1911 over claims in North Africa. In 1908, Russia almost fought Austria-Hungary about territories in the Balkans (southeast Europe). Two wars in the Balkans in 1912 and 1913, made possible by a crumbling Ottoman Empire, involved all

---

[3]"Bellicose" means looking for war. So maybe "bellicose idiot" is redundant.

the nations in that region. Only careful negotiations managed to prevent a much bigger conflict.

So, here's what we've got by 1914: trigger-happy European nations, jealous and bitter about colonial holdings and overly armed with powerful, experienced military forces. They all wanted to expand and protect their territories, in and out of Europe. They had partly used alliances with each other to do that. Thankfully skillful, well-clad diplomats had prevented these smaller conflicts from exploding into something larger. But reasonable diplomats seeking to avoid war were fighting against a massive tide of nationalism and naïve belief in progress.

The war began in the Balkans. On June 28, 1914 the Austro-Hungarian Empire sent Archduke Ferdinand, the heir to the throne, to oversee military exercises in Sarajevo. Serbia was not happy. After all, that area had been part of the Greater Serbian Empire back in the Middle Ages, and June 28 was a national day of mourning in Serbia for a battle they lost in 1389 in Kosovo. Yes, folks were still pissed about a defeat 525 years ago. Serbian nationalists, perhaps with the blessing of their government, assassinated the Austrian heir and his wife. Oh, no you didn't! Now, it's on!

Needless to say, Austria-Hungary was angry and wanted into Serbia to investigate the assassination. Here "investigate" basically meant "invade." Now, the Austrians weren't going to attack Serbia without German backing. Big bro Germany gave them what's become known as a "blank cheque" of support.[4] Serbia was ready to resist Austria-Hungary after confirming that *their* big brother, Russia, had their back. When Serbia didn't accept all of Austria-Hungary's demands, the Austrians declared war on July 28. Russia knew this move meant war with Germany. And let's face it, Russia is big, cold, muddy, and they were not ready to move their military quickly. So, on July 30 Russia began mobilizing its troops toward Germany. Okay, thought Germany, it's going to take the Russians a while to get here; in the meantime, we need to knock out France.

That was Germany's von Schlieffen war plan (named after the general who created it): quick victory over France to secure the western flank (or side of their military) and then take care of business with the slow Russians in the east. On August 3, Germany declared war on France. However, France had been building up fortifications since 1871 along its border with Germany, so that quick route to Paris was closed. The Germans thought, hey, why not zip through Belgium? How much resistance can *they* offer? At this point Germany, France, Austria-Hungary, and Russia were all at war. And still the question hung in the smoky air: What. About. The Brits? The UK warned everyone to respect Belgian neutrality (since many goods came into the UK via Belgium and Holland), which major powers had agreed to in 1839. But the Germans had to stick to their plan, man! On the night of August 3–4, Germany invaded Belgium and the United Kingdom immediately declared war on Germany. The Ottomans and Japanese got into the game, expanding the fighting further. And, of course, most of these countries had significant

---

[4]Yet another old metaphor that may not work as well in a world where few people write cheques *or* checks anymore. Basically, it meant Austria had Germany's full support.

colonial holdings around the world. So, by August 1914 it was safe to say that the world was at war.

Maybe the arms race, nationalism, technology, imperialism, and sheer naiveté (read: stupidity) across Europe meant this war was pretty much bound to happen. Certainly, most folks in Europe thought so and were damn glad about it. Still, it's important to note two things about how the war started. First, most of the powers involved helped cause the war. That blame game matters because, when the war ended, Germany got blamed for everything and handed the massive bill to pay for it all. Those moves nearly destroyed the German economy and created the atmosphere in which a World War I veteran named Adolf Hitler mixed anger and pride into a violent combination in the 1930s. Second, the monarchs of Europe might have found a way to call the whole thing off. After all many of them were related and could have literally called their relatives to try to defuse this thing. Seriously, the monarchs of Britain, Germany, and Russia were cousins! I'm sorry, but what's the point of having an incestuously related European aristocracy, if they can't talk things over and stave off a little thing like a world war?[5]

Definitely *not* all quiet on the Western Front[6]

Boy, people were excited about the start of the war. Super excited. Hundreds of thousands of people poured into the streets to celebrate. Men volunteered all over Europe. It was going to be great! And they'd be home for Christmas. Ultimately what counted was not enthusiasm, strategy, or will. The Great War was about numbers. Already in 1914, the Allied Powers (France, Britain, Russia, and amigos) had 199 divisions ready to go, compared to just 137 from the Central Powers (Germany, Austria-Hungary, Ottoman Empire, and their buds). More importantly the Allies had twice as many people (279 million) than the Central Powers did (120 million). These numbers more or less guaranteed that the Allies would win. But let's not spoil anyone's fun at this point. Four years of non-stop mechanized death. Welcome to the Great War!

Things started out exciting enough. Germany amassed a million-and-a-half solders to invade Belgium, which was protected by a brave force of 217,000. But France managed to speed troop reinforcements to the front lines. The Russians, on the other side of the continent, actually got moving way faster than even they had expected. In short, Das German-Plan-to-Whip-France-Quickly and then get ready for the Russians did not work. So, it's a two-front war for you, Germany. By late October 1914, movement in Western Europe was basically over. From the English Channel to the Swiss border, Europe was divided by 350 miles of trenches and barbed wire and guns pointed at each other. Between 1914 and 1918 there was no more than ten miles of movement along this line. And so the armies of France, Belgium, Britain, Germany, and Austria-Hungary

---

[5]To be fair, Tsar Nicholas II did exchange telegrams with Kaiser Wilhelm, though it didn't do any good.
[6]Reference to Erich Maria Remarque's great 1929 novel about the war, *All Quiet on the Western Front*.

settled down for three-and-a-half years of slaughter. The combination of stationary stalemate, deadly weapons, and powerful states caused the massive carnage of this war. In the first five months alone France lost 995,000 men; Germany lost 667,000 men; the UK, 96,000; and the Belgians, 50,000, or a quarter of their military. Yep, five months down—only forty-nine to go!

Fighting on the eastern front was a little more fluid and a little less sustained. There were fewer trenches than in the west, in part because the battle lines were much longer. Transportation was less reliable in Russia, Austria, and Serbia, and the weather was worse. Still, early eastern front battles also demonstrated how deadly this war would be. For instance, in September 1914 Austria-Hungary took 1 million soldiers into western Russia (basically Poland) and lost a battle from which they would never fully recover: 200,000 soldiers dead and 100,000 prisoners of war (POWs). Victory for the Russians cost almost 180,000 lives and 45,000 prisoners. The Austrians similarly lost 227,000 men in a tactical victory against Serbia, whereas the defeated Serbs only lost 70,000 soldiers. All across Europe battle lines got fairly firm and lots of soldiers died. That's the main story of the would-be glorious and quick fight of 1914. Nobody was going home by Christmas—or for the next three Christmases.

We call this big conflict a *world* war for three reasons. First, because countries around world fought each other. (Duh.) Japan, for example, expanded their own empire by taking over some of Germany's bases in China and elsewhere in Asia. Battles in the Middle East and North Africa between the Allies and the Ottomans especially mattered for the oil supplies necessary to fuel mechanized warfare. Second, large, powerful navies fought each other at various places around the world. The British boasted the largest naval force in the world and got help from sea-faring allies France, Russia, and Japan. Germany's buddies—Austria-Hungary, Turkey, the Ottoman Empire—weren't so much salty nautical types. Nevertheless, Germany used submarine warfare to challenge British control of the North Atlantic.

Third, European colonies and colonial subjects around the world fought each other. In Africa British and French forces took over most German colonies in less than a year, but fighting continued off and on for the entire war. It may seem hard to believe, but colonial powers conscripted millions of colonized subjects to serve in this war all over the world. (Or maybe it's just about what you'd expect from those imperialist bastards.) Two million Africans served as soldiers, for example, and 200,000 of them died. India alone sent a million men to fight and work for the British war effort. Some of these guys might have hoped that their support and sacrifice would earn them independence or greater rights after the war. Ha! We'll see in Chapter 13 that the Great War did empower independence movements, but the fighting usually encouraged imperial powers to dig in their heels.

Anyway, that's 1914. And now for a quick synopsis of the rest of the war:

- 1915: Pointless attacks, tens of thousands of soldiers perish, no movement.

- 1916: Verdun, the Somme. See 1915, only worse. Much worse.

- 1917: lots of stuff happening, but no end in sight, despite the Russian Revolution.

- 1918: One big boy out (Russia), one big boy in (USA). Continued carnage until Germany passes out, exhausted.

You may already be skimming over all the numbers. Frankly, listing one massive tally of dead after another starts to minimize the losses. But there really wasn't much exciting board-game- or video-game-like movement in this war. Just a lot of guys mostly staying in the same place using huge weapons against each other. You can barely talk of battles won or lost. Often "victories" cost so many men and such trust in military leadership, that they could do as much damage to a country's morale as a defeat. So, the number of casualties ends up telling more about how the fighting was going that what one brave battalion or bold attack did.

Let me just share a few important details about how the war went. I'm serious when I say not a lot changed in 1915 and 1916. But the battle of Verdun (February–December 1916) subjected soldiers to ten months of non-stop shelling and warfare. Ten months, twenty-four hours a day! No human had ever endured something like that. In the related Battle of the Somme (July–November 1916), during the first week alone, the British fired 1,627,824 rounds of ammunition. On the first *day* of that battle, 19,240 British soldiers died and 38,300 were captured. Both Verdun and the Somme were technically Allied victories, yet the cost was so great that popular support began to waiver in the United Kingdom and elsewhere. Also, in the bloody year of 1916, Russian Tsar Nicolas II assumed command of troops directly at the front and left things back home in the hands of his ultra-reactionary, clueless wife and the mystical monk Rasputin. That didn't go well, as we'll shortly see. Plus, in September 1916, Russia notched perhaps its greatest victory in the Brusilov Offensive against Germany and Austria-Hungary. The death of 1.2 million soldiers (!) and capture of another 212,000, however, seemed like a failure back home and substantially weakened the Russian monarchy.

In 1917 several important events actually changed things. First, in the spring, French military mutinies or "strikes" forced the French command to improve conditions and promise only to attack when there was legitimate hope for victory. French soldiers, living and dead, might have wondered why that rule took so long. Next, while tanks and planes did not greatly affect battles, the broader use of tanks in 1917 demonstrated that they might overcome the trench warfare stalemate. Airpower had already proved essential for intelligence, but in 1917 the Germans especially began to have airplanes strafe ground targets at the start of an attack and kill anti-tank guns.

Third, the USA declared war in April 1917 against the Central Powers. The Yanks brought enthusiasm that European forces had long since lost, as well as supplies and more bodies for the grinder. Americans had been divided about the war since 1914 but had been mostly in favor of staying out. In January 1917, British intelligence intercepted a telegram from Germany offering support for Mexico to invade the USA, if the USA entered the war. In addition, German spies had been caught along the East Coast carrying out or planning acts of sabotage. Messing with our house?! That got the Americans mad. Also, Germany's aggressive submarine warfare kept sinking American ships. In fact, German sub attacks in February and March of 1917 finally prompted the USA to declare war. It took a while to raise an army, but eventually in 1918 the USA sent an army of

4 million men and a navy of 80,000. While many of them never saw action, their presence greatly relieved and revived Allied fighting.

(Fourth) The Russian Revolutions

Two Russian revolutions in 1917 radically altered the course of the Great War and the entire twentieth century. Conditions for revolution go back into the nineteenth century. By the end of the nineteenth century, Russia's state-supported industrialization had made it one of the leading industrial nations, although the vast majority of Russians still farmed like peasants. The super-autocratic Tsarist regime stifled almost all political reform movements. That suppression encouraged activists, especially Marxists, to believe that the only solution was to overthrow the government violently and install a totally new system. Certainly, those were the aims of socialist revolutionary leaders like Vladimir Lenin, Leon Trotsky (1879–1940), and others. The tsarist government had also failed to modernize its military very much, and they began World War I with very old-fashioned military leadership. Both defeats and victories steadily undermined trust in the Tsar, the government, the military, and the war effort overall. Russia had more people than its enemies but did not equip them well. For instance, many soldiers were sent into battle without guns. When they asked why, they were told just to pick the weapon of a fallen comrade and carry on. Not the best for morale. In short, the war made clear how backward, out of touch, and vulnerable the tsarist regime was.

By 1917, the war effort had taken a massive toll on Russian soldiers and civilians. In February of that year, the Russian autocratic regime collapsed as a result of popular protests led by women, soldiers, and workers. Even the Russian elite realized the Tsar could no longer rule. How backward was the tsarist regime? Well, for one thing they were thirteen days behind the rest of the world. Seriously. Almost all of Europe had changed from the old, Roman Julian calendar to the Gregorian calendar a few hundred years back. The Gregorian calendar acknowledged the fact that the Earth takes 365 *and a quarter* days to orbit the sun and added an extra day (February 29) every four years (leap year) to calculate for that quarter day. Russia, however, remained with the ancient Julian calendar. One neat trick, though: you could mail a letter from Moscow and it would arrive in Berlin before you sent it.

The revolution began on February 23, 1917 (or March 8 everywhere else). After some skirmishes, Tsar Nicholas II abdicated, and on March 3 (or March 16), a new Provisional Government took control of the massive Russian empire. This new government consisted of politicians representing the entire spectrum of political opinions in Russia, from those wanting the monarch back to radical socialists. Most members were liberal politicians who wanted some form of constitutional democracy. Led by the left-leaning politician Alexander Kerensky (1881–1970), the Provisional Government had a much harder time ruling than it did taking power.[7] Russia's allies in the war recognized the new government, and the Provisional Government continued fighting.

---

[7] Ain't it always so?

One immediate challenge to the Provisional Government was a totally new form of political authority: "councils," or *Soviets* in Russian, that began springing up across Russia, especially in big cities. These Soviets were self-governing organizations connected to workplaces, schools, or towns. The biggest and most powerful was the St. Petersburg Soviet. Kerensky was one of the few people serving in both the Provisional Government and the St. Petersburg Soviet. Many soldiers, sailors, and workers supported the Soviets, so there were really two sources of power in 1917 Russia: the Soviets and the actual government. Lenin and other socialist revolutionaries began to call for "all power to the Soviets" and wormed their way into these new organizations.

Lenin was watching all this from afar. He was in exile in Switzerland during the war. When revolution broke out in Russia, Lenin was chomping at the bit to get back into the action. However, a little thing called the Great War blocked his way. Lenin urged the Soviets to push for "peace, land, and bread." "What?" said German leaders, "you had us at 'peace'!" So, the Germans arranged for a sealed car to take Lenin and his wife, Nadya Krupskaya (1869–1939), who was also a Marxist revolutionary leader, back to St. Petersburg. Later Lenin's opponents would call his move treasonous.

When Lenin arrived in St. Petersburg in April, he didn't even get off the train before giving his first speech to revolutionary supporters. Directing the most radical of the socialist parties, the Bolsheviks,[8] Lenin again called for "peace, land, and bread" and "all power to the Soviets." Needless to say, Lenin's ideas didn't sit well with the Provisional Government. But his Bolsheviks did help save the Provisional Government's hide, when right-wing forces tried to overthrow it in August and reinstall the tsar. That move further empowered the Bolsheviks.

Meanwhile, the Provisional Government kept Russia in the war, losing more and more soldiers every day. At the same time, the St. Petersburg Soviet kept calling for peace. Across Russia peasants used the uncertain times to grab land since they cared more about land than rights and votes and whatnot. You can imagine this land grab did not help Russia's already weak military. Sample letter to soldier at the front: "Revolution here at home is great; we are grabbing land and abusing aristocrats. How goes all the death in the trenches? Did they give you a gun yet?"[9] Desertions, mutinies, revolutionary Soviets, and above all, the continued weight of war weakened the Provisional Government and strengthened the Bolsheviks. The night of October 25–26 (November 6–7 for the rest of y'all), the Bolsheviks took over the Russian government. They faced little resistance since most people had given up on the Provisional Government and were willing to let the Bolsheviks give it a go.

"Peace, land, and bread," Lenin had been hollering more or less since the war had begun. So, the new Bolshevik government quickly asked Germany to negotiate peace terms. Now, you don't just go pulling out of a war and expect everything to go back to normal. Germany used whatever leverage they had against Russia. The two sides met in the Polish town of Brest-Litovsk, and the Germans laid down some severe demands. The

---

[8]"Bolshevik" meant the "minority" group among Russian socialists.
[9]Fabricated letter of course, silly. Russian peasants couldn't read.

resulting March 3, 1918[10] treaty cost the Russians dearly. They had to give away their portion of Poland, as well as Estonia, Finland, Ukraine, and some territory in the northwest and southwest. They also had to pay the insane sum of four to five billion gold rubles. In all, Russia lost 56 million people or a third of its population and 1.3 million square miles of territory, which included a third of its farmland and the vast majority of its iron and coal production. Basically, the treaty pushed Russia back to its seventeenth-century borders. Germany and Austria-Hungary quickly set up friendly dictatorships[11] or monarchies in the occupied territories. This deal only lasted for a few months until the war ended, but the Treaty of Brest-Litovsk was super harsh, way worse than the Versailles settlement or really anything in modern history. It made lots of Russians mad at the new Bolshevik regime and probably helped cause the Russian Civil War of 1918–21. But for now, Russia was out. It was a single-front war for the Central Powers, but the Americans were coming.

The end

By 1918, Germany was increasingly fighting alone. Austria-Hungary was falling apart and being invaded by Italy, which had switched sides and joined the Allies. The Ottoman Empire too was slowly sinking. In 1918, Germany planned to attack in the west before too many Americans could strengthen the Allies. But all that land they took from Russia wasn't going to administer or defend itself, so Germany could not send all its troops from the east to help with the final push in the west. When Germany attacked in March 1918, it initially recaptured all the land it had lost since 1916. A big Allied push in August 1918, heavily supported by US troops, drove the Germans back and pretty much sealed Germany's fate. In October, Bulgaria and Turkey collapsed, and the Italians finished off Austria-Hungary, allowing various national groups to declare independence and chopping up that centuries-old empire.

A lot happened in Germany in the fall of 1918, including a revolution that ended the German Empire and the war. On September 29, the German High Command asked for a new democratic government to be formed so those pour souls would have to bear the shame of defeat. Military leaders who had run the entire war were already blaming leftist revolutionaries for stabbing Germany in the back, even before revolution broke out. On October 28, a major sailor mutiny started in Kiel and quickly spread among other soldiers, who were joined by many frustrated workers. Revolutionary councils (modeled on the Russian revolutionary Soviets) spread across Germany. The Allies agreed to an armistice instead of pressing for unconditional surrender. That decision certainly saved lives by ending the war sooner, but it allowed the German army to retain its dignity and

---

[10]Actual date. The Bolsheviks moved the country to the Gregorian calendar at last. They decreed that, when Russians went to bed on January 31, 1918, they would wake up the next morning on February 14, 1918. Welcome to the modern world, comrades. And Happy Valentine's Day.
[11]"The Friendly Dictatorship" sounds like a good name for a band btw.

lent credibility to those claiming that Germany had been undermined by socialist revolutionaries.

This "stab in the back" theory was of course ridiculous. It would be like picking a fight, winning at first, then losing, and then calling for someone else to take the final punch and ask for mercy. After the war, conservatives would use this myth to claim that Germany might have won the war, had it not been for those nasty socialist revolutionaries. They cast doubt on the new democratic system. Young Adolf Hitler, who, despite being an Austrian, had volunteered for the German army, would later make especially good use of this "stab in the back" story. By early November mutinies and revolutionary protests led to the proclamation on November 9, 1918 of a German Republic. *Auf wiedersehen* to the Kaiser!

At this same time, German representatives (the civilians noobs, not the military morons who had lost the war) were in France negotiating very unfavorable terms of an armistice, including the surrender much of Germany's navy, all of its submarines, and many planes and guns. At 5:00 a.m. on November 11, 1918, British, French, and German representatives signed an armistice ending the war and declaring that fighting must cease by 11 a.m. that day—the eleventh hour of the eleventh day of the eleventh month.

Now, you might think, after four years of warfare and the death of millions of soldiers, the folks involved would pick up the phone and tell everyone to put down their damn guns down right now. Nope. In those last hours of fighting, between 5:00 a.m. and 11:00 a.m., close to 11,000 soldiers were killed, wounded, or went missing, including French, American, and Canadian soldiers killed within minutes of the 11:00 a.m. cease-fire. So, we end as we began, with bellicose idiots pointlessly killing each other. At least the celebrations of peace in 1918 were about as big as the celebrations of war had been in 1914.

Several treaties signed in 1919 formally settled peace terms between combatant nations. Most important was the one signed that June at Versailles between Germany, Great Britain, and France (with the USA and Italy involved too). The Versailles Treaty included several important components that would weaken Germany and bolster nationalist sentiment against the democratic regime there:

- Germany gave up 25,000 square miles and seven million people, as well as the gains from that crazy March 1918 Treaty of Brest-Litovsk.

- France would occupy parts of western Germany and have access to coal and industry there.

- Germany surrendered all its colonies.

- The German military was capped at 100,000 men.

- In the area along the Rhine River, the border between most of Germany and France, Germany could not station troops or build fortifications for fifteen years.

- Most importantly, Article 231 blamed Germany for causing the war and demanded they pay France and Britain 132 billion Marks ($31 billion or £6.6 billion then or about $442 or £284 billion today) in gold, material, or other tangible items (i.e., not paper money or credit).

Utterly defeated, alone, and trying to start a new government, Germany had to agree. With hindsight we can see how disastrous these terms were. Even then, some folks thought they were too harsh. But the treaty did temporarily have the desired effect of weakening Germany and helping the British and French economies a little. Germany got all the blame because it was the only nation left standing of the Central Powers.

Austria-Hungary and the Ottoman Empire splintered into smaller nations in part because US President Woodrow Wilson insisted on the right to national self-determination (one of his "Fourteen Points" aimed to guide the post-war peace). The new nations created also included significant protections for minority groups. A reliable racist, though, Wilson did not believe such rights applied to dark folks who were subject to colonial rule. The post-war peace treaties in fact reaffirmed European colonial holdings. The Versailles Treaty also formally established a new international body, the League of Nations. Another one of Wilson's bright ideas, the League was supposed to foster international cooperation and prevent war. We'll see how that one turns out, especially since the USA never signed it. These grand ideas—national self-determination, international cooperation, Western control of the world—echoed the Enlightenment thought that had informed ideas and politics from the "long nineteenth century." The failed peace after World War I ensured that they would continue to shape European politics and economics, for good and for ill.

The peace treaties ending the war showed, as well, that most European nations would be dealing with its aftermath for years to come. Peace treaties are by design about what has happened in the past. But these treaties imprinted anxieties and ideas from the nineteenth century onto the twentieth century. In that way they helped engender economic upheaval, ideological conflict, and another world war. Put simply, peace never really had a chance.

And under the heading of "just when you thought it couldn't get any worse," an influenza pandemic swept through the world in 1918 and 1919. This H1N1 flu infected perhaps 500 million people and took as many as 50 million lives worldwide. The disease hit young adults especially hard, so World War I soldiers faced yet another deadly gauntlet as the war was ending. Influenza killed more US soldiers, for example, than the war did. The recent Covid-19 coronavirus pandemic has generated a lot more interest in the 1918–19 flu pandemic, which probably first jumped from birds to humans in Kansas. That pandemic taught the world about social distancing, quarantining, and the importance of hygiene and vaccines. This often-ignored part of the Great War's history in fact significantly shaped modern medical history and practice. One slight silver lining in a very dark cloud.

Gender and the Great War's legacy

This chapter has featured just about enough insane numbers revealing how men killed each other, so let's wrap up by considering the war's impact on women. First, the Great War defined important concepts like "civilian" and the "home front," which war-time propaganda constructed as "feminine." Men were at the (battle) front fighting, so that left women and children at home. Any man at home who was unable to fight (too old, infirm, disabled, etc.) was thus part of the feminine home front. The home front served as motivation for the men fighting: women and children needed to be kept safe from the violence of war.

In reality, "civilians" were just as essential to a massive struggle between industrial nations as soldiers were. Women and men back home made the materials necessary to wage non-stop war. And of course, in many places, military forces plowed through or dug into areas where civilians lived. In fact, militaries targeted civilians in the Great War with air bombings, concentration camps, and blockades aimed at reducing food supplies. These ideas redefined concepts of warfare in the twentieth century. The battle front was definitely a "masculine" place, but the home front was in fact more complex in terms of gender. What would happen when men had to find their way after the war in that supposedly feminine home front?

Have I mentioned that lots of soldiers died? American writers like Gertrude Stein (1874–1946) and Ernest Hemingway (1899–1961) used the term "the lost generation" in the 1920s to refer to people who felt lost after the war. But especially in Europe, the term had a more literal meaning since so many men died in battle or returned scarred for life. If experience in the war defined this "lost generation," then it must have been for dudes only. And yet men and women alike had to navigate changed societies after World War I. Of course, all the death meant there were more women in Europe after the war, which shaped marital and sexual politics. Women, who had helped keep enormous industrial war machines going, moved into public life in the 1920s. Most countries even let them vote. That fact caused some conservatives to worry about an overly "feminine" society in Europe.

Plus, how did men fit into this society when they could no longer define themselves by the uniform they wore or the gun they held? One response was to intensify, even mythologize masculinity. Some super-tough guys would, oddly enough, look back fondly to the hyper-masculine camaraderie of the war as a model for politics and social organization. Their concepts also drew from the men-only ideas of the Enlightenment.

Finally, we can say very broadly that people after World War I lived in a "mass" age. Mass politics, mass culture, mass media, mass hysteria, etc. This total war had certainly made governments far more engaged in the lives of both soldiers and civilians at home. New forms of entertainment (movies, radio, records, cheap literature) were aimed at very large audiences instead of narrow sets of consumers. Likewise, many countries in Europe gave men and women the vote and offered them welfare benefits. This shift toward greater political engagement required politicians and government leaders to appeal to the masses. Since both mass culture and mass politics included women in large numbers for the first time, some observers concluded that this "mass" age was fundamentally feminine. For some folks, this shift indicated a more diverse, inclusive, and positive direction for Europeans. For other misogynist observers, "feminine" mass culture and politics behaved like emotional and weak women, and should be treated thusly. What this divide meant we'll see in the next chapter.

CHAPTER 10
BETWEEN THE WARS WITHOUT A CENTER, OR: UP THE CREEK WITHOUT A PADDLE

Jazz was the perfect music for European life after the Great War. It was fun; you could dance to it. It was American, so it was different. Jazz featured syncopated rhythm—stressing the weak beat—and jazz musicians played ahead, behind, and all around the beat, so it felt less predictable. They improvised and used call and response, playing to each other or to a crowd. Jazz originated in New Orleans in the 1910s, mostly from African-American musicians mixing blues, ragtime, folk songs, and old slave songs. Jazz was (and is) most exciting live, but most people experienced it through records and radio. That experience was new and exciting too, and very American. Yes, America was coming to Europe all right, with jazz and movies and gadgets and efficiency. Many Europeans developed a love-hate relationship with the United States after World War I. Jazz music's excitement, novelty, *and* contradictions embody much of what happened in the 1920s.

Except most Europeans really didn't know anything about jazz. They *thought* they knew jazz but usually heard watered-down, whitened-up, and Europeanized imitations. Hardly any real American jazz or jazz musicians made it to Europe. Virtually all jazz performers in Europe were Europeans who had probably learned from sheet music—not the best place to dig that swing. And Europeans didn't hear much real jazz on records either. Racist record companies in the USA did not export or promote the music of Black Americans. At best most Europeans heard sweet white American dance bands like Paul Whiteman's. Europeans often assumed a jazz band leader to be a dude with a violin. A violin! Really Europeans heard what we might call commercial dance music, which often used elements of jazz, like syncopation, saxophones, and strong drums. But it wasn't jazz. The so-called "jazz craze" in many places in Europe that excited young people and scared conservatives was actually a "dance music craze." The "jazz age" of the 1920s was mainly the creation of media. Real jazz didn't make it to Europe until the 1930s, 1940s, or even 1950s.

This jazz mix-up points to the broad yet vague impact of "America" in Europe. In many ways "America," could be whatever you wanted it to be—the crazier, the better. Ideas about jazz also show that even the changes of this period were shaped by existing assumptions and prejudices. And folks' getting worked up over "jazz" also indicates how important mass culture became during this era.

Building the argument

In some ways this chapter tells two simple stories: (1) the conditions in Europe after World War I set the stage for World War II, and (2) our trusty Enlightenment ideas helped split the world again into sides killing each other. At the same time, the 1920s and 1930s were crazy decades in which much changed in Europe. Fawning over movie stars, the whole nation listening to your leader on the radio, buying things because advertisements told you to, women and men both working: these are hallmarks of the modern, mass age. We recognize those activities. The years after the Great War were really the first era most of us can understand. It was both optimistic and scary.

This chapter covers the years between the two world wars or the "interwar" period. It deals, first, with the aftermath of World War I. The boys may have come home, but they were different, and society was different. Maybe there never really was "peace" after World War I. And how about those Enlightenment ideals that helped cause the war? Plenty of Europeans doubled down on ideas like communism, fascism, democracy, capitalism, nationalism, etc.—regardless of their flaws. We see in this chapter, in other words, the ongoing dual nature of Enlightenment ideas. They can free you or mess you up. Many people loved the freedom but once again failed to see how bad the mess-ups could be. We will look closely at examples in Italy, Germany, Russia, and Spain. By the late 1930s ideological and political conflicts set up another show-down, World War II.

One of the legacies mentioned at the end of last chapter was that Europeans after World War I were living in a "mass" age. Mass politics and support for powerful governments made ideologies into super-deadly weapons. Mass consumerism and culture shaped people's daily lives. Also, the post-World War I period was kind of a roller-coaster, and there was a huge plunge right in the middle: the Great Depression. That massive economic upheaval impacted almost every person in Europe. We'll see here how this major economic shift altered politics and daily life alike. Yet Europeans were still grabbing as much fun as they could, even when political conflicts were exploding. Dancing on the volcano.

"The centre cannot hold;" in fact, the centre is a joke!

We learned in Chapter 8 that, around 1900, some intellectuals realized there were no common values or experiences that united most Europeans. Maybe there never was, but in the nineteenth century, many Europeans believed generally in broad ideas like Christianity, the Enlightenment, and progress. Thinkers such as Nietzsche, Freud, and others poked holes in those beliefs. In 1921 W.B. Yeats warned:

> Things fall apart; the centre cannot hold;
> Mere anarchy is loosed upon the world, . . .
> The best lack all convictions, while the worst
> Are full of passionate intensity.

World War I, as we saw in the last chapter, for damn sure demonstrated that there was no common good to which Europeans were all working. There were three major responses to this conclusion after the Great War: pacifism (opposing war), using states to promote ideology, and escapism (having fun).

First, no more war. A few authors, intellectuals, and political leaders said what lots of Europeans had discovered: war sucks. German writer Erich Remarque (1898–1970), Robert Graves (1895–1985) from the United Kingdom, and Czech author Jaroslav Hašek (1883–1923) all used satire and dark humor to show the absurdity of war.[1] In 1928 a couple of well-meaning fellas, the US Secretary of State, Frank Kellogg (1856–1937) and the French President Aristide Briand (1862–1932), convinced world powers to sign a treaty outlawing war as a foreign policy tool. Isn't that sweet? You know how that turned out, but the Kellogg-Briand did actually reflect some common values among the fifty states around the world who signed. Way to keep that id in check, says Freud. Given the insane violence of the twentieth century, maybe more folks should have bought into those values, if only for the purpose of personal survival.

Second, powerful states meant powerful ideologies. Big ideologies that proposed to make the world better weren't going to advance themselves. Increasingly mighty states pushed these concepts. Now, Enlightenment thinkers never said that only big ole states, armed to the teeth, could realize their causes. We can thank the French Revolution and Napoleon for that. By the twentieth century, though, political ideologies were the tools of states. So, for a broad Enlightenment idea to get any traction, it needed a state, with laws, police, military, propaganda, etc., to get the job done. Advocates of the ideologies of this era—communism, fascism, capitalism, and democracy—all believed that the world would be better, if everyone organized themselves like they did. Put those things together—universalist ideology + strong nationalist state—and you've got a recipe for some major conflict. That combo allowed people to feel personal pride in their country *and* believe they were advancing all of humanity.

Finally, some folks said, screw it all, let's have fun! Kinda hard to blame them after the First World War really. Now, make no mistake: things were not great financially for lots of people in Europe after World War I. But consumer mass culture grew big enough in the 1920s so that even people barely making it could escape their troubles and go to the movies occasionally or listen to the radio. Certainly consuming movies, cheap literature, and radio programs gave people a little joy in the midst of difficult times. But mass culture also tied them together. And those links could go either way. People in Germany, for example, might have felt a connection when they laughed at the same Disney cartoons that people in Poland or the United States did. At the same time, mass culture had already served nationalist aims during World War I and would continue to provide states with powerful ways to motivate and connect their people, often against enemies. No surprise.

---

[1] Remarque, *All Quiet on the Western Front* (Germany, 1929); Graves, *Good-Bye to All That* (United Kingdom, 1929); Hašek, *The Good Soldier Ševejk* (Czechoslovakia, 1921–3).

So, About Modern Europe ...

The new woman

Women's lives changed as a result of the Great War, and not just because all of the dead men. Women's contributions to that total war had enabled states to fight for as long as they did. Clearly women could make an industrial economy hum as well as men could. Women also fought alongside men in revolutionary movements that grew out of the conflict, especially in Germany and Russia. After the war, women in most European countries earned the right to vote. When male workers returned from fighting, women were often expected to exit the work force. In many places the number of women in the workforce fell after World War I. In the United Kingdom, for example, there were more women working in 1911 than in 1921 or 1931. In Britain and elsewhere healthcare for women and children got worse in the interwar era, at the very same time that many regimes were pushing women to have more babies. In fact, most regimes of the interwar period—liberal, communist, fascist, monarchical, whatever—all defined women as baby-making machines.

After the First World War pretty much every country in Europe needed more people. And guess who could do that? Most states, more generally, encouraged women to be "homemakers," a relatively new concept at this time, and they viewed men as the "breadwinners." States didn't simply reflect old-fashioned gender roles and misogynist assumptions about women. They actually implemented policies to reinforce gender divisions that limited women's opportunities. With all the political and social upheaval after the Great War, many European leaders hoped that reinforcing traditional gender structures would bring a sense of normalcy and order to people's lives. Guys naturally benefitted most from such policies and plans.

Sometimes the ladies did okay, though. Especially in big cities across Europe, "emancipated" women offered a new role model. This "new woman" of the 1920s had her own job, often in an office or store, cut her hair short, wore stylish yet comfortable clothes. She could drive a car and smoke in public. She was in charge of her own sexual identity and activity. In short, the "new woman" rejected many traditional assumptions about women, especially the biological notion that woman = having kids. The image of the "new woman" image inspired many people in the 1920s, although few women could afford the leisure and material objects the stereotypical "emancipated" woman had.

In reality, this image was largely a creation of advertisers and mass media.[2] For most women life changed in smaller, more mundane ways. The ability to participate in politics was huge. Women could entertain themselves with mass culture, which appealed to women and men alike. And even though women were pushed out of some jobs, they did land employment elsewhere because of economic changes. Especially in urban areas across Europe, women worked in factory jobs and new white-collar office jobs. Left-wing political parties particularly pushed for better health care for women and children, for more reproductive rights, welfare assistance for widows and mothers. So, even if the "new woman" concept served advertisers best, the changes she embodied were real.

---

[2] Ain't it always so?

168

Conservatives were not impressed. To them the "new woman" demonstrated how out of whack European society had become. Conservatives after World War I had lots of reasons to freak out, but changes in gender roles was at the top of the list. Big surprise. They felt threatened by women's ability to vote or work or control their own sexual identity. Fascist politicians—the new conservatives of the interwar period—had very schizophrenic ideas about women. They wanted women to participate in politics and actively sought their votes in many places. Yet fascists also celebrated very traditional ideas—myths, really—about society and gender roles. Basically they wanted to use woman's new participation in democracy to end democracy, so they could then celebrate women as baby makers and home makers.

In response to the "new woman" concept, fascists sort of saw themselves as "new men." They were tough dudes who wanted to make the camaraderie of World War I trenches the basis of modern politics, guys who would use the powerful tools of mass politics to identify a common enemy and unite people. They believed that reinforcing traditional gender roles would strengthen the nation state. Women did gain some power in fascist states, but they were never going to be in charge.

So, what even *is* fascism?

Hopefully by now, other big political ideologies are clear enough. Democracy grants citizens the right to vote for leaders and/or policies. Capitalism protects private property and promotes free trade. Liberalism assumes that liberties or freedoms should be enshrined in laws. Socialism promises to end class conflict and economic injustice. Communism uses the state to force socialism. Feminism argues that women should have the same rights and opportunities as men. Nationalism believes that a strong state best embodies the traditions and aspirations of a group of people. Thus endeth the summary of major European political ideologies.

Fascism combines some of these ideas. Above all, fascism promoted a strong state as the embodiment of a people's will.[3] Start with a little capitalism: fascists believed in private property and that society was naturally organized hierarchically, mainly by income. Add a dash of communism: the state had the right to use some private resources to benefit everyone, including the poor. Cut the liberalism, though: fascism saw individual rights and expression embodied only in the state. Heavy on the nationalism. Fascism was chiefly about a strong, authoritarian state that suppressed opposition and created a sharp unity among citizens. Fascists in the twentieth century often built authority from traditional power bases: religious groups, large landowners, supporters of monarchy, and the military. Once in power, though, they frequently weakened those groups. The roots of fascism go back to familiar nineteenth-century suspects: top-down nationalism, Social Darwinism, imperialism, Nietzsche's idea of will, charismatic leaders. But really fascism was about power: getting it, holding it, using it. Maybe the best way to describe fascism is through a picture.

---

[3] Yeah, well, if "people's will" means "the will of the leader who gets control."

Figure 10.1 Fasces.

The term fascism comes from the ancient Roman symbol of the *fasces*, a bundle of sticks that was traditionally paraded in front of the Caesar in public. Each of the sticks represents one segment of society, like accounting or sports or churches. Each of those sticks is vertical; it's organized hierarchically from the top government leader down to the lowest person in that group. All these groups in society work together for a common cause. They are united by nationalism, the rope or band that binds the sticks together. Nationalism gives these groups and thus individual citizens a common purpose. Obviously a bundle of sticks is much stronger than a single stick. The axe represents war, which fascists believed was the greatest activity of the state and the thing that best brought people together.

Fascism began in Italy. The first fascist party formed there in 1915. After the war Benito Mussolini (1883–1945), a journalist, teacher, and former socialist, gathered forces in Italy that opposed Marxism, liberalism, old-fashioned conservatism, and internationalism into the National Fascist Party. They all wore matching black shirts. In 1922 they got carried away at their meeting in Naples and just took over the city. It went pretty well, so they headed north to the capital. This "March on Rome" had broad support from the military and many others in Italy, and it forced the Italian king to hand power over to Mussolini. He and his fellow Fascists quickly installed a nationalist dictatorship, got rid of opposition,[4] and began expanding Italy's borders and its overseas empire. Sale of black shirts skyrocketed. To stand out, Mussolini sometimes appeared shirtless.

This fascism thing turned out to be a pretty flexible and appealing ideology, especially when it resulted in gaining political power. And who doesn't like getting power? Dudes

---

[4] Jailed, exiled, murdered—the usual.

across Europe would get together, don matching shirts,[5] waive flags with ancient, mystical symbols, and claim that they best represented their nation. Fascism offered conservatives a way to feel modern, aggressive, and full of progressive purpose. They also used Social Darwinism to justify pushing weaker countries around and colonizing non-Western places. Fascists grabbed power in a number of other countries in the interwar period: Germany, Austria, Greece, Portugal, Spain, and Yugoslavia. And fascist parties popped up in almost every country—even liberal bastions like the UK and France. Folks like Adolf Hitler admired what Mussolini did, although Hitler used race to define his party and political aims more than other fascists did. World War II basically brought an end to fascism everywhere except Spain.[6] So, fascism was a pretty short-lived ideology, but it sure did a lot of damage.

Blame it on the Great Depression

The classic narrative of interwar Europe goes something like this: European economies sucked after the Great War, but the Americans were having a ball. When the Americans realized their "roaring twenties" fun was based on (fake) Monopoly Money,[7] the Stock Market crashed. And since Western economies were linked, the Depression that started in the USA spread to Europe. Governments struggled to solve big problems, especially unemployment of 25 percent or more, and extreme political solutions like fascism and communism became more appealing. Those ideologies then trained their sites on each other and went to war. The Depression, in other words, pushed ideologies to the extreme and helped prompt conflict that turned into another world war.

While that story simplifies a lot of crazy stuff, it does capture the importance of major economic swings in this era. It also shows how connected the economies of Europe and the United States were. Who loaned money to whom changed after the Great War. The United States went from being a debtor nation (largely *taking* money from wealthy European investors) to being a creditor nation (serving as the sugar daddy *giving* money to struggling European economies). Today we talk a lot about globalization, but already in the 1920s Western economies relied upon each other and their colonies in important ways. And governments were quite involved in people's economic lives. Most European states after World War I offered some social welfare benefits like support for retirement, unemployment benefits, or assistance with healthcare. Governments also helped direct investment in increasingly large and complex industrial economies. So, yeah, if one major economy fell apart, others were going to suffer too.

---

[5]Ideally black or brown. Serious colors. I don't know of any fascists in yellow, green, or pink, but I'd like to believe those guys might have been a little more fun.

[6]Francisco Franco ran a fascist regime in Spain from about 1937 until his death in 1975. Portugal was sort of fascist until 1974.

[7]An appropriate description. Lizzie Magie created The Landlord's Game in 1903, and Charles Darrow turned it into the popular game Monopoly in 1932; it was a big hit during the 1930s (Mary Pilon, "Monopoly," *The Guardian*, April 11, 2015).

Plus, nationalism usually flew in the face of real economic cooperation. And God knows nationalism was burning after World War I. In fact international economic cooperation and banking policies were some of the things that interwar nationalists raged against the most. International economic cooperation was necessary, but it pissed off nationalists, who attacked that international system as a way to gain power. (This may sound familiar to twenty-first-century American and British readers.) This basic tension of nationalism vs. internationalism was a major problem after World War I. Nowhere was that more evident than in Germany.

The Weimar Republic and Third Reich

You knew we'd talk about Germany, right? I mean, this chapter is about the period between the two world wars, and Germany was, like, right in there for both of those. At the end of Chapter 9, we saw that Germany was left holding the tab after the massive bar fight that was World War I.[8] The German revolution at the end of the war finally stopped the fighting, but the Social Democratic leaders of the revolution had to take the blame for the war and figure out how to pay for it. Conservatives in Germany immediately blamed them for stabbing Germany in the back. And when some French African soldiers were stationed in the occupied Rhineland area on Germany's western border, conservatives really freaked out. Their presence crystalized right-wing ideas about race, gender, and the Versailles Peace Treaty.

In 1919, German political thinkers gathered in the city of Weimar to write a constitution for the new republic. That's why we often call the German government after 1918 the *Weimar Republic*. It's just a nickname. The technical name was still the German Empire. No one changed their business cards. The Weimar Republic protected rights and offered universal adult suffrage and generous social welfare benefits. The Weimar constitution in fact created one of the most progressive democracies in the world. Right on, Germans. So how did this situation produce Hitler and the Nazis?

Well, things didn't start off so well for the Weimar Republic. Getting blamed for the worst conflict in human history and having to pay for it will do that. Germany was supposed to pay $31 billion in gold or other tangible goods in war reparations. No way that was happening, so the French took over some of Germany's prime industrial area to extract that fee directly. Not a popular move in Germany. When gold and industrial goods began to flow out, the only way for Germany to keep paying war reparations was to print money and buy foreign currency. That made things worse. Starting in late 1921, Germany experienced *hyperinflation*, which meant the value of its currency fell exponentially. By November 1923, one US dollar would get you 4.2 trillion German Marks. A loaf of bread would run you about 4 billion Marks. It was often cheaper for people to burn cash as fuel.

---

[8]And yes, there are a lot of good memes about World War I as bar fight.

This hyperinflation was tough on everyone, but especially if you had any savings. I mean, having a 100,000-Mark savings account in 1920 defined you as wealthy. Three years later you couldn't even buy a cup of coffee with that. Hyperinflation thus hit the middle class especially hard, which weakened their belief in the Weimar Republic. In 1924, US banks restructured Germany's reparations payments, stabilizing Germany's economy and setting up a period of relative peace and success there for the rest of the 1920s. The same conservatives who were mad about the "stab in the back" and the hyperinflation now couldn't believe that big, awesome Germany had to be bailed out by *the Americans*. The shame! This bailout also created a kind of dicey economic circle in Figure 10.2.

Here's how the economic impact of the Great War helped empower the Nazis. See, wars are expensive, but the First World War really cost a lot. The British and French had to borrow money from American banks during the war. So, they were bleeding Germany in order to pay debts to America. But now the Americans were helping to fund the Germans. Money just flowed in one big, happy circle. And it was happy for a while. Times were pretty good in Germany in the mid 1920s. Their politics kind of worked; Nazis and other annoying groups were weak. German films were great again; the beer flowed. The international community accepted Germans back into the fold. Unfortunately, the happy circle of cash flow was built on US stock speculation and inflated stock prices. And when the US Stock Market crashed in October 1929, it messed up this whole system. Banks failed everywhere and so did companies; industrial production plummeted. As companies weakened or failed, they laid people off. By 1930 or so, unemployment was up to 25 percent or more in most Western countries, including Germany. People called for political change everywhere.

Enter the Nazis and the Commies! In Germany the political extremes had long been saying that the whole system of democracy didn't work, and folks started listening to them. The Communists on the far left and the Nazis on the far right gained popularity by attacking the Weimar Republic and by fighting each other in the street. The Nazi Party

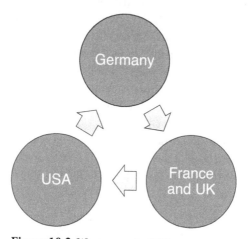

Figure 10.2 War payments, 1920s.

gained the most in this crisis climate since most Germans feared the dire effects communism had had in the Soviet Union.

In the 1932 national elections, the Nazi Party won 37 percent of the German vote, which was a large plurality, or the largest share of votes. The next closest party was the Social Democratic Party, which earned about 20 percent of the vote. Since the Nazis won the most votes, the German President asked their party leader, Adolf Hitler, to form a government. Hitler became Chancellor (Prime Minister) in January 1933. So, that's how the Nazis came to power in Germany. They were elected by the book, and Hitler became Chancellor through the normal means of a parliamentary democracy. Why did so many Germans support the Nazi Party? Five main reasons, more or less in order of importance:

1. Anger at the Versailles Treaty and especially the economic problems it caused.
2. Fear of communism.
3. Nationalism.
4. Radically new solutions to political, economic, and social problems.
5. Antisemitism.[9]

Popular perceptions of the Nazis might lead you to believe that the Nazis convinced Germans to blame everything on Jews. Certainly, Hitler and most Nazi Party members saw an imaginary conflict between Jews and Germans (or "Aryans") as the major fault line in German society. And plenty of Germans were, like many Europeans, mildly antisemitic enough consider some of the Nazi arguments against Jews. But the other reasons listed here motivated voters much more. And Hitler didn't "brainwash" Germans into hating Jews. No, it's more complicated and depressing that we go from Germany as a generally tolerant democracy to a regime that carried out the Holocaust.

And now, meet the *Third Reich*! That was another nickname. The first Reich, in case you're curious, was the Holy Roman Empire (or *Reich*, which existed 800 to 1806), and the second Reich was the German Empire (1871–1918). Calling the Nazi government the "Third Reich" connected it to these historical regimes. Have you ever wondered where the term "Nazi" came from? Hitler's party was named the N̲a̲tionalso̲z̲ialistische *Deutscher Arbeiter Partei* (or National Socialist German Worker's Party). So, yeah, even for Germans, "Nazi" was much easier. Anyway, Hitler and the Nazi Party may have come to power all legit and legal-like, but things did not stay that way. In February 1933, only about a month after Hitler formed a government, the German Reichstag (parliament) caught fire. We're still not sure who did it, but the Nazis quickly blamed communists. Parliament voted to give the Chancellor and President emergency powers, something written into that fine Weimar constitution. They used these powers to attack leaders of the Social Democratic Party and especially the Communist Party and eventually outlaw these groups. The government also passed "Laws for the Protection of the State and

---

[9]You might be used to seeing it written "anti-Semitism." I'm calling it "antisemitism," because there's no such thing as Semites to be against. So the term "antisemitism" recognizes that it's a real sentiment—hatred of Jews—with a bogus name.

People (*Volk*)" that removed Jews from most government positions. You have now exited the land of political legitimacy and legality. Welcome to authoritarian dictatorship.

But most Germans didn't care. They were loving it. Stuff was getting done, baby! The Nazis had made their plans clear, and they weren't good for communists or gay men or Jews. The regime didn't hide what they were up to. You bet they opened concentration camps. You could take tours and read newspaper articles about them. Most Germans, then and later, saw the 1930s as pretty good times, when the economy was improving and their country was flexing again.

All the bad, scary stuff the Nazi regime is rightly infamous for—persecuting minorities, war, genocide—took time to develop. For instance, after the 1933 laws that stripped Jews of some rights came the 1935 Nuremberg Laws, which officially made Jews second-class citizens. In November 1938 the state supported attacks on Jewish shops and synagogues. This event, known as "The Night of Broken Glass" (or *Kristallnacht*), demonstrated that Jews' property and rights no longer mattered Germany. At the time, Jews comprised less than one-half of one percent of the population. Unfortunately, not enough of the rest of the 99.7 percent of the population cared to halt the regime's persecution. And, yes, maybe they could have. If you think the regime didn't listen to its populace, I would offer the example of the regime's murder between 1939 and 1941 of around 250,000 mentally handicapped citizens. Eventually, individuals and religious leaders spoke against this action, and the regime stopped it in 1941. Stopped. Popular support might have been manipulated, but it mattered in Hitler's regime.

The Third Reich was powerful, technologically sophisticated, ruthless, and focused on advancing the Nazi ideology, but it only accomplished as much as it did because of broad support for its policies. Certainly this regime used fear, but millions of Germans gladly and proudly helped Hitler's government. After all, the Nazis seemed to be solving problems. Unemployment went down; eventually Germany broke the Versailles Treaty everyone hated. There were cheap radios, affordable Volkswagens,[10] and the Autobahn! Honestly the Third Reich was doing the same thing economically everyone else in the West was doing, using government spending to help revive the economy. Getting out from underneath the massive burden of the Versailles Treaty helped, so the country could dig into its significant industrial economy. Some of this stuff should look like, yes, Enlightenment ideas: nationalism, fixing the economic system, making politics work better, even engineering society to benefit most citizens (at the expense of some minorities). Right? After 1933 things just kept getting better for most Germans.

And Hitler was at the center of it all. In 1934 he assumed the title of *Führer* or "Leader." He made great promises—break the Versailles Treaty, put Germans to work, rearm Germany, take back lost territory—and delivered every time (at least until some setbacks in World War II). Oddly enough, Hitler did not oversee a tightly organized system. In fact, the regime was built partly on competition within the government. That was an

---

[10]The name means "people's car," and Germans could buy them for about 1000 Reichsmarks or $140, which is about $2,500 or £2,000 today.

inefficient way to rule, but it made Hitler the ultimate arbiter and, we'll see in Chapter 11, helped fuel mass murder during the Second World War.

Meanwhile, back in the USSR

When you think of the Soviet Union, I bet you think about:

- One-party or one-man dictatorship.
- Police state.
- Cold.
- Powerful military.
- Lots of red.
- Aggressive ideological nationalism.
- State-regulated economic egalitarianism.

Soviet Russia claimed to be a *Marxist* state, so where do we find such ideas in Marx? We don't. All the fundamental characteristics of the Soviet Union came from leaders' attempts to adapt Marxist ideas to Russian conditions. That's right: the USSR was not very Marxist. See, Marx anticipated socialist revolutions in Western Europe first. But Lenin and his pals were not willing to wait a hundred years for Russia to catch up with the West. So, Lenin first decided that peasant farmers could be solid proletariat workers. *Voilà*, large working class. Next, Lenin directed a dedicated revolutionary elite, a vanguard, to stir up support for socialism and then make a revolution happen. That flew in the face of Marx's idea of spontaneous, inevitable revolution. Once in power, things got real for the Bolsheviks.

After the Great War ended, they had to fight a civil war from 1918 to 1921 against Everyone. Else. In. The. World. And I do mean everyone. During the Civil War every other political group in Russia, from moderate socialists to raving monarchists, attacked the Communists.[11] So did troops from the USA, UK, France, Czechoslovakia, Poland, Italy, China, and Japan, among others. Bad news for Communist leaders, who were mainly a bunch of bespectacled intellectuals. But they managed to win by making drastic changes. First, they nationalized (which means: took over) all private property under the name of "war communism." Okay, government-controlled resources? Check. Next, Leon Trotsky, Lenin's right-hand man, created a powerful Red Army by recruiting former tsarist officers and using traditional military hierarchy and discipline. Ready to fight a civil war? Done. Finally, the new regime created a new secret police based mainly on the old tsarist secret police. Way to stamp out opposition? Affirmative.

---

[11]They changed their name from "Bolsheviks" to "Communists." "Bolshevik" meant "minority," which wasn't very inspiring. And calling themselves "Communists" helped solidify their false narrative that they were putting Marx's plans into place.

These emergency measures worked so well that Soviet leaders kept most of them going after they won the Civil War. They did pull back some control of the economy and allowed people to own and use some private property. Yes, other political parties were outlawed, but the Communist Party gave people a forum to argue and hash out the best direction for the country. Likewise, Soviet citizens gained a bit more cultural freedom in the 1920s, as long as their work promoted the revolution or the collective. Not exactly a liberal democracy, but this Union of Soviet Socialist Republics (USSR), as it was now called, empowered citizens to help build socialism. Sounds like some Enlightenment action to me! Even after Lenin died in 1924, Soviet leaders continued to balance capitalism and state-run socialism. Times were pretty good in the mid-1920s Soviet Union. Until Uncle Joe came to town.

Josef Stalin (1878–1953) had worked with Lenin since 1905 and served important roles in the new Bolshevik regime. Stalin was close to Lenin but definitely not one of his likely successors. In fact, Lenin didn't fully trust Stalin (go figure!). After Lenin died, Stalin used his position as Communist Party Secretary to outmaneuver other leaders. By 1928 he was the head of the USSR and quickly got rid of opponents. In fact over the next six or seven years, Stalin knocked off anyone whom he thought might have ever been or could be an opponent. He exiled, jailed, and killed thousands of the very revolutionaries who had helped build the Soviet Union, often after elaborate show trials.[12] Stalin also created a cult around Lenin (easier to do with a dead guy) and gradually installed himself as Lenin's natural heir. He tended to shoot those who thought otherwise.

Stalin was of course violent, paranoid, and jealous, but he recognized something his fellow Russian revolutionaries did not: Russia could not expect communist revolutions elsewhere to help them and would have to go it alone. Stalin decided that Russia must catch up with the West by industrializing at a break-neck pace. First they had to squeeze all they could out of the farmers who still made up the vast majority of Russia's workforce. To do that, Soviet leaders began an enormous process called Collectivization. They brought farmers together to work in factory-like "collective farms" instead of on inefficient little private plots. This idea did not go over well with peasant farmers, who had always only dreamed of owning more land. They burned their crops and killed their livestock rather than let the government take them. Way to stick it to the man, peasants! Unfortunately, all that burning, killing, and craziness led to a great famine, especially in Ukraine, from which 5 or 6 million people died. It was bad. So bad that, in 1943, when things were mighty bleak for the Allies during World War II, Stalin told British Prime Minister Winston Churchill (1874-1965) that, "this is bad, but not as bad as Collectivization was."

Never one to dwell much on past mistakes or murders, Stalin forged[13] ahead with industrialization, even while Collectivization was literally going up in flames. Pushing these two major economic changes at once seriously upended Russia's social order. To

---

[12]For example, Stalin kicked out his main rival, Leon Trotsky. Eventually Soviet agents tracked him down and murdered him in Mexico in 1940 with a pick axe!

[13]Btw "Stalin" means "steel" in Russian, so "Stalin forged" is kind of a joke. I warned you about the history dad jokes . . .

make matters worse, the police were ordered to shoot thousands of people who might be resisting collectivization and industrialization. "But, comrades, we don't have thousands of people resisting in our districts," some officers told their superiors in Moscow. "Oh, sure you do," replied leaders, "find 20,000 enemies of the state to kill by Tuesday, comrades." Right, and this being scary times in Russia, the district cops would go shoot 21,000 to show their enthusiasm. Here's how the new math worked in Stalin's Russia: collectivization and industrialization = support for Mother Russia = support for Stalin. Therefore, *not* supporting these economic changes = treason/opposing Stalin = death.

I have bad news: it worked. Sure, millions of people from all levels of society died or got sent to Siberia, but the Soviet Union somehow turned into a powerful industrial nation by the mid-1930s. Production in all areas, even agriculture, rose dramatically. Whole new industries popped up that had not existed in the 1920s. Westerners knew things were tough in Russia but couldn't help but admire all the Soviets had accomplished. (Tight media censorship kept images of dead, starved peasants out of Western newspapers.) That might have been one of the reasons they eventually allied with the USSR against Germany. Stalin's repressive Soviet Union of the late 1930s was radically different than Lenin's more open-ended regime of the early 1920s. It was much stronger, far more centralized, and even less Marxist. Of course Stalin and other Soviet leaders always used Marxist language, but the lived reality in the USSR was far from the classless, stateless utopia Marx had imagined. In fact (spoiler alert!) the growing gulf between utopian Marxist rhetoric and people's daily lives will ultimately undermine the Soviet Union later in the twentieth century.

The Spanish Civil War as dress rehearsal for World War II

Tensions between these big ole ideas came to a head in Spain. In the mid-1930s, Europe's two powerful authoritarian states, Nazi Germany and Soviet Russia, were defining themselves against each other. The Nazis claimed to be the only force stopping communism from taking over Europe, and the Soviets said they were leading the fight against fascism. By 1936 they were already fighting each other indirectly in the Spanish Civil War. Lots of other people were too. Troops from France, Italy, Britain, Mexico, and the United States fought in the Spanish Civil War. Just an old-fashioned, international, ideological, Spanish hootenanny!

The conflict in Spain began in 1931, when socialists and liberals won a majority in national elections, created a Republic, and kicked out the king. Spanish conservatives—especially the Church, large landowners, and military officers—opposed this new regime. By 1936, these conservatives rallied around General Francisco Franco (1892–1975) and tried to overthrow the Republic. While the Republic had fairly broad support among Spanish citizens, its leaders were often divided. Plus, the groups supporting Franco had greater resources, including support from fascist Italy and Nazi Germany—like German planes and air force personnel. *Gracias.* Fascists in Spain used those planes to carry out, among other things, the first aerial bombing of civilians in the Basque town of Guernica

EXPOSITION INTERNATIONALE PARIS 1937

114. - VUE D'ENSEMBLE PRISE DU TROCADERO

Figure 10.3 Paris World Expo, 1937.

in April 1937. This bombing was particularly terrifying and disturbing since it was totally unexpected. The attack showed that civilians were becoming targets in war, not just collateral damage. Go look up "Guernica" by Spanish artist Pablo Picasso (1881–1973) to see his abstract, modernist mural commemorating the attack. It's a great example of how well non-realistic art portrayed emotions like terror and surprise.

Picasso's mural first appeared at the 1937 Paris World Expo. This image from the Expo (Figure 10.3) offers a pretty good sense of how things stood in 1937. On the left we see the solemn, square Nazi German pavilion with a big eagle on top. (Compensating for anything, Herr Hitler?) Right across the way you have the dramatic Soviet pavilion with flowing figures holding up a sickle, the symbol of the USSR.[14] Squeezed between these representations of fascism and communism is the Eiffel tower, a symbol of French democracy. Since fascists and communists were already at war in Spain, this image encapsulates Europe's major ideological conflict, which threatened to spill into another world war.

Up next: World War II

Remember that time in 1914 when Europeans anticipated a war and then got super excited when the fighting began? This time people again recognized the possibility of

---

[14]The image of a man and woman working together indicates that, yes, women had official equality in the Soviet Union. But if the symbol had been a broom, dish, or diaper, the dude would not have been holding it! In other words, equality to work *outside* the home did not mean equal sharing of duties *at* home.

war but knew it would be a mess. Most folks in Europe viewed the possibility of war in the late 1930s with resignation or dread. Little did they know how bad it would be. In the last chapter, we took apart the start of World War I because other nations—not just Germany—were to blame for its start? Well, this time it was totally the Germans' fault.

Germany's expansion in the late 1930s kicked off a conflict that would pit the Axis Powers (Germany, Italy, Japan, etc.) against the Allied Powers (United Kingdom, France, Russia, the United States, and Co.). Now, if you get technical about it, this *world* war had already started in 1931, when Japan invaded China. But the alliance system that made the war into an international conflict grew out of Europe. Hitler and the Nazi Party had made very clear that they thought Germany should break the Versailles Treaty and be able to rearm. The Third Reich began quietly rearming soon after the Nazis came to power, purchasing, for example, some really bad-ass "tractors" from the Krupp arms manufactory. In 1935, Hitler formally announced that Germany would ignore restrictions on the German military and begin rearming. That year the United Kingdom signed an arms agreement with Germany that ensured the British navy would always be five times larger than the German navy. The agreement gave tacit approval to Germany's breaking the Versailles Treaty. Both sides laughed up their sleeves at the other. "Silly Brits," the Germans snickered, "they don't realize that airplanes, not ships, matter now." "Silly Germans," the Brits chuckled, "you need sea power to control an empire and wage world war." In the next chapter we'll see who has the last laugh.

In 1936, Germany reoccupied the area along the Rhine River that had been demilitarized after World War I. The move was dicey. In fact, German generals told Hitler, "look, buddy, we can't beat the French here, so if they call our bluff and we get humiliated again, your ass is gone." "No worries," responded Hitler, "no one will go to war over land that is already German." Score one for the Führer, and German troops moved into the Rhineland. Germany continued to expand based mainly on the idea of national self-determination. In March 1938, Germany annexed Austria into the Third Reich. Hitler was Austrian, after all, and made clear that he wanted to create a Germany for all German speakers. Now, please don't get all *Sound of Music* on me here and claim that the Austrians resisted like the von Trapp family did. Austrians welcomed the German military with flowers at the border. In fact, the only problem the German military experienced when they "invaded" Austria was running out of gas because they faced no resistance and thus got *farther* than expected! To cap it off, Hitler spoke in Vienna to the largest crowd he ever addressed. Later Austria would claim to be the first victims of Nazi aggression.[15] Ha!

Next, the 3 million Germans living in the Sudetenland, or the western-most part of Czechoslovakia, wanted to join the Third Reich. That area had been given to the Czechs after the First World War for geo-military reasons. In September 1938, German, French, and British representatives met in Munich and agreed to let Germany incorporate the Sudetenland. Note that the Czechs were not invited to what became their funeral. British Prime Minister Neville Chamberlain (1869–1940) returned home especially pleased,

---

[15]To be sure, Austrian communists, gay men, gypsies (Sinti and Roma), and especially Jews suffered.

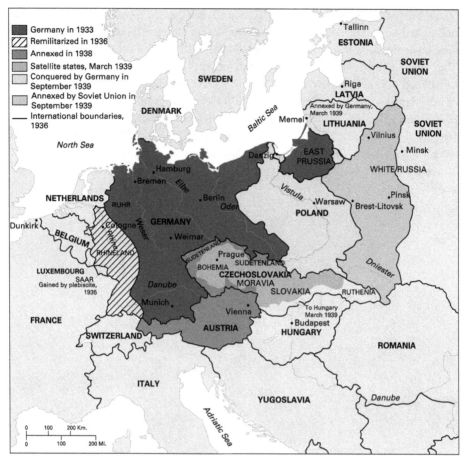

Map 10.1 German expansion, 1936–9.

claiming that Britain would have "peace with honor." In October, the Sudetenland joined the Third Reich. In March 1939, the Slovaks bolted and formed their own country. The Germans then took over the rest of what had been Czechoslovakia. Oops. So, some British and French thoughts on German foreign policy aims:

- Break Versailles Treaty: well, okay, maybe we were a little harsh in 1919.
- Create greater Germany: makes us uncomfortable, but we kinda get the idea.
- Need for Lebensraum or "living space" beyond Germany: now, hold on a minute.

Germany said it was done taking over places, but …they did want the Polish city of Danzig too because it was also mostly German. The Allies chose to take a stand and protect Poland against Nazi aggression. If fighting broke out, Germany would once again have to fight a two-front war: British/French in the west and Soviets in the east. That implied alliance was one of the reasons the British and French could (finally) stand up boldly to Germany.

So the world was shocked to learn in August 1939 that the Germans and the Russians had signed a non-aggression pact. These two powers, who hated each other intensely and seemed about ready to go to war throughout the 1930s, agreed not to fight for ten years. They also divided Poland between each other. The United Kingdom and France threatened war, if Germany attacked Poland. But Germany was feeling good, with its eastern flank secure. So, on September 1, 1939 Germany invaded Poland on the pretense of reclaiming Danzig. World War II had begun. Before the invasion, maybe a half million Jews lived in Germany. The Third Reich conquered its half of Poland in about three weeks, at which point the Jewish population shot up to 2 million. As we'll see next, the war and the Holocaust were closely linked, often in surprising ways. But definitely not good ways.

CHAPTER 11
DOWNHILL ALL THE WAY: WORLD WAR II AND THE HOLOCAUST

Critics call the 1942 film *Casablanca* one of the greatest Hollywood movies of all time for good reason. It features a terrific cast, is shot well, has memorable music, and centers on a poignant romance. *Casablanca* is also driven by a major ideological conflict at the heart of World War II: fascism vs. democracy. About two-thirds of the way into the film (around seventy-two minutes into it, a moment often called the "golden section" of many pieces),[1] these two concepts do battle through music. The two male protagonists are discussing the woman they both love upstairs at the nightclub one of them owns. They hear downstairs a group singing the German military song "The Watch on the Rhine." Now, Casablanca was in the French colony of Morocco, which at this time was controlled by the Vichy French government, the part of France the Germans did not take over in World War II but still influenced. German soldiers therefore were "honored guests" but not necessarily loved. Neither man is pleased to hear a bunch of Germans belting out a nationalist tune. Rick, the nightclub owner, tries to avoid politics but helped the Republicans in the Spanish Civil War. Victor is a Czech resistance leader who escaped from a German concentration camp and is trying to flee to America to continue his work against the Germans.

Upon hearing the Germans singing, Victor walks up to the house band and demands that they play "La Marseillaise," the French national anthem and French Revolution song of liberty, equality, and fraternity. The band leader looks over to Rick for approval, and Rick nods. That nod actually marks the turning point of the whole film, when Rick's idealism overcomes his cynicism and bitterness. The band starts playing "La Marseillaise," and pretty much everyone in the bar joins them, eventually drowning out the Germans with emotional, enthusiastic singing. I don't think the filmmaker, Michael Curtiz, intended it, but there's a fabulous moment when these two songs, performed in the same key, perfectly mash up. As the French song takes over the German one, other characters besides Rick begin to change and support the French ideals. You can find this scene online easily.

An American film made as the USA was entering the war, *Casablanca* portrays World War II as a conflict between liberating Enlightenment ideals represented by the French anthem of freedom vs. controlling militarism embodied in a nationalist German song.

---

[1] You can find countless examples of the "golden section" in music, literature, film, and other forms of culture. Often at that point about 67 percent into it, something dramatic happens that changes the meaning of the piece and sets up a dramatic end. Go check out your favorite movie or song or book: I bet you'll find that something critical happens at almost exactly two-thirds of the way into it.

There's no mention of Jews or genocide in this movie, nor does communism figure here. Nevertheless, the film makes clear that this war was about universal ideals. Unlike the First World War, which Europeans fought over vague ideals like culture, nationalism, imperialism, and pride, this conflict pitted big ideas that were absolute and designed to fix all of humanity. Plenty of people who thought that the Great War was a stupid waste nevertheless concluded that this conflict was about the fate of everyone in Europe and maybe the world.

Building the argument

This chapter is kind of the golden section of this book.[2] World War II and the Holocaust reflect the most violent expression of Enlightenment ideas in the modern world. By now you shouldn't be surprised that the Enlightenment can do crazy good and crazy bad. Chapter 10 illustrated the major ideological conflict in Europe between fascism, communism, democracy, freedom, and capitalism. And let's not forget our powerful, omnipresent friend nationalism. These concepts battled each other big time in the Second World War. This chapter also traces the continued growth of powerful states. In the First World War, European nations realized how to make use of citizens and material resources in total war. World War II shows what happens when states mobilize to an even greater extent for ideological conflict. States also used propaganda far more effectively in World War II (like in *Casablanca*). This conflict continues, as well, the story of science as a secular religion in the modern world. Unfortunately, science comes off looking kinda bad in World War II since combatant nations mostly used it to develop more effective technologies to kill and control people.

The Second World War was of course a total war. While fewer soldiers were killed than in World War I, way more civilians died. All together about 60 million people perished (maybe more, depending on how you count), and around 60 percent of those were civilians. Military forces intentionally aimed to kill civilians. Just as home and battle front were closely linked, so too were the various areas or "theaters" of war—Europe, Asia, North Africa. We remain focused on Europe but will consider the impact fighting elsewhere had on the war's outcome in Europe. Alliances morphed some over the war, but basically you got your Allied Powers (Britain, France, Russia, USA, and friends) vs. the Axis Powers (Germany, Japan, Italy, and others).

Finally, this chapter emphasizes the close link between the war and the Holocaust. As the originator of the war and the genocidal mass murder we call the Holocaust, Germany receives close attention in this chapter. We learned last chapter about the Third Reich's development and geo-political aims in the 1930s. Here we'll consider Germans' motives for murdering over 6 million Jews and about 5 million other people the Third Reich

---

[2]Seriously, the math works out. This chapter is about two-thirds of the way through the book, and the year 1942 is about two-thirds of the way through the main years I'm covering. It's magic!

deemed "unworthy of life." How did those genocidal actions fit with the fighting of a world war? We also look at the experiences of Holocaust victims.

The blitzkrieg bop: speedy German victories, 1939–41

When we last left our story, Germany had invaded and quickly taken over half of Poland by mid-September 1939. *Blitzkrieg*, by the way, means "lighting war" and involved bombing enemies before attacking with quick-moving, mechanized ground forces; it was very effective for Germany. Generally the lines of battle in the Second World War moved much quicker than in the First. Anyway, the UK and France had promised to stand up to Hitler, to support the Poles, to teach the grabbing Third Reich a lesson. Two days after Germany invaded Poland, the British and the French got right to it and declared war on Germany. That'll show 'em! Then these allies gathered their strength, and did nothing. I mean really, did you expect them to jump in between Germany and Russia, both of whom were happily carving up Poland? Not a lot happened outside of Poland in the winter of 1939–40. Well, German warships and submarines began attacking French and British ships around the world, including passenger liners. The German military in Poland immediately began clearing space there for bringing Germans to live there. And, yes, "clearing space" meant exiling and killing civilians, especially Jews. In other words, the very first volleys showed what kind of war it would be: brutal, mechanized, international, fast-moving, and aimed at civilians.

In the spring of 1940, Germany was ready to turn west. This time their pact with Russia meant they wouldn't have to fight a two-front war (at least not yet). Germany pretty quickly ran over Norway, Denmark, Luxembourg, the Netherlands, and Belgium. In May, German forces invaded France and were headed to the English Channel to cut off and capture the bulk of the British army, which was trapped there. Effective defensive fighting plus a herculean effort by the British air force, navy, and, like every little private British boat on the southern coast managed to get over 300,000 soldiers (some French, mostly British) out at Dunkirk.

Despite this major setback, German forces made it to Paris by June 14, 1940. Two weeks later, Germany forced French leaders to sign an armistice in the same railroad car in which Germany had to surrender in 1918. Ouch. Along the way they massacred black soldiers from French colonies, continuing to signal their racialized war aims. After declaring martial law in Paris, Hitler visited the city for the first time and checked out the sites. Like any good tourist, he took a picture with the Eiffel Tower and sent it back to his girlfriend. Seriously. See Figure 11.1.

This picture naturally alarmed people when it was released to the press around the world. It's still pretty alarming today! Aside from the obvious shock of Germany's quick defeat of France, the image seemed to say: you're next, Britain. From June through September, German bombers pounded the southern half of the United Kingdom, in hopes of convincing British leaders to pull out of the war. Instead, the Battle of Britain strengthened British resolve and increased assistance from the USA. Because of weather

Figure 11.1 Springtime in Paris. Wish you were here. Did I mention I own this now?

and conflicts elsewhere, Germany had to put off invading Britain. And, although they didn't admit it, they had to notch this one as their first big defeat. Still, Germany and Hitler in particular were patting themselves on the back by the end of 1940. The Third Reich had conquered seven countries, including one major enemy, France. It had also radically expanded the territory to be supplied and the number of "state enemies"— above all, Jews—it controlled in Europe.

Also in 1940, fighting in Africa and the Middle East began to influence German war plans. Controlling a big empire and waging war around the world demanded a large, steady supply of oil and control of important transportation avenues. Plus, believe it or not, Hitler really wanted to invade Russia—you know, the largest and coldest country on earth. Germany therefore tried to take over Middle Eastern and North African oil fields. The British had colonized many of these oil-rich countries and fought Germany in all those spots. The Italians, bless their hearts, tried to help Germany. Frankly, Italy wasn't really super ready for war, but Mussolini wanted to press Italian interests in Africa and in the Balkans.

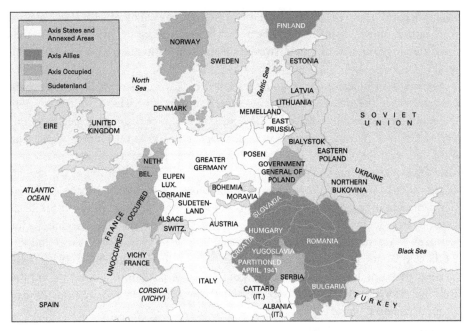

Map 11.1 Europe, spring 1941.

In the summer of 1940, Italy took over British Somaliland, Ethiopia, and Libya but were driven out by British forces. Likewise, Italy tried to capture Greece but couldn't hold it either. Eventually Mussolini had to ask, um, well, you know, if, like, Germany could, uh, maybe help out a bit? Hitler was concerned that losing these strategic colonies would endanger oil supplies and maybe get Mussolini kicked out of power. So of course German troops came running. In North Africa in particular, the great German general and strategist Erwin Rommel (1891–1944) helped retake Libya and push British forces back into Egypt. By spring of 1941, Germany was mainly focused on the upcoming invasion of Russia and had to pull troops from Africa, strengthening the British position there. Also a coup in Yugoslavia demanded Italian and German invasion, which turned out to require many more troops than anticipated. In short, Germany entered the big game of invading Russia a little more distracted and less prepared than planned.

This time it's totaler war!

Chapter 9 described the Great War as a total war, one in which all state resources went toward the fighting. Well, the Second World War made the first one seem, I'm afraid, not quite so total. The majority of deaths in World War II were civilians for three reasons. First, the war was highly mechanized and fast moving. Even when soldiers tried to avoid harming civilians, the fact that millions of soldiers moved across Europe, often in airplanes, tanks, and trucks, meant that civilians got in the way. These forces bombed each other and, as in World War I, shelled the hell out of each other with very big guns. And as they moved soldiers often helped themselves to crops, livestock, and other foodstuff along the way, or they destroyed them. Civilians in many places suffered as a result.

Second, the Holocaust. Other countries killed civilians as part of the war, but only Germany made the systematic murder of several groups of people an explicit war aim. Other military forces committed atrocities. Russian troops, for example, killed Poles and treated German civilians especially violently (rape, murder) as they moved west at the war's end. But the fact that the Third Reich murdered over 11 million people for ideological reasons, mostly during the war, accounts for a large portion of the civilian deaths. Shortly we'll dive deeper into the Holocaust. It's important here to note that German soldiers began murdering civilians as soon as the war started. The Third Reich stated clearly that it wanted to create "living space" (*Lebensraum*) in Eastern Europe for Germans to resettle there. That meant that soldiers were instructed to expel and kill Polish clergy and elites, as well as Jews, when they invaded in September 1939. These murders were not just war-time atrocities of revenge or passion. They were part of the Third Reich's war goals. The Nazi state aimed in this war to create a European society free of racial "enemies," above all Jews.

Third, civilians were targets. Let's be clear: everybody was killing civilians. Above all, military forces dropped bombs on cities. Now, air forces certainly aimed at strategic targets: military bases, factories making war materials, and railroad lines transporting troops. And civilians died around those places. But both Allied and Axis war plans intentionally destroyed enemy cities, regardless of their military value. Both sides hoped that bombing civilians and razing cities would weaken their enemies' will to fight. That did not happen. Bombing mostly led to shaking fists against the sky and bold speeches, and then more bombing followed. The Allied fire-bombing of Dresden and American use of nuclear bombs on Hiroshima and Nagasaki were exclamation points at the end of the war to this policy of bombing civilian populations. Beyond death and destruction, bombing civilians made the war a daily part of many Europeans' lives, usually in horrific ways—although some folks found airplane dogfights pretty entertaining.

This total war reached deep into the lives of people at home. Even in places where there was no fighting, the line between battle front and home front was fluid. Within a year of the war's outbreak, Russia and especially Germany occupied large parts of Europe. In the ideological context of this war, that occupation was rarely pleasant, even for those not killed or imprisoned. Most occupied populations suffered in small, daily ways—less food, curfews, forced labor, having to tell their occupiers how awesome they were. Occupied populations often resisted their new lords through small acts like work slowdowns or more dramatic organized paramilitary groups. In many cases, the amount of daring, armed resistance has been greatly exaggerated since World War II ended. Those stories make exciting novels and movies and more satisfying explanations of people's behavior than the dull, dispiriting reality that most people cooperated with occupying forces. What would you rather tell your grandchildren, that you risked your life to resist evil Nazi invaders or that you hunkered down and looked away when they took your Jewish neighbors?

And governments restricted consumption. All governments used rationing policies to limit use of food and materials that might help the war effort. Rationing was especially important in places like the United Kingdom, which had imported large portions of its food and suddenly had to survive on much smaller internal food production. In many places in Europe and the United States, people planted "victory gardens" to supplement rationed food. Rations varied all over Europe and changed during the course of the war. Germany, for example, introduced rationing even before invading Poland but generally provided fairly high levels of rationed food for citizens, at least until 1943, when things got tough. Even the U. S. of Consuming A. began rationing food and important war-related materials (gas, oil, rubber, leather, etc.) not long after entering the war in December 1941. And, friends, when Americans can't buy anything they want, you *know* it's a total war! Food rationing usually involved getting a card that stipulated how much of various products you could buy. It was illegal for anyone to sell you more than your allotment. Of course people developed barter systems and black markets to get around restrictions, especially for special occasions.

This all-out total war again greatly impacted gender relations. Even more than in the First World War, governments relied upon women to keep huge war machines going. Again women flooded into factories, and again the "home front" became "feminine" in contrast to the "masculine" war front. Women also served military forces indirectly and, in a few cases, directly in battle. Even as women became more and more important for war efforts across Europe, the hyper-masculinity that defined the war itself ensured that women's roles remained mainly supportive and secondary.

While women had more opportunities for public service, the war also reinforced patriarchy and enhanced men's appreciation of the fraternity of war.[3] That fraternity was natural and necessary, but it also sharpened gender differences and pushed some aspects of toxic masculinity during the war, especially rape. Soldiers took advantage of women sexually for all kinds of reasons, as has almost always been the case during wartime. But the Enlightenment ideologies that drove World War II aims were all built on visions of the world that were partly rooted in fraternity.[4] Fascism and communism especially drew inspiration from the experiences of World War I "front generation" soldiers. All sides treated civilians as enemies to various degrees, so sexual violence against women became an implicit and sometimes explicit war tactic. In short, this total war served both to empower women and reinforce misogynist stereotypes, but the extent of the war's reach significantly reshaped gender relations during and after the fighting.

Also, this total international conflict connected different theaters of war much more directly than in the First World War. There was fighting all over Europe, in North Africa, the Middle East, in Southeast Asia, China, all around the Western Pacific, in Sub-Saharan

[3] I'm looking at you, HBO's *Band of Brothers*.
[4] Recall that fraternity was one of the rallying cries for the liberal democratic ideas of the French Revolution.

Africa, and even some in (or near) South America. All the major combatants fought significantly on at least two fronts. As in World War I, colonial subjects fought each other and for their colonizers. Both the experience of fighting and watching colonial powers fall to Japan would kindle anti-colonial sentiments in many places after the war, as we'll see in Chapter 13. World War II drew soldiers and civilians into battle from all corners of the globe and demonstrated how increasingly connected events and developments around the world had become.

And the rematch for the heavyweight title: Third Reich vs. USSR

Invade Russia? Seriously? Hadn't the Napoleonic Wars and World War I taught Germany anything? Were they really going to fall for one of the classic blunders and get involved in a land war in Asia?[5] Not surprisingly Hitler and most of his generals assumed they were so much more awesome than those previous loser invaders and could therefore bring it to the Russians! Germany most certainly did bring it to the Russians, coming pretty close to capturing Moscow at one point. But in the end the Russian Big Three turned Germany back: cold, space, and human resources. The Third Reich had always planned to invade Russia. That August 1939 non-aggression pact mainly allowed both sides to get ready. Battles elsewhere delayed the German invasion of Russia, "Operation Barbarossa," until June 1941. Hitler and the German military suffered some major illusions about how it would go (see if these sound familiar): they could win quickly before winter set in, Russian soldiers suck, quick attacks would end the Soviet regime, and *natürlich* Germany vould master ze logistics of such a massive operation. German leaders also made plain to their allies that police forces would follow the military and murder Jews in occupied territories.

Indeed, Germany's invasion of the Soviet Union directly connected the war and the Holocaust for three reasons. First, attacking Russia meant that the Germany military would spread into lands where the vast majority of Jews in Europe lived—the rest of Poland and the western part of Russia. See Map 11.3 below. Second, Nazi ideology basically equated communists and Jews. Propaganda had consistently labelled the Soviet Union a "Jewish" regime. But, third, Germany's failure to conquer Russia would force leaders to find more efficient, deadlier ways to get rid of Jews and other "state enemies." So, yeah, Germany's invasion of Russia was kind of a big deal for the whole war. It was stupid, but that's never stopped super tough guys with armies, guns, bombs, and other dangerous stuff at their disposal before.

For sure, the Germans didn't go in there weak. They invaded on June 22, 1941 with 3 million soldiers and another half million from Finland and Romania.[6] Things went really

---

[5]Just gonna say: if you've never seen the 1987 film *The Princess Bride*, from which this line is taken, you're missing out.

[6]Do not think it escaped Hitler that he rocked into Russia with almost six times as many men as Napoleon had 129 years earlier. Well, Hitler didn't go personally, because he wasn't that kind of leader. Hmm, maybe that explains something.

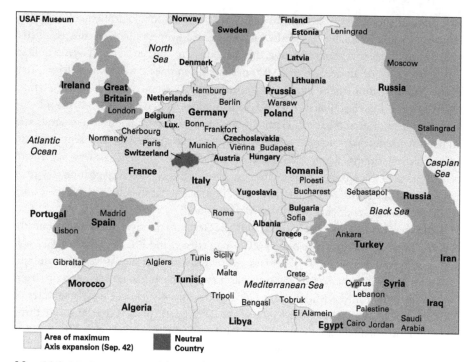

Map 11.2 Maximum extent of the German Empire, 1942.

well for Germany initially. Stalin had helpfully killed all his top officers in the late 1930s and ignored intelligence from France and the United States. Oh, yeah, Germany definitely won the first six weeks, totally killed it. Unfortunately for them, invading a country with eleven time zones is a marathon, not a sprint. And even at the start, some of Russia's ultimate advantages were clear. The massive Russian landmass meant that they could move industrial production behind the lines over and over again and still have, like, half of Asia to spare. And Russians once again burned crops and killed livestock to slow down invaders.[7] Plus, Russian officers may have been inexperienced, but Russian soldiers fought hard. Turns out they weren't cool with Germans invading their land. Also, Slavic folks like White Russians and Ukrainians could have been German pals, but the Germans had other plans:

Ukrainians, White Russians, Latvians and others: OMG, Germans, it's great to see you! Thanks for liberating us from these awful Russian communists. You know how much commies suck, eh?

Germans: *Ja.* Did we mention you're racially inferior? Please line up against this wall.

---

[7]Remember that time in 1812 when the same thing happened to Napoleon?

Third Reich soldiers saw Russians as military, racial, and ideological enemies, so they murdered some Russian POWs. Always great record keepers, the Germans calculated that, within the first year of this battle, they had killed or starved to death over 2 million Russian POWs, or an average of 10,000 per day seven days a week. Guess what? That made Russian troops fight harder and encouraged Russian troops to treat German POWs worse. The Third Reich also used Soviet soldiers and civilians as slave labor in the occupied territories and back in Germany, forcing them to do the most dangerous and difficult work necessary for war while starving them to death. And they sent plenty to concentration camps, where they suffered and died. World War II was filled with atrocities on all sides. But Nazi Germany connected military and racial goals in ways that made systematic murder—not just soldiers killing each other in battle—a central feature of German action. Suddenly Stalin looked pretty good!

Did I mention that Russia is big and cold? The Germans discovered that pretty quickly. See, the Russian autumn more or less = German winter, and Russian winter = German nightmare. And by late 1941, Germany was stretched thin across very hostile and chilly territories into the Soviet Union, just as they were having to pull some troops from that front to fight in the Middle East. German forces got within seventy-five miles of Moscow in late 1941. They tried to starve out Leningrad (or St. Petersburg) for three years and lost 850,000 soldiers in the 1943 Battle of Stalingrad. Throughout the Russian invasion and especially at these major battles, Germans marveled at Russia's ability to keep fighting and keep bringing more materials and men (and sometimes women!) to fight.

The Third Reich's failure to conquer the Soviet Union was *the* turning point in the war. Especially after the massive defeat in February 1943 at Stalingrad, Germany began contracting, and the USSR began expanding. German leaders knew that a two- and possibly three-front war was inevitable, especially since the United States had declared war on Germany in December 1941 as part of its response to Japan's attack on Pearl Harbor. (And in 1943 Allies sent some troops into Italy, as Mussolini's regime fell apart.) The war in Russia would claim the vast majority of wartime soldier casualties, starting in 1942. Back home in Germany, life changed after the 1943 Stalingrad defeat. You may think that in the Third Reich lurking Gestapo agents were tossing German citizens who listened to British radio or made fun of Hitler's mustache into camps. That was not the case (mostly) for the first decade of the Third Reich, but, yes, starting in 1943 the regime clamped down on even the smallest challenges.

Holocaust = World War II = Holocaust

The Holocaust resulted from the combination of a long-term, slowly-developed, rational plan *and* a quick maniacal solution. Scholars have long debated the definition and scope of the Holocaust, but let's call it here Nazi Germany's systematic removal and murder of "state enemies," above all Jews, from 1939 to 1945. We have already seen that German leaders connected the Reich's eastward expansion with the murder of

Jews, Slavic civilians, Russian POWs, and others. German plans included kicking out and killing people in their occupied territory to create space for Germans to move in. As always, it's helpful to consider the long-, medium-, and short-term causes of the Holocaust.

Long-term plans

Hitler and other Nazi leaders had stated in the early 1920s that Jews were the enemy of "Aryan" Germans and should be removed from Europe, if not the Earth. Most Germans didn't really share this goal, but few people in the Third Reich opposed laws that made Jews into second-class citizens. Decrees in 1933 prevented Jews from holding civil service positions. The 1935 Nuremberg Laws formally made Jews second-class citizens. Further restrictions followed the violent November 1938 *Kristallnacht* attacks on Jewish shops and synagogues. The systematic murder of citizens actually began with the killing of mentally and physically handicapped Germans in the fall of 1939. But enough Germans, especially Catholic leaders, freaked out over this program that the regime stopped it in 1941. If you want to keep score, this will be the only time that Germans actively resisted and curbed the Holocaust.

Medium-term plans

Well, they weren't exactly *plans*, but it's important to understand that the strangely chaotic and competitive nature of the Third Reich intensified the Holocaust. One historian has argued that the Third Reich operated as "government without administration," that it was not well-organized and effectively administered.[8] The regime often duplicated functions, which was inefficient and caused disruptive turf wars. Rather than working out clear, competent administration, Hitler preferred these messy competitions. Then he could pick the idea he liked best, and it became official policy. Such bickering ensured that all Third Reich leaders were more concerned about beating out the other guy and winning the Führer's favor than doing what made the most sense.

Hitler always rambled and hollered about an expanded Germany and the desire to get rid of Jews, but he did not explain how to accomplish those aims. In fact, one Nazi Party guy said it was the duty of everyone in the Third Reich "to work towards the Führer along the lines he would wish."[9] Not exactly top-down totalitarian control. But that perspective helped build a whole regime on Hitler's vague yet terrifying vision, while relying upon others to fight for the best way to make it happen. This kind of administrative context had dire implications for victims of Germany's genocidal plans. In 1941 and 1942, when the whole war was in flux, Nazi leaders were duking it out to see who could come up with the best solution to their invented "Jewish problem."

---

[8] Jane Caplan, *Government without Administration* (Oxford: Oxford University Press, 1989).
[9] Ian Kershaw, *Hitler 1889–1936: Hubris* (New York and London: Norton, 1998), xxix.

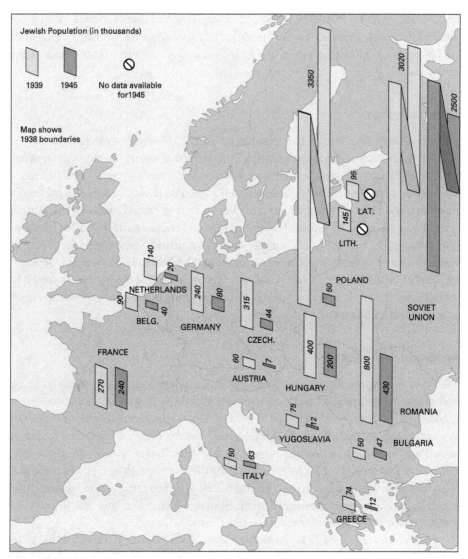

Map 11.3 Number of Jews in Europe.

Short-term plans, namely, conditions of war

So, big Nazi ideas laid out the general aims of what became the Holocaust, and messy Nazi administration created the environment in which those ideas developed. The war then determined the scope of the Holocaust and how it was implemented. We've already seen how brutal the war was on all sides, even if Germany won the Worst Behavior Award. And the mechanized death of this war empowered individuals to slaughter large numbers of people easily, including civilians. German soldiers were thus accustomed to killing soldiers and civilians alike without remorse.

The Third Reich expanded rapidly across Europe from late 1939 until early 1942, and then it slowly collapsed from 1942 to 1945. This process meant that very quickly the Nazi regime took over the territory containing the majority of European Jews. They immediately began the process of removing them but then had to come up with other ways to get rid of them as their empire contracted. The war aim of creating a Jew-free space for German expansion meant that genocide drove decisions as much as military goals did.

The period from late 1941 to early 1942 was especially important. The United States' entry into the war in December 1941 guaranteed a multi-front war and meant that Germany would have to fight two nations with enormous resources (USA and USSR). In January 1942, Third Reich leaders met in Wannsee, a suburb of Berlin, to draw up detailed plans for the Final Solution of the "Jewish problem." They considered what may seem like some wacky ideas. "Hey," said one fella working toward what the Führer wanted, "we got France in our pocket; let's send all the Jews to the French colony of Madagascar ...oh, wait, we forgot to defeat Britain, so we don't control the high seas. Sorry."[10] "Oh, oh, I've got a better idea," said another man in uniform, "let's ship the Jews to Siberia. It's cold and huge and who cares what happens to them." "No can do," said another guy, "we just failed to take Moscow, so we don't exactly have control of Siberia."

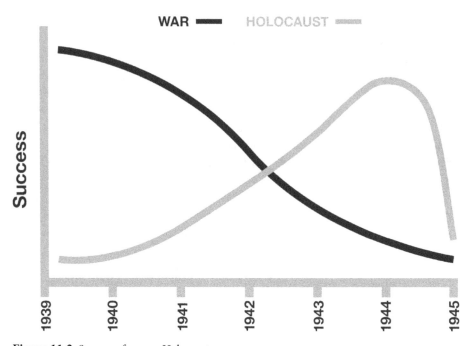

Figure 11.2 Success of war vs. Holocaust.

---

[10]Too bad the Brits weren't there. Remember in Chapter 10 when the British believed they had gotten the better end of that 1935 arms agreement with Germany because they kept a bigger navy? Um-hm.

So, they decided to move Jews from all over Europe to death camps in Eastern Europe and murder them, all 11 million of them. They would also attack others they considered threats to German purity: Gypsies (the Sinti and Roma people), gay men, the mentally handicapped, Slavic leaders like intellectuals or Catholic priests, Jehovah's Witnesses, and others. Starting in the fall of 1941, the men running Auschwitz had been perfecting the use of poison gas Zyklon B to kill mainly Russian POWs. This quick, industrial, scientific method of murder enabled fewer soldiers or camp workers to murder many people efficiently, releasing more military personnel to fight. And it took the lives of thousands of people per day at Auschwitz and other death camps.

Motives of perpetrators

In March of 1942, about 20 to 25 percent of the eventual victims of the Holocaust had been killed and 75 to 80 percent still lived. By February of 1943, those numbers had flip-flopped.[11] So, what happened during these intense eleven months? The simple version you can see in the chart above: pressure from the flagging war effort pushed more urgent and technologically efficient methods of killing. During this period, Nazi Germany used both the efficient method of gassing victims and the old-fashioned method of having soldiers shoot them in the back of the head. The experience of one police battalion, detailed in Christopher Browning's *Ordinary Men*, offers insight into what motivated regular soldiers to murder 83,000 Jews by shooting them individually.

These guys were "ordinary" in practically every way. They were old enough—in their thirties or forties—not to have been educated in the Third Reich. They came from a variety of political backgrounds and were members of Nazi organizations at about the national average. Almost all were married, and most had kids. They had joined a police battalion in order to avoid the worst fighting on the eastern front, so they were not gung-ho warriors. They heard Nazi propaganda at home and in the field but didn't seem to respond too much to that info. Were they forced to go commit these horrible deeds? Did they fear they would suffer if they chose not to pull the trigger? No, their commanding officer gave them opportunities not to participate. And the dozen or so men who chose not take part in the shootings suffered no negative ramifications for their choices. So why did the rest do it? Certainly they were influenced by the brutality of this war and angry that the Allies were bombing their families back in their hometown of Hamburg. But ultimately the greatest motiving factor was peer pressure.

Peer pressure? So, men committing the worst atrocities ever were motivated by the same pressures that teenagers feel at parties when the booze or weed comes out? Sort of. That group of fellow soldiers was critical in the midst of war; they needed to have each other's back. They were given gruesome, unpleasant orders. Sure, they could refuse, and a few did. But those who opted out still had to live with the rest of the guys who carried out the orders. Asking your fellow soldiers—your protection group in a hostile

---

[11]Christopher R. Browning, *Ordinary Men* (New York: HarperCollins, 1992), xv.

environment—to do something you could not or would not, would weaken their trust and support in you.

Eventually this battalion wiped out village after village of Jews in Poland. They got used to murder and wanted to do a "good job" of even this awful task. About a quarter of the victims of the Holocaust died in this face-to-face manner. And while the motives Police Battalion 101 do not apply to every person who carried out the Holocaust, understanding their actions sheds light on how ordinary people did extraordinarily horrible things. Certainly murderous antisemitism and rabid belief in Nazi ideology drove some men, especially the SS[12] soldiers tasked with organizing and directing the Holocaust. But killing over 6 million Jews and 5 million other people required the assistance of millions of regular soldiers and civilians.

Once you realize the scope of the Holocaust, the distinction between the "good" German army and the "bad" Nazi organizations breaks down pretty fast. And other groups assisted the Germans. People in occupied territories like France, Poland, and Ukraine helped Germans find and haul away their Jewish neighbors, sometimes grudgingly, sometimes gladly. So did allies like Hungarians, Romanians, and Italians. In Eastern Europe, where the bulk of the killing took place, Germans relied upon enthusiastic antisemitic helpers for rounding up and killing Jews. In short, millions of "ordinary people" helped carry out this worst genocide in human history. That fact made it messy and difficult to assign blame after the war. It's also way more disturbing than some simplistic, inaccurate view that a few bad men did it all or coerced Germans and others into such violence.

Experiences of Holocaust victims

Here's a big understatement for you: the Holocaust dramatically reshaped life in Europe, especially in central and eastern Europe, where the bulk of the victims had lived and the bulk of the killing occurred. Above all, Jewish life there was forever altered. About 3 million Jews, for example, lived in Poland when Germany invaded in September 1939. Maybe 200,000 remained in 1945. The Holocaust is such a horrific event and offers such profound and disturbing lessons, that it's easy to treat victims as numbers or bodies. We also need to understand the experience of the human beings who became victims of genocide.

By the early twentieth century, Jews in many European countries enjoyed civil liberties and more or less equal rights, despite persistent antisemitism. Thanks, Enlightenment! By the late 1930s, though, Nazi ideology and German expansion had made Jews second-class citizens in Germany and elsewhere in central Europe. Thanks, Enlightenment. In Eastern Europe, antisemitism was woven into politics and policies. There Jews could thrive only in limited urban professions (mainly commercial, cultural, and banking) or

---

[12]SS = *Schutzstaffel* or "security squadron." It was the most elite organization in Nazi Germany that had traditionally protected Hitler and directed the Holocaust. They usually wore black outfits, often made by Hugo Boss. Yep.

in *shtetls*, poor and isolated villages of Jews usually left alone by governments and gentiles. The Soviet Union had formally liberated Jews. By the 1930s, Russian Jews had the same opportunities to advance within the system of Stalinism, and they had the same opportunities to suffer greatly from it.

At the start of the Second World War, therefore, Jews in Europe lived with varying degrees of success and integration into their larger national societies. Jews also differed widely in their religious practice. Most Eastern European Jews remained strictly orthodox. In larger cities across Europe, many Jews lived mostly or entirely secular lives. Plenty of people in Germany and other Western European countries, in fact, came from families that had converted to Christianity, sometimes a generation or two back. Some of these people didn't even consider themselves Jewish. But the Nazis did.

When Nazism became policy in Germany starting in 1933, it signaled a new, deliberate form of antisemitism, one that (falsely) claimed to be rooted in science. This aggressive, proactive ideology ultimately threatened Jews' existence far more than the old-fashioned, quasi-religious antisemitism of Eastern Europe from which Jews could usually hide. When the Germans moved in, the impact on Jews was usually swift and terrible. German conquerors drew upon underlying antisemitism in many European countries, especially in the East. They usually got plenty of help locating Jews, and sometimes in killing them. In conquered Western lands, German leaders mostly rounded up or identified Jews for later movement. In the east the killing rolled right along with the tanks.

Especially as the Third Reich expanded in 1940 and 1941, so did the scope of the Holocaust. In addition to the systematic shootings by average soldiers like Police Battalion 101, SS troops ran mobile killing that pumped carbon monoxide back into buses and slowly asphyxiated victims. In 1941 and 1942, Jews and other victims of Nazi genocide were being murdered in relatively small groups. But especially after the January 1942 Wannsee Conference planning, the Third Reich began rounding up Jews from all over Europe. Some were housed temporarily in super crowded ghettos, where disease and malnourishment killed thousands. Other racial "enemies," above all Jews, were sent directly to the growing number of camps set up mainly for industrial murder.

German concentration camps sprang up everywhere in Europe and murdered prisoners in a variety of ways. All camps used slave labor that killed thousands of people through exhaustion, starvation, and disease. Some large camps like Auschwitz, Treblinka, and Chełmo, mainly located in Poland, expanded to become cities of 100,000. Here science, technology, bureaucracy, and smart business contracts united to create mechanized death unlike the world had ever seen. At its peak function in 1943 and 1944, the Auschwitz camp killed as many as 10,000 people per day (416 per hour). About half the victims of the Holocaust perished this way. Camp prisoners, usually Jews, helped usher victims of all ages into gas chambers, waited for the gas to asphyxiate them, then removed their contorted bodies, and burned them in efficient crematoria. For miles around these camps the ash of burned bodies fell like snow year round. And, yes, people near and far knew what was happening, at least around them. Most people outside German political and military leaders, though, could not have known the full extent of this expansive genocide.

Some Holocaust victims escaped or, in a few cases, fought back. In April and May of 1943, for example, a few hundred armed Jews resisted the German military's final round-up of the Warsaw ghetto. It took three weeks for the mighty German military to destroy the ghetto and kill those in the uprising, and this action inspired other violent resistance elsewhere in Eastern Europe, even in a couple of the death camps. Most Jews were rounded up with their families for immediate execution or deportation to camps, something that discouraged violent resistance.

Jews were the largest but not the only victims of Nazi violence. Hitler and others created a hierarchical world view based on traditional, Christian antisemitism, traditional prejudices against "others," and Social Darwinist ideas of eugenics. The Aryan/German was at the top, and the Jew was at the bottom of this scale. Along the way sat many other groups of people who threatened the Third Reich's racially purity—Africans, Slavs, and some Asians (though not Germany's pals, the Japanese). Other major victims of the Holocaust included the Sinti and Roma peoples, often called "Gypsies." About 250,000 of them perished in the Holocaust. As with Jews, German conquerors could rely upon established prejudice in central and eastern Europe to help round up and get rid of these people. The Sinti and the Roma have the unfortunate distinction of being the one group that, rather than being commemorated after the Holocaust, were persecuted in many places in Europe until the 1970s. Something similar happened to gay men too.

In the final, bizarre, yet telling chapter of the Holocaust, camp leaders often led prisoners out of camps to wander around in order to avoid the oncoming Red Army. Nazi leaders understood that there could be no hiding their genocidal actions. Many camp leaders elected not to run and avoid the Russian forces that would surely deal severely with them. Instead they continued to kill prisoners through these so-called "Death Marches" during the freezing winter of early 1945. About a quarter of the total victims died during these marches—that's close to 3 million people! If there was any doubt about the connection between Germany's military and genocidal aims, the Death Marches make clear that many German leaders were more determined to continue killing racial "enemies" than saving themselves from military capture.

And the dramatic finish

The image of armies slowly closing in on Germany is compelling and basically what happened at the end of the war. However, German leaders continued to hold out hope for some miracle change, like the British quitting or that the powerful V2 rockets would turn the tide or that maybe German scientists would figure out how to create a nuclear weapon first. On that last score, it helped the Allies that racist laws in Germany had kicked out top-notch Jewish scientists. By late 1942 or early 1943, however, it was fairly clear that the Allies would eventually defeat Germany. Some German soldiers, including teenage boys, fought to the death, like their Führer had instructed. Other soldiers had long realized that Germany was doomed and that (whisper voice) the Führer had no idea what he was doing. By 1943, Allied forces completely controlled the skies of Europe, and

Germany was having to pull resources from other theaters to defend against the relentless bombing attacks. German guns were in fact firing more shells into the air than on the ground. In July 1943 the Allies invaded Italy. The Italians surrendered, and Mussolini was imprisoned. In the spring of 1945, he tried to escape and was caught by communists and executed; his body was hung upside down in Milan. *Ciao, Duce*!

German forces held Italy for a while but gradually yielded to advancing Allies. On June 6, 1944 a huge Allied force invaded Normandy, France and, after heavy fighting, gradually reclaimed France.[13] Meanwhile, the Russian army advanced into Ukraine, Poland, and then eastern Germany. By late 1944, the Allies were therefore pinching Germany. In the Pacific, American and some British forces continued taking over islands controlled by Japan, but the Allies were committed to winning the war in Europe first. In late April 1945, Allied forces had surrounded Berlin. Hitler and several of his entourage, holed up in a bunker under Berlin, committed suicide. On May 8, 1945 General Alfred Jodl (1890–1946) surrendered unconditionally for Germany, ending the war in Europe.

Allied leaders met in July 1945 in Potsdam to deal with the war's aftermath, and they sent an ultimatum to Japan to surrender or face the power of a new kind of weapon. Russia also declared war on Japan. When Japanese leaders refused to surrender, the United States—after consulting with its Allies—dropped a nuclear bomb on Hiroshima on August 6, 1945. The blast killed about 70,000 people immediately and injured that many more. About 70 percent of the buildings there were destroyed. When Japan still refused to surrender, the United States dropped an even bigger nuclear bomb on Nagasaki three days later. While these weapons did not cause as much damage as some major firestorm bombing raids, they demonstrated the power of a terrible new weapon. US President Truman (1884–1972) had authorized more nuclear bombings of Japan. However, the Japanese surrendered August 10, 1945, ending the Second World War.

And the final tally: 60 million dead, many more injured, a definitive notion of genocide, massive numbers of refugees around the world, and at best a pause before a new kind of tension that would become the Cold War. No rest for the wicked. World War II ended perhaps more dramatically than it began, ushering in a new, nuclear age and sealing this cataclysm with the only use of atomic weapons (so far!). As Allied soldiers pieced together the extent of Germany's genocide against over 11 million people, the world had to look into perhaps the darkest human abyss ever.

Dramatic trials in Nuremberg after the war by the Western Allies held the German leaders (who didn't kill themselves or escape) accountable for war crimes, waging a war of aggression, and crimes against humanity. There were some quick trials and executions in eastern Europe, under Russian direction, shortly after the fighting ended. Only much later, in smaller individual trials, would anyone hold the perpetrators of the Holocaust responsible for their actions. Of course, the extent of those somehow involved—soldiers, civilian contractors, informants, government officials, much less the millions who chose not to say anything—made real justice impossible.

---

[13]Stalin's response: about damn time!

CHAPTER 12
THE COLD WAR AS A LINE IN THE SAND

He's more than a hound dog, folks. Elvis Presley (1935-77) explains the Cold War! Yes, the history of rock and roll can demonstrate how the Cold War developed, especially for average Europeans. In Germany, in particular, rock and roll and American popular culture helped define the two sides of the Cold War. Rock and roll had a pretty checkered history, literally. A few American DJs started using the term "rock and roll" in the early 1950s to describe new music that mixed rhythm and blues, rockabilly, country, and gospel. See, young white consumers, especially in big American cities, were not going to buy the music of African-Americans or rural Americans. "Rock and roll," though, covered up those racial and rural roots and made this new music palatable for affluent white record-buyers. Young listeners also liked the term's sexual implications. American conservatives weren't fooled and often used racist terms to describe rock and roll. In Germany things were a little more complex.

By the mid-1950s, when Elvis and other rock and rollers hit Germany, leaders in both East and West Germany were concerned. They worried that American music and popular culture would replace one of the few things they still had after the awfulness of the Third Reich, namely, German culture.[1] East and West German leaders also feared that this music would whip kids into a sexual frenzy, instead of encouraging them to settle down and start families, something leaders desperately needed after World War II had killed off almost 9 percent of the German population. And like their American counterparts, German leaders had some pretty racist thoughts about rock and roll. But the whole, uh, Nazi thing meant that they couldn't really use race to attack rock and roll. They *could* talk about gender, however. They described Elvis's moves and look as too "feminine" and said he wasn't setting a good example for upstanding, German dads-to-be. But then capitalism came to town.

In the late 1950s, West German and East German leaders diverged in their thoughts about rock and roll. Certainly, it helped that Elvis served in the US Army in West Germany at this time.[2] West German leaders changed their minds about American popular culture for a number of reasons. They began to see it as a vehicle for helping young West Germans become good little consumers. They realized that it wasn't thwarting their sexual development (quite the contrary!) or turning teens into rebels. Capitalism is, after all, about buying stuff, and Elvis taught people how to do that and thus strengthened the capitalist economy of West Germany. For East German leaders of

---

[1] They really went nuts over Chuck Berry's 1956 "Roll over Beethoven"!

[2] Yeah, the biggest star in the world accepted his draft notice, joined the Army in 1958, and hardly performed for two years. Imagine Beyoncé or Justin Timberlake taking two years off to serve in the US military or Adele in the Royal Air Force!

course, that argument only made Elvis and American consumer culture worse. So, that's right, baybuh, the King of Rock and Roll helped solidify Cold War division from the bottom up. The Cold War was a big-time political struggle between two superpowers. It was also about different ways that average folks lived – what they bought, how they spent their free time, whom they admired.[3]

Building the argument

Okay, destructive international war, genocide, ideological battles, killer science, super-powerful states, mass politics. Can we just move beyond all that? Well, the Second World War really put the Enlightenment to the test. People fought and died by the millions—like 60 million dead, or about 3 percent of the world's population! And that number included over 11 million murdered in the greatest genocide of human history, the Nazi Holocaust.[4] World War II was very much an ideological war *and* a fight over good, old-fashioned nationalism. The thirty years from 1914 to 1945 might make people think twice about those fine Enlightenment originating in the eighteenth century. The Cold War grew directly from the Second World War. And just like after World War I, those in power intensified their commitment to Enlightenment ideas.

Friends, this time nothing short of the whole world is at stake. Let's meet our two contenders. In the blue corner we have the United States of America, armed with democracy, capitalism, Coca-Cola, good times, and the most advanced military on the planet. In the red corner stands the Union of Soviet Socialist Republics, ready to rumble with communism, a planned economy, Uncle Joe Stalin, moving songs, a humongous landmass, and the Red Army (a close second in military might). And, well, nobody else really matters. For the first time in world history (more or less), there were two superpowers. And they forced pretty much every other country to pick one side or another because both the USA and USSR believed that making the whole world just like them would benefit everyone. The good news is that these two sluggers never actually fought each other. The bad news is that they prompted a bunch of wars in which they indirectly battled each other several times, and their nuclear weapons that could destroy the world scared the hell out of people. But, hey, we got some good music out of the deal. Hello, silver lining.

The Cold War was a long-term conflict from the late 1940s to late 1980s. We're going to look at the impact of big ideas on people's daily lives (so, top down) *and* the way that everyday life shaped Cold War ideologies (or, bottom up). Here's the basic storyline. Before World War II even ended, the USA and USSR were already squaring off.

---

[3]Props to Uta Poiger for this idea in *Jazz, Rock, and Rebels* (Berkeley: University of California Press, 2000).
[4]Some scholars argue that Stalin's purges, dislocation, and famine represented a greater genocide. True, more people perished in those events of the 1930s, but the Soviet state was not always intentionally and systematically killing millions of people. The Holocaust was a targeted mass murder of very distinct groups by Germany's leadership.

From the war's end until Stalin died in 1953, both sides greatly expanded their military capacity, tried to contain each other, and extended their influence to many parts of the globe.

The Cold War became the new international norm by the late 1950s. In the 1960s and early 1970s there were some moves toward regularizing or even improving relationships between the two sides. From about the mid-1970s to mid-1980s, relations between the USA and USSR felt like a roller-coaster. Overall, major events like the Korean War (1950–3), the Cuban Missile Crisis (1962), and the Vietnam War (1955–75) punctuated this era of international tension. The Cold War conflict helped shape the process of decolonization, the subject of Chapter 13. It finally came to an end around 1989 to 1991, which we'll cover in Chapter 14. The Cold War jacked up the competitive differences between different Enlightenment ideals enough to threaten world destruction. You can see that in post-war politics and hear it in the jumping sounds of rock and roll.

Mega-nationalism after World War II

God knows we've seen a lot nationalism in this book, but the super-charged nationalism of the Cold War was bigger and badder, basically dividing the world in half. In some ways, US and Soviet nationalism after World War II was no different than what we've already seen: love of homeland, rooted in language and culture, plus feelings of superiority. Basically the same line since the French Revolution. Around World War II, though, came a new brand of ideological nationalism, one that assumed that the world would be a better place if everyone adhered to their system. Super Enlightenment! Even Nazism assumed that a racial hierarchy was good for everyone, including the losers at the bottom. The Soviets and the Americans continued this universalist trend, each arguing that their system should be applied to every place on the planet. A few countries tried to steer a "third way" between the two superpowers with limited success. As we'll see in the next chapter, the many new nations emerging from imperialist rule represented one ideological battleground after another for each superpower's attempt to control the world.

The massive destruction and moral certainty of World War II spawned the Cold War. We've already seen political leaders screaming about their amazing ideologies, regardless of the lived experience, and sometimes shooting anyone who disagreed. All the death, destruction, and uncertainty convinced US and Soviet leaders that they had to take extreme measures to avoid another war like that one. Even before World War II ended, Allied leaders—Churchill, Stalin, and US President Franklin Roosevelt (1882-1945)—had agreed that Europe would be divided into spheres of influence. They also agreed that the Soviet Union, which had suffered greatly from two German invasions in less than thirty years, should have a protective buffer zone.

That "buffer zone," we'll see shortly, meant that Poland, Czechoslovakia, Hungary, Romania, Bulgaria, Albania, Yugoslavia, and eventually East Germany would become known as the Eastern Bloc and be sort of an extension of the Soviet Union. The victorious powers would occupy and divide Germany for a while, and they agreed that the world needed a United Nations. Something like that. These vague agreements set the stage for the eventual Cold War conflict.

The fact that the USSR had more or less fought Germany alone for about three years during the war also amped up expectations and mistrust between these allies. I bet you don't rank Josef Stalin high on your list of Trustworthy World Leaders. And rightly so. Murdering many members of the party that brought you to power and a good chunk of your military officers will earn you that reputation, not to mention causing the deaths of something like 20 million people due to famine you helped create. Nevertheless, it's important to note that Stalin also had reasons not to trust his buddies Churchill and Roosevelt. I mean, they were allies and had all declared war on Germany. But except for a little Italian action in 1943, it took three years for the Western Allies to open a second front in Europe. Meanwhile, the Soviet Union lost something like 27 million people in the war, almost 14 percent of its entire population and about ninety times the number of Americans who perished! At least 11 million Soviet soldiers died in what was by far the most brutal front of the war. That's thirty-seven times the US military losses, if you're curious.

We saw in the last chapter that Germans routinely killed Russian prisoners of war as military and racial enemies, including making them the first victims of Zyklon B gas chambers in Auschwitz. The Soviets were thus victims of both World War II fighting *and* the Holocaust. Now, there were good reasons the British and Americans held off invading Europe until June 1944, and Stalin sure did some dumb things that weakened his war efforts. But the Eastern Front was simply the worst part of history's most awful war. So maybe we can also understand that Uncle Joe mistrusted the West too. Plus, the Soviet economy and social fabric was wrecked, unlike that of the USA. In short, the Allies battling Germany mainly just shared a common enemy. When fighting ended in 1945, the mistrust, expectations, and desire to build a new world in their image took over.

Pretty quickly the two superpowers began spreading their ideologies. They created military alliances more or less to split Europe in half between the North Atlantic Treaty Organization (NATO) in the West and the Warsaw Pact in the East. Then they started exporting their ideas to other countries, sometimes by invitation, sometimes with guns. What ideas exactly are we talking about here? The USSR and USA articulated distinct ideologies that came straight from—you guessed it—the Enlightenment. The chart (Figure 12.1) below might help explain.

These are the theories, and theories don't always work out in practice. Both sides believed fervently that implementing these ideas everywhere would improve the whole world. American and Soviet leaders were willing to undermine existing governments, support rebels, assassinate leaders, fight limited wars, and do pretty much anything necessary to see their ideas beat out the other side's. Above all, they tried to expand their economic and military systems. They sought new trading partners, markets, and access to natural resources, as well as military allies. Leaders on both sides often overlooked their new-found pals' lack of ideological purity, in return for economic or military cooperation. In the 1950s and 1960s, for instance, the United States routinely supported

Map 12.1 NATO vs. Warsaw Pact.

dictatorships that abused human rights in order to gain new economic and military partners. And the Soviets didn't worry much about wealth redistribution or lack of aid to workers when they found countries that would support their trade and military policies. Meet the new boss, same as the old boss.

The cynical exploitation of Enlightenment ideas to enhance the strongest people in the world was certainly nothing new, nor was their belief that their systems should apply to everybody. But the scope was greater in the Cold War, especially with mighty military alliances. The truly global reach of Europeans and Americans by the 1940s meant that these ideas were debated and fought over all around the planet. Plus, World War II and its aftermath weakened formerly great powers like Britain, France, and Germany. Only the massive USSR and USA had the resources and the supreme confidence to declare that their ideas should rule the world. Oh, and they also had a ton of weapons, including nukes.

Superpower	Economic Organization	Political Organization	Social Organization	Military Relations
Union of Soviet Socialist Republics (in the red corner)	Collectivism, tightly controlled by the government with the aim to maximize equality	Single-party rule in a centralized state where opposition is violently suppressed	Social equality (in theory) of men and women, regardless of ethnic background	Military well integrated into political leadership, large standing armed forces, leading member of the Warsaw Pact
United States of America (in the blue corner)	Free-market economy with limited government interference, aim to maximize opportunity	Multi-party democracy with a blend of centralized and de-centralized rule, based on rights and freedoms (with some exceptions)	Technically equal opportunity for men and women and all races, *but* that had historically (and even Constitutionally) been chiefly limited to white men	Military well integrated into political and economic leadership, large standing armed forces, leading member of NATO

Figure 12.1 Cold War superpower comparison.

High stakes and crazy culture in this MAD world

If controlling the world is your aim, then wrecking the world may be your game. Nuclear weapons can do that, you know. Fortunately, the USA and USSR never went to war with each other. That's why George Orwell coined the term "cold war" in October 1945. But this Cold War prompted plenty of "hot" conflicts in which the superpowers battled each other through proxies. There were the big conflicts, like the Korean War (1950–3), the Vietnam War (1955–75), and the Soviet-Afghan War (1979–89), as well as many smaller battles in Africa (Ethiopia, Angola, Congo), Central and South America (Cuba, El Salvador, Nicaragua, Chile), Asia (Cambodia, Laos, Iran), and Europe (Greece). Israel, which became a state in 1948, uniquely galvanized Cold War political tensions, and was a part of repeated conflicts in the Middle East.

In most of these battles, as we'll see in the next chapter, the United States and Russia arrogantly assumed that anti-colonial movements were just squabbles over which team—USA or USSR—these fine new nations would join. Usually the Soviet Union and United States just sent money, weapons, and maybe some military advisors. But sometimes initial "investments" morphed into actual American or Soviet boots on the ground. And that never worked. Those troops always left in defeat or worse. That lesson from the Cold War has influenced much foreign policy since the end of the Cold War. At least, sometimes.

One of the reasons the USSR and US never fought each other was because of the bizarre concept of Mutual Assured Destruction, aptly abbreviated as "MAD." The idea was that the United States and Soviet Union had so many nuclear weapons that an attack by one side would prompt massive retaliation from the other and they would destroy each other. Therefore, neither superpower would actually be dumb enough to use nukes.

The United States had of course dropped atomic bombs on Japan in August 1945. Russia successfully tested a nuclear bomb four years later.

Very quickly both sides began building hundreds of nuclear weapons, which could be delivered by airplanes, missiles, submarines, grandmothers, whatever it took. The US military in particular came up with some hare-brained ideas about putting nuclear warheads on land mines, torpedoes, and even portable launchers that a couple of guys could carry around. Other countries (Great Britain, France, China, India, Pakistan, North Korea, and probably Israel) have since produced nuclear weapons too. By the early 1960s, when both the USA and USSR kept portions of their nuclear arsenal ready to go at all times, the MAD policy had become semi-official doctrine. It's a crazy combination of irrational and rational assumptions. If you want to see a hilarious take on the MAD concept, check out Stanley Kubrick's 1964 film *Dr. Strangelove*.

I was a teenager in the 1980s and remember feeling a strange kind of patriotism in knowing that the USA had enough nuclear warheads to destroy the world thirteen times over, whereas the Soviet Union could only do it eleven times. Take that, Ruskies! Those figures were exaggerated, but there were around 70,000 active or stock-piled nuclear weapons in the mid-1980s (and the Russians, in fact, had more, although American weapons were more efficient killers). For sure by the 1960s, a full-fledged nuclear war with all the weapons unleashed would have killed hundreds of millions of people and made portions of the globe uninhabitable for a long time. Likewise, when people asked me as a teenager what I wanted to be when I grew up, I gave some ambitious answer (doctor, engineer, rock star, etc.) and qualified it by saying, "as long as there's not a nuclear holocaust." I wasn't particularly morbid; it was just something we lived with. I was also perversely proud to live in a big city that would get hit hard by Russian bombs because I thought instant vaporization was better than surviving a nuclear war and watching my appendages fall off. Too many apocalyptic books and movies about a post-nuclear-war world, I guess.

I wasn't alone. Popular culture, in fact, both shaped and reflected people's experience of the Cold War. We've already seen that culture, especially mass culture, became a more important way for people to define and express themselves in the twentieth century. The Cold War era coincided with an explosion in mass culture *and* the ability to enjoy it. Even the less affluent and more heavily censored Eastern Europeans had greater access to free time activities. Plus, all countries involved in World War II had really leaned on mass culture as propaganda. In a hypothetical conflict like the Cold War, it was probably even more important for governments and cultural elites to mark clear battle lines. I mean, it's pretty clear who the enemy is when they're shooting at you. Folks in an imagined war need a little more urging to rely on ideals, policies, fears, and hopes. Thank God movies, music, TV, literature, theater, and other kinds of culture can help get you revved up for an imagined battle.

And what better way to encapsulate the complexities of international geo-politics than in a ninety-minute movie or a two-and-a-half-minute pop song! Or through the life of a sexy spy like James Bond, perhaps the best-known and most suave Cold Warrior, created by Ian Fleming (1908–64). Other writers across the West used the anxiety and mystery of the Cold War to craft a non-stop stream of spy novels and movies. The French author Gérard de Villiers (1929–2013), for example, wrote 200 novels in one spy franchise and sold 120 million books in multiple languages. The stories of Soviet writer Yulian Semyonovich Semyonov (1931–93) featured various Russian and Eastern Bloc characters and adventures, often set amidst the Cold War. Movies and TV shows in almost every country involved likewise dramatized the Cold War—or at least turned it into entertainment.

Popular music often expressed feelings about the Cold War. For example, it's hard to imagine opposition to the Vietnam War in the West without protest music. And the strange combination of legitimate fear and frivolous fun—like dancing on a volcano— gave 1980s new wave music one of its important qualities. Cold War muse Nena described life after nuclear war in "99 Red Balloons" (1983): "it's all over, and I'm standing pretty/In this dust that was a city." Maybe the fact that I loved German music about nuclear war said something about me back in the day, and about my eventual interest in German history. But we'll leave that alone now. It's a very, very MAD world.

The division of Germany as Cold War split

Oh, Germany again. I know, but it's hard to ignore that place in the twentieth century. Germany was Ground Zero for the Cold War, mainly because it was Ground Zero for World War II. And plenty of espionage novels imagined it as Ground Zero for World War III. How Germany split into two nations tells us a lot about the Cold War. We saw in Chapter 9 that many countries, including Germany, deserved blame for instigating World War I. But there's no doubt that Nazi Germany began the Second World War. And while all combatants were brutal and targeted civilians, the genocidal policies and actions of the Third Reich single it out as the baddest of the bad. The Allies were justifiably angry but knew that imposing harsh sanctions had backfired after World War I. So, at the end of the war, Allies worried about how to punish *and* rehabilitate Germany. Russia, Britain, and the USA had agreed in 1945 (at conferences in Yalta and Potsdam) that Germany would be occupied and divided for a decade in order to denazify the place. But the idea that it would turn into two distinct countries was not part of the plan.

Germany was in big trouble at the end of World War II. While it took a few years for the Allies to figure out the extent of the Holocaust, it was evident that the German leadership, armed forces, and average citizens had carried out a campaign of mass murder against innocent people, especially Jews. And the German military had waged the most destructive war ever. The Nuremberg Trials of 1945 and 1946 found some Third Reich leaders guilty of war crimes. The more disturbing trials for the Holocaust came later, especially in the 1960s. The fact that all that support for Hitler vanished, like, the second he committed suicide in April 1945 tells you that most Germans realized they had messed up big time. They could see it all around them, after all. Most major German cities had been bombed extensively. About 90 percent of the structures in Cologne, for example, had been destroyed! The US and British firebombing of Dresden in February of 1945 killed at least 25,000 people and levelled large portions of that city.[5] Germans would much later, in the 1990s, tentatively talk about themselves as victims of such attacks. But in late 1945 Germany was occupied by the Allied powers (France, Britain, Russia, and America) and totally in the doghouse.

Germany's division came in six steps that reveal the growing tension of the Cold War. If you keep score, you'll notice there are moments along the way when both the Ruskies and Yanks deserve blame for the split. First, the World War II Allies had sharply different visions of how to remove the destructive influence of Nazism. The Soviets viewed denazification as dramatic and simple: execute some leaders, imprison others, forbid lesser offenders from participating in public life, and replace the Nazi political system with communism. Boom, done. The Westerners assumed it would be messier. They considered Germans' motivations for joining Nazi organizations and knew they needed the leadership of some former Nazis. And like the Soviets, the Western allies wanted to repair German society by replacing fascism with *their* political system of multi-party democracy.

Second, in 1946 both sides started to harden their ideologies. The Soviets began to coordinate their zone politically and economically. They forced the German Social Democratic Party (SPD) to merge with the Communist Party to form the Socialist Unity Party. Other political parties in the Soviet zone were "coordinated" into submission under this Socialist Unity Party. Plus, the Soviets began to create in their zone the same top-down economic structures used in the Soviet Union – collective farms, centralized factories, nationalized industries, etc. They were making similar moves across Eastern Europe. The British and Americans responded. Former British Prime Minister Winston Churchill, for instance, gave a speech in March 1946 at Westminster College in Fulton, Missouri, USA where he coined maybe the most famous phrase of the Cold War: "From Stettin in the Baltic to Trieste in the Adriatic," he said, "an 'iron curtain' has descended across the continent," and the countries behind it are "all are subject, in one form or another, not only to Soviet influence but to a very high and in some cases increasing measure of control from Moscow." Oh, snap!

Step number three: important events in 1947 marked a significant shift in the US view on the Cold War. In March that year, US President Harry Truman described a new American foreign policy in a speech to Congress. The "Truman Doctrine" made containing communism and promoting freedom the cornerstones of American action in the world. In June 1947, US Secretary of State George George Marshall (1880–1959) unveiled an extensive economic aid package aimed at rebuilding war-torn Europe. From 1948 to 1952, the "Marshall Plan" directed $12 billion from the USA into countries across Europe. All countries were offered it, but those under Soviet influence declined

---

[5]And it was the inspiration for Kurt Vonnegut's crazy, sci-fi, semi-autobiographical 1969 novel *Slaughterhouse Five*, which oddly captures the insanity of World War II.

the capitalist-oriented aid. (And when the Yugoslavs accepted some, Stalin got furious and kicked them out of the Commie Club.) This project helped Western Europe recover, brought Western allies closer together, and demonstrated that working with the United States benefitted Europeans' material lives. The years 1946 and 1947 were pretty awful for many Europeans: they were hungry, tired, cold, and still living in rubble. But even average folks could see that two distinct sides were taking shape.

Fourth, in June 1948 there was a big announcement from the Western zone: hey, world, meet the new German currency, the *Deutschmark*! This new currency helped get rid of public and private debt, avoid the crazy inflation of the early 1920s, and cut down on the black market undermining post-war economic recovery. The *Deutschmark* turned out to be the most stable currency in Europe until the Euro took over in 2002. The Russians of course couldn't abide a capitalist-run currency, so they cut off direct access to West Berlin. And, yes, they could do that because the western part of that divided city was a tiny island in the middle of the Soviet zone in the east. British and American air forces responded by flying supplies into West Berlin for almost a year. That "Berlin Airlift" turned what used to be Nazi Town into a symbol of freedom and made (Western) Germany a major ally in the growing Cold War conflict. It was also a big ole middle finger to the Russians.

Still with me? Step five in the German Partition Dance: in May 1949 the Western allies and their German counterparts founded the Federal Republic of Germany (a.k.a. West Germany). The new nation boasted a parliamentary democracy with standard Western liberties and a market economy. West German leaders still hoped for a unified Germany at some point. But, alas, in October 1949 the East Germans created the German Democratic Republic, complete with a Soviet-style political and economic system. So, there you go: four years after the war, German mitosis, two Germanies, both of which became important partners in their bloc. They hated each other of course. These two neighbors with the same language and often same families didn't even recognize each other until 1972.

But wait, there's more! Step six: in 1955 both nations joined the military alliance of their preferred superpower, the Warsaw Pact and NATO. Both Soviet and American troops decided to stay for a bit longer. The Russian military was chilling in Germany until they got booted in the fall of 1990, and the US military is still there today. That kind of presence shows how important both Germanies were.

Finally (bonus step seven!), the August 1961 construction of the Berlin Wall literally sealed the division of Germany in concrete. East German soldiers and construction workers began work in the middle of the night on August 13, 1961. Until then, East Germans could get into West Berlin and thus West Germany relatively easily. So, the East Germans said they needed to build a wall to keep out the "fascists." Right, right. And the fact that 30,000 East Germans left for West Berlin in July 1961 alone had nothing to do with it! Anyway, East Germany completed the wall dividing the two cities in two weeks. It took several more years to secure and arm the border between the two nations. We rightly think of the Berlin Wall as an icon of the Cold War. It prevented the free flow of people, goods, and ideas between a divided city for almost thirty years. And it was the site

Figure 12.2 Cold War in concrete, or: the Berlin Wall. © Everett Collection Historical / Alamy Stock Photo.

of some pretty bad-ass Cold War moments, like an East German police officer jumping over barbed wire to defect in 1961, President John F. Kennedy's 1963 "Ich bin ein Berliner" speech,[6] and David Bowie's 1987 concert.

By 1961, when the Wall went up, the Cold War was a lived reality for Berliners, Germans, Europeans, and much of the world. Already both the USA and USSR had intervened in a number of conflicts around the world. In October of 1962, the two sides came the closest during the entire era to actual war over whether the Soviets had the right to install nuclear weapons in Cuba. The German division became a literal border, highly guarded and dangerous, as well as figurative line in the sand. The Berlin Wall symbolized how far both sides would go to continue the ideological and military division of the Cold War, and how average people managed to continue living their lives in this new, tense world.

---

[6]And yes, "ich bin ein Berliner" literally means "I'm a jelly doughnut." A "Berliner" is a pastry like a jelly doughnut. In German you actually should say "ich komme aus Berlin" to mean "I'm a Berliner." But the Berliners in the audience knew what Kennedy meant, and they loved it—though not the same way they loved jelly doughnuts.

So, About Modern Europe ...

The state and the good life

But, hey, it wasn't all doom and gloom. East and West European states after the Second World War were committed to helping their citizens prosper. And generally things got better for most Europeans. Government involvement and international trade especially helped create fairly strong economies across the continent. In Western Europe, analysts called the major growth in the 1950s and 1960s an "economic miracle." Some economies expanded by as much as 10 percent per year. Oddly enough, the places most destroyed by the war grew the most: they had nowhere to go but up. Also, the war's destruction forced modernization. For example, a Rolls-Royce plant in Derby that had survived the war unharmed could continue to use facilities built in the 1930s, whereas BMW in Munich had been levelled and had to build new, more modern factories with updated technology in the 1950s.

As well, some economic bad habits—labor-management conflict, nationalist policies, trade wars—had been discredited because they had contributed to the war. In their place, most West European countries created *social market economies*: capitalist market economies with significant government intervention. Governments used progressive taxes to give citizens health care, universal education, tuition-free universities, (retirement) pension plans, unemployment benefits, and child credits to incentivize having kids. They built protections for farming and other industries, capped work week hours, and guaranteed holiday and vacation pay. These benefits redistributed wealth, expanded opportunities, and ensured that economic growth benefitted the vast majority of citizens. They were expensive and required high taxes, but the war's destruction had a curious levelling effect for many Europeans that made such moves more acceptable. And, unlike in the Eastern Bloc, these were vibrant democracies, so citizens could use votes to determine how their governments shaped the economy.

Foreign trade provided a great economic stimulus across the West. Money from the Marshall Plan helped spur growth and made Western Europeans stronger trading partners. Growing economic cooperation within Europe slowly turned into the European Economic Community (1957), the European Free Trade Association (1960), and the European Union (1993). The cornerstone of these associations was a partnership between, yes, France and West Germany, countries that had fought each other since Napoleon. Their cooperation highlighted how discredited economic nationalism was after World War II.

By the early 1960s most Western European nations, some of whom had been killing each other only twenty years earlier, were acting as a single trading bloc with virtually no tariffs or restrictions between them. This Common Market, as it came to be known, created friendly trading partners within Europe and collectively made these countries one of the most powerful players in the world market. And, as we'll see in the next chapter, the end of colonial rule often turned out to be an economic boon for most Western nations.

Many European countries invited people from their former colonies or non-Westerner allies to come to Europe as foreign workers. All that economic expansion, coupled with the population decline after the war, created major labor shortages in many Western European nations. Basically, white Europeans were doing well and needed someone to do their crappy jobs (cleaning, construction, fast food, other manual labor). These new immigrants—known as "guest workers"—fulfilled that need, brought new energy to European societies, and reinforced international trade. Their welcome did not last, but in the 1950s and 1960s especially they provided another boost to European economic growth.

Ultimately, economic cooperation and expanded trade caused wages in Western Europe to rise more than prices, which meant good times. It meant people had more money to spend—even after paying hefty tax bills—and saw their success and affluence tied in some way to that of their fellow citizens. Their governments were using portions of individual wealth to build a better society but still allowed plenty of economic freedom and encouraged innovation. It didn't last forever, but this synthesis of capitalism and socialism worked pretty well for a while. Enlightenment ideals getting it done! In sum, Western European economies, with some help from governments, produced a higher standard of living for most citizens, as well as more free time to enjoy this affluence.

Across the Iron Curtain the concept of "free" was in shorter supply, but Eastern Europeans also benefitted from economic growth after World War II. Remember, things sucked pretty much everywhere in Europe after the war. Big ole government intervention in your economic life, even with a Russian accent, might not seem so bad, if it helped you feed your family or keep warm. The USSR applied its Stalinist recipe to Eastern Bloc countries in the late 1940s and early 1950s: highly centralized authority, a planned economy, collectivization, industrialization, powerful communist party, and a militarized society.

These command economies, directed by and connected to Moscow, helped pull people out of post-war deprivation. These were not consumer-oriented economies of course, and that would become a problem by the 1970s. Eastern Bloc economies did, though, encourage consumption (not the same as consumerism) by strengthening existing industrial and farming capacity. Things expanded and improved even more after Stalin died in 1953.

Nikita Khrushchev (1894–1971), who basically headed the USSR from 1953 to 1964, began to move the Soviet Union in a different direction in 1956. He denounced some of the more egregious abuses of Stalinism and encouraged Eastern Bloc countries to play to their economic differences. That call appeared to allow more economic freedom. Industrial bases like Czechoslovakia or East Germany could focus on industry, whereas more agrarian nations like Hungary and Romania could improve their farming. And like in the (western) European Common Market, trade within the bloc benefitted individual countries.

But, turns out some of the Eastern Bloc folks misread what Khrushchev meant. They thought he was giving them the green light to build their own versions of socialism. When Hungary tried to do that in 1956, the Soviets sent in the tanks and stopped any real economic or political innovation. They halted changes in Poland too. Nevertheless, Soviet leaders and their partners in Eastern European countries did, as a result, begin to pay more attention to consumer goods by the late 1950s. The 1960s in the East might not have amounted to an "economic miracle," as in the West, but many Eastern Europeans saw their standard of living improve under these command economies. Eastern Bloc regimes had to remain sensitive to consumer demand since their ideology claimed to be building the best life ever for workers. Welcome to communism, comrades: give the state total support and it will care for you.

Very publicly, scientific competition and the space race embodied Cold War competition and its impact on average citizens. When the Soviets launched *sputnik* (which means "satellite" in Russian) in 1957, the Americans freaked out. It may seem hard to believe in the twenty-first century, but Westerners legitimately thought that the Soviet system might prove to be superior since the Soviet model was kinda rocking it in the late 1950s and early 1960s. In one of the more iconic moments of the Cold War, Khrushchev, while talking to Western ambassadors in November 1956, cried "we will bury you!"[7] Put aside your knowledge of who won the Cold War. Many people in the West in the 1950s thought the Russians might do it, especially after they managed to launch a satellite into orbit first.

The space race was yet another contest of the Cold War. Who can launch a monkey into orbit first, or a man? Who can orbit the Earth the most number of times? Who can put a man on the moon first? Typical Cold War pissing contest. But the different impact of the space race in West vs. East tells you something about the two systems. The West got Tang and smart phones, whereas the Soviets got a bigger military and bankruptcy. That's a bit of a simplification, but the US and Western space programs did help produced new consumer goods. The Soviet space program grew from a command economy that focused less on consumers and thus did not put as many new gadgets, food, or general improvements into the hands of Eastern Bloc citizens. We'll see in Chapter 14 that the expense of keeping up with the Americans in space helped undermine Soviet authority. The scientific knowledge gained by pushing into space has taught people many things about the universe and our place in it. Of course both sides of the Cold War used that information to make more dangerous weapons. But the fact that average citizens benefitted so differently from the space race demonstrates perhaps the biggest distinction between the Soviet and Western systems.

Yeah, but what about Finland? Huh? I know, not a place that's figured into our story here. But its curious history during the Cold War offers a good conclusion to this section on states. Finland illustrates that, while Europe was split, there was grey between the black and white of the Cold War division. (Maybe more like purple, since we've been using red and blue to represent Team USSR and Team USA.) Finland had been part of the Russian Empire since the early nineteenth century but broke away in 1919 in the wake of the Soviet Revolution. Finland actually fought in World War II against both the USSR and the Third Reich. After the war Finland almost joined the

---

[7]Or something like that, depending on how you translate. Entertaining but inaccurate urban myths have Khrushchev banging on the desk with his shoe during this outburst. That would have made a good story, but Nikita was too portly to reach his shoes under the desk!

Eastern Bloc but maintained its democratic and capitalist institutions and remained with the West.

In fact, both Western Europeans and the Soviets used Finland to advance their agendas. Militarily it remained neutral.[8] Urho Kekkonen (1900–86) served as president from 1956 to 1982, a super-long tenure that made people in and out of Finland question the country's full commitment to democracy. But he managed to play the two sides off each other to benefit Finnish interests. The Soviets certainly influenced Finnish politics, yet Finland joined the European Free Trade Association and participated fully in the capitalist trading bloc. (And in the 1990s the Finnish company Nokia invented some of the first cell phone systems.) Finland's democratic social market economy worked pretty well during the Cold War, revealing what might have happened if Eastern Bloc states had been able to forge their own paths yet remain friendly to the Soviet Union.

And what happens when things aren't so good?

Both East and West European states made themselves anchors of prosperity in their societies. That's fine in good times but can bite you in bad times. On both sides of the Iron Curtain, government intervention in citizens' economic lives was supposed to improve things. And mostly that worked during the 1950s and 1960s. However, when economies went south, guess who got blamed? Starting around 1968, people found different ways to express frustration toward their governments.

The most dramatic example of protest in the Eastern Bloc was the so-called "Prague Spring" in 1968 in Czechoslovakia. Once again silly Eastern Europeans misread signs from Moscow. The Czech Communist Party elected a reformer, who started creating "socialism with a human face"—basically decentralizing some of the Czech economy and political system, even introducing some democracy. They weren't becoming capitalists. Really they were looking more to the original ideas of Marxism. Remember how much Soviet power had warped those? Young people, intellectuals, and artists especially got excited about opportunities to improve their society. And how do you think the USSR responded? Yep, sent in the tanks, squashed it.

Plenty of citizens throughout the Eastern Bloc had already become disillusioned about communism by this point. All these regimes claimed to be models of socialist equality that would benefit everyone. Yet the minimal reforms of the 1960s only helped a little. By the early 1970s, Czechs and many other Eastern Europeans saw few opportunities to improve things and were not super engaged in politics. The distance between those experiences and utopian Marxist talk from leaders just kept getting wider. The repression of the Prague Spring showed that the USSR didn't really care much about the ideology they preached. As a result, Eastern Europeans became increasingly cynical

---

[8]They weren't alone. Other neutral European countries (then and now) include Switzerland, Austria, Ireland, Sweden, Lichtenstein, and Malta, as well as the Pope's own little country in Rome, Vatican City.

Figure 12.3 Brace yourself: it's the Sex Pistols.

about the system in the 1970s and 1980s. But they had very few outlets to express that frustration. We'll see how that blows up in Chapter 14.

Western Europeans, on the other hand, had many more venues to discuss problems, especially when their economies slowed down in the 1970s. A host of reasons caused those "economic miracles" to falter in the 1970s: rising energy costs, competition from expanding Asian economies, high labor costs, government price controls, bell-bottom pants, and so on. High unemployment, inflation, limited opportunities, and lower wages undermined people's faith in the Western economies. And just like in the East, governments had to accept some the blame since they had previously taken the credit for the good times. Live by the sword, die by the sword. Westerners protested in vocal and dramatic ways, including riots in 1968.

Perhaps the noisiest response to the 1970s economic downturn was punk music, which began in Britain in the mid-1970s.[9] Please go turn on, very loudly, "Anarchy in the UK" or "God Save the Queen" or any other song off the Sex Pistols' 1977 album *Never Mind the Bollocks, Here's the Sex Pistols*. They only made one album; it was all they needed to tear music apart. Their angry lyrics and music loudly rejected the British establishment that seemed to have promised that all would be well in jolly olde England. Some artists invited Westerners to escape the problems of the world through beauty, drugs, imagined

---

[9]I know you can argue that the Ramones started punk music first in the USA. A fair point, but the Sex Pistols' vision of punk included non-traditional chord progressions and politically charged lyrics, which became hallmarks of punk thereafter.

utopia, or whatever. The Sex Pistols wanted Europeans to take seriously the failing legacy of ideas that were supposed to improve life for everyone. Other punk bands like The Clash pointed out racism in Britain and Western Europe in the 1970s, especially when all those helpful "guest workers" became scapegoats for lost jobs and wages.

In short, people recognized the distance between big ideas and the reality of their everyday lives. In the Eastern Bloc the government controlled people's daily lives, yet citizens often had to buy things on the black market to make ends meet. That situation seemed a far cry from the worker-peasant socialist utopias their government raved about. In the West some folks realized (again) that capitalism and democracy do not work out the same for everyone. The difference between rhetoric and reality was greater in the East, and Western Europeans had more outlets to express concern and suggestions. Nevertheless, citizens blamed their governments, quietly or loudly, for creating expectations that could no longer be met in the 1970s.

Elvis has left the building

Of course, the Cold War soldiered right along. The big-ticket conflict between USA/capitalism/democracy and the USSR/communism/single-party rule continued, as did the arms race and the wars. But as I said about rock and roll, we see a slightly different Cold War, when we compare that ideological conflict with how average people actually lived. All the nukes just made the struggle more interesting. In Chapter 14 we'll see how it all ends, especially when rhetoric and reality in the East grow too far apart in the late 1980s. There was no corresponding kick in the head to Western ideology. But Chapter 15 will demonstrate that in the later part of the twentieth century, identity politics—focusing on the rights of certain groups instead of large-scale change—became the new rallying cry for reforming Western society.

Does that mean the end of Enlightenment ideology? Don't you fret. The Enlightenment has survived worse, so no, it's not going to end with the twentieth century. But the Cold War certainly showed just how far these Enlightenment ideals like communism, capitalism, and democracy could go. The Cold War was a fifty-year experiment with limited military conflict about two different ways for states to manage economic and social lives. It divided the world, created tons of weapons, and connected Europeans' daily lives to ideology. It also helped make consumerism the number one activity in the western world. Those trends still shape the world today.

CHAPTER 13
THE LONG, STRANGE, AND NOT-SO-COMPLETE DEATH OF COLONIALISM

In 1947 the Bulawayo Sweet Rhythm Band recorded the instrumental song "Skokiaan." When it dropped on a South African label in 1954, it became an international hit. It's a catchy tune you can find online. The song is named after illegal, home-brewed alcohol from Zimbabwe, where the Bulawayo Band lived. Actually, the country was called Rhodesia back then, after the late nineteenth-century British adventurer, miner, and white supremacist, Cecil Rhodes. Rhodesia was the scene of some pretty awful abuses of colonialism. In fact, white settlers there declared independence from the United Kingdom in 1965, in order to continue their white-dominated rule rather follow the British lead and gradually return colonies to native peoples. In 1980 native people did finally gain independence, after a fifteen-year civil war, and renamed the place Zimbabwe. Not a nice place in the the 1940s and 50s. But that's where the Bulawayo Sweet Rhythm Band recorded their happy hit.

The song features a bouncy sax solo on top of syncopated strummed banjo doing a basic I – IV – V chord pattern and simple percussion. The song is an interesting example of give and take between music of Africa and the West. The banjo comes from West Africa. Slaves in the Caribbean and North America played them, and then white Americans began mass producing them in the 1840s. They became a regular part of North American popular music by black and white people (and, I'm afraid, white people dressing up like black people). Early jazz in the 1920s relied heavily on banjos. "Skokiaan" uses the banjo much like in early jazz, and the saxophone melody also takes cues from American jazz. The chord progression is basic blues. This song thus shows how African musicians used this African-American instrument to create something that blends East African music and American jazz. And then white folks in the United Kingdom, United States, and elsewhere bought lots of their records, giving African musicians a measure of success, something that didn't often happen. At the same time, black US musicians like Louis Armstrong and white US musicians like Bill Haley recorded their own versions of "Skokiaan" and probably made more money than the Bulawayo Sweet Rhythm Band did.

That back-and-forth story is a bit like how decolonization worked. Europeans first took things from non-Western colonies, then the non-Western folks figured out how to use the set-up against Europeans and do their own thing, but ultimately the Europeans got the better end of the deal. What's new, right?

Building the argument

This chapter traces the end to Europeans' direct political control of the world, something they had been flailing at since the 1500s. It follows the process of former colonies becoming independent states, mainly from the 1940s to the 1970s. Our trusty Enlightenment helps explain. People in Africa and Asia wove their own experiences and aspirations together with Enlightenment ideas to create a potent rejection of European authority. In some cases, Islam or Hinduism helped. Recall in Chapter 7 that imperialism reflected the dual nature of the Enlightenment—the tendency both to liberate and control. Those same contradictory impulses influenced the process of decolonization. Sometimes colonial subjects used nationalism and liberalism to advocate for freedom from European colonial masters who had, oddly enough, employed the same concepts to justify their taking over many parts of the world. Sometimes Europeans used Enlightenment ideals to explain their reasons for departing. We will therefore look at the various motives behind liberation movements and the reasons imperial rulers let their colonies go.

This chapter mostly focuses on events after World War II, though we'll briefly explore events before that. Since the British and French controlled the largest colonial empires, we'll pay special attention to how they concluded their colonial experiments. We study other European empires too. And we'll spend some time considering how colonial independence movements fit with the Cold War. Remember how quickly Europeans carved up Africa (Chapter 7)? The pace of decolonization after the Second World War was just about as fast. The vast majority colonies gained their freedom between 1945 and 1975. Boom!

Unfortunately, Europeans' quick grab of colonies, their limited investment in them, and their hasty exit did not serve these new nations well. The end of colonialism often meant unrest, strife, and political turmoil in many former colonies. Plus, Westerners used their old colonial trading patterns to set up new beneficial trade arrangements. Decolonization actually solidified economic divisions in the world, which allowed the wealthier, mostly white Northern Hemisphere to make bank at the expense of the poor, mostly dark Southern Hemisphere. We will consider the legacy of imperialism in Europe, something that points toward issues in Chapter 15.

This chapter, like the book overall, mainly looks at Europe. In the larger history of imperialism, the experiences of people throwing off the yoke of colonialism matter at least as much as how white folks reacted. But as I've said before, it's important for us to understand the European perspective on this process.

From imperialism to decolonization to post-colonialism

Now, we went through all the imperialism vs. colonialism stuff in Chapter 7. Although we usually describe what happened in the modern era as imperialism, we don't call its end de-imperialization. We call it *decolonization*. In some cases, European *colonists* did leave areas in which they had settled or worked out how to remain in a new, independent nation. But mostly the process involved small numbers of Europeans who had ruled over large numbers of non-Western people giving up that control. The process of decolonization partly mirrored how Europeans originally took over. Chapter 7 offered

COLONIALISM   POST-COLONIALISM

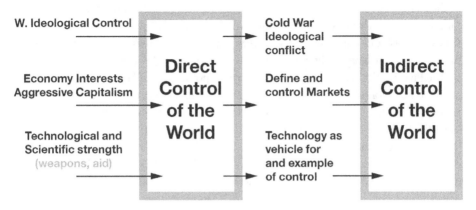

Figure 13.1 Colonialism, decolonization, post-colonialism.

three broad reasons for Europeans' grabbing land around the world in the nineteenth and twentieth centuries:

1. Economic motivations, namely, expanding markets, often driven by industrialization, and aggressive capitalism.
2. Ideology, specifically, nationalism, racism, Christianity, and the desire to "civilize" the world (i.e., bringing Euro ideas with guns).
3. Scientific and technological strength, which enabled small numbers of Europeans to control large numbers of colonial subjects and to use science to improve things in colonies.

Decolonization was similar. Europeans got out sometimes for economic reasons, sometimes because of political, social, and economic changes back home or in the world. Colonialism (or imperialism) was more than just one group of people controlling another. Their interaction shaped both sides. Decolonization, therefore, reveals how Westerners have continued to control most things in this world right up to today. Check out the chart in Figure 13.1.

Put another way: decolonization used the methods of colonialism to give Europeans (and Americans) *indirect* control of the world, especially financial resources. Let's see how it happened.

How it went down: an overview of decolonization

By the twentieth century taking and losing empires was nothing new for Europeans. The British had of course lost the United States of America in the eighteenth century. A few

French colonies in the Caribbean used the 1789 Revolution to declare independence, which didn't always last but scared Europeans[1] and inspired independence movements in the western hemisphere. In the nineteenth century, Spain and Portugal lost almost all of their empires in Central in South America to independence movements. The colony Liberia, a haven in West Africa for former slaves, declared independence from the United States in 1847 and has remained free ever since. Most of these earlier independence movements drew from Enlightenment ideas of freedom and nationalism.

The First World War marked a major turning point in colonial relations. On the one hand, some colonial subjects fought for their colonial masters, both at home and in Europe, as we saw in Chapter 9. Afterwards, many of these men were disappointed to learn that fighting had not earned them any more autonomy or rights. Some colonies became "protectorates" and changed hands. Big whoop; Western powers remained in charge. On the other hand, colonial subjects saw in World War I that their masters were not invincible. And all the European powers fanned nationalism in enemies' colonies. After the war, some of US President Woodrow Wilson's fine, fine Fourteen Points stressed the right to national self-determination. One even insisted that the needs of native populations be considered in colonial issues. Sure thing, Woody. In reality, the post-World War I settlement reinforced colonial authority. Several colonial powers did integrate native populations further into colonial rule, though. Also, around this time the Soviet Union began the flirtatious relationship between anti-imperialist independence movements and communism. (Never mind that the USSR was itself one hell of an empire.) In short, the Great War both raised and dashed hopes regarding independence.

The political and economic storms that battered Europe in the 1920s and 1930s made some imperial types wonder, hmm, should we be spending money controlling people far away when our own folks are standing in soup lines? Other Europeans decided to lean more heavily on their colonies for economic benefits and as status symbols. In the 1920s, local leaders in India and some other colonies began independence movements, often melding religious and cultural inspiration with Enlightenment notions of nationalism. The tense period leading up to World War II was not the most hospitable environment for independence movements. Italy's 1935 attack on Abyssinia (Ethiopia) was the first of many imperial invasions by fascist governments.[2]

The Second World War was the real push for colonial change. We saw in Chapter 11 that fighting in North Africa, the Middle East, and throughout Asia helped determine the outcome of the war. Combatants again supported nationalist and anti-colonial movements to weaken their opponents. Perhaps most importantly, Japan's imperial expansion in the East revealed the weakness of Western colonial powers. In fact, World War II in Asia was in many ways a war about colonies. Western Allies called the war a battle for liberation and fought to free subjected people from expanding German and Japanese empires. Colonial subjects, who fought in greater numbers than in World War I, liked that idea. They certainly expected changes after the war. If World War I opened

---

[1]Because this move showed that Enlightenment ideals could even help liberate black slaves!
[2]I mean, if democracies like Britain and France can have colonies, why can't fascist dictatorships?

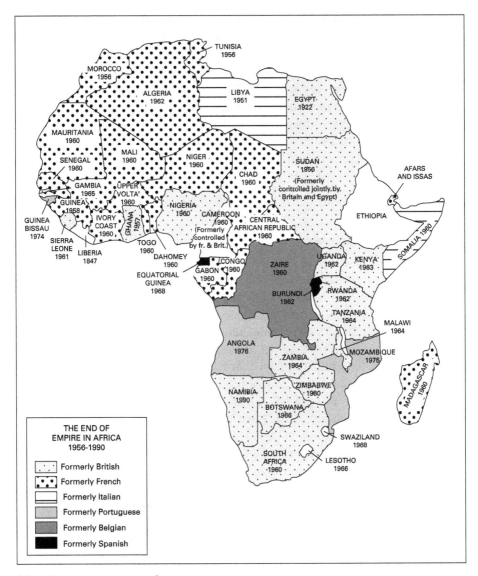

Map 13.1 New nations in Africa.

Pandora's Box of colonial liberation, then World War II smashed that box and made sure those ideas were out there for good.

Most colonies went through three general stages of resistance. First, traditional elites fought the modernization that empires brought, seeking to protect native culture. In a few rare cases—e.g., Ethiopia and China—that resistance more or less kept colonizers out. Second, a Western-educated middle class in the colony used modernization to challenge and replace traditional elites. These new leaders often adopted Western dress and lifestyle. Colonial rulers felt mighty good about themselves when they saw their subjects trying to imitate them and hoped that giving some subjects the Western goods would make them more loyal to colonial rule. But many of these native leaders discovered that putting on a suit or speaking with a perfect accent or earning a degree did not change their skin color or power dynamics. When Mahatma Gandhi (1869–1948), who had studied law at University College London, realized that fact, he pushed for Indian independence. Third, national liberation usually came through mass revolution. Local Westernized elites developed connections to the masses and between traditional native and Western modernized culture. The differences between those two cultures created powerful anti-colonial movements but also built tension into the very fabric of such movements and the new states that resulted.

And the Cold War …

The simple way to describe the relationship between the Cold War and decolonization goes like this. Cold War ideological division meant that every independence movement and every new post-colonial state had to decide which side it was on: Team USA or Team USSR. That decision earned them money, support, and weapons from their Team Captain but obliged them to support their side against the other Team. The slightly less simple version reveals that the Cold War line was not so clear. Independence movements and new post-colonial states often played the two superpowers off each other. In many cases new states managed to get financial support and weapons from both Team USA and Team USSR. Oh, and Team USSR had a sub-team/rival Team called Team PRC (People's Republic of China). Team PRC joined the game in 1949, when Chinese communists led by Mao Zedong (1893–1976) won the long-running civil war in China and proclaimed it a People's Republic.[3] Some clever post-colonial states got assistance from all three teams! It was an exciting and scary time to become an independent nation. One African historian put it really well: "Gaining your independence during the Cold War was like getting your driver's license in the middle of a demolition derby."[4]

Freedom movements and newly independent states also shaped the Cold War because they forced the superpowers and their allies to acknowledge that ideology was more important than racial, ethnic, or religious differences. Liberation movements and new states pushed the traditional definitions of nationalism. And a few larger post-colonial states like India joined with other so-called Third World Countries[5] like Brazil to try to forge a "third way" between the United States and Soviet Union. Sometimes that worked.

---

[3] Said the Soviets in response: hey, great to have another commie buddy, sort of.

[4] Erik Gilbert and Jonathan T. Reynolds, *Africa in World History from Prehistory to the Present* (Upper Saddle River, NJ: Pearson, 2011), 385.

[5] First World = Western capitalist democratic countries, more or less Team USA. Second World = communist state-run economies, led by Captain USSR, though Team PRC wanted to be Captain too. Third World = less industrially developed countries almost totally in the southern hemisphere. Guess who came up with this handy division of the world?

Given that most colonial powers—the UK, France, Belgium, Holland, and Portugal—were capitalist countries, it may come as no surprise that communism held some appeal for anti-colonial movements. After all, communists had been attacking imperialism since the nineteenth century. Lenin had labelled imperialism the highest stage of capitalism. And in the early Soviet days, before Stalin was in charge, the USSR tried to give the many parts of the Russian empire some options for how to work with Russian leaders. True, the USSR absorbed countries after World War II and bullied its way into Eastern Europe. But they still kept up that good ole Marxist talk about freeing people from the clutches of imperialists.

Leaders of anti-colonial movements in Asia and Africa were no fools: they knew that rhetoric was overblown. Nevertheless, communism seemed to offer a way to throw off imperial controls *and* industrialize quickly—sort of like the Soviets had done themselves. The British managed to keep many former colonies connected through a commonwealth organization, so they helped recruit new nations to Team USA. The fact that France and other colonial powers often clung too long to their colonial holdings did not help the cause of Western capitalist nations. Let's look at what happened in a little more detail.

The (mostly peaceful) end to British Empire

The two main colonial powers—France and Great Britain—handled independence very differently, in part because they had handled colonialism very differently. Although the UK had ruled some colonies (North America, India) quite directly at times, the Brits generally set up various forms of indirect rule in their colonial empire. That method made for smoother transitions from colonies to independent states. France, on the other hand, tried to assimilate its colonies and make them a part of greater France. That sounded pretty awesome to the French. I mean, they considered themselves basically the purveyors of Western culture, and who wouldn't want to be French after all? But first, how did the Brits come to terms with the fact that after World War II they weren't the greatest power on the planet anymore?

Now, let's be clear: the British Empire was the biggest. Even before the late nineteenth-century "scramble for Africa," they controlled an empire, they liked to say, on which the sun never set. Grabbing large chunks of Africa only enhanced their position as Empire Number One. By the twentieth century the British Empire included one-quarter of the world's population! The "jewel" of Britain's empire was India, and that's also where resistance to the Empire began. A combination of Enlightenment ideas, local religious traditions (Hinduism and Islam), and indigenous leadership began to work against the Empire in the later nineteenth century. In 1885, local leaders, representing all Indian religious groups, came together to form the Indian National Congress. The very idea of an Indian nation was a new, Western concept. Indeed, the English language helped unite disparate groups in India. So just like young master Napoleon had helped forge German nationalism, British ideas gave Indians the ability to imagine an Indian nation without the British in charge. Karma's rough sometimes.

Now, it wasn't all kumbaya among Indian groups. Hindus and Muslims in particular remained divided in many ways.[6] Gandhi tried to unite Hindus and Muslims, but even his powerful leadership couldn't do it. Colonial India slowly split into mostly Hindu India and mostly Muslim Pakistan. British victories and defeats in World War II inspired Indians to push for independence. When a new Labour government replaced Churchill's grand coalition at the end of the war, they recognized the need to grant independence quickly. After hasty preparations, on August 15, 1947 India and Pakistan became independent nations. Religious and ethnic violence broke out in both countries, and Gandhi was assassinated (by a fanatical Hindu) in 1948, even as he appealed for secular unity in India. Despite ongoing religious conflicts in India, it has become the largest democracy in the world. And India served as a one of the most important inspirations for independence movements around the world against the United Kingdom. Other Asian British colonies like Ceylon, Burma, and Malaya in the 1950s transitioned fairly smoothly from colonies to independent nations.

Independence movements soon sprang up in British African colonies, and they became independent nations between 1957 and 1964. What would you call that, the Scramble to *Free* Africa, the Scramble to *Flee* Africa? The British had been there less time and sent fewer settlers than in Asia. The old "anchors" of British Africa, South Africa and Egypt, had already gained independence in 1910 and 1922 respectively. Each of those cases tells a unique story about decolonization. White leaders in South Africa—a combination of Dutch and British settlers—created a nation based on white supremacy, doubling down on that ideology, as more native people were gaining independence in Africa. We'll return to South Africa below.

The UK basically saw Egypt as the Suez Canal + pyramids + sand. In 1869 they had built, with their French pals, the 120-mile (193 km) Suez Canal that connects the Mediterranean and Red Seas. It was kind of a big deal: ancient pharaohs and other ambitious dudes had been trying to pull this feat off for millennia. Above all, this waterway gave Britain and France easy access to Asia, instead of forcing them to sail all the way around Africa. In the twentieth century the Brits weren't about to let any local yahoos control the Canal. Even after Egypt became independent in 1922, the UK worked out a deal to remain in control of the Canal. That agreement lasted until 1956, when Egypt took over the Suez Canal. Controlling the Suez Canal made Egypt a powerful country in the Cold War since both sides needed to connect Europe and Asia and protect oil supplies. Britain's loss of the Canal emboldened nationalism everywhere, especially in the Arab world.

British resignation and their tradition of empowering native leadership helped push independence in Africa. In February 1960, British Prime Minister Harold Macmillan (1894–1986) explained to the South African Parliament that a "wind of change" was blowing through Africa, the same nationalist "wind" that had originally inspired Europeans and, more recently, Asians to create nation-states. He said that British policies

---

[6]And that tension continues right up to today.

should accept this "fact." White-supremacist South African leaders opposed such a proposition.

Native leaders and populations in British Africa took the speech as a green light for independence. Ghana had already declared independence in 1957. Macmillan headed the Conservative Party, which had consistently supported imperialism. But rather than fight or delay independence, Macmillan pragmatically reversed Conservative thought and encouraged quick independence. Local leaders in Nigeria, Uganda, Tanganyika (which eventually became part of Tanzania), Kenya, Malawi, and Zambia were ready to go and created independent nations by 1964. White leaders in Rhodesia and South Africa held out, though eventually both moved to majority-black rule.

Together, independence movements in Asia and Africa and Macmillan's "wind of change" speech helped nudge most remaining British colonies toward independence. In the Caribbean, Jamaica, Trinidad, and Tobago became independent in 1962. The Bahamas became independent in 1973; Bermuda remained a British dependent but was self-governed starting 1968. Belize in Central America declared independence in 1981. In the Mediterranean, the multi-ethnic colony Cyprus became independent in 1960 after negotiations between Greece and Turkey. Malta became independent in 1964. In the unique case of Hong Kong, the island remained under lease to the British—yes, the Chinese leased an island with millions of people—until 1997. The United Kingdom had formed the British Commonwealth in 1946, and most former colonies found that remaining within that very loose federation benefitted them. After 1965 the group became just The Commonwealth. This organization allowed the British to continue to push gently ideas like democracy and rule of law among their former colonies. Sometimes that worked. Today there are fifty-four countries in the Commonwealth.

Decolonization altered the United Kingdom itself in important ways. One of the more interesting (and danceable) results was the creation of various forms of pop music that blended white and black culture. Ska, one of the most durable genres of dance music, began in Jamaica in the 1950s and helped spawn reggae and two-tone. Ska's shuffle rhythm and accentuated upbeats reveal its African, Latino, and New Orleans jazz roots. Jamaican immigrants brought ska and reggae to the UK in the 1960s and 1970s. In the late 1970s and early 1980s "two-tone" (black-white) bands like Madness and The Specials mixed ska and punk to emphasize cultural and racial harmony in the face of tensions about immigration and multiculturalism.

And the French depart (kicking and screaming)

The French had slightly different relations with their colonies, which partly explains why decolonization there proceeded differently—generally more violently. France got into the colonial game for the same reasons everybody else did: they wanted more money, thought they were wonderful, sought status symbols, and so forth. French colonial acquisition, though, was often spurred by an odd combination of certainty of civilization and defeat in war. This book has been filled with concepts of French Enlightenment, philosophy, ideas about government, human rights, and other highfalutin thinking. And we've seen some French beat downs, too. By the early nineteenth century France had lost most of its North American empire to the British or Americans or independence movements. France took most of its modern empire in Africa and Asia in the late nineteenth century, spurred in part by their loss of the 1871 Franco-Prussian War.[7] Likewise, their defeat to, ahem, the Germans again in 1940 encouraged the French to hang on to their empire after World War II. Many French leaders concluded that the world needed French civilization more than ever.

You may find it odd to know that the French didn't describe their colonial holdings as an "empire." That term had some, well, *Napoleonic* implications France wished to avoid again. (You know, taking over the world, creating French and German nationalism, and then falling apart.) So, they called colonies "France overseas"—as opposed to "metropolitan France" at home. France tried to bring its civilization, ideas, and government to the world. *Plus ça change, plus c'est la même chose!* That process meant that "France overseas" had some representation in the French Chamber of Deputies. So, although the relationship was unequal, France tried to incorporate colonies into French political life. France was quite involved in administering their colonies, especially economically. In short, France had more invested in its colonies than the British did. They would not let them go without a fight, and the process of decolonization altered life in France "overseas" and at home or "Metropolitan France."

In 1946, the new Fourth French Republic created the French Union, which further connected overseas colonies to Metropolitan France and made everyone citizens. This new Union included colonies all around the world, including the Caribbean, the Middle East, Africa, southeast Asia, the south Atlantic and the south Pacific. But the two most important cases of French decolonization were in Indochina (Vietnam, Laos, Cambodia) and North Africa, especially Algeria.

France had, since the late nineteenth century, tried to rule Indochina more or less directly. But already during the First World War, nationalists led by Ho Chi Minh (1890–1989) realized that communism, coupled with nationalism, offered a powerful ideology to challenge French control. The Japanese conquest of this area during World War II galvanized opposition there to imperialism. But the conflict in Indochina, especially Vietnam, was unique among colonial struggles because it became a direct battleground in the Cold War. At the end of World War II, the United States pushed for ending colonialism. But after the successful Chinese communist revolution of 1949, American leaders reversed course and viewed Vietnam and other European colonies as necessary bulwarks against communism's spread.[8]

France tried to recapture northern Vietnam, which communists had liberated from the Japanese. In a very clever move, Ho proclaimed the "Vietnamese Declaration of

---

[7]Remember that time when a bunch of mustached, victorious Germans proclaimed the German Empire in the Hall of Mirrors in Versailles?
[8]The USA feared that communist China would knock down Vietnam, then Cambodia, Laos, Thailand, Burma, India, and who knows what's next! That's the "domino theory" for you.

Independence," which used some of the ideas from and same language as the 1776 US "Declaration of Independence." By 1954, the French had failed and left after 16,000 of their best troops were captured by Vietnamese fighters. American advisors and soldiers gradually took over, made things worse, and then also fled in 1975. North and South Vietnam united that year to form an independent nation.

The situation in French North Africa was equally complex. Well, maybe it was complex from a French perspective because they agonized over what to do. From the perspective of people in North Africa, it was pretty simple: white folks had moved in starting in the 1830s and stayed, and we don't want them here anymore. French settlers moved especially to Algeria, where they made up about seventeen percent of the population by the 1940s. As in Indochina, French losses and occupation during World War II weakened their colonial position and strengthened nationalist movements against them. In Algeria, nationalists built their opposition to France in large part around Islam: their faith served to unite the masses and provide an alternative legal and social structure.

Just as France was leaving Vietnam with its tail between its legs (1954), the Algerian National Liberation Front (FLN) began a popular uprising in Algeria. Eventually France sent half a million troops there, some of whom had fought in Vietnam, but could not put down the increasingly broad resistance. After eight years of fighting and terrorism between the French and Algerians, Algeria became an independent state in July 1962. To say that white French settlers had worn out their welcome is an understatement, and almost all of them hightailed it out of there. Clearly this conflict reshaped the lives of native Algerians and demonstrated the appeal of political Islam all across North Africa and the Middle East. The crisis over Algeria also caused France's government to fall in 1958[9] and nearly got President Charles De Gaulle (1890–1970) assassinated. As the British had done, the French fairly quickly granted independence for several sub-Saharan African colonies in the 1960s.

These major colonial losses rocked life in mainland France. The French had to recognize the limits of le grandes idées of the Enlightenment—or perhaps, more darkly, their repressive service in imperialism. Their mission to conquer and then civilize parts of the world didn't work.[10] Colonial subjects used the very ideas of liberty, fraternity, and equality from the French Revolution to ask the French to get the hell out. And Islamic nationalism proved that French religious tolerance only went so far. The tension between secular French culture and Islam has continued to haunt France, a topic we'll address in Chapter 15.

Some scholars have argued that the French soothed their losses by buying things starting in the 1950s. Oui, France is losing its colonies and maybe its status as a world power. Sucks, but hey, how about a fine French Citroën car for the hardworking husband and a nice refrigerator for the wife? Don't laugh. Western capitalist economies needed people to buy things, and one way to offset the losses (and markets) of a colonial empire

---

[9]The crisis was huge. Basically, a military coup overthrew the government of France and created a whole new government, the Fifth French Republic.
[10]Napoleon chuckles in his grave.

was to encourage more domestic consumer spending. And as we've seen before, some people thought reinforcing traditional gender roles could help make French men and women feel better in a time of uncertainty. Certainly, advertisers appealed to gender differences to sell things (still do). France's economy grew strong in the 1950s and 1960s as a result of this gendered, inward economic turn and because they renewed connections with trading partners in Europe. And there you have a basic summary of life after World War II in Western Europe: if your ideals don't work, you can still buy stuff.

Other empires fall

Since the British and French at one point together controlled almost a third of the world, it's easy to forget about the other European empires. And maybe folks in Holland, Belgium, Portugal, and Spain don't mind everyone overlooking their imperial history. But the end to these smaller empires also reveals something important about decolonization and Western ideals. The Dutch East Indies colonies (and a few others around the world) had brought wealth to Holland since the late sixteenth century. We saw in Chapter 7 that Dutch colonial leaders worked closely with Islamic subjects to enable them to make the *hajj* or pilgrimage to Mecca. Dutch leaders eventually realized that some Muslims were using Islam to promote independence movements in the twentieth century. Japanese occupation of Dutch colonies during World War II further stimulated nationalism there, as did British and French support for independence movements to weaken Japan. After the war, Dutch forces fought for four years to beat back nationalism in Indonesia. They finally agreed to Indonesian independence in 1949, in part because the United States threatened to cut off Marshall funds, if they remained in Indonesia. The Cold War strikes back!

Belgians had a strange relationship with their few colonies. In the 1870s, the Belgian King Leopold II basically took over a large chunk of central Africa that became the Congo all for himself. Really. And it was awful. Some of the worst abuses and exploitation of the colonial era occurred there: amputations, forced child labor, starvation. As many as ten to fifteen million Africans died in what might have amounted to genocide. Things had gotten better by the 1940s, and a Congolese independence movement took cues from nationalist movements elsewhere and began working with the Belgians toward independence. In 1960 they proclaimed the Democratic Republic of Congo. The Belgians had also not done too well with the German colonies Rwanda and Burundi they got after World War I. While the majority Hutus and minority Tutsis hated each other before the Europeans showed up, the Belgians pitted the two against each other for their colonial benefit. After Rwanda and Burundi became independent states in 1962, the two ethnic groups clashed violently. Eventually in Rwanda the Hutus tried to commit genocide against the Tutsis in 1994.

Portugal earned the distinction of having the first and last European colonial empire. Way back in the fifteenth century, even before Columbus, Portugal was colonizing spots around the globe: North and South America, all around Africa, Arabia, Southeast Asia, East Asia, and Oceania. They were kind of a big deal in the early modern period. Portugal was the first European power to establish trade relations with and routes to China. Also, more than other imperial powers, Portuguese imperialists mixed with native populations, especially in Brazil. In the nineteenth century they lost many of their colonial holdings to independence movements and other colonial powers. By the mid-twentieth century, Portugal was a fairly poor, fascist-ish country, but still an empire, dammit!

Even after the wave of 1960s African independence movements, Portuguese leaders tried to hold onto their colonies. They fought costly and ugly wars that ultimately resulted in independence for Guinea-Bissau in 1974 and Mozambique and Angola in 1975. Their other tiny island colonies around the world also broke away around this time too. These conflicts and the civil unrest they caused in Portugal helped end the forty-year authoritarian *Estado Novo* regime there. Portuguese mismanagement set these former colonies up for many problems that lasted into the 1990s. Like Portugal, Spain had lost most of its colonies by end of the nineteenth century. Spain's remaining twentieth-century colony, part of northern Morocco, joined Morocco in 1956.

South Africa was a unique example of decolonization. That nation, led by a white minority, had gained independence from the United Kingdom in 1910. As black nationalism swept across Africa after World War II, whites in South Africa reacted by strengthening their long-standing racial hierarchy. By 1948, the government had codified white supremacy through their policy of *apartheid*. Like other twentieth-century racist laws (e.g., US segregationist laws or Third Reich Nuremberg Laws), these statutes made non-whites in South Africa second class citizens. Regulations restricted where non-white people could live and work, whom they could marry, use of public facilities, and their participation in government. Classic example of using Enlightenment ideas to support laws for control! Members of the growing (British) Commonwealth opposed such measures, so South Africa left the Commonwealth in 1961.

Non-whites (and sympathetic white people) in South Africa organized increasingly effective campaigns for civil rights there, receiving support from other African nations and some Western powers. Internal agitation and external pressure eventually forced South African leaders to work with native groups, especially the powerful African National Congress (ANC) in the late 1980s. In 1990 South African police released the ANC's leader Nelson Mandela (1918–2013) from prison after twenty-five years. Four years later he was elected president of South Africa's first majority-black government. Quite a turnaround! Thereafter, South Africa's Truth and Reconciliation Commission began a fascinating and somewhat successful experiment in coming to terms with the abuses of *apartheid*. The Commission investigated and reported on human rights abuses in South Africa since the 1960s. It offered a way to share black victims' stories and rehabilitate their lives. The Commission also granted amnesty to some white South Africans who had committed abuses but apologized publicly and requested amnesty. Plenty of people criticized this process as too lenient. But the Truth and Reconciliation Commission offered one model for both acknowledging and trying to overcome the many abuses of the colonial era.

And here's a curve ball at the end. What if we look at the fall of the Soviet Union as decolonization? We'll talk more about that process in the next chapter. It's certainly true that the USSR *was* an empire—not just in controlling Eastern European client states, but within its own borders. Remember the discussion in Chapter 5 on Russian nationalism as imperialism? Various Soviet constitutions said at least on paper that the republics that made up the USSR could just take off any time they wanted to. But I ask you: do you believe that Stalin would let any of them go? Didn't think so. Nationalism in the 1980s, which flared up in southwestern provinces and in Eastern Europe, helped to destabilize the Soviet Union. In several places Islam motivated some citizens to challenge Soviet leadership, and within four years—bada-boom-bada-bing!—the USSR had broken apart into a dozen countries. Smells like decolonization to me. Russia's massive empire had taken over three hundred years to build, but it dissolved in four years. The Enlightenment strikes again!

Post-colonial legacies inside and outside Europe

Perhaps this won't come as a surprise, but colonial powers left behind some messes. Most former empires also struggled back home to come to terms with their losses, or at least changed some. Let's look at what the process of decolonization left behind in Europe and in newly independent states.

Multi-racial societies

Multi-racial societies actually took root in many European countries for the first time. Small numbers of non-white people had lived in Europe before. But most former colonial powers invited people from colonies to come as guest workers, especially during the booming 1960s. Many of these people stayed, built lives in Western Europe, and gradually helped turn these places into multi-cultural societies. We will see in Chapter 15 that their welcome waxed and waned. But non-Western culture and religion were there to stay.

Significant political transformation

Decolonization altered politics in a number of European countries. I've already mentioned that the 1958 Algerian crisis brought down the French Republic and that colonial wars undermined the Portuguese regime. Portugal's transformation—known as the peaceful "Carnation Revolution"—simultaneously ended imperialism, brought down a forty-year fascist-type regime, set up democracy, and moved Portugal toward joining the European Union. In other countries, decolonization revised political fault lines and altered political discourse. In the UK, for example, the Conservative Party grew stronger because they had led the African decolonization process, and support for imperialism no longer divided that Party. Many Dutch people were ashamed of their country's violent colonial exit and embraced the liberalism and tolerance for which Holland has been known ever since. In 2011 and 2020, Dutch leaders publicly apologized to the Indonesian people for violence and atrocities in the 1940s. Belgian leaders also apologized in 2019 for kidnapping mixed-race Congolese children in the 1940s and 1950s. And while the Belgians did not commit genocide in Rwanda, that shadow (and the legacy of colonial atrocities) hangs over Belgium's attempt to function as a multicultural society.

Multinational corporations

Multinational corporations grew stronger as a result of decolonization. Western empires pulled out of colonies in part because large international—or *transnational*—corporations realized they could make more money through favorable trade agreements with non-western countries than dealing with European empires. Many former colonies have had a hard time attracting investment, especially once Cold War money dried up in the late 1980s. Starting in the 1970s, large corporations seeking cheap resources and labor have been some of the few organizations willing to invest in former colonies. By the turn of the twenty-first century, the top 300 of these large businesses controlled a quarter of the world's assets, and some of their annual sales are larger than the Gross Domestic Products of small countries. So, they have been able to come and go in the post-colonial world as they wish. Is this set up an economic improvement over imperialism? Tough to say.

Greater investment in Europe

Former European imperial lords often cried on each other's shoulders about losing their status as bad-ass international empires. The Brits clung to their Commonwealth as a symbol of their continued world status. Whatever. One way former empires handled this new normal was to realize that maybe nationalist chest-beating in Europe had not yielded such great results.[11] Witness movements toward the European Union described in Chapters 12 and 15. That common market also strengthened many of the economies that were weakened or at least altered by the end of empire. Nationalism has by no means disappeared in Europe (cough, cough, Brexit, cough, right-wing movements in Hungary, Austria, France, Holland, Germany, etc.). But the combination of decolonization and the Cold War forced many Europeans to recognize connections across the continent and focus resources on European markets. It was crazy times: French and Germans working together, lowering military spending, free love, dogs and cats living together!

Ethnic violence

Ethnic violence has rocked some former colonies. Imagine if powerful South American countries invaded Europe and quickly divided up the whole continent, creating colonial borders defined by how far one imperial army got before another stopped it. Those borders would likely have nothing to do with ethnic or religious differences in Europe.

---

[11] And the dead from both World Wars and colonial struggles all cried, "Amen!"

Plus, the new colonial masters might think, "man, all these folks are white, look pretty similar, and worship the same God. So, no big deal for people who are Dutch, German, French, Belgian, Italian, Swiss, or whatever to be lumped together, right? Who cares if y'all have loved or hated each other; time to work together for your new bosses." Or the new bosses might realize, "oh, this one group of white people who are into wine and stinky cheese doesn't like this other group who prefer beer and sausage; let's make use of that hatred to strengthen our control over them." Then imagine that after a while the South Americans decide that controlling this place was pretty lame and very expensive, so they peace out. "Right," they say as they depart, "we've left you folks some nice borders for new states. You white people can get along and work it out. Bye now." That happened in Africa and Asia. So, raise your hand if you're surprised that violence erupted between various groups in former colonies. Sometimes European colonial masters stoked ethnic tensions; sometimes they tried to dampen them; sometimes they even helped overcome them. But for sure the ethnic violence and even genocide in portions of Africa and Asia stemmed partly from how Europeans marked up and administered colonies.

Shaky democracies, shaky governments

Colonial masters could debate which of them created democracy, but they agreed that it was the best system of government. Totally the best; fist bump![12] And after the Second World War the USA didn't let them forget it. So, most post-colonial governments began as democracies. Departing imperialists often told former colonies, rather condescendingly, that they should set up a fine democratic government. (Never mind how undemocratic most of them had been in the colonies!) In some new states it worked out okay, like in India, South Africa, and Indonesia (although democracy sometimes served to repress people in all of those places at various points). But most post-colonial democracies devolved into one-party or one-man dictatorships or civil war. Most former colonies lacked a clear sense of *national* identity, so democracy often played out as ethnic struggles. Especially in Africa, coup d'états were common, like fifty-six of them across the continent between 1952 and 1994. Since the 1990s many of those nations have stabilized and improved the lives of citizens. Still, the hypocritical preaching of European powers to former colonies about awesome democracy often rang hollow and did not help create effective participatory government in new states.

Limits to development

Colonial rulers liked to brag about how much amazing Western development and industry and stuff they were bringing to their colonies. They were going to *civilize* these poor folks, and that meant modern medicine, science, industrial development, plastic bottles, and other amazing things! In the end, though: not so much. Except the plastic bottles: lots of those, I'm afraid. Europeans mainly created infrastructure so they could

---

[12]Portugal and Spain look down in shame.

extract resources from colonies. They built awesome roads leading from ports or airports to mines or oilfields, but not between groups of people actually living there who might want to work with each other. Likewise, former colonies understandably hoped to modernize and industrialize but often had to borrow money from wealthier nations or accept aid with political strings attached. These conditions could put new nations into debt (to Western banks of course) and force them to try to make big economic changes to pay back what they owed. When that didn't happen, these countries found themselves in greater debt – and still without modern, industrialized economies.

Greater north/south economic disparity

Being ruled by someone else sucks, in part because colonial powers create unequal trading relationships with their colonies and just take stuff from them. All those unfair economic practices did not simply go away when empires ended. Instead they remained the easiest, go-to way for countries to trade with each other. Former colonies struggling to industrialize and modernize could only offer the same raw materials, cheap goods and labor, or natural resources to world markets they had before. In other words, the end to colonialism did not mean the end to colonial economic relationships. In fact, some people have argued that it's gotten worse for new nations. Certainly, globalization has offered new opportunities to people in some countries, especially in Asia, to participate in the international industrial or service economy. But rather than balancing out differences between wealthy northern hemisphere economies and poorer ones in the southern hemisphere, post-colonial developments have often expanded the gap between the rich north and poor south.

Mixed blessing for the Cold War

Decolonization both strengthened *and* weakened Cold War divisions. On the one hand, new independent nations had to pick a side, so the teams got bigger. And both the Soviets and Americans used conflicts about and after colonialism to advance their ideology. Vietnam was only the most overt example of a colonial struggle becoming a Cold War battle. On the other hand, the appearance of dozens of new nations, especially in the 1960s and 1970s, naturally created a new dynamic that altered the geopolitics of two international superpowers. So-called "Third World" nations became more numerous than "First" and "Second World" powers. And in some ways, decolonization brought the two superpowers together. US veterans of the Vietnam War, for instance, found that they had much in common with Soviet veterans of the Afghan War. Likewise, continued unequal trading relations between north and south jointly benefitted the USA and USSR and their allies at the expense of newly independent nations.

Islamic nationalism

Using Islam to define a nation was nothing new. Even the earliest mediaeval Muslim *caliphates* (religious empires) did something like that. But the modern concept of a nation is a little different. Modern, Enlightenment-oriented nations assume a secular connection between citizen and state. Leaders of some independence struggles discussed in this chapter looked to Islam to unite and motivate the masses. Of course, in multi-religious colonies like Nigeria and India, religion could divide new nations as well as unite them. Above all, Islam gave moral and historical authority to many people fighting against colonialism. Some European colonies had suppressed Islam or encouraged Christianity, which allowed independence leaders to fight for religious freedom. We can't go so far as to blame the rise of radical Islamic terrorism in the late twentieth and early twenty-first century on colonialism. But there's no doubt that anti-colonial movements and new states informed by Islamic law have created a model for using religion and violence to achieve political ends.

CHAPTER 14
THE END OF HISTORY, OR SOMETHING LIKE THAT

So, 1989 was a pretty big year in Europe. Mass protests and government reforms ended communist regimes in Eastern Europe, and Russia was changing too. Right in the middle of it all, Francis Fukuyama (b. 1952) said that these events marked the "end of history." Fukuyama, an employee of the US State Department, argued that history was about conflict between major ideologies or world views. Since communism seemed to be crumbling in Europe, that left no more major ideologies to compete with Western liberal economic and political systems. Liberal democracy had basically beaten fascism in World War II and was about to whip communism. Game over. No more competition between major ideologies means no more history. Guess that means it's about time to wrap up this book!

Fukuyama got his ideas from the nineteenth-century German philosopher Hegel. (We met him in Chapter 6 as someone who had influenced Karl Marx.) Like Hegel, Fukuyama thought that ideas drive what people do and thus drive history. Wait, does that mean I've written a Hegelian textbook? Kind of. And yes, our focus on ideas helps explain why the "short twentieth century" ends in 1989. We've looked at many ideas in this book. Fukuyama only cares about the really big ones, the ones that apply to everyone. People fighting and killing for the big Enlightenment concepts of the twentieth century—capitalism, communism, democracy, fascism—believed the whole world would be better, if everyone signed up for those ideas. The end to the Cold War in this chapter marked a major change in European history. I don't think it represents "the end of history," but it's an interesting idea to consider.[1]

Fukuyama's timing was perfect. He gave a talk about the end of history in February 1989 and got an article out by June of that year, when all hell was breaking loose in Eastern Europe. Fukuyama's piece allowed people in the West, especially folks in charge in the United States and United Kingdom, to feel really good about themselves. They were going to win the Cold War and win history! Although Fukuyama was reaching a little bit, his argument emphasizes the importance of events described in this chapter. And his claim also supports the main argument of this book, that ideas matter and have helped shape why people in the past did what they did.

Building the argument

This chapter details the fall of communist regimes in Eastern Europe and Russia. The end to the Cold War, around 1989 to 1991, appeared to come very fast, but the origins

---

[1]Maybe that's a history nerd thing, though.

of these massive changes had deeper roots. Above all, these big, swift changes resulted from the huge gap between the rhetoric of communism and the realities of life in communist countries. We will look at these big political changes and their impact on people's everyday lives. Some of these political changes came from the top down, especially from reforms initiated by Soviet leader Mikhail Gorbachev (b. 1931). But political dissidents and popular protests pressured regimes to change and helped make those changes possible.

We'll start with the dizzying events of 1989 and work backwards. The concept of the "Eastern Bloc"—Poland, East Germany, Czechoslovakia, Hungary, Romania, Bulgaria, and Yugoslavia—seems to imply one big, similar-looking place with the same systems imposed by the Soviet regime. Certainly the changes we're looking at were connected and influenced each other. But the longer and unique roots of each country matter. Eastern Europeans had, at various points in the Cold War, resisted or altered Soviet authority. The different ways they had done so ultimately shaped how communist regimes fell apart and how the Soviets lost control of the Eastern Bloc. The Soviet Union hoped that reforms in Eastern Europe would help save the ailing Soviet system, but instead—surprise!—those reforms ultimately destroyed the USSR.

I believe I've said this before, but this chapter and book are focused on Europe. We must nevertheless note that similar, dramatic popular protests rocked China in 1989, too. However, that pro-democracy movement had quite a different outcome. The Chinese military killed thousands of protesters in Tiananmen Square in June 1989, and the communist party still rules China today. There was, in other words, no guarantee that Eastern Bloc governments, when challenged by their citizens, would respond peacefully. In fact, the history of communism since World War II made most people in and out of Eastern Europe worried that reform movements would be violently squashed the way they had been for forty years. The fact that these repressive, violent regimes ended in 1989 with only leader losing his life (Nicolae Ceausescu of Romania) testifies to the unique nature of this revolutionary period.

What exactly happened in 1989?

Major public protests undermined regimes in Eastern Europe and ultimately helped to end the Cold War. The main political change that year was that virtually all the Soviet satellite states in Eastern Europe ended communist party rule, and most of them held free elections. These events pointed toward an end to the Cold War conflict. That came technically in 1991 when the Soviet Union broke apart and the United States was the only remaining superpower. Events of 1989 also represented one of colonialism's last gasps, although communist control in the Eastern Bloc from the 1940s until 1989 was very different from other instances of colonialism. Really Fukuyama was making a point about a big shift in 1989 more than he was actually claiming that historical development ceased. Certainly this year marked a major change in the ideological battles and impact of the Enlightenment that have been a part of this whole book. Take a look at some of the crazy list of events from that year:

February	
Hungary	Constitutional changes end Communist Party's monopoly and institute multi-party system; new parties begin
Poland	Communist Party begins discussions with opposition
USSR	First multi-candidate election in Soviet history begins
March	
USSR	Open elections for seats in national Congress; Boris Yeltsin elected deputy of Moscow with ninety percent of vote
April	
Poland	Solidarity legalized as political party; agreement for free, open national elections
May	
USSR	Gorbachev elected Chairman of Congress in open and televised elections
Latvia, Lithuania, Estonia	These Baltic countries declare sovereignty from USSR
June	
Poland	Solidarity Party wins ninety-nine of one hundred parliamentary seats
(China	Chinese government kill thousands in Tiananmen Square massacre)
July	
USSR	Mass strikes settled by negotiation for first time
August	
Czechoslovakia, Hungary	Refugees from East Germany occupy West German embassies in Prague and Budapest
Poland	Solidarity-led government takes power; Tadeusz Mazowiecki becomes the first non-communist Prime Minister in the Eastern Bloc
September	
Hungary	Government opens border to Austria
East Germany	Communist leaders begin dialogue with opposition leaders
October	
East Germany	Weekly mass demonstrations force long-time leader Erich Honecker to resign
Hungary	Communist Party disavows Lenin, changes name to Hungarian Socialist Party; new constitution allowing multi-party elections
Czechoslovakia	Mass public protests, clashes with police; Velvet Revolution begins
November	
East Germany	Berlin Wall opens, unrestricted travel to West; government resigns
Czechoslovakia	Mass demonstrations causes Party leadership to resign; constitutional changes end one-party rule; free elections begin
Bulgaria	Chairman and Communist Party overthrown
December	
Czechoslovakia	Former dissident Václav Havel elected President
United Kingdom	Peter Murphy releases *Deep*; not technically relevant here, but one of the best albums of the year; plus, I saw him on tour
Romania	Mass protests and military crackdown; long-time dictator Ceausescu deposed and executed on Christmas Day

Figure 14.1 I can't believe all these events happened in just one year!

I mean, any *one* of these events was big news. The idea that they kept coming, one after another, was hard for most people to grasp. News spread across Eastern Europe, first informally and then more officially as censorship began to falter. Western media had always penetrated a little into the East but became even more available in 1989. Probably the best example of one event leading to others is the impact of Hungary's opening its border to Austria in September. Since citizens could already travel freely within Eastern Bloc countries, that move allowed East Germans to head into Czechoslovakia and then Hungary, then to cross the border into Austria and go right into West Germany for the first time in thirty years. Once the Hungarians were letting folks into Austria, it became pretty pointless for East Germany to keep its massively armed border with West Germany closed. R.I.P., Berlin Wall. And almost immediately East and West Germans began talking about reunification, which seemed both natural and totally shocking at the time. In 1989, I was actually taking a modern European history class. More than once my professor rolled into class to say, man, if we want to talk about history, we gotta talk about what's happening right now because it's definitely history!

And these events happened so fast! Yes, all of them built upon conditions and long-term developments in each country. But almost immediately in 1989 events in Eastern Europe were just tumbling forward. British historian Timothy Garton Ash quipped: "what took ten years in Poland, took ten months in Hungary, ten weeks in East Germany, and ten days in Czechoslovakia."[2] And then about ten hours in Bulgaria and ten minutes in Romania.

The basic story: revolutionary change in 1989

It goes something like this. Things were rolling along in Eastern Europe. Folks did okay in the 1950s and 1960s, but in the 1970s and 1980s communist regimes could not and did not respond to citizen needs. Eastern European and Soviet leaders had demonstrated, though, that they were willing to use violence to stop reform movements or protests. People across the Eastern Bloc were increasingly frustrated by the massive gap between regimes' utopian Marxist rhetoric and daily life of hardship and repression. A new Russian leader, Mikhail Gorbachev, started making some changes in the late 80s, changes that finally empowered citizens especially in Eastern Europe to express their frustration. Long-term trends (discussed below) blew up these short-term opportunities for reform. By the end of 1989, regimes had changed in almost every Eastern Bloc country. We can see why now, but no one expected it back then. And it was looking like the USSR itself was next. Wow.

Most people know that the Berlin Wall fell in November 1989. The Wall was the most obvious example of that Iron Curtain that Churchill had talked about, and it was a powerful image. I mean, it's one thing to hear about free elections in Poland or negotiating strikes in Russia. But *seeing* a bunch of ecstatic East Germans high-fiving security guards, embracing West Germans, and taking turns with a pickaxe to tear down the Wall? Now, *that's* some political change right there! If you've seen videos of that event, you probably agree. And in fact, those images inspired further changes in Eastern Europe in 1989.

---

[2]*The Magic Lantern* (New York: Random House, 1990).

Media coverage made plain that the old ways were over in Eastern Europe. But how did we get there, and seemingly so quickly?

The Soviet Bloc, or Eastern Bloc, was a group of satellite states the Soviet Union influenced in Eastern Europe. Like an imperial power, Russia exerted varying degrees of control in these countries. All of them, including the USSR, talked a lot about socialism and communism, but they were all really just authoritarian Stalinist states. People in each of the Eastern Bloc countries, though, had resisted Soviet authority at various points in different ways. Those ways of resisting ultimately shaped the end of communism in that country. At the same time, the fact that these systems had become fairly similar by the 1980s meant that changes in one place could be implemented fairly easily in another.

We saw in Chapter 12 that both East and West European countries sometimes had trouble living up their promises. Life had gotten better for most Europeans in the 1950s and 1960s. When growth slowed down in the 1970s, people tended to blame their governments, especially in Eastern Europe, where the government literally ran the economy. If people got mad about their economic situation in the West, they could vote politicians out or write about problems or make punk music. Those options weren't really available to folks in the Eastern Bloc. Some Eastern Europeans found ways to improve their lives and their society. But many people in these countries became increasingly disillusioned with the ideology that was supposed to be making their life awesome. Communist societies, starting with the 1917 Russian Revolution, always had to manage the distance between utopian Marxist rhetoric and the reality of a highly controlled society. That gap got bigger starting in the 1970s, and most Eastern Europeans felt powerless to do much about it. When they had tried to change their systems in the 1950s and 1960s, their Soviet masters sent in the tanks. So, yeah, there was a lot of cynicism in Eastern Europe by the 1970s.

Women's experiences in these regimes are particularly telling. Technically communist ideology liberated women and gave them the same opportunities as men. Certainly, women could work and support themselves in Eastern Bloc countries in ways that had not been possible before the Second World War. Most of these countries also passed laws to enhance women's control of their bodies and sexuality, including liberal rules about birth control, maternity leave, abortion, and divorce. But they didn't pass laws about who did the housework! These hard-working, liberated female workers still had to go home and do the domestic work their mothers and grandmothers had done—hand washing clothes and cooking meals with few machines and products to make this work easier. It wasn't all doom and gloom: some scholars have argued that economic independence freed women for more romance and better sex.[3]

Women did manage to move into politics and serve in Eastern Bloc governments. Communist ideology, though, recognized women's issues as merely one part of the larger struggle to improve all workers' lives. And women in Eastern Bloc governments would

---

[3]Take that, capitalists! Here's a book title you didn't expect: *Why Women Have Better Sex Under Socialism* by Kristin Ghodsee (New York: Nation Books, 2018).

weaken their authority by drawing attention to "women's issues" or their own domestic situations. Plus, state-run economies focused on heavy industry and the military. The Cold War was on, baby, and wasn't going to be won with washing machines, make-up, or tampons.[4] Because Eastern Bloc regimes paid little attention to women's needs, they had to get creative and resourceful to find or create beauty products, cooking materials, and clothing items.

The fact that most women there lacked sanitary napkins didn't bring down Soviet Bloc regimes, but ignoring citizens' needs eroded faith in these governments. Of course, Western democracies weren't passing laws about feminine supplies either. But they weren't dictating production and preventing companies from responding to women's needs. You live by the sword, you die by the sword. If communist governments were going to take credit for the grand economic improvements of the 1950s and 1960s, then they had to deal with the frustration women (and men) felt about government decisions to focus more on tanks than washing machines. With virtually no public outlets for expressing frustration, women could only roll their eyes and complain to each other. In short, women both benefitted and suffered from communist emancipation. That tension highlights the growing credibility gap in the Eastern Bloc between the liberating rhetoric of Marxism and the often difficult reality of everyday life in a controlled economy. What do you know? It's the dual nature of the Enlightenment once again!

Hopefully by now you've realized that understanding major, dramatic changes demands that we consider long-, medium-, and short-term causes. Events from 1989 to 1991 in Europe were certainly as major as the French Revolution or World War I. We've already covered the long-term gap between communist rhetoric and lived reality. Now let's look at the medium- and short-term causes:

- Medium term: during the Cold War, Eastern European states worked out different relationships with their Soviet bosses, and the pressure of Cold War spending pushed all these economies to the breaking point. Plus, Eastern European and Soviet regimes regularly used violence to control citizens, most notably in 1953, 1956, 1968, and 1981.
- Short term: Gorbachev, as head of the USSR, allowed reformers to make changes, and local activists ran with those opportunities.

Let's consider these medium- and short-term reasons for change under four headings.

1. Previous conflicts and political disillusionment

Citizens in most Eastern European countries had resisted Soviet authority at some point since 1945, and that history shaped how events of 1989 went down. Rewind to the end of

---

[4]In June 1959, Soviet Premiere Nikita Khrushchev and US Vice-President Richard Nixon (1913–94) actually got into a "kitchen debate" at a Soviet exhibit in New York City. The two leaders argued ideology by discussing, among other things, which system provided women better equipment for housework. Women in both places thought: um-hmm, whatever.

World War II. Churchill and Roosevelt were not willing to risk a new fight to stop Stalin from creating a "buffer" of sympathetic states in Eastern Europe. By the early 1950s folks in Eastern Europe knew who was in charge. But they still at various points tried to exert some authority. No one was trying to leave the Soviet sphere of influence or turn capitalist or cozy up to the Americans. They just wanted to create their own form of communism. You go, Eastern European satellites!

Yugoslavia, one of Russia's solid allies during World War II, was the only Eastern European country that was communist but *not* controlled by the Soviet Union. In 1946 they signed right up for the Stalinist program. They copied the Soviet model of connected socialist republics that crushed any nationalist aspirations and held one-party elections. But in 1948, Yugoslavia took some Marshall Plan money from the USA to rebuild. "Not on my watch," said Uncle Joe and kicked them out of the Commie Club. At that point Russia was not strong enough to send in the tanks and bring the Yugoslavs back in line. So this unique communist country with four different languages on its currency got to go its own way. Although there was no resistance to *Soviet* authority, ethnic and nationalist tensions that had been suppressed in Yugoslavia erupted in 1989, caused civil war, and eventually broke Yugoslavia into seven separate nations.

Next, East Germany became maybe the jewel of the Soviet Bloc. You know Stalin wasn't the only person in Russia thinking, "suck on that, Adolf, we got some of Germany as part of our gang now!" However, East German strikes in 1953, demanding more authority for unions and social democratic parties, turned into a full-blown rebellion that the Soviet military had to put down. The peak of the uprising, June 17, became the national holiday in West Germany to show solidarity with rebellious East Germans. That connection between popular East German resistance and reunification defined events in East Germany in 1989. These 1953 events also prompted East German leaders to increase their surveillance of citizens, which ultimately became one of the most hated features of this political system. By the 1980s there was one employee in the Stasi, East Germany's State Security Service, for every 180 citizens!

In Poland and Hungary in 1956, dissidents and some communist leaders made the mistake of taking seriously Russian statements about greater autonomy and decentralization. In February 1956, Khrushchev encouraged all Soviet Bloc citizens to move away from Stalinism and help create better communism. "Well, all right," thought folks in Poland and Hungary, "let's get right on that!" Workers led the way in Poland that summer, advocating for unions and better working conditions—you know, the kind of thing you'd expect in a worker's utopia like communist Poland. Some Polish leaders followed suit. Workers and reformers in Hungary got excited and began doing the same thing. The stiffs in Moscow freaked out. That was *not* what Khrushchev had meant, comrades! The conflict in Hungary actually turned into a real rebellion with popular resistance, government reforms, and military conflict. The Soviets sent in the tanks, crushed the rebellion, executed reformers, and reinstated Soviet control. Eventually, the Soviet Union allowed leaders in both Poland and Hungary a little more freedom to determine policies. In Hungary particularly, the rebellion helped create "goulash communism," a form of Soviet-style rule that nevertheless included some Hungarian ingredients.[5] Mixing ideological elements would inspire protesters to build something new in the 1980s.

I mentioned the "Prague Spring" of 1968 in Chapter 12: yet another case of hopeful Eastern Europeans misreading signs from Moscow. Czech protestors and leaders only wanted to create "socialism with a human face," to try to do what they thought the Soviet Union was after. Nope. After a couple of months, the Soviets sent in the tanks, punished protesters, and reorganized leadership in Czechoslovakia. Many citizens turned away from politics and just resigned themselves to dealing with their situation. Interestingly, this crackdown made *cultural* resistance more important in Czechoslovakia. Here's a great story: the hippy, prog-rock, jam band, the Plastic People of the Universe formed in 1968 during the "Prague Spring." If you check out their wacky music and lyrics about drinking away your problems, you'll realize why the Czech regime was not a fan. Members of the Plastic People got in trouble a lot. In 1976, the band and other underground artists were arrested for taking part in an outlawed festival. In protest, a host of artists signed the Charter 77 that called for greater cultural freedom. A well-known playwright named Václav Havel (1936–2011) signed the Charter and was eventually put under house arrest for doing so. Havel became a leading spokesman in the 1980s against the Czech communist regime and perhaps the most important protester of 1989. He was elected President of post-communist Czechoslovakia in December 1989. So you see, supporting weird, freedom-loving bands can get you elected president.

That's not how you get elected president in Poland, though. Here's how it goes there. You'd think the Poles would have learned their lesson in 1956. But a couple of things in 1978 got them worked up again. First, a former Polish priest became Pope John Paul II. While communism was officially atheist, Soviet leaders had realized that repressing religion too much in Eastern Europe would backfire. Catholicism thus remained an important feature in Polish life, and folks there were inspired by John Paul's spiritual revival. Also in 1978 a group of workers created a national organization to unite trade unions. Still going for that old Marxist ideal, eh? One of the leaders was an electrician named Lech Wałęsa (b. 1943). Wałęsa's group eventually became the national organization Solidarity and pushed for reform in Poland. They wanted to make communism actually about workers. Afraid not, comrades. In 1981, the Soviets sent in the tanks, declared martial law, arrested Wałęsa and others, and banned Solidarity. Wałęsa couldn't even accept the Nobel Peace Prize he won in 1981! He and other Solidarity leaders remained active in the 1980s and led protests against the communist regime in 1989. In June 1989, Solidarity won ninety-nine out of one hundred seats in the newly democratic Polish legislature, and Wałęsa became the first freely elected President of Poland in 1990. So, there's another way to become president: work as an electrician, support unions, and protest.[6]

---

[5]By Cold War standards, this name is considered clever since goulash is one of Hungary's most famous dishes. It's a paprika-spiced soup with chunks of meat, potatoes or vegetables, and whatever else you want. See how that works as a funny political metaphor? Cold War standards for humor were admittedly pretty low.
[6]Yeah, I don't think that plan's going to work everywhere either.

All these movements tried to improve communism, not abandon it. In other words, plenty of people in Eastern Europe wanted to make good on Marxist ideas of egalitarianism and liberation. But they ran into the fact that the Soviet Union just wasn't Marxist. It was a powerful empire that used Marxist ideals to benefit a class of rulers and Party members. Every time reformers tried to get more Marxist than the USSR, they got slapped back. Those recurring blows to idealism meant that, by the 1980s, not many people in the Soviet Bloc really believed in socialist ideology. But people in Eastern Europe remembered the methods and ideas that had challenged the USSR and used them in the late 1980s. Like Havel and Wałęsa, some people who had led protests before became the leaders of events in the late 1980s. In sum, both cynicism about politics *and* hope for reform inspired people to change things in 1989. Hope and hopelessness. Sounds like the 1980s.

2. Economic difficulties

Governments can usually handle cynicism and hopelessness, as long as the economy is okay. By the 1970s, many people in the Eastern Bloc had given up on the ideals of communism. Eastern Bloc civil society wasn't dead, but it connected citizens less and less with their governments. Economic stability therefore served as the main way to legitimize Eastern Bloc governments. Even if consumer choice had never been great in communist countries, citizens there appreciated total employment, free education, and a robust welfare state. Especially in the 1950s and 1960s Eastern Bloc economies improved the lives of most citizens. That began to change in the 1970s for several reasons. Some of the problems that slowed Western economies in the 1970s also plagued Eastern European countries. Both sides, for example, had about maxed out post-war efficiency. Newer economies around the world were taking market share. Energy costs went up. But mainly communist economies ground down because of their screwed-up systems.

Right. So, we've already established the first economic problem: the difference between ideals and reality. Next, these top-down planned economies couldn't change very easily. Following the Soviet model, they all planned everything for five years. Everything. If planners happened to miscalculate how many socks their citizens would need or how much beef, then there were sock and beef shortages. It was very difficult for these massive plans to adapt to changing conditions. Capitalist systems did not satisfy everyone either, but certainly individuals or companies in the West could more easily respond to changing economic necessities or wishes. Plus, all Eastern Bloc economies prioritized heavy industry and military products. Thanks again, Soviet tradition. Cold War military demands pushed consumer needs to the side.

Focusing on heavy industry created other problems. One of the more powerful economic spurs to action in the 1980s was environmental degradation. All industrialized economies have wreaked havoc on the earth; there's no two ways about it. Folks in the West began to realize that in the 1970s. Green political parties cropped up[7] in the

---

[7]See how I did that? "Green ... cropped up." Clearly getting to the end of this book.

early 1980s, bringing greater attention to environmental problems and calling for governmental regulation and economic changes. Needless to say, in the East there was nowhere to talk about this stuff, much less any environmental movements or Green parties or even slightly green-*grey* parties. Questioning your country's economic focus meant questioning communism, which could get you in trouble. So workers suffering from unhealthy factory environments, for instance, had to suck it up for the great communist utopia in which they lived. Or folks dwelling near brown coal plants belching out carcinogenic pollution had little recourse but to suffer and die early.

Eastern Bloc countries also missed out on much of the post-World War II international development and expansion we now call globalization. Yes, communist countries around the world worked together economically. Eastern Bloc countries benefitted from some of the post-colonial trade relationships described in the previous chapter since some of those new states threw in their lot with Team USSR. But the Eastern Bloc countries could not engage very much with international trade, the main economic development that helped advance Western economies. As well, communist countries isolated themselves by choosing not to trade with "imperialist" (capitalist) nations, and Western nations were wary to trade with them or invest there. For one thing, Soviet Bloc currencies did not trade on the international currency market. Pretty hard to buy and sell stuff when your money's no good in many places around the world.

Finally, the Soviet Union encouraged Eastern European economies to specialize. See, *that's* what Comrade Khrushchev was talking about in 1956, not *political* reform. Leaders from Moscow thought that more industrialized countries like East Germany, Czechoslovakia, and Poland could play to those strengths, while more agrarian societies like Hungary, Romania, and Bulgaria could keep on rocking in the farm world. That sounded good in Moscow, but it made the USSR more dependent upon a system of satellite economies and encouraged very uneven economic development across the Eastern Bloc. These bigger structural economic issues were less obvious when things were good, but the problems inherent in Eastern Bloc economies became more obvious when growth slowed. And censorship could not keep out all information from the West. By the 1970s Eastern Europeans knew that they were falling behind the West in terms of material life. All the while their leaders kept going on about how much better things were than in the West. Uh, credibility gap much?

3. Pressure of the Cold War arms race

Alright, the ideological conflict between the USA and the USSR was sort of a war, or at least a massive arms race. And it was damn expensive. Both sides were trying to outdo each other with more and cooler military technology. Ultimately, the USA and its Western allies had more resources to fight this conflict. The Soviets and their allies had to devote much larger chunks of their economy to military growth. The USSR was spending like 20 to 30 percent of its gross domestic product on the military during the Cold War, whereas the United States spent 5 to 10 percent. There's a scene in Stanley

Figure 14.2 Cold War competition on the Silver Screen in *Dr. Strangelove*.

Kubrick's great Cold War black comedy, *Dr. Strangelove*, when the Soviet ambassador complains that "in the end we could not keep up with the arms race, the space race, and the peace race. At the same time our people grumbled for more nylons and washing machines." The Soviets in the film have decided to create a much cheaper "doomsday weapon" (a bunch of buried nuclear weapons that could end life on earth) in order to keep up with the USA. You really should watch this movie some time; I think I've said that already. Anyway, the Cold War arms race put greater pressure on the Soviet Union and its allies than on the West. After the Cold War, Western leaders rightly noted that this pressure helped weaken Eastern Bloc economies.

Soon after the Cold War ended, I saw Margaret Thatcher (1925–2013) give a talk about the Cold War arms race.[8] Thatcher had served as British Prime Minister from 1979 to 1990 and was, with US President Ronald Reagan (1911–2004), right in the thick of the final stages of the Cold War conflict. She said that she and Ronnie used the arms race to help win the Cold War and, well, "you're welcome." True enough, but Thatcher was taking credit for having *planned* to use the arms race to help end the Cold War. That's what we call a *post hoc* fallacy—where you see that one thing followed another and assume therefore that the first thing caused the second. We might also fault her for *teleology*,

---

[8]She came to my college. Thatcher was a chemist by training and donned a lab coat and did experiments with chemistry students, which I thought was pretty cool. Needless to say, I was not one of those chemistry students.

where you see history's development as an inevitable march to where we are today, instead of random events that we can only put in order with hindsight. I mean, you can't look at the results of something and then say that you totally *meant* to do something to make it turn out that way. That'd be like saying, "yeah, yeah, I *meant* to break that window last weekend because I knew it would allow me to befriend a nice public safety officer, help me redirect my financial resources, and build character." Thatcher was correct, though, that the Soviets could not keep up with the arms race and try to provide goods in a planned economy. And every time one side created some new nuke or stealth plane or computer system, it raised the stakes for the Cold War. It also put more dangerous weapons in the hands of nervous people and increased the economic pressure on both sides. Ultimately, Team USSR just couldn't keep doing that.

The Cold War arms race pressure further expanded the gap between Marxist rhetoric and lived reality, too. After all, Marx had promised the state would wither away and claimed that nationalism and militarism were tools of the bourgeoise to hold on to power. Uh, yeah, that's not what anyone in the 1970s and 1980s was seeing in or out of the Soviet Bloc. It was more accidental than Thatcher and Reagan later claimed, but the Cold War arms race did ratchet up pressure on the Soviet Bloc that further strained that system by the 1980s.

4. Gorbachev's "Frank Sinatra" policy

"Start spreading the news." No, not *that* Sinatra standard. Gorbachev preferred "My Way." That's what he told Eastern European countries: go make communism *your way*. Look, Gorby wasn't naïve. He recognized that the Soviet Union and its allies faced some serious problems by the 1980s. They could send rockets to Venus but not provide citizens with basic kitchen appliances. They had loads of doctors and hospitals but an increasingly sick population. Alcoholism was about as rampant as cynicism. Rather than sweeping these problems under the commie carpet, Gorbachev went kinda nuts and started looking around for ways to improve things. In particular he proposed two major changes: *perestroika* or "restructuring" and *glasnost* or "openness."

The restructuring he suggested was to dial back the control the central government exercised over the economy of the USSR and even its Eastern Bloc allies. Wait, could the head of the Soviet Union be proposing *less* government control? Pretty radical stuff. Gorby also called for more socialism and more democracy. Well, there's one thing that folks on *both* sides of the Iron Curtain could agree upon: those two things do *not* go together! Okay, maybe there are elements of socialism in Western European social market economies. But more socialism and more democracy in the Soviet Union? You be crazy, Gorbachev! Y'all been beating down socialism and democracy since 1917. But Gorbachev was serious. He wrote a book, he toured places, he actually listened to people.

Okay, how about *glasnost* or openness? Khrushchev had been a little more open. But really what went on inside the Soviet system was hard to read. I mean, intelligence agencies across the Western world actually employed people called "Kremlinologists."

Figure 14.3 Mikhail Gorbachev and Ronald Reagan.

They analyzed the smallest information or symbols coming out of the Kremlin, the building that housed the Russian central government, in order to figure out what the hell the Soviets might be doing. So, now the leader of the USSR is saying they want to be open? What's more, Gorbachev called for criticism of Soviet policies, for removing the censorship that had prevented open discussion about problems. He wanted dissent, challenge, and discussion. He believed they would ultimately strengthen the Soviet system. This was big stuff. Gorby was really undoing the whole way the Soviet government had functioned for seventy years. He wanted to find a way to make the ideals of Lenin and maybe even Marx more real in the Soviet Bloc. He knew how disillusioned people were.

It gets better. Gorbachev recognized that Eastern European countries could be more nimble and would be better places to try out new ideas than big ole superpower Russia. So he went there and asked Eastern Europeans to give suggestions to the USSR. You saw that right: the Soviet Union asked Eastern Europeans how to fix communism. Eastern Europeans had thoughts:

Eastern Europeans: Thanks, but we've been through this before.

Gorbachev: No, really this time we totally want your input, your experimentation.

Eastern Europeans: Okay, but our suggestions have not, uh, been well received before.

Gorbachev: Right. Sorry about that, but this time we mean it.

Eastern Europeans: So, even if we suggest, like, new forms of government, you're not going to send in the tanks?

Gorbachev: Not anymore; we're done with that.

Eastern Europeans: Really? You will actually listen to us? You want our ideas?

Gorbachev: Yes, please! We need to fix communism.

Eastern Europeans: Okay, let's start with this: please get the hell out.

Gorbachev: Hmm, not quite what I was expecting.

Together, perestroika, glasnost, and the "Sinatra policy" began to create space for considering real changes in the Soviet Bloc. Gorbachev meant it. He even gave a speech to the United Nations on December 7, 1988 explaining that the Soviet Union would no longer use its military to subdue or influence its satellite states. Nice. He was, however, rather naïve in expecting that everyone in the Soviet Bloc loved communism the way he did. He underestimated how just cynical people had gotten about the system.

And Gorbachev majorly underestimated nationalism. Turns out that communism had not gotten rid of nationalism. In fact, forty years of *Soviet* nationalism crushing national self-determination in Eastern Europe had actually *strengthened* nationalism. Russia would find out about that in 1991, when twelve of the fifteen Soviet Republics bolted and formed new countries. Cough, cough, decolonization. So instead of Gorby getting a bunch of ideas to fix communism, he helped start nationalist revolutions across Eastern Europe. Regrets, he's had a few.

Nationalism and ethnic tension in Eastern Europe quickly ran through the stages we talked about in Chapter 5. Liberating Enlightenment nationalism gave Eastern Europeans inspiration to break free from Soviet control. Lots of things were going on there around 1989, but certainly nationalism was a driving force in all those events. It didn't take long for the violent, repressive, "Othering" form of nationalism (also courtesy of ye olde Enlightenment) to cause more conflicts. For example, not long after the peaceful, popular "Velvet Revolution" in Czechoslovakia, the Slovaks wanted their own country, and the place split into two separate republics. More dramatically, in Yugoslavia nationalism that had been suppressed since the 1920s—sometimes violently— came roaring back. That country ultimately broke into seven republics, in a couple of cases after bloody civil wars. Those conflicts included human rights violations and genocide.

One more thing that Gorbachev underestimated: the appeal of consumerism. Remember that Eastern Europeans' various attempts at reform from the 1950s to the early 1980s really aimed to make socialism better. They were not trying to leave the Eastern Bloc and be like Western countries, much less like the USA. They may have envied some of the West's material wealth, but most reformers believed enough in socialist ideals not to run into the arms of consumer capitalism.

Well, the decades of cynicism about communist economics had kind of changed that. Plus, capitalism was in some ways easier to implement than democracy. And you can't fault the Eastern Bloc folks for mistaking capitalism for democracy. Many people still do that today. And why not? Consumerism has been such a powerful force in the modern world that many people already by the 1980s saw it as a form of economic democracy. We could debate whether that's true or not, but it's easy to see why the ability to purchase what one needs and even what one wants held great appeal for folks living under austere Eastern Bloc economies. They may have fought for freedom and democracy. But those things are harder to appreciate sometimes than a new washing machine, sanitary napkins, or fruit in the wintertime.

So, here's an interesting counterfactual idea: if Eastern European countries *had* been able to reform communism in the 1950s, 1960s, and 1970s, maybe the Cold War wouldn't have ended. Or maybe it would have changed dramatically or even ended much earlier. Or maybe there would have been world peace! Okay, time to stop.

Watch the Soviet Union crumble

It probably comes as no surprise that, after these reforms and changes in Eastern Europe in 1989, the USSR was bound to experience similar trauma. Russia has rightly been a major actor in this book, especially in the twentieth century. You could easily argue that the Russian Revolution of 1917 was one of the most important events of that century. If the French Revolution was Enlightenment with guns, then the Soviet Revolution was Marxism with lots of guns. Or at least *mistaken* Marxism with guns. We've seen how far that regime veered from actual Marxist ideas. Historians of the future may look at Russian history and say that the Soviet Union was just another example of its empire or another way this massive place has expanded and contracted over the centuries. That's true to some extent, but Fukuyama was right that *the* ideological conflict of the twentieth century was communism vs. capitalism/democracy. It shaped how governments and average people around the world behaved. The Cold War from the late 1940s to the late 1980s most clearly encapsulates this long battle. That conflict more or less ended when the Soviet Union collapsed in 1991.

Basically, all that crazy change in 1989 Eastern Europe spread back to Russia. The Soviet Union had dominated the governments and lives of Eastern Europeans since World War II. Then suddenly Gorbachev basically let the Eastern Bloc go. He had asked them for suggestions to fix the USSR, and he got 'em: we want nationalism and consumerism, comrade! Those two concepts struck at the heart of the Soviet empire since it was based on controlling nationalist sentiment and consumer behavior in the name of Marxist ideology. We saw above that previous conflicts with the Soviets shaped the massive changes of 1989 in Eastern Europe. In many ways the quick fade of the Soviet Union in 1991 goes back even further. We learned in Chapter 5 how Russia grew into a huge, multi-national empire by the nineteenth century. Soviet leaders in the early twentieth century used communist ideology to suppress

So, About Modern Europe …

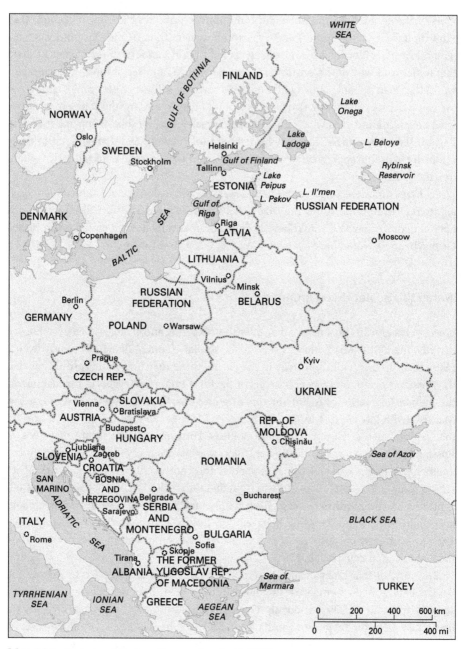

Map 14.1 Central and Eastern Europe after the Cold War.

252

nationalism and try to connect at least 120 different ethnic groups in the USSR. That worked, until it didn't.

When ethnic groups in the Soviet Republics around the edges of Russia saw that Eastern Europeans were peacing out, they starting doing the same thing. In fact, people in many parts of the Soviet Union (Latvia, Lithuania, Estonia, Azerbaijan, Armenia, Georgia, Ukraine, Moldova, and Belarus) were already protesting by 1988 against Russian control. Thanks, *glasnost*! As in other decolonization processes we studied in Chapter 13, Islam inspired folks in some of the southwestern Soviet republics. After long-time dissidents like Andrei Sakharov (1921–89) and new reformers like Boris Yeltsin (1931–2007) were elected in 1989 to the Soviet Congress, reform really got going. Protests expanded that year especially in non-Russian parts of the country, and sometimes Soviet authorities put them down violently. Nationalist parties won majorities in six Soviet Republics in February 1990 and declared their sovereignty from the USSR.

In June 1991, Boris Yeltsin was elected President of Russia, the biggest of the Soviet Republics, and declared Russia independent of the Soviet Union. What?! Russia out of the USSR? Eventually, they joined with two other nearby republics to form the Russian Federation. In August 1991, hardline communists, who were angry that Gorbachev was letting the USSR fall apart, tried to take over the government. Yeltsin and other reformers stopped them, but it was clear that Gorby's time was up. In the autumn of 1991, giddy republics were pretty much running out of the Soviet Union. The United Nations and European Union began recognizing these new countries. In early December the USSR ended the 1922 treaty that had connected all the Soviet Republics. On Christmas Day of 1991, the Soviet flag flew for the last time over the Kremlin. The next day the Soviet Council of the Republics voted the USSR out of existence.

Well, how did all this change work out?

Mixed bag but generally improved. Most of the Eastern European nations managed to transition fairly successfully to market economies and democratic political systems, while the new states from the shards of the Soviet Union have not fared so well. Most post-communist countries in Eastern Europe have seen significant improvements in people's standards of living, consumption, and health. It took a while, though. The first decade after communism was pretty rough since there was no blueprint for how to make this transition. And there was no huge pot of money like the Marshall Plan after the Second World War to help pay for changes. Most Eastern European countries have built have successful democracies and boast less income disparity than other capitalist economies. However, since 2016 right-wing parties that oppose liberalism have gained ground in some of these countries—as they have in other places. Nationalism and xenophobia have sometimes channeled popular resentment in East Europe toward perceived "enemies" in and out of the country. We'll talk a little more about that in the final chapter. By most measures, though, former communist countries in Eastern Europe have made the move from being post-communist experiments to "normal countries."

The former Soviet republics have mostly backed away from democratic and free market reforms, usually into some form of dictatorship. Of the fifteen former republics of the USSR, only the Baltic states (Latvia, Lithuania, and Estonia) have effectively functioning democracies and free market economies. Three of the former Soviet states—Turkmenistan, Uzbekistan, and Tajikistan—rank as some of the worst places in the world for political and civil rights. The Russian Federation has become more autocratic, less economically free, and increasingly militaristic. Unfortunately, these post-Soviet state developments are more in line with trends across the world in the twenty-first century. Around 1989 the world seemed to be getting more free, more democratic, and providing more civil rights. Since 2005, however, the number of countries with these features has been slowly declining.

One final point about Fukuyama. In his 1989 essay he addresses two potential ideologies that might challenge liberal democracy: nationalism and religious fundamentalism. While both of these ideas have continued to cause major conflict in the world, they do not in Fukuyama's mind represent real threats to the universalist ideology of liberal economic and political systems. Nationalism isn't really an ideology, he argues. It's usually just a wish to be independent of someone else or dominate someone else. Religious fundamentalism has mainly flourished in the Muslim world and holds little appeal from non-Muslims. Maybe so, Mr. Hegelian Fukuyama. But those trends have been important elements for identity politics. We'll turn to that in our final chapter. I'll let you decide if it's post-history.

CHAPTER 15
YOU DO YOU: IDENTITY POLITICS

I love playing German hip-hop for my students. The music begins and they bob their heads appropriately and smile that, finally, I'm playing music they know. But then some dude starts rapping in German! Usually they snicker at the very idea of *German* hip-hop. I quickly become the obnoxious professor and explain that, you know, German works well for poetry and rap because all the verbs end with "en" and usually come at the end of sentences, so it rhymes well. Then we get on to why German hip-hop matters.

Hip-hop has become the main language of pop, coolness, and youth around the world.[1] White and black Germans have used hip-hop to express important points about being German since the 1980s. Check out Samy Delux's 2009 "Dis wo ich herkomm," which talks about "this is our Germany, your Germany," the land "where I come from," a fairly powerful message from a black German. Eko Fresh, who is Turkish-German, kicks it up a notch with his 2018 "Aber" or "But . . ." This song features a white German rapper and a Turkish German rapper talking about what they dislike about each other's culture. It's based on Joyner Lucas's 2017 "I'm Not a Racist." The white guy says, "I'm not a Nazi, but . . ." and lists problems he sees with Turks in Germany, and then the Turkish guy says, "I love Germany, but . . ." and talks about the problems in the country and oppression of Turks. Then the often hilarious Eko Fresh ends things on a positive note about multi-racial Germany and says "but y'all will work it out."

Since the 1990s, artists all across Europe, especially those of color, have used hip-hop to express identity. In fact, music and popular culture generally have become some of the main "political" venues in the West for dealing with self-expression and difference. We've already seen culture, especially music, do that pretty regularly in this book. Remember Beethoven's reaction to Napoleon or "Skokiaan" as an example of decolonization. Especially since World War II, popular culture has been closely connected to Enlightenment issues for two related reasons. First, consumerism—defining yourself in part by what you buy—has become *the* most common ideology in the West, especially since 1990. Second, the big, dual impacts of the Enlightenment—liberation and control—have since the 1970s largely come down to issues of identity politics. Identity politics means people working out how specific social groups defined by race, gender, religion, ethnicity, sexuality, ability, and so forth can express their experiences and be free to live as they wish. It may be imperfect, but popular music offers a way to consider these issues. Certainly straight-up political conflicts over Enlightenment ideas haven't always gone so well: ahem, nationalism, imperialism, world wars, Holocaust, Cold War, etc. So maybe it's time to give something else a try. Especially if it has a good beat.

---

[1] A few years ago, Gennie, the "queen of Mongolian hip-hop," argued that this music expressed what it meant to be Mongolian today.

Building the argument

Who's glad this is our last chapter? It's okay to admit. I'll confess that it's not been easy to sustain an argument this long. But I'm hoping that this book's main point—that big ideas have shaped how people behave in the West—has become pretty clear. This final chapter is a little different. Unlike previous chapters, it's not squarely focused on a set time period. The main emphasis is the late twentieth century to the present. But we consider the longer history of identity politics, or the way that certain groups (often defined by gender, race, sexuality, cultural identity, or other characteristics that matter to them) behave together politically.

Identity politics have raised some pretty potent issues: who gets to define or name whom, how much we should live and let live, how much should governments should protect rights, especially of minority groups, and whether Enlightenment thought oppresses more than it liberates. Identity politics have been important, hot-button topics in the Western world for some years. Consider the #MeToo movement, Brexit, Black Lives Matter, conflicts over immigration, laws about transgender rights or same-gender marriage, independence referendums, fat- or slut-shaming, or discussions about NATO and the EU's purpose. All these contemporary issues stem in some way from identity politics. This chapter looks at how we got here and what it means.

Naturally, we want to trace the history of identity politics and consider how our beloved Enlightenment figures in here. Naturally. Enlightenment thinkers imagined new ways for people to define themselves and relate to their larger society. The liberating side of the Enlightenment promised opportunity, equality, and state-guaranteed rights. Yet states and elites continued to limit who actually got rights and protection. Especially in the nineteenth century, rights were more about *individualism*, which isn't quite the same thing as identity. Next, world-breaking Nietzsche and mind-bending Freud messed all that up. Their highly personal, internal definition of the individual kick started the modern concept of identity. They helped us appreciate the difference between *public* individualism and *private* identity.

Then both of those concepts took some heavy blows in the first half of the twentieth century. World War II and its aftermath, though, strengthened the concept of identity around the world. Some developments like the Cold War, NATO, and the European Union proposed new connections and ways for identity to work in Europe. Other movements like decolonization, civil rights, women's and gay rights helped make identity a label *and* a way of doing politics. Until about 1968 many people pushing liberation assumed they were all working toward the same big ole freedom for everyone. Conflicts and protests in 1968 in East and West Europe gave some people hope for big change. But, ultimately: not so much. By the 1970s that dream of large Enlightenment liberation for everyone splintered into more narrowly defined identity politics.

The failure of would-be revolutions and big reforms encouraged more people to focus instead on improving the lives of specific groups, like ethnic or racial minorities, women, or queer folks. The liberating promise of Enlightenment thought could still inform these movements, yet the Enlightenment's tendency to define and control had often limited the same individuals pushing identity politics. In short, identity politics help us see the continued dual impact of Enlightenment thought in the modern world.

Identity before World War II

Identity politics may be fairly new, but identity is not. Duh. We can identify concepts of identity and individualism in plenty of ancient thought. Yes, even people long, long ago understood themselves to be individuals. They didn't go around using the pronoun "we" or thinking, "wait, am I you? Are you me?" The modern concept of individualism and identity, though, came partly from the Enlightenment tension between the individual and society. Surprised? All our Enlightenment dudes were, in one way or another, interested in that relationship, and we've been working through that topic for much of this book.

In the nineteenth century, Enlightenment ideas about individual identity mainly benefitted the white men with property who were becoming more important in European society. Middle-class guys were really into protecting individualism. And that individualism—wouldn't you know it?—was mostly what privileged white men were supposed to be: autonomous people with enough property and smarts to engage in a free, open, democratic society. No doubt that sounded good to women and people of color too. But we've seen throughout this book how the assumptions of the Enlightenment liberated white men with property and limited everyone else. Identity politics, especially in the twentieth century, eventually opened up the liberating promise of Enlightenment thought to everyone by empowering people who had not traditionally been the cool kids of European society. These uppity folks pushed governments to recognize and protect minority rights.

The modernist thinkers we learned about in Chapter 8 helped define identity more personally and internally starting the late nineteenth century. Nietzsche, Freud, and other Killers of Santa Claus said that what you feel and want reveals who you are as much as what you think and do. Identity for them was about who you understand yourself to be. Freud explained that we have multiple identities—our deepest irrational desires (the id), the rational Self struggling with those desires (the ego), and our public Self that engages with others (the superego). Even if we just simplify things to the personal vs. the public Self, that perspective explains a lot about how identity politics work. In many ways the ultimate goal of identity politics is to match those two things up. I'm pretty sure Locke, Montesquieu, Rousseau, Smith, and those guys did not quite think like that. (Well, maybe Rousseau did.) But certainly, this idea of the private individual being free to define the public individual reflects the ongoing power of Enlightenment thought.

In the early twentieth century, some activists pushed these ideas into actual identity politics. In 1903 W.E.B. Du Bois (1868–1963), a Black American sociologist and activist, published *The Souls of Black Folk*, which argued that people of color living in majority white societies had to consider how they view themselves vs. how white society views them. In other words, identity functions differently for groups without power. Du Bois helped encourage black liberation in the USA, Europe, and Africa. Around the same time, the German doctor and sexologist Magnus Hirschfeld (1868–1935) did some of the earliest scientific research on homosexuality. He spent his career using scientific evidence to dispel myths about homosexuality and trans-gendered people and to challenge violently repressive laws against them. Finally, in the years before the First World War, women's suffrage movements grew in strength in the Western world. British activist Sylvia Pankhurst (1882–1960) particularly revised expectations about women's public behavior in order to highlight the hypocrisy of British ideals. She and others ultimately helped women secure the right to vote after the First World War in most Western countries. Pankhurst also connected women's rights to those of other groups with little power, campaigning for workers and against imperialism.

Subsequent ideological conflicts—above all two world wars—made identity politics even more urgent. In some ways the big ideas at stake in the 1930s and 1940s—communism, democracy fascism—intensified concerns about identity. Communism in the USSR made workers' identities into weapons to fight fascism. On the one hand this super simple concept empowered all citizens of the Soviet Union. On the other hand, this fight also meant that citizens had to suppress feeling like a woman, an ethnic minority, a religious believer, or anything else besides "worker." During the Second World War, the Western Allies enlisted many types of people to support democracy, and those folks got to thinking that maybe, at last, they deserved some rights too. The experience of diverse forces defending democratic ideals would have profound effects after the war.

Fascism and especially Nazism really intensified government-defined identity in violent ways. The Third Reich's racist vision of the world assumed that people = their racial identity: Aryan, Jew, Slav, etc. Like communism, Nazism believed that single definition was more important than anything else. So, whether Jews *felt* Jewish or not didn't matter. They were racially defined enemies and had to be eliminated. Nazi ideology maintained that women had a primary duty to the race, to reproduce, and they were treated accordingly in the Third Reich. Gay men, on the other hand, prevented reproduction, so the Third Reich tried to "rehabilitate" them or killed them. The Holocaust thus fundamentally redefined identity by demonstrating how much harm could result when a powerful state made one type of identity *the* definition of citizenship and a reason for mass murder. The attempted Nazi genocide of Jews and others made clear how important it was for minority groups to obtain rights and protections from governments. Plenty of Jews concluded thereafter that only a Jewish state could protect them from antisemitism. Within three years of the war's end, Jewish refugees from Europe and elsewhere had created the state of Israel. Israel's history since 1948 has of course been complicated, and its leaders have had to deal with various identity issues too.

In all these cases the experience of World War II made people think differently about identity. The violent suppression of identity in the Soviet Union and especially the Third Reich demonstrated how easily big bullies could beat up small groups of individuals. Repressed groups began to realize they would need to advocate for themselves and find new ways to secure rights and protection.

Identity after the Second World War

Recall that in Chapter 13 colonial subjects after World War II were, like, "okay, we fought for y'all (again), died for ya'll (again); time to loosen the reins or let 'em go"? There was a lot of that going on after the war. Women, workers, African-American soldiers, cowboys, Indians, other colonial subjects all expected that their support for and sacrifices in the war merited full citizenship, just like the white guys. Sometimes that happened.[2]

We'll return to decolonization in a moment, but two general trends after World War II also helped refine ideas about identity. First, some of the larger political developments we've studied pushed integration. The post-war superpowers brought people together in military alliances, economic cooperation, and ideological unity. We saw how that worked in Chapter 12. Supra-national—that is, above the nation—organizations minimized national difference. In many places, people could instead stress regional and local identities. West Germans, for example, had to be careful about expressing *national* pride for historical reasons (ahem, World War II, Holocaust) and current alliances (Cold War, American troops stationed there). So, while Germans couldn't sing their national anthem, it was fine to belt out regional songs. Similarly, Romanians living in Transylvania could celebrate that region without offending national communist or Soviet authorities. (I'd like to tell you that they did so by dressing up like Count Dracula, but it was usually more benign cultural festivals than gothic role-play.)

Second, consumerism. Hopefully the last three chapters have demonstrated that Europeans were into buying stuff—though maybe a little less in Eastern Europe. During good times and bad, what people in Europe bought helped them define who they were and their connections with each other. We've seen this trend growing since the 1920s. The varying ability to consume made Europeans more aware of economic and class differences. Plus, people's overall standard of living was going up, and that gave them more disposable income to purchase markers of identity—clothing, music, food, movies and television, furniture, etc. Consumption thus gave specific groups ways to express themselves and even use their buying power for political purposes. Let's look more closely at a couple of the biggest impacts on identity in Europe: decolonization and political integration.

Decolonization, immigration, and multicultural Europe

Clearly the end to Europeans' empires shaped how they thought about *national* identity. They were both sorry and glad to lose colonies. But in many cases relations between European powers and their former colonies continued. Indeed, those relationships often helped fuel economic growth in the 1950s and 1960s. I think we've established that

---

[2]The US military, for example, desegregated in 1948, giving American men of all backgrounds the same opportunity to serve. In 1979, women could enlist equally and, in 2013, serve in combat.

World War II killed a lot of people. So, as European economies expanded after the war, they faced a labor shortage. And increasingly educated and affluent Europeans weren't so into the low-end jobs like cleaning toilets and serving fast food. They invited "guest workers" from various places outside of Europe to come help out, often drawing from established colonial relationships. Pakistanis, Indians, Caribbean people, and sub-Saharan Africans, for example, often worked in the United Kingdom, thanks to the 1948 British Nationality Act, which allowed Commonwealth citizens to settle there. North Africans and Southeast Asians went to France. Ethiopians, to Italy, etc. West Germans had no colonies but welcomed workers from Turkey, with whom they strong relationship. The Turkish-German rapper in Eko Fresh's "But . . ." makes this point.

This immigration, which lasted until the early 1970s, helped drive economic reconstruction in Western Europe. "Guest workers" were often men who were there to earn money for families back home. But almost immediately, and especially starting in the 1970s, families came to join these workers.

"Hold on," said some Western European leaders, "maybe you didn't understand the first part of 'guest worker.'" European governments and employers needed *temporary* help, thank you very much. And when their economies slowed down in the 1970s, suddenly those crappy jobs that immigrants had filled didn't look so bad. In fact, as unemployment rose, some Europeans got mad that immigrants had jobs at all. Never mind that Europeans had invited them to do so and probably still didn't want to clean toilettes.

Meanwhile, immigrants were settling in, sending kids to school, and contributing to society. By the early 1980s, most Western European countries were embroiled in debates about immigration, settlement, and identity. The British had restricted non-white immigration in 1968 with the Commonwealth Immigrants Act, basically reversing their 1948 open-door policy. Other governments began passing laws to limit immigration, and popular culture became a battleground for racial conflicts. In the UK, for example, some punk musicians formed ska bands that promoted racial harmony, while others crated skinhead "oi" music that was often violently white supremacist. For the first time really, these countries had to wrestle with problems and promises of a multicultural society.[3] Eastern European interaction with non-Europeans visiting or moving there during this time was much more limited and shaped by communist ideology. Overall post-colonial migration connected three important issues: (1) the racist, colonial past, (2) present-day economic pressures, and (3) long-term issues of integration and ideas about civilization. This combination could be explosive, especially starting in the 1990s. Together these issues also reveal an interesting liberal paradox: many Western European states offered open markets but closed states. Yep, the Janus-faced Enlightenment is still at it.

---

[3] The American response: welcome to our world.

Let's get together: forces of integration in Europe

But listen, man, there were good vibes going on too. Some of the developments we've already studied encouraged European integration and thus created new contexts for identity politics. It may be strange to say, but the Cold War kinda brought people together. Yes, yes, it was a line in the sand and all that. But on both sides of that line, people had to come together, even if it was against a common enemy. This conflict emphasized economic identity, that is, the ways that various groups contributed to the dominant ideology.

Folks in the Eastern Bloc were encouraged to look beyond racial differences and see common goals with new socialist/communist nations. Communist ideology claimed that Eastern Europeans and former colonial subjects in Africa and Asia shared the bond of being oppressed by the imperialist West. Stick it to the man! Eastern Bloc countries even embraced American jazz as the music of those oppressed by white imperialists. Some of these new allies moved to Eastern Europe, though far fewer than the migration of "guest workers" to the West. The sometimes warm blanket of communism minimized identity conflicts in the Eastern Bloc. But not forever. Xenophobia surged in Eastern Europe after 1990 because Eastern Europeans had not worked through the prejudices and conflicts that come with a multicultural society.

Meanwhile out West, them cowboys was raising a posse too. Their ideological spurs were jingling and creating one kind of common identity—a steely-eyed capitalist. Sometimes those confident capitalists could welcome strangers to town as folks that would help build a strong economy. And one way that former imperialists could make themselves feel better about the whole colonial exploitation thing was to invite some former colonial subjects to participate in economic development. More than a few former white imperialists felt pretty good about helping out poor, dark folks. For sure that experience of immigrating to Europe helped shaped the identities of non-Europeans. But this multicultural interaction also added a new dimension to white identity. For some Europeans it was the first time they had thought much about being white or about the role of race in their society.

The European Union (and its predecessor organizations) especially created a mechanism for economic integration in Western Europe. I mean, it was built upon cooperation between former enemies Germany and France. By the 1980s, this group contained twelve nations that were increasingly functioning as a common economic market. The EU certainly never ended nationalism but did minimize economic expressions of nationalism. In some ways this trend toward economic integration gave both immigrants and white Europeans the opportunity to define themselves as something other than just political citizens. At the same time, the EU has also allowed white citizens in charge to open their markets while closing their states to immigration. In other words, the EU's very function as an integrating organization has, oddly enough, actually allowed nationalist and even racist sentiments in flourish in Europe. Presumably that was not the plan.

So, About Modern Europe ...

Gender and queer rights

It should no longer be a shock that the Enlightenment has been kinda schizophrenic, especially when we look at the Big E's record on women's rights. From the very earliest examples of Locke talking about all men being equal, Enlightenment thought contained the potential to liberate *and* limit women. Until the mid-twentieth century, however, the Enlightenment tended to reinforce rather than reject long-standing prejudices against women. The assumptions built into most Enlightenment ideas assumed women to be examples of the "darkness" that needed to be controlled or overcome. Queen of the Night anyone? And yet many advocates for women's rights, starting in the eighteenth century, continued to say that, yes, these concepts of individual freedom and equality can and should apply to women. We saw in Chapter 6, for example, that supporters laid out a platform for women's rights in 1848 in Seneca Falls, New York. Women finally gained the right to vote in many Western democracies in the 1920s, in part thanks to their contributions to the Great War and the efforts of suffrage movements since the early 1900s.[4] This "First Wave" of feminism had broad roots in ideas of equality but mainly looked narrowly to getting women voting rights. Mission (mostly) accomplished in Europe. At the same time, plenty of women earned some freedom in industrial societies another way: they got jobs that gave them more economic independence.

We've already seen how the two world wars significantly reshaped women's experiences and even basic ideas about gender in Europe. The blustering, trigger-happy ideologies of these decades also offered women some opportunities. Communism liberated women, at least on paper, and sometimes even let them take up arms. That also happened, by the way, in the Spanish Civil War in the late 1930s, where states had less influence. Even fascism gave women very narrowly defined power as mothers and heads of households. Of course, the main way that women earned greater authority during this period was doing the work that men left behind when they went off to fight. Symbols of women's contributions like "Rosie the Riveter" (Figure 15.1) redefined traditional gender roles *and* demonstrated that more women had economic independence.

After the war women in Europe had to fight against many men's (and women's) desire to return to traditional values. The chaos of war and subsequent massive changes made traditional gender relations seem reassuring to many people in Europe and the United States. In 1949 French philosopher Simone de Beauvoir (1908–86) published *The Second Sex*, a book that challenged women to defy those social assumptions. Her ideas, along with others like the 1963 *Feminine Mystique* by American writer Betty Friedman (1921–2006), helped spark the Second Wave of feminism. Feminists after World War II identified a variety of social, economic, and political barriers to women's equality. Many of the

---

[4]Women also got the vote in the USA in 1920. But, believe it or not, one of the first places in the world to allow women to vote was in the Wyoming Territory in the western part of the United States. Women could vote there starting in 1869! I'm afraid some of the reasons reflect a rather limited view of Enlightenment liberation: politicians there hoped that white women would offset any voting power of Black or Chinese men. You win some, you lose some.

Figure 15.1 Rosie the Riveter during World War II.

women's rights movements across Europe focused on improving issues particular to women, such as access to birth control and abortion.

Feminists in the 1960s sometimes worked with other liberation groups, such as those advocating gay rights or racial equality. At the same time, women who were involved in broader progressive movements (for racial equality or workers' rights or against the Vietnam War) often found themselves doing the usual "women's work" in those settings too. Having to serve the coffee or be secretaries or clean up after meetings for radical causes didn't strike these activists as real change. Progressive movements, in other words, both inspired and annoyed women into focusing more on their own concerns and lack of authority.

By the 1970s, many activists had concluded that they should work specifically for changes to benefit women—equal pay, reproductive rights, maternity leave and health care, and greater protection from sexual assault. Middle-class white women had generally led the push for women's rights. After all, they had the resources, education, and connections to wage that fight. But women of color became more aware of their unique challenges starting in the 1970s. Black feminists in the United States particularly articulated the ways that race and gender *together* shaped their experience. Now, that perspective was not the same for, say, Ethiopian women in Italy or Sumatran women in Holland. But this idea that race and gender and even class together shaped experience increasingly defined identity politics starting in the 1980s. Being aware of how forces of prejudice come together has become known as critical race theory or *intersectionality*.

These ideas point out the problems and promises of identity politics: multiple identities define people's experiences, yet activists sometimes divide into ever-smaller groups with narrow aims. We can see one example, though, of how broad Enlightenment ideas have specifically benefitted women in the German Green Party. This group, which formed in the late 1970s chiefly to promote environmental issues, also recognized early on the need to ensure gender equality. The Party introduced a quota system within its own ranks to ensure that 50 percent of their representatives were women. They have used a similar means to help elect Germans of color.

Queer rights in Europe began by combating the idea of homosexuality as a *negative* identity—an illegal activity, a medical issue, strange or problematic behavior. The original meaning of "queer" was basically just odd or suspicious, and many people used that term to define gay people as abnormal. In the 1940s and 1950s, gay men particularly fought to be "normal" members of society, to challenge definitions of homosexuality as something medically pathological or illegal. Most European nations had long-standing rules outlawing homosexual activity. Gay men in Germany, for instance, were prosecuted for a century under a law passed in 1871. The Nazi regime imprisoned and murdered gay men as threats to their hyper-masculine vision of Aryan racial purity. But unlike many victims of Nazism, gay men continued to face persecution after World War II. Some West German gay men even had to complete prison sentences originally handed out by the Third Reich! East Germany, though, legalized homosexuality. By the 1970s most countries began relaxing restrictions against homosexuality. In 1973, the American Psychological Association, like other groups in Europe, finally removed homosexuality as a pathological disorder. Right, so for most of Western history, being gay was considered a disease and illegal, not to mention challenging traditional religious morality!

Many people date the start of the gay rights movement very specifically to the night of June 28, 1969 in Greenwich Village in New York City, when patrons of a gay bar, the Stonewall Inn, fought police and rioted against constant police harassment. Thereafter, activists crafted a more radical assertion of gay rights, sometimes connecting with broader progressive movements. Embracing the term "gay" instead of "homosexual" in the 1970s reflected a move away from pathological and legal definitions. It also demonstrates the power of naming for identity politics.

Now, let's be honest here: plenty of folks do not worry about how they are identified because they don't have to. Many of them don't quite get all the fuss about what name someone is called. But very often the power a majority group holds to name a minority group also determines that minority group's rights, opportunities, and even legality.

Calling someone a "homosexual" in the twentieth century somehow made them a part of diseased and illegal activity—whether the person saying it meant to or not. Using "gay" instead allowed non-straight people to define themselves a little more. But that term also reflected the fact that gay *men* had largely defined the struggle for rights and created some tensions with lesbian women. Like I was saying above: intersectionality.

The drive for gay rights thus both drew from broad liberation movements and created more narrowly focused advocacy groups. The 1980s HIV/AIDS crisis, especially in the USA, caused a backlash against gay men but united gay men and women and radicalized gay politics across the Western world. Yep, good ole Janus-faced action here. Queer rights advocates could connect with each other and with other liberation movements. *And* they recognized the ways in which their experiences were quite distinct from other oppressed groups. In fact, the term "queer" in the 1990s appropriated a formerly derogatory word to unite various non-straight people. Today the increasingly common use of "LGBTQ+" (lesbian, gay, bi, trans, queer, and others) or "LGBTQIA+" (which includes inter- and asexual) seeks to connect pretty much all non-heterosexual identities.

Since the late 1990s, gay rights advocates in the Western world have generally been fighting (again) to be considered "normal," especially to have the right to marry and have children. You know, the stuff that straight people do all the time, sometimes by accident. By the 2010s twenty-nine European countries had legalized same-sex marriage or partnership. Oddly enough the old imaginary iron curtain matters here a little. Many of the former Eastern Bloc countries still have laws against same-sex unions or even laws outlawing homosexuality. Some of those rules actually go back to pre-Soviet days.

Integration and disintegration: the 1990s to today

So, identity politics changed in the 1990s. The end of the Cold War altered the dynamics of integrating political organizations like the European Union. The end of East-West European division also meant that Eastern Europeans could no longer simplistically define all racial difference through communist platitudes; xenophobia and conflict have increased as a result. Across Europe the reality of women and people of color thriving in and even leading some European societies redefined assumptions about national and European identity. Queer rights advocates pushed for both real protections and real equality. How have these various movements fared since the 1990s?

After the end of the Cold War, identity politics have become one of the main ways to expand the promise of liberal democracy. Fukuyama would be proud. The explosion around 1990 of political systems based on liberal politics and economics didn't last long, as we saw at the end of the last chapter. How about consumer capitalism? Keep on rocking in the free (market) world! Since you are what you buy, baby, plenty of identity groups have used purchasing power to express themselves or even shape government policies. But if you're ultimately trying to secure rights and protections for a group defined by race, sexuality, gender, religion, ability, etc., you need a political system that takes rights and protections seriously in the first place. Consumer capitalism ain't enough. Liberal democracies are rooted in Enlightenment ideas about treating all individuals equally. Identity politics force these systems to recognize that they were mainly set up to treat straight white men equally. Everyone else: we're working on it. That's been one of the main story lines of this book.

Identity politics encourage liberal democracies to promote *equity*, not just equality. What's the difference? *Equality* means treating everyone the same, while *equity* recognizes the fact that different people may need different things to succeed, especially when some people really haven't been treated equally. Equality is basically a negative right—that people and government should let you do your thing. Equity is a positive right—that governments or other organizations must recognize that some groups who've long been denied equality may need some more assistance even to get to an equal playing field. Both of these goals are pretty much only possible in liberal democracies.

Identity politics, though, force majority populations to realize the limits and weaknesses of their wonderful democracies. That's why that white German rapper got mad at the Turkish German rapper who said "I love Germany, but …" How well have European states been able to handle these difficult issues since the 1990s? Policy-wise it's gone pretty well but politically it's been rocky. European states have in fact become more multicultural, improved rights for women and sexual minorities, and made some adjustments to their overall national identity as a result. However, the political cost has been fairly high. Concerns about identity have intensified and often polarized political debate. Right-wing parties have grown in many countries, usually by rejecting aspects of identity politics, especially immigrant rights.

Europe has become more integrated and connected since the 1990s. Most obviously the end of the Cold War ripped down the old iron curtain of ideological division. In 1991, the Warsaw Pact, the military alliance of the Soviet Union and its Eastern Bloc allies, folded. The Western equivalent, NATO, had already incorporated one former Warsaw Pact member, East Germany, in 1990. Hungary, Poland, and the Czech Republic joined NATO in 1997, and nine more Eastern European countries signed on in the 2000s.[5] Other former Eastern Bloc or Soviet countries hope to join in the future. Membership in NATO does not guarantee civil rights, but the organization is committed to promoting human rights among its members and where it conducts military operations.

More significantly, the European Union has connected governments and people. The 1992 Maastricht Treaty formalized the European Union and started the process of creating a single currency among members. This treaty also emphasized the economic rights of EU citizens to have free movement of goods, services, capital, and people. In 1995, six more countries (Austria, Finland, Sweden, Norway, Iceland, and Lichtenstein) joined the EU as full or partial members. Thus, by the end of the twentieth century, eighteen countries, or the majority of West and Central Europe, had united in a common economic market and lose political federation. Almost immediately after the Cold War's end, Eastern European nations applied for membership in the EU. Joining the EU demanded significant political

[5]Montenegro, one of the former Yugoslav republics, joined in 2017, bringing the total number to twenty-nine.

and especially economic restructuring. By 2007, ten more former Eastern Bloc countries had become members. That meant most of Europe was functioning as a common market for the first time since, like, I don't know, the Roman Empire, or maybe ever! The 1997 Treaty of Amsterdam expanded the EU's authority over its member states to include civil and criminal laws and regulations about immigration. By 2002, the Euro had replaced local currencies in almost all member nations. *Adieu*, Francs, Deutschmarks, Lira, etc.!

All this groovy integrating has had very mixed results for identity politics. Overall the expansion of NATO and the EU minimized national identity in the 1990s and 2000s. That massive shift meant more cooperation between European nations. Maybe you're used to seeing Germany and France as BFFs, but that friendship has overcome 200 years of history. Less nationalist Othering in Europe—defining who you are by emphasizing who you're not—has cut down on tension in Europe. The tensions between European nations since the 1990s have often centered on economic disputes, especially who's keeping the EU fiscally strong vs. who's weakening it. From the sixteenth through the middle of the twentieth century, wars between European nations were, as we've seen, all too common. But since the late 1990s the idea of these countries actually fighting each other is—shockingly—pretty much unthinkable.

The European Union has, though, created a new venue for a slightly different kind of nationalism. The (barely) failed Scottish Referendum to leave the United Kingdom in 2014, for example, aimed to create a new nation within the context of the European Union. Catalan's (thwarted) attempt in 2017 to leave Spain did something similar. In both of these cases, the powerful supra-national EU has actually enabled further nationalist splintering. The much more significant vote in 2016 for the UK to leave the European Union—"Brexit" or "Britain's exit"—is a whole other beast. It's moving forward, but ultimately God only knows how it will turn out. In many ways Brexit reflects bad ole nationalism: the odd combo of post-World War II British resentment at losing an empire and much older English aspiration to "splendid isolation." Good luck with that, mates.

Above all, European integration has reset terms for immigration. Really when we talk about migrants to Europe, there are about three-and-a-half waves. We've already covered the first one and a half waves, when Western European nations invited "guest workers" and their families followed. Next, in Wave Two in the 1990s, people from Eastern Europe and slightly more distant former Soviet Republics[6] spread into Europe through legal and illegal means. Wave Three also started in the 1990s, when immigrants came from places facing war and poverty, especially the Middle East and Central Asia—most notably Iraq, Afghanistan, and Syria. Many of these people have come to Europe seeking political asylum from dangerous places. As with previous waves of immigration, men often arrived first and then brought their families.

Europeans have been fighting about immigration since the 1980s, but these early twenty-first-century immigrants have dramatically politicized and polarized debates about immigration in Europe. Since the European Union shapes borders and immigration

[6]Azerbaijan, Georgia, Armenia, and the 'Stans: Turkmenistan, Uzbekistan, Tajikistan, Kazakhstan, and Kyrgyzstan.

policy for member states, it has been at the heart of this debate. Indeed, plenty of "Brexiters" assumed their vote was a way of telling the EU that Britain should be able to define its own border policies. Hungarian border closings in 2016 made that claim even more dramatically.[7] Ironically, the EU has mainly tightened, not loosened, immigration policies. In fact, some EU regulations passed in 2000 have allowed member states to push nationalist agendas that further limit immigration. Other laws have tried to solve national tensions about immigration (usually unsuccessfully).

These conflicts have heightened identity politics within European countries. Majority (white) populations in Europe have had to rethink their image of national identity. Some people have embraced a more multicultural vision of their country. Remember the example I mentioned in Chapter 13 about Dutch people leaning into liberalism as a way to deal with guilt about their colonial past? Okay, but then in 2004 anxieties about Islam and integration blew up in Holland, when a man advocating radical Islam killed a provocative television journalist who had railed against Muslim immigrants.

Political movements especially on the right have made immigration a powerful "wedge issue" that has forced discussion about whether a country is Christian or white or tolerant or something else. By the early twenty-first century, many of those first-wave "guest workers" were actually integrated, contributing, multi-generational members of Western European societies. But they still looked different from the majority and often practiced a different religion (usually Islam). The growth of more recent asylum-seekers and other immigrants has intensified conflicts in most European countries about ethnic and cultural difference. Some white Europeans have embraced their "Christian" roots, at least culturally. Many new immigrants and established non-white Europeans have embraced Islam as a way to define themselves. Eastern and Central Europe especially has long been a site of conflict between Christianity and Islam. As "European citizenship" has expanded, so have these religious-cultural conflicts.

Religious and ethnic self-definitions in the twenty-first century highlight the tensions that have developed in these (now) multicultural states. Even as economic and foreign-policy nationalism seems to be receding a little,[8] nationalist sentiments about identity from the political right have been driving politics in Europe, especially in the 2010s. Expressions of identity sometimes embrace national or ethnic definitions—feeling German or Hungarian or British in the face of big ole EU policies. And non-white folks have been doing the same—feeling Syrian or proud to be a Turk. At the same time, larger identities like being Christian or Muslim or secular, have also become ways for majority and minority groups to define and defend themselves. The wars that the USA and its European allies have been waging in Iraq, Afghanistan, Syria, and elsewhere have only heated up these conflicts over religion and culture, as have the terrorist groups those conflicts have helped to spawn. One of the best examples of recent debates about identity was the big bruhaha in France over headscarves.

---

[7] There was a lot of resistance to and fighting about immigration in 2016, wasn't there? That same year the USA elected Donald Trump President. 'Nuff said.
[8] Maybe? Hopefully? Who knows really.

Scarves and human rights: Islam in Europe

Should women or girls be able to wear headscarves (*hijab* in Arabic) in public places? That question was hotly debated in France from 1989 to 2003. Identifying the main issue at stake would probably depend upon whom you asked. Were these conflicts that consumed French media and politics about religious tolerance, religious freedom, secularism, women's rights, or race? Yes. In March 2004, the French government passed a law prohibiting students from wearing "conspicuously" religious signs in school. While those symbols could include skullcaps for Jewish boys or turbans for Sikh boys, almost all the attention focused on Muslim girls' headscarves.

The government argued that headscarves (or "veils" as they were often called) violated the separation of Church and state, a long-standing French Enlightenment value. Officials also maintained that those scarves kept Muslim women subordinate to men, something that the egalitarian French Republic could not allow. More generally supporters of the law viewed it as a way to assert tolerant modernity over intolerant Islam. Similar legislation was considered or passed in Belgium, Holland, Australia, Bulgaria, and Germany around this time. The increased tension in the 1990s surrounding Muslim citizens and newer immigrants made the debates in 2003 more intense than in 1989.

This conflict in France brought together the two major strains of identity politics we've considered in this chapter. Certainly, the debate was about the role of Islam and how its adherents could practice their faith. But it was also about women: did they have the right to express faith publicly with a headscarf, or was doing so just a sign of being subservient to men? Supporters of the ban mainly argued that they were promoting religious tolerance and gender equality. Out of five-and-a-half million Muslims in France, maybe 400,000 Muslim women (and even fewer Muslim girls) wore *hijabs* at this time. Why did the French government pay so much attention to such a small and relatively powerless minority? Again, answers would vary, depending upon whom you asked. But for sure the law demonstrates the importance of intersectional ways that prejudice, discrimination, and identity work.

These are complicated issues that can't be summed up in a few paragraphs. Ultimately, the law was fueled by racism, post-colonial frustration, nationalism, and the odd bit of sexism. It allowed majority citizens to assert their identity as defenders of tolerance and women's rights, but also to emphasize that Islam was not the majority religion of France. Muslims generally, but especially women, could in turn use the headscarf as a symbol of power and to express their identity. *Viva la différence!*

Who are you anyway?

I chose to end this book with identity politics because they sort of push Enlightenment ideas to their logical conclusion. Those big concepts, which have driven much of what we've studied, have now become extremely personal. It's like the Enlightenment Dudes (Locke, Rousseau, Smith, and Company) and the Irrationalist Fellas (Nietzsche, Freud, and Friends) finally made up. Yes, logic, rational self-interest, good systems, and all that matter, but so does how you feel, what you've experienced, and what you want. Aww, it's like a Hallmark movie, where everything works out in the end. Well, maybe.

The political turmoil of the 2010s—Brexit, threats to the EU's existence, attacks on immigrants, US President Trump, debates about same-sex marriage, reactions to the Covid-19 pandemic, terrorist attacks, etc.—don't feel so Hallmark. And those issues all concern identity politics in some way. They're made particularly potent by economic concerns. How far do citizenship rights extend anyway, and who pays?

Identity can inspire a demand for dignity or the politics of resentment. At least that's what Fukuyama identified in his 2018 book on the subject.[9] Once again, Fukuyama may be more provocative than right, but he gives us something to consider.

Identity can, for better or worse, work a bit like nationalism. It can offer an empowering group definition. Minority groups in modern Europe have often had to draw sharp distinctions between their public and private behavior, so they could adhere to strict older, straight-white-guy definitions how to behave publicly. Identity politics offer them the ability to be more or less the same person in public and private—at least theoretically. Sometimes that stuff pisses off majority folks, and especially the white guys in charge. They occasionally see requests for *equity* as a challenge to the basic concept of *equality* that's at the heart of liberal, Enlightenment democracy. And so both majority and minority groups appeal to freedom, equality, fairness, and all those other awesome Enlightenment ideas. Then they fight about them. This book has shown that's nothing new. But if they can do it without violence, then maybe we're getting somewhere.

---

[9]Fukuyama, Francis. *Identity: The Demand for Dignity and the Politics of Resentment.* New York: Frarrar, Straus and Giroux, 2018.

EPILOGUE: NOW WHAT?

Seriously, this really is the last chapter. And it's super short. For a history book, an epilogue is a place to sum up, connect to the present, and look ahead. But don't worry: I'm not going to try to predict the future. Studying history can help explain how things are today. But using that information to say what's going to happen in the future has always been a little dicey.

This book has shown that big ideas, especially those from the Enlightenment, have shaped the lives of Europeans. And other lives too: the United States has played an important role here, and Europeans of course spread their ideas to much of the world, whether people wanted 'em or not! Enlightenment ideas have been quite Janus-faced or dual-natured. They have both liberated and controlled people. These concepts have offered average people and oppressed folks a way to get more respect, material wealth, and influence in their society. At the same time, powerful people have used Enlightenment ideas to define, restrict, and harm some people. These ideas and their scientific roots reshaped modern Europe and the world in profound ways. Hopefully that's clear by now. I hope, as well, that "building the argument" in each chapter has helped you follow the larger story and maybe taught you a little something about how to make your own arguments.

I've tried to show how important big ideas continue to be in the twenty-first century. The last few chapters on decolonization, the end of the Cold War, and identity politics especially follow Enlightenment thought into the twenty-first century. For better or worse, Enlightenment thought still shapes many of the big and small things we continue to debate. Take the example of climate change.

Almost every scientist and most people in the Western world today understand that humans have influenced our natural environment, often in negative ways. The question is what to do about it. In other words, we're debating how to make use of scientific data. How do we use information to change human behavior? How can laws help do that? Sounds pretty Enlightenment to me. Even the bizarre debates about *whether* humans have impacted the climate are still about how to use science to shape the behavior of people, businesses, governments, and other organizations.

Since the natural environment doesn't follow the arbitrary national borders we've drawn on maps, improving the environment is an international issue. Discussions about national sovereignty vs. international needs or organizations also connect to Enlightenment ideas. Enlightenment thought since the eighteenth century has basically assumed that nation states are the best places to grow rational economic systems to improve people's lives. No doubt, powerful industrial economies have raised the living standards of many people, especially in Europe. But, oops, turns out that industrial process has had significant, disastrous impacts on the natural environment and is not sustainable. Most Enlightenment thinkers, especially pro-industrial economists, failed to consider limits to natural resources and how humans work with nature. Plus, wealthy countries in the northern hemisphere seem to be saying to poorer nations in the southern hemisphere: whoa, that industrial stuff was okay for us but isn't going to work for the whole world!

What to do? We look to science, laws, national and international organizations for ways to minimize and reverse the negative direction of climate change. Everyone's heard the phrase "think globally, act locally." That connection is built upon the Enlightenment assumption that the right system can empower individual people to do good and improve things. So, the Enlightenment may have screwed up the environment, but we're hoping that an Enlightenment framework of rational planning can fix things too. We'll see.

You know, maybe Enlightenment thought is starting to wear out its welcome a bit, no matter how flexible and useful it's been. Perhaps it's time for some new ideas. I said in the Introduction that this book lays out just one way to consider modern European history or history generally. I want to close by sharing a couple of very different ways to think about history. One caveat, though: both of them assume that a rational, scientific worldview helps us best understand history. So maybe these perspectives are really significant extensions of the deep concepts we've considered in this book. Whatever the case, these ways of approaching history ask us to reconsider our place in this world.

1. The Anthropocene

You may have heard of this idea, pronounced "AN-thro-pu-seen." It's a scientific term that proposes that humans' massive changes to nature mark a whole new geological era. Now, geologists and other folks studying the Earth don't go lightly adding geological eras. They're called "eras," because they're, like, tens of thousands or millions of years long. And the idea of the Anthropocene remains controversial. Nevertheless, the concept forces us to think very differently about human history. It's a more radical version of environmental history.

Humans have been the leading species on Earth for maybe 70,000 years (when we first created language) or at least 12,000 years (after the last ice age). But our radical use of technology to alter the natural environment really began with industrialization in the nineteenth century. Many scholars point to the first detonation of a nuclear weapon in 1945 as a point when humans possessed technology powerful enough to alter radically or even destroy much of life on Earth. Plus, human population growth and desire for energy began dramatically killing off other species starting around the mid-twentieth century.

This concept certainly demands that we ask hard questions about how we can sustain continued human growth and technological advancement in the future. Survival, anyone? Viewing history through this Anthropocene lens would prioritize our study of how human activities have historically influenced the natural world. This perspective would encourage us to see ideas and technology not as the drivers of history but as tools humans have developed to alter and master their environment. Some of the history covered in this book would remain important—economic theories, massive wars, industrialization, population growth, imperialism. But we might treat political ideologies like democracy, socialism, or capitalism as means to influence or use the environment. Same with nations and other governmental organizations. All history is political. This perspective makes the political point that we must consider the relationship between humans and nature in the past. Doing so might help us better understand our current predicament and make better decisions in the future to sustain human and other life on this planet.

2. Big History

This perspective also studies human activity as part of a larger story, in this case, like, the whole 13.7 billion-year history of the universe! Imagine if mine was a Big History book covering time from the Big Bang to the present. If we scaled the book out proportional to the time it covered, then modern European history we get like three words on the very last page![1] If history from the perspective of the Anthropocene emphasizes human impact on the natural world, then Big History considers human history as one tiny little part of a much, much larger story of the universe. I'm not sure which one is more troubling. Sometimes Big History feels like metaphor. We might, for example, compare the gravitational formation of atoms into stars in the early universe with the process of communities coalescing around farming in the Agricultural Revolution.

For sure Big History forces us to rethink how we define "history." Usually history has been based on written or other kinds of sources. Not too many records from the Neanderthals, however, much less in the first 3 million years after the Big Bang. Even if we scale back the cosmological story and just try to place human activity within a longer storyline, we have to think differently about what matters and how we explain historical development.

But people don't think in geological or galactical time. They think in terms of a few generations back or forward, maybe very vaguely about a couple thousand years of history. Big History forces us to consider the relationship between what we're doing today and big things that happened in the past. And yes, when you're talking about billions of years, "today" can mean the last few centuries or even millennia. If we wish to be more than a little blip in the story of the Earth or the universe, we need to understand how to help our species and world survive. Maybe this perspective can help us figure out what has enabled humans do well for a few thousand years. Big History allows us to compare human and cosmological patterns. Perhaps those natural patterns that helped, you know, create the universe might be better models for human society than what some smart guys in the eighteenth century imagined.

---

[1] It's sort of like those analogies you may have heard before: if the Earth's history was a calendar, then humankind would only appear in the last minute before midnight on December 31.

Done!

Well, I guess the epilogue of a history book *does* involve a little looking at the future. Even if Anthropocene History or Big History minimizes the long-term implications of Enlightenment ideas, these concepts we've studied continue to shape how we treat each other and our planet. Enlightenment thought gives us ways to control, alter, and harm the natural world that don't seem to benefit most people or the environment. Fortunately, it also offers us a way to value all of humanity and perhaps the planet we share. You should now be equipped to know the difference. I hope this book will encourage you to go out and do the right thing.

FURTHER READING

1. (Re)birthing New Ideas in the Renaissance

Brown, Judith C. and Robert C. Davis. *Gender and Society in Renaissance Italy*. New York: Longman, 1998.

Hale, John. *The Civilization of Europe in the Renaissance*. New York: Atheneum, 1994.

King, Margaret. *Women of the Renaissance*. Chicago: University of Chicago Press, 1991.

King, Margaret L. *A Short History of the Renaissance*. 3rd edition. Toronto: University of Toronto Press, 2016.

Lee, Alexander. *The Ugly Renaissance: Sex, Greed, Violence, and Depravity in an Age of Beauty*. New York: Doubleday, 2014.

Moller, Violet. *The Map of Knowledge: A Thousand-Year History of How Classical Ideas Were Lost and Found*. New York: Doubleday, 2019.

Nauert, Charles G. Jr. *Humanism and the Culture of Renaissance Europe*. Cambridge: Cambridge University Press, 1995.

Quilligan, Maureen, Walter Mignolo, and Margaret Rich Greer, eds. *Rereading the Black Legend: The Discourses of Religious and Racial Difference in the Renaissance Empires*. Chicago: University of Chicago Press, 2007.

Spiller, Elizabeth. *Reading and the History of Race in the Renaissance*. Cambridge: Cambridge University Press, 2011.

2. Science is a Human Invention

Clark, Henry C. *Compass of Society: Commerce and Absolutism in Old-Regime France*. Lanham, MD: Rowman & Littlefield/Lexington Books, 2007.

Huff, Toby E. *The Rise of Early Modern Science: Islam, China, and the West*. Cambridge: Cambridge University Press, 1993.

Hunter, Lynette and Sarah Hutton, eds. *Women, Science and Medicine 1500–1700: Mothers and Sisters of the Royal Society*. Gloucestershire: Sutton, 1997.

Jacob, James R. *The Scientific Revolution: Aspirations and Achievements, 1500–1700*. Atlantic Highlands, NJ: Humanities Press, 1998.

Kuhn, Thomas. *The Structure of Scientific Revolutions*. 2nd edition. Chicago: University of Chicago Press, 1970.

Levack, Brian P. *The Witch-Hunt in Early Modern Europe*. 3rd edition. Harlow: Longman, 2007.

Masood, Ehsan. *Science and Islam: A History*. 2nd edition. Duxford: Icon Books, 2017.

Principe, Lawrence M. *The Scientific Revolution: A Very Short Introduction*. Oxford: Oxford University Press, 2011.

Ray, Meredith K. *Daughters of Alchemy: Women and Scientific Culture in Early Modern Italy*. Cambridge, MA: Harvard University Press, 2015.

Teich, Mikuláš, *The Scientific Revolution Revisited*. Cambridge: Open Book Publishers, 2015.

3. The Enlightenment Will Free You and Mess You Up

Brewer, Daniel. *The Enlightenment Past: Reconstructing Eighteenth-Century French Thought.* Cambridge: Cambridge University Press, 2008.

Curran, Andrew S. *The Anatomy of Blackness: Science & Slavery in an Age of Enlightenment.* Baltimore: Johns Hopkins University Press, 2011.

Edelstein, Dan. *The Enlightenment: A Genealogy.* Chicago and London: University of Chicago Press, 2010.

Garcia, Humberto. *Islam and the English Enlightenment, 1670–1840.* Baltimore: Johns Hopkins University Press, 2011.

Goody, Jack. *The Theft of History.* Cambridge: Cambridge University Press, 2006.

Kant, Immanuel. "An Answer to the Question: 'What is Enlightenment?'" In *Practical Philosophy.* Edited by Mary J. Gregor. Cambridge: Cambridge University Press, 1996. 11–22.

Sala-Molins, Louis. *Dark Side of the Light: Slavery and the French Enlightenment.* Translated by John Conteh-Morgan. Minneapolis and London: University of Minnesota Press, 2016.

4. Now, *That's* a Revolution! (France, 1789)

Beckstrand, Lisa. *Deviant Women of the French Revolution and the Rise of Feminism.* Madison and Teaneck: Fairleigh Dickinson University Press, 2009.

De Tocqueville, Alexis. *Old Regime and the French Revolution.* 1856.

DiCaprio, Lisa. *The Origins of the Welfare State: Women, Work, and the French Revolution.* Urbana and Chicago: University of Illinois Press, 2007.

Dubois, Laurent. *A Colony of Citizens: Revolution and Slave Emancipation in the French Caribbean, 1878–1804.* Chapel Hill: University of North Carolina Press, 2004.

Jones, P.M. *The French Revolution 1787–1804.* London: Pearson, 2003.

Neely, Sylvia. *A Concise History of the French Revolution.* Lanham: Rowman & Littlefield, 2008.

5. I've Got a Fever, and the Only Prescription is More Nationalism!

Anderson, Benedict. *Imagined Communities: Reflections on the Origin and Spread of Nationalism.* Revised edition. London, New York: Verso, 1991.

Blackbourn, David. *The Long Nineteenth Century: A History of Germany, 1780–1918.* New York: Oxford University Press, 1998.

Chapman, Tim. *The Congress of Vienna 1814–1815: Origins, Processes, and Results.* London: Routledge, 1998.

Crews, Robert D. *For Prophet and Tsar: Islam and Empire in Russia and Central Asia.* Cambridge, MA: Harvard University Press, 2006.

Hobsbawm, E.J. *The Age of Revolution: 1789–1848.* Cleveland and New York: World Publishing, 1962.

Kappeler, Andreas. *The Russian Empire: A Multiethnic History.* Translated by Alfred Clayton. Harlow: Pearson, 2001.

Patriarca, Silvana. "Indolence and Regeneration: Tropes and Tensions of Risorgimento Patriotism." *The American Historical Review* 110. 2 (2005): 380–408.

Smith, Anthony D. *Nationalism: Theory, Ideology, History.* Cambridge: Cambridge University Press, 2001.

Tolz, Vera. *Russia.* London: Arnold, 2001.

6. Industrialization, or: Welcome to the Machine

Burnette, Joyce. *Gender, Work and Wages in Industrial Revolution Britain*. Cambridge: Cambridge University Press, 2008.

Hobsbawm, E.J. *Industry and Empire: From 1750 to the Present*. Harmondsworth: Penguin, 1969.

Satia, Priya. *Empire of Guns: The Violent Making of the Industrial Revolution*. New York: Penguin, 2018.

Solow, Barbara L. *The Economic Consequences of the Atlantic Slave Trade*. Lanham: Lexington Books, 2014.

Stearns, Peter N. *The Industrial Revolution in World History*. Boulder: Westview Press, 1993.

Steinberg, Marc W. *England's Great Transformation: Law, Labor, and the Industrial Revolution*. Chicago and London: University of Chicago Press, 2016.

Teich, Mikuláš and Roy Porter, eds. *The Industrial Revolution in National Context: Europe and the USA*. Cambridge: University of Cambridge Press, 1996.

7. On the Road Again: The Ideas and Violence of Western Imperialism

Adas, Michael. "Imperialism and Colonialism in Comparative Perspective." *The International History Review* 20, no. 2 (1998): 371–88.

"Colonialism vs. Imperialism," http://internationalrelations.org/colonialism-vs-imperialism/, accessed October 22, 2019.

Conklin, Alice L. and Ian Christopher Fletcher, eds. *European Imperialism, 1830–1930: Climax and Contradiction*. Boston and New York: Houghton Mifflin, 1999.

Padgen, Anthony. *Lords of all the World: Ideologies of Empire in Spain, Britain and France c. 1500–c.1800*. New Haven and London: Yale University Press, 1995.

Roberts, Richard L., Emily Lynn Osborn, and Benjamin N. Lawrance, eds. *Intermediaries, Interpreters, and Clerks : African Employees in the Making of Colonial Africa*. Madison, Wisconsin: University of Wisconsin Press, 2006.

Saïd, Edward W. *Orientalism*. New York: Pantheon Books, 1978.

Smith, Woodruff. *The German Colonial Empire*. Chapel Hill: University of North Carolina Press, 1978.

8. Look, We've Got to Talk About the Enlightenment

Freud, Sigmund. *Civilization and its Discontents*, 1930.

Freud, Sigmund. *The Interpretation of Dreams*, 1900.

Fritzsche, Peter, ed. and trans. *Nietzsche and the Death of God: Selected Writings*. Boston, New York: Bedford/St. Martin's, 2007.

Gay, Peter, ed. *The Freud Reader*. New York and London: Norton, 1989.

Horkheimer, Max and Theodore Adorno. *Dialectic of Enlightenment*. New York: Continuum, 1972.

Kierkegaard, Søren. *Either/Or*, 1843.

Kierkegaard, Søren. *Fear and Trembling*, 1843.

Lukács, Georg. *The Destruction of Reason*. Translated by Peter Palmer. Atlantic Highlands, NJ: Humanities Press, 1981.

Nietzsche, Friedrich. *Beyond Good and Evil*, 1886.

Nietzsche, Friedrich. *On the Genealogy of Morals*, 1887.

Further Reading

Nietzsche, Friedrich. *Thus Spoke Zarathustra*, 1883–4.
Schopenhauer, Arthur. *The World as Will and Representation* , 1818, expanded 1844.

9. World War I: The War That Did Nothing but Changed Everything

Fitzpatrick, Sheila. *The Russian Revolution 1917–1932*. Oxford: Oxford University Press, 1982.
Figes, Orlando. *A People's Tragedy: The Russian Revolution, 1891–1924*. London and New York: Penguin, 1998.
Fussel, Paul. *The Great War and Modern Memory*. Oxford: Oxford University Press, 1975.
Grazel, Susan R. and Tammy M. Proctor, eds. *Gender and the Great War*. Oxford: Oxford University Press, 2017.
Morrow, John Howard. *The Great War: An Imperial History*. London: Routledge, 2004.
Proctor, Tammy M. *Civilians in a World at War, 1914–1918*. New York: New York University Press, 2010.
Tucker, Spencer C. *The Great War 1914–18*. Bloomington and Indianapolis: Indiana University Press, 1998.

10. Between the Wars Without a Center, or: Up the Creek Without a Paddle

Beddoe, Diedre. *Back to Home and Duty: Women Between the Wars, 1918–1939*. London: Pandora, 1989.
Caplan, Jane. *Nazi Germany: A Very Short Introduction*. Oxford: Oxford University Press, 2019.
Chadwick, Whitney and Tirza True Latimer. "Becoming Modern: Gender and Sexual Identity after World War I." In *The Modern Woman Revisited: Paris Between the Wars*. Edited by Whitney Chadwick and Tirza True Latimer. New Brunswick: Rutgers University Press, 2003. 3–20.
Crampton, R.J. *Eastern Europe in the Twentieth Century*. London and New York: Routledge, 1994.
Gruber, Helmut and Pamela Graves, eds. *Women and Socialism/Socialism and Women: Europe Between the Two World Wars*. New York and Oxford: Berghahn, 1998.
Kitchen, Martin. *Europe between the Wars*. 2nd edition. Harlow, UK: Pearson Longman, 2006.
Robinson, J. Bradford, "Jazz reception in Weimar Germany: in search of a shimmy figure." In *Music and performance during the Weimar Republic*. Edited by Bryan Gilliam. Cambridge: Cambridge University Press, 1994. 107–34.
Tucker, Robert. *Stalin as Revolutionary* and *Stalin in Power*. New York, Norton, 1974 and 1990.
Weitz, Eric. *Weimar Germany: Promise and Tragedy*. Princeton: Princeton University Press, 2007.
Wigger, Iris. *The 'Black Horror on the Rhine': Intersections of Race, Nation, Gender and Class in 1920s Germany*. London: Palgrave Macmillan, 2017.

11. Downhill All the Way: World War II and the Holocaust

Bauman, Zygmunt. *Modernity and the Holocaust*. Ithaca, NY: Cornell University Press, 1991.
Bergen, Doris L. *War & Genocide: A Concise History of the Holocaust*. 3rd edition. Lanham: Roman & Littlefield, 2016.
Browning, Christopher R. *Ordinary Men: Reserve Police Battalion 101 and the Final Solution in Poland*. New York: HarperCollins, 1992.
Caplan, Jane. *Government without Administration: State and Civil Service in Weimar and Nazi Germany*. Oxford: Oxford University Press, 1989.

Kershaw, Ian. *Hitler 1889–1936: Hubris.* New York and London: Norton, 1998.

Timm, Annette F. and Joshua A. Sanborn. *Gender, Sex and the Shaping of Modern Europe: A History from the French Revolution to the Present Day.* 2nd edition. London: Bloomsbury, 2016.

Wasseterstein, Bernard. *On the Eve: The Jews of Europe before the Second World War.* New York: Simon & Schuster, 2012.

Weinberg, Gerhard L. *World War II: A Very Short Introduction.* Oxford: Oxford University Press, 2014.

Wiesel, Elie. *Night.* Toronto and New York: Bantam, 1982.

12. The Cold War as a Line in the Sand

Bren, Paulina and Mary Neubuger, eds. *Communism Unwrapped: Consumption in Cold War Eastern Europe.* Oxford: Oxford University Press, 2012.

Immerman, Richard H. and Petra Goedde, eds. *The Oxford Handbook of The Cold War.* Oxford: Oxford University Press, 2013.

Orwell, George. "You and the Atomic Bomb." *Tribune* (London). October 19, 1945.

Poiger, Uta. *Jazz, Rock, and Rebels: Cold War Politics and American Culture in a Divided Germany.* Berkeley: University of California Press, 2000.

Siracusa, Joseph M. *Into the Dark House: American Diplomacy and the Ideological Origins of the Cold War.* Claremont, CA: Regina Books, 1998.

Westad, Odd Arne. *The Cold War: A World History.* New York: Basic Books, 2017.

13. The Long, Strange and Not-So-Complete Death of Colonialism

Anderson, Benedict. *Imagined Communities: Reflections on the Origins and Spread of Nationalism.* Revised edition. New York: Verso, 2016.

Chamberlain, M. E. *Decolonization: The Fall of European Empires.* 2nd edition. Oxford: Blackwell, 1999.

Cooper, Frederick and Ann Laura Stoler, eds. *Tensions of Empire: Colonial Cultures in a Bourgeois World.* Berkeley: University of California Press, 1997.

Reynolds, Jonathan T. *Sovereignty and Struggle: Africa and Africans in the Era of the Cold War 1945–1994.* New York and Oxford: Oxford University Press, 2015.

Ross, Kristin. *Fast Cars, Clean Bodies: Decolonization and the Reordering of French Culture.* Cambridge, MA.: MIT Press, 1995.

Shipway, Martin. *Decolonization and its Impact: A Comparative Approach to the End of the Colonial Empires.* Oxford: Blackwell, 2008.

Thomas, Martin, Bob Moore, and L. J. Butler. *Crises of Empire: Decolonization and Europe's Imperial States, 1918–1975.* London: Hodder Education, 2008.

Wilson, Henry S. *African Decolonization.* London: Edward Arnold, 1994.

14. The End of History, or Something Like That

Ash, Timothy Garton. *The Magic Lantern: The Revolution of '89 Witnessed in Warsaw, Budapest, Berlin, and Prague.* New York: Random House, 1990.

Bohlen, Celestine. "Behind the Electoral Curtain of Post-Soviet Regimes." *New York Times.* October 16, 2019. 7.

Further Reading

Drakulić, Slavenka. *How We Survived Communism and Even Laughed*. New York: Harper, 1993.

Fukuyama, Francis. "The End of History?" *The National Interest* 16 (Summer 1989): 3–18.

Gorbachev, Mikhail. *Perestroika: New Thinking for Our Country and the World*. New York: Harper & Row, 1987.

Mason, David S. *Revolution in East-Central Europe: The Rise and Fall of Communism and the Cold War*. Boulder, CO: Westview Press, 1992.

McNeill, John Robert., and Corinna R. Unger. *Environmental Histories of the Cold War*. New York: Cambridge University Press, 2010

Sarotte, Mary Elise. *1989: The Struggle to Create Post-Cold War Europe*. Princeton and Oxford: Princeton University Press, 2009.

Shleifer, Andrei, and Treisman, Daniel. "Normal Countries: The East 25 Years After Communism." *Foreign Affairs* 93.6 (November/December 2014): 97–103.

15. You Do You: Identity Politics

Amer, Sahar. *What Is Veiling?* Edinburgh: Edinburgh University Press, 2014.

Burma, Ian. *Murder in Amsterdam: Liberal Europe, Islam, and the Limits of Tolerance*. New York: Penguin, 2007.

Crenshaw, Kimberlé Williams, et. al., eds. *Critical Race Theory: The Key Writings That Formed the Movement*. New York: New Press, 1995.

Elliot, Anthony, ed. *Routledge Handbook of Identity Studies*. London and New York: Routledge, 2011.

Geddes, Andrew. *The Politics of Migration and Immigration in Europe*. London: Sage, 2003.

Gilroy, Paul. *There Ain't no Black in the Union Jack: The Cultural Politics of Race and Nation*. 2nd edition. London: Routledge, 2002.

Monod, Tariq and Pnina Werbner, eds. *The Politics of Multiculturalism in the New Europe: Racism, Identity and Community*. London: Zed Books, 1997.

Richardson, Diane. *Rethinking Sexuality*. London: SAGE Publications, 2000.

Scott, Joan. *The Politics of the Veil*. Princeton: Princeton University Press, 2007.

Epilogue: Now What?

Chakrabarty, Dipesh. "Anthropocene Time." *History and Theory* 57.1 (March 2018): 5–32.

Christian, David. *Maps of Time: An Introduction to Big History*. Berkeley: University of California Press, 2004.

Ellis, Erle C. *Anthropocene: A Very Short Introduction*. Oxford: Oxford University Press, 2018.

Harari, Yuval N. *Sapiens: A Brief History of Humankind*. New York: Harper, 2015.

INDEX

INDEX

INDEX

use of more effective technologies in World
  War II to kill and control, 184
  See also Scientific Revolution; technology
scientific method, 24–6, 39, 94
  use of by Freud, 133
Scientific Revolution, 1
  bloody impact of in World War I, 148
  dated from about 1500 to 1700, 24
  defining truth, 41
  industrialization growing out of, 94
  Renaissance leading to, 23, 25, 26, 27 fig., 31, 41,
    42
  science coming of age while people fought over
    religion, 26–7
  witches and women of science, 32–4
  See also science; technology
Scottish Referendum, 267
The Scream (painting by Munch), 143, 143 fig.
Second French Republic. *See* French Republics
The Second Sex (De Beauvoir), 262
Second World Countries, defined, 224 n.5
Second World War. *See* World War II
secularism, 55, 70, 133, 139, 198, 226, 268, 269
  conflicts with religious thought, 9–10, 78
  and the Enlightenment, 3, 137, 236
  and the French Revolution, 71, 77
  and humanism, 21, 31
  and Islam, 229
  and Marxism, 107
  meaning of secular, 7 n.2
  and the Renaissance, 5, 8, 31, 32
  and science, 24, 25, 33, 184
segregation from 1990s to today, 265–9
  segregationist laws in US, 231
self-determination, 90, 92, 162, 222, 250
Semyonov, Yulian Semyonovich, 208
Seneca Falls, New York and women's rights, 108–9,
  262
Sepoy Mutiny (1857), 120
Seven-Week War, 87–8
Seven Years War (1756–63), 60
Sex Pistols (punk band), 216 fig., 216 n.9, 216–17
Sforza, Caterina, 33, 34
Shakespeare, William, 6
"Shooting an Elephant" (Orwell), 128
"short twentieth century." *See* twentieth century
Sieyès, Abbé, 62
"Sinatra Policy" of Gorbachev, 248–50
Sistine Chapel ceiling painting, 17, 18 fig.
Ska (dance music), 227
"Skokiaan" (song by Bulawayo Sweet Rhythm
  Band), 219, 255
Slaughterhouse Five (Vonnegut), 209 n.5
slavery, 20, 30 n.4, 35, 48, 63, 97, 104
Smith, Adam, 45, 49, 50, 94, 97, 99, 257, 269
social constructs, 48–9, 49 n.4

Social Contract (Rousseau), 49
Social Darwinism, 112–13, 118, 138, 141, 141 fig.,
  199
  and fascism, 169, 171
  reinforcing racism, 91–2
Social Democratic Party (SPD) (Germany), 172,
  174, 209
socialism, 1, 3, 94, 103, 108, 129, 178, 213, 243, 273
  advocating for workers' rights, 93
  and capitalism, 99, 213, 250
  on causes of inequality, 99
  in Czechoslovakia, 214, 244
  defining, 99, 169
  democratic socialism, 109, 127
  in the Eastern Bloc, 209, 213, 215, 217, 241, 244,
    245, 250, 261
  efforts to minimize inequalities in industrial
    society, 108
  and the Enlightenment, 42, 86, 94, 213
  evolutionary socialists, 108
  and the French Revolution, 73, 75, 81
  growing out of Enlightenment, 94
  and industrialization, 93, 94, 104
  and Karl Marx, 105–8
  Marx's version of, 94, 105–8, 176
  and meaning of Bolshevik, 159 n.8
  Nietzsche on, 133, 137
  revolutionary socialists, 108
  socialist revolutionaries, 117, 158, 159, 161, 176
  in USSR, 177, 213, 241, 243, 248, 250
Socialist Unity Party in Germany, 209
social market economies, 212, 215, 248
social organizations, 8, 14, 42, 54, 131, 134, 139,
  163
social welfare, 103, 151, 171, 172
Society of Jesus "Jesuits," 29 n.3
sociology, development of, 139–40
Solidarity (Wałęsa's group in Poland), 244
Somme, Battle of, 149, 149 n.1, 156, 157
The Souls of Black Folk (Du Bois), 257
Sound of Music (musical), 180
South Africa, 116, 116 n.5, 126, 153, 219, 226–7, 231,
  234
South Africa Company, 116, 126
Southeast Asia, 122, 125, 189, 228, 231, 260
  See also Indochina, French decolonization in
Soviet-Afghan War (1979–89), 206
Soviet Union. *See* Russia/USSR
space race, 214, 247
Spain, 10, 20–1, 234 n.12
  Catalan's attempt to leave, 267
  as a colonial ruler, 35, 230
  and decolonization, 222, 231
  fascism in, 171, 171 n.6, 178–9
  and France, 72, 78
  Spanish Civil War, 178, 262

CPSIA information can be obtained
at www.ICGtesting.com
Printed in the USA
LVHW080436070323
741095LV00004B/111